THE CLAIRVOYANT EYE

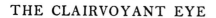

The
Clairvoyant Eye

The Poetry and Poetics of Wallace Stevens

JOSEPH N. RIDDEL

Louisiana State University Press   Baton Rouge

To Kevin and Valerie

and most of all
To their Mother
"And for what, except for you, do I feel love?"

Second Printing 1967

Library of Congress Catalog Card Number: 65-24679
Manufactured in the United States of America by
The Parthenon Press, Nashville, Tennessee
Designed by Jules B. McKee

Published with the assistance of a grant from
the Ford Foundation.

Preface

*T*he following pages are intended primarily as readings, individually and chronologically, of Stevens' poems. I say primarily because they include, I hope, several other things about Stevens, not the least being a tentative account of his theory of imagination and how it relates to the changes in and development of his style. I am equally concerned with the contours of Stevens' development as a representative modern imagination whose poetry, in its various adjustments to the modern world, spells out the crucial problems of the self-conscious man in a time which has lost, as Stevens puts it, the old "nostalgias" and can find no adequate forms of belief to replace them.

I have chosen to concentrate on Stevens' poems as individual and complete "acts of the mind" rather than to approach his work thematically, for two reasons. In the first place, he is a poet whose public reputation rests primarily on a few poems. In the second, the thematic approach tempts one to reduce his themes to formula, the imagination-reality opposition, and to read the poems as variations on that *ur*-poem. Also, I have

v

tried as much as possible to see Stevens' poems in their historical and philosophical perspective, and thus to discriminate between the qualities of images and metaphors which critics, too often, have assumed bear the same value from his early to his late work.

I wish to present as many of Stevens' poems as possible and to treat them not only as total and complete forms but also as part of the larger, coherent structure he envisioned for them. Moreover, convinced that Stevens' greatest achievement rests in his longer poems, I want to isolate those for extensive commentary and yet acknowledge their place in the larger corpus. If this forces an imbalance in the developing argument, as it does perhaps in the case of the lengthy examination of "Owl's Clover," it is a risk I choose to take because of the special role the long poem plays in each one of Stevens' volumes. ("Owl's Clover," by the way, is a poem that has either been condemned as an utter failure and dismissed or, as in at least two books on Stevens, treated as his finest achievement—neither judgment, I think, being defensible.)

The Introduction and Chapter 1 comment on Stevens' "theory of poetry" and its relation to the continuity of his development. Chapter 1, though not a point-by-point examination of Stevens' prose, studies the philosophical and aesthetic generalizations of the prose. The subsequent chapters treat the poetry in five separate phases. Each of these chapters is designed to culminate in the examination of a long poem (and occasionally two) which sums up the volume or phase and provides point of departure or transition to the next. Each begins with a brief commentary on the particular history, the informing ideas, and the characteristic mode of the poetry under consideration. So far as possible, as I have said, I treat poems individually rather than by extensive cross-reference of images and themes. Nonetheless, the chapters are designed to use the minor poems by way of introduction, leading toward the major statements, and to approach the various phases in terms of basic and distinct preoccupations. The integration of minor and major themes, minor and major forms, I take to be the complex and vital world of Stevens' total invention—the world, as I shall argue, in which he has projected his own life in poetry. My thesis, if I may claim one, is that Stevens' total work constitutes metaphysically the act of creating oneself (always, of course, within naturalistic possibility) and living (figuratively, but in a very real sense, actually) in poetry.

Acknowledgments

During my work on the several forms and drafts of this study, I have incurred more debts than can adequately be discharged in acknowledgments. The greatest of these is, without qualification, to Frederick J. Hoffman whose good will and devotion I have too often tried. The energy he has expended on my behalf, and his faith in my work, can be repaid, if at all, only in the publishing of this book. Whatever virtues it has originate from the example of professional integrity which he manifests to his students and demands of his friends, as well as from the kind of discipline his own work represents. The faults of this book, let me add, are not his responsibility—a cliché I prefer to insist on.

I am grateful for the helpful criticism and encouragement of my former colleagues at Duke University: Grover Smith, Louis Budd, Herbert Schneidau, Bernard Duffey, Oliver Ferguson and Donald Reiman. Among Stevens critics and enthusiasts who have had occasion to read and to criticize parts of the manuscript are Louis Martz, Samuel French Morse, Roger Mitchell, Wilson O. Clough, and Frank Doggett, along with the many anonymous readers who perused and commented on my contributions to the learned journals. Stevens' daughter, Holly Stevens Stephenson, has been a cherished supporter of my project. She is at present working on a collection of her father's letters and has been helpful in answering inquiries and in verifying conclusions that otherwise might be based on hearsay evidence. The letters used herein are quoted with her permission. Jackson Bryer, who collaborated with me in doing a checklist of Stevens criticism, has been a valuable contributor of detail and a model of scholarly efficiency. My thanks, also, to my typists, Mrs. Ann Clark and Mrs. Grace Hawke.

Two others deserve my very special gratitude: Roy Harvey Pearce, for his encouragement, but no less for his sharp and discerning criticisms that have saved me numerous embarrassments; and Melvin J. Friedman, for the kind of friendship, the sustained faith and prudent advice, which makes this profession ultimately so rewarding.

I trust that the dedication speaks for itself, so that I need not confuse my wife's many efforts on behalf of the manuscript with her true contribution.

Among the many libraries which were responsive to my requests for materials and assistance were those of the following universities: Wisconsin, Duke, Yale, Harvard, and Dartmouth. The Duke University Research Council financed the typing of the manuscript and assisted in the purchase of materials. Kimball Elkins of the Harvard Archives kindly supplied me with information about Stevens' curriculum. I wish to thank the following journals for permission to print here parts of essays that first appeared in their pages (the work, in almost every case, has been extensively revised): *PMLA, ELH, Modern Philology, Twentieth Century Literature, Wisconsin Studies in Contemporary Literature, New England Quarterly, Texas Studies in English,* and the *South Atlantic Quarterly.*

I am grateful to Alfred A. Knopf, Inc., the publishers of the poetry of Wallace Stevens, for permission to quote from the following copyrighted editions: *The Collected Poems of Wallace Stevens* (1954); *Opus Posthumous,* edited, with an introduction, by Samuel French Morse (1957); and *The Necessary Angel: Essays on Reality and the Imagination* (1951). All page numbers of Stevens' poems refer to these volumes; citations are in the text. In order to reduce the number of parenthetical interruptions, I have cited poems to be discussed in detail and at length only once, at the beginning of the reading. I have tried to cite all quotations and titles for which the reader may desire the larger context, as well as those fragments and phrases of quotations which point beyond the immediate argument. Otherwise, I have omitted citation of basic and recurrent phrases which should be familiar to readers of Stevens, or which have been established earlier in the text. The key:

Collected Poems   (CP)
Opus Posthumous   (OP)
Necessary Angel   (NA)

Contents

THE CLAIRVOYANT EYE

*O*ur author's vision, fixed as it is on concrete images and expressed in detached epigrams, does not always extend to the philosophical relations of his thoughts. Yet he offers, perhaps unconsciously, an admirable variation on that revolution of thought which is associated with the name of Kant. He proposes to us as the work of human intelligence what is commonly believed to be the work of God. The universe, apart from us, is a chaos, but it may be made a cosmos by our efforts and in our own minds. The laws of events, apart from us, are inhuman and irrational, but in the sphere of human activity they may be dominated by reason. We are a part of the blind energy behind Nature, but by virtue of that energy we impose our purposes on the part of Nature which we constitute or control. We can turn from the stupefying contemplation of an alien universe to the building of our own house, knowing that, alien as it is, that universe has chanced to blow its energy also into our will and to allow itself to be partially dominated by our intelligence. . . .

We see that the "Cosmos" here invoked is not inconsistent with the "Nothingness" before described. It is a triumph amid illusions, an order within chaos, *la gloire du néant.*

SANTAYANA: on the poetry and thought of Jean Lahor

Introduction

Ourselves in Poetry

He never felt twice the same about the flecked river,
Which kept flowing and never the same way twice . . .
This Solitude of Cataracts

*W*allace Stevens wrote in mid-career, "The need of the poet for poetry is a dynamic cause of the poetry that he writes" (OP 229). Stevens' achievement is testimony to that need. So are his difficulties and limitations. More than any other poet of his generation—more than Eliot or Pound, more even than Cummings, more than MacLeish or Aiken—Stevens found poetry a way of life. And while the terms in which he celebrated that mode were very much like those of his peers, expressing his belief that above all else poetry could help us "to live our lives" (NA 36), Stevens addressed himself more uncompromisingly than any of the others to defining those terms. "Poetry is the subject of the poem" he wrote in a now-famous but little-understood line which describes at once the amplitude and limits of his verse—a line which, though it may reveal the secret to the inner world of Stevens' poems, has impressed his commentators as unwholesomely singleminded. The consequences for his poetry, especially as he developed and refined this theme, were an intensification of thought and stripping of style that invariably left admirers

3

as well as critics one step behind him. For this reason, among others, Stevens has experienced a belated reputation.[1]

Since his death, however, Stevens has grown from a poet nearly anonymous into a kind of poet-prophet for his age—from a poet known for a few remarkable anthology pieces into the great apologist for modern poetry, for the poet, and hence, as he said, for "any man of imagination." Both images of Stevens—the one of puckish outsider which he occasionally presented in his earliest poems, and the one he now manifests to literary history, the insider of modernism—are perhaps, like most images, slightly askew yet true enough. It is my purpose here to examine the growth and development of what Stevens liked to call the "life of the imagination," as it is recorded in individual poems and in their relationships. My premise is that the one image grows out of the other, as one of Stevens' poems very often grows out of a previous one: that Stevens' achievement must be measured in the continuity and development of his work, as it expresses a life lived in the mind, a life not only recorded but realized in poetry. In this corpus of poetry he fulfills his own need; but more than that, he realizes his belief that poetry is the provenance of man's being as well as the highest form of articulating that being. In an age angrily secular, romantically antiromantic, and resignedly naturalistic, this was a credence nowise popular or well-founded and hardly conducive to the ordinary life of poetry. For it demanded that the poet justify his poetry even as he wrote it, to prove the poem by way of proving himself. Such was Stevens' task as he inherited it from his romantic predecessors and shared it with his peers.

This premise does not go unchallenged. With good enough reason, many critics have considered Stevens a poet notable for a handful of exquisite poems and a canon full of indifferent ones, a poet who above all failed to develop.[2] Or else, a poet of greatly limited though challenging ideas which hardly changed even when subjected to different angles of vision and voiced in divergent styles. Or, more rarely, a poet almost pure, who could live apart in the sound of words even as he insisted that the "greatest poverty is not to live/ In a physical world." The question of Stevens' development is indeed crucial. To deny him that, it seems to me, is to deny his greatness: not only because it assumes that in his first volume, *Harmonium* (1923), Stevens reached the pinnacle of style and idea, but because it implies that *Harmonium*'s strengths (the alternating gaiety and world-weariness, the musical range, the *brio* and wit, the impeccable craftsmanship) are the measures, not to say forerunners, of his failure to mature. Yet it seems equally questionable to praise him as a philosopher; for his thought, if consistent, is hardly systematic. Though he is, I shall argue, a philosophical poet. Nor does it seem praise to applaud his defense of the romantic in the face of the overwhelming distrust of romanticism that characterized his age, and ours. The romantic, ever young, ever intent on recreating himself (or trying to) in his own style, develops if at all with curious inconsistency: (1) maturity of style is rarely accompanied by change or maturity of idea; or (2) thought moves toward an orthodoxy and conservatism which emasculates style; or (3) repeated apocalypse runs afoul of repeated despair, thwarting a sustained and maturing vision. I would hesitate to insist that the second happened to Wordsworth, but the first fairly well describes the purest American romantic of this century, E. E. Cummings, and the last, if not exactly Coleridge's fate or Shelley's, was Hart Crane's. None of these adequately measures Stevens, whose development from a poet of great sensuous energy into a poet of reflection and statement has often forced the critics to opt for either one or the other, but seldom for both.

I am prepared to accept Stevens' own suggestions of how his poetry developed: that it did develop and mature rather than simply change, and that the evidence of this development lies in neither his ideas as such nor in basic stylistic changes as such, but in the inner life of a changing and aging sensibility. "The imagination changes as the mind changes" (NA 151), he once remarked, further implying that the mind changes itself in its imaginative acts. It is no proof of Stevens' maturing that he abstracted the tissue of ideas (his aesthetic) repeatedly stated in his late poems from the vivid experiences of his earlier ones, or that his late abstractions are simply enlargements and proliferations of his earlier images. There is every indication that his ideas in the abstract were fully formed (if not clearly refined) in the early poems, and fully in-form them. Stevens did more as he developed, however, than peel away the rich texture and expose the core of abstractions. His development is manifest in an evolution of style, and thus of the self it expresses, in a continuum of poems that become a body of poetry, a total structure. Moreover, the single poem, as distinguished from poetry,[3] constitutes but a moment of reality, an achieved form in the ever-flowing life of imagination, as Stevens conceives the incessant conjunctioning between mind and world. The poem is a form, life come to order in a vivid abstraction (in metaphor, the sound of words), and thus to reality. Life is a rhythm, a grammar, of forms. The poet's total achievement, his "book," is a life manifest in forms, and hence the fullest realization of the life of the imagination which Stevens insisted is the life we live everyday.

Now this romantic notion is repugnant to the traditional conceptions of poetry, inverting as it does the ratio of poetry to life. There is no apologizing for it on the grounds that it is one man's faith, no more than on the grounds that the romantic metaphysics or epistemology on which it builds is *ipso facto* true. For now it is enough to insist on Stevens' premise. This is the burden he placed on poetry, its centrality in his life, which allowed him to shift with ease between the masks of amateur and professional poet. And it is from this perspective, as I see it, that we can do most justice to Stevens' full contribution to poetry. We can understand the demands he made of it and, ultimately, of his readers, who in sharing the life of his poems would share, as he felt, not the reality of one lone mind but the potential reality of all. But this is to jump ahead into the labyrinths of later Stevens, which are made out of the forms of the earlier.

Stevens began writing poetry while a special student at Harvard (1897–1900), serving a brief tenure as president of the *Advocate* in which he published stories and editorials as well as verse.[4] But it was some fourteen years after leaving Harvard that his first mature poems appeared and nine years after that, as he neared forty-four, that he published his first book. This casual, and even mannered, indifference to reputation eventually inspired some uninspired doggerel by Amy Lowell, at the very time Stevens was thinking in terms of a first book:

> He has published no book and adopts this as pose
> But it's rather more likely, I think, to suppose
> The particular gift he's received from the Muses
> Is a tufted green field under whose grass there oozes
> A seeping of poetry like wind through a cloister.[5]

This, and much more, appears to borrow heavily from a Stevens letter to William Carlos Williams, which Williams had published in the "Preface" to *Kora in Hell* (1920).[6] Williams had written to Stevens suggesting that the latter collect his several published poems into a volume. Stevens' reply casually admonished Williams about his attitude toward a "book," citing the desultory quality of Williams' *Al Que Quiere!* (1917). Williams, insisted his critic, had become modish in refusing to adopt a mode and had ended with a medley of verse, not a book of poems. It was a question largely of point of view, Stevens opting for the unifying center of the poet's voice, Williams for a potpourri of observations and impressions that approves this plural world of things and the poet's intense fascination with them. Summing up, Stevens was firm: "I have a distaste for miscellany. It is one of the reasons I do not bother about a book myself." A book of poems, he added, "is a damned serious affair."

In part pose, of the fastidious kind that was to damage his reputation as a serious poet, Stevens' attitude is nonetheless revealing of the coherence he sought in poetry. A "book of poems" for him had to be in itself a fully realized form (as witness even his lasting interest in the fine art of bookmaking), but above all it should not be miscellaneous. This passion for order is clearly evident in his original intention to call *Harmonium* "The Grand Poem: Preliminary Minutiae," which allows one to speculate that even as he appreciated the collection's unity he envisioned it as the rudiment of a greater Poem. That his *Collected Poems* was at one time to be called "The Whole of Harmonium" indicates that he viewed his total Poem—like Mallarmé's "Oeuvre" perhaps—as something more than a collect of poems. Stevens' *Collected Poems* composed a life in poetry—the total being of the poet, like Susanna's beauty in Peter Quince's harmonies, attaining its "immortality" of form. At the same time, it is the life of the intermediate forms, the poems as individual acts of the imagination, to which we must attend; for Stevens was not one to allow great systems or visions to subsume life itself, or subsume his individual poems. The edges are never tucked in; there are always a few poems remaining, something posthumous even to complete (or almost so) the circle left incomplete by the *Collected Poems*. "I say live by literature," Stevens wrote, "because literature is the better part of life, provided it is based on life itself" (OP 222; see also OP 158). Stevens was a poet who knew very well how man aspired toward final forms, to know the absolute, to complete the circle.

And he knew just as well how this aspiration reached beyond life, willing a negation to it and its poems.

Stevens implies, nevertheless, that his poems as individual pieces take on a new import in the continuous life of the whole. Only if we honor them in this way can we understand the occasional indifference to the strict, formal coherence of his "book" which allows him to publish casual exercises beside highly ambitious and carefully designed poems, or build large structures out of the notations of a commonplace book. For unlike Williams' medley of poems, Stevens' "book" coheres to the unifying self from which all forms issue. It is in this sense alone that Stevens' development becomes meaningful: the evolution of a style is for him the process of creating a sensibility; every act of imagination is an act of life (what Valéry called the self as architect), an aesthetic adventure in search of form or wholeness. Those acts which issue in minor exercises are no less essential than those leading to the larger structures. This is more than is normally allowed the poet; for he may abuse the privilege of insisting his every utterance is significant because it is his. And so for him it would seem to be. It is true enough that a severely discriminating assessment of Stevens' many poems would find distressingly few with the mark of unquestionable posterity on them, and those not necessarily the famed anthology pieces. But Stevens asks, with Whitman, that we read through the poems to the self they body forth, to see the parts in the whole and the whole in the parts, and to discover the sum that exceeds the parts. Indeed, his willingness to let his poems stand for what they (and he) were at the time of their composition, with a minimum of revising, would suggest his satisfaction that poetry must be the "cry of its occasion,/ Part of the res itself and not about it" (CP 473). This is the very opposite of James updating his sensibility, or Yeats remaking his earlier self, or Auden his ideology. The minor exercises, the casual asides, along with the stately, elaborating, enlarging meditations—this collage of perceptions and thoughts, images and metaphors—finally compose their separate occasions into the continuous and developing life of the mind. Hence my intention in this study to approach the poems individually and chronologically, yet in the light of the complete consort.

The reception of *Harmonium* reveals the wisdom of Stevens' editors in refusing his title of "Grand Poem." For even in the most generous of reviews, and there were several, it was considered a miscellany, a book of poems all too insular.[7] Stylistically, *Harmonium* was at once traditional and experimental: it flouted Eliot's and Pound's denunciation of romantic effusiveness, implied that Imagism was as subjective as objective, deliberately mixed American vernacular with Gallic elegance, and had some of its finest moments in the "archaism" of blank verse. Confounding critics, it did not altogether satisfy Stevens. His subsequent development, consistently stripping away the panoply of this style, clarified the intrinsic themes—broadly, as Stevens never tired of saying, the relations between imagination and reality. But at the same time it reminded Stevens' readers of what had been lost. For his ideas, undressed, fell upon hard times. In the antiromantic thirties, when to live in poetry was to be a moral pariah, Stevens ran afoul of the Marxists as well as the humanists. And later, when the vogue of a romantic, personal poetry returned, a younger generation of poets could take *Harmonium* as a revealed word, only to find that the author of those exquisite exercises had adopted the mode of an intellectual poetry, the very mark of modernist orthodoxy against which it was revolting.

The reception of Stevens' books, which I have recounted elsewhere,[8] constitutes in itself a significant footnote to contemporary literary history, if only in its revealing contradictions. Recognized everywhere and at all times as a poet of consequence, Stevens was until the last decade and a half almost always considered out of the mainstream; the consistency of his attention to one theme was thought at first to allow him too much freedom, and at last too little. As his poetry entered its period of greatest change and complexity, in the late thirties and early forties, he was considered a poet who had not changed, because, unfortunately, he seemed to be saying increasingly in his prose essays that his later reflections on poetics were simply abstractions from his earlier adventures in imaginative perception. On the other hand, Stevens' increasing stature among critic-scholars is largely the result of their esteem for his later work, which has tended to put off his peers. And younger poets, finding *Harmonium* inimitable, were not always at ease with the discursiveness or impersonality of the late vintage.[9] Randall Jarrell, musing on this problem of influence, was not comforted: "If someone had predicted to Pound, when he was beginning his war on the iambic foot; to Eliot, when he was first casting a cold eye on post-Jacobean blank verse; to both, when they were first condemning generalization in poetry, that in forty or fifty years the chief—

sometimes, I think in despair, the only—influence on younger American poets would be this generalizing, masterful, scannable verse of Stevens', wouldn't both have laughed in confident disbelief?" [10] Perhaps Jarrell is thinking of Theodore Roethke, though Roethke is much more passionate, more tortured, more Yeatsean; perhaps Richard Eberhart, though again he is more academic and, recalling Frost, more given to a poetry of anecdotal and dramatic reflection; perhaps Howard Nemerov or Delmore Schwartz; perhaps, almost certainly, Richard Wilbur. But no matter. The thing about Stevens' late poetry that stamps itself indelibly on the poetry of the forties and fifties is its spirit not its mode. For the mode, whatever else one says about it, may be disastrous to the imitator.

Yet the task of judging Stevens now seems a question of assessing this "masterful, scannable" verse, not its generalizations but its intrinsic style. That is to say, the later poetry as it grows out of the earlier becomes the normative activity of any imaginative mind, not the special perceptions of a private sensibility, and hence a metaphor for the possibilities of the human mind creating the forms of the world in which it lives. If it echoes the earlier themes, if it parades many of the familiar images in but slightly different dress, the later style issues in a different poetry: its images are refined and memorable, not immediately felt; they are no longer the tenor of perception but the vehicle of meditation. The poem becomes an action rather than a perception, a process rather than a form. Whether one calls it a poetry of meditation, or of process (a poetry constantly becoming),[11] it cannot, I think, be wholly measured by the traditional forms, largely romantic meditations, which it so readily suggests. It is a poetry which not only extends and completes the essentially traditional style of *Harmonium,* but provides the standard by which the early poetry must be understood. *Harmonium,* in other words, must be seen in the light of the whole rather than the whole in the light of *Harmonium.* For only in this way can we see how integral and necessary it was to the later poetry, and equally, why it was a poetry, as Louis Martz has claimed, that Stevens had to outgrow, and did.[12]

Moreover, when seen in its totality, Stevens' work reaches its heights in the long poem—or more precisely, in the incessant short lyrics and meditations which gather magisterially into a whole. The movement of his *Collected Poems* is always toward the long poem, about which the separate, minor pieces cluster, providing the landscape of a mind rich in particulars but nonetheless composed or moving toward composure. This is another way of seeing the ordonnance of the canon, as well as that of the individual books, each of which is summed up in or leads directly to a long poem. It is a way of coming to terms with a poet who, even when absorbed in relating himself to the rich diversity of his world, knew that the life of the mind was a constant search for order, or form, and hence an examination of itself in the act of finding "what will suffice" (CP 238–40). Or to put it another way, the phylogeny of Stevens' long poem, from the pseudo-narrative of "The Comedian as the Letter C" (a poem of man in the world) to "An Ordinary Evening in New Haven" (a poem of the world in man), constitutes the making of a self in poetry and provides us with a perspective from which to judge Stevens' Grand Poem. "The mind of the poet," he wrote in an essay, "describes itself as constantly in his poems as the mind of the sculptor describes itself in his forms, or as the mind of Cézanne described itself in his 'psychological landscapes'" (NA 46). Thus his analogy between style and sensibility, between poem and poet, in whose "indirect egotism," as Stevens calls it, we discover not only one man's mind but mind itself. We find "ourselves in poetry."

The critic of Stevens is confronted with a number of basic contradictions. He is and is not an intellectual poet, is and is not a "pure" poet. He is a romantic, but disconcertingly impersonal; a traditional poet, yet experimental; an imagist, but also a symbolist of sorts; a lyrical and meditative poet who wears equally well the masks of clown and pedagogue. The fact is, he can be at any one time any and all of these, which should, I think, give pause to those who would either praise his poetics or censure his obsession with one limited and vague idea. Stevens resolves the contradictions in a poetry which is neither pure lyric nor intellectual argument, but which at any one time may pose as either. Accused, especially in his early poetry, of being a hedonist pure and simple, Stevens was no less a reflective poet from first to last. The experience of his poetry, even at its most militantly antirational, is within the mind rather than at the tip of the senses. If Dr. Williams' purpose in poetry was, as he said, to bring an "environment to expression," [13] by way of making it the poet's possession, Stevens' was to bring a mind to expression, by way of understanding how much its ambience was of its own making, and thus what reality obtained in the imagination's transformations.

Compared with Williams or Marianne Moore, contemporaries whom he most nearly resembled, Stevens was never an objectivist or descriptive poet. "Not all objects are equal," he once wrote *en passant*. "The vice of imagism was that it did not recognize this" (OP 161). This attitude defines his style from the beginning and separates him fundamentally from Williams. Indeed, his lifelong quarrel with Williams was on this point of how far the imagination could or should remake the world: that is, evolve a qualitative reality of mind from the quantitative reality of pure perception, yet still savor the essential life of things as they are. *Harmonium* set beside Williams' *Spring and All* or the purely descriptive poems of *Al Que Quiere!* clearly evinces the inwardness of Stevens even in the period when his primary task was to relate the self to its physical world. Stevens was never, like Williams, so much astonished by the "thinginess" of nature as by the creativeness of imagination.[14] He was never so much attracted by the discovery of "things as they are" (relationships like red wheelbarrows glazed with rain water beside white chickens) as by the discovery of himself in the act of discovery (as in observing his own imagination in the life of seascapes off Tehauntepec).

Stevens' images are, essentially, metaphors of consciousness, or states of consciousness. They are the products of a perception, but a perception refreshed; moreover, they exist not in static arrangements (fixed perceptions) but in a state of process or flow, describing the landscape of a sensibility rather than the landscape of a physical world. Stevens' images adhere to a world of things—as often ordinary and commonplace as exotic and rare—with striking fidelity, but only in the sense that they catch the moment in which mind and thing marry. What Stevens does, of course, is fuse his images into new arrangements, new patterns—he "cures," so to speak, the ordinary by looking at it in an extraordinary (which is to say, individual) way. His way of seeing the world, while suggesting an impressionistic method, is more like that of Klee; the extraordinary is the ordinary as perceived from the inside rather than the outside: for example, the form of a thing, its appearance, may be seen to suggest motion rather than fixity, or nature looked at in terms of its incongruities rather than its congruities. When in "Connoisseur of Chaos," for instance, Stevens notes the geographical and linguistic incongruity in the obvious fact that African violets can be grown in Connecticut, or the humor in the fact that his English friend in Ceylon does not like tea (CP 215), he provides evidence enough of the truth he lived by—if man will but look at his world intently enough, he will see that it is more than it appears and hence he will be free of its dominion. He will make it his. The fact that people do build pagodas in Reading, Pennsylvania, is a kind of poetry, the alteration of the landscape by an act of the mind, as well as the starting point of a poem; it is evidence enough to qualify Tocqueville's prophecy that there could be no poetry, in the traditional sense, where all things are considered equal. The poetry of self, which Tocqueville said could be the only viable poetry of democracy, works to give back to things their uniqueness. The introduction of a sensibility into the world transforms things—or better, transforms the arrangement of things from the natural to the human—but more important, transforms the world in which one dwells, the mind. Stevens' essay "Effects of Analogy" treats at length, but with wayward authority, this quality of the image as a subjective "attitude," as the analogy of an emotion, in style as well as sense (see NA 111, 127–28). If Williams, as was said of E. E. Cummings, often sees the world through the eyes of an innocent child,[15] Stevens sees it through the eyes of a self-conscious middle-aged man (or a spectator in the "Theatre/ Of Trope") who knows what it is like to experience the child's vision only because he knows he is seeing a fiction of his own making. It is this self-consciousness, which Williams and Miss Moore almost managed to suppress in their earliest poems, that characterizes Stevens' poetry from the very first. His full flowering in the meditative vein was natural and inevitable, and not a sudden break from his early mode.

Both Miss Moore and Williams, perhaps she more so than he, did develop toward a reflective poetry. Williams had experimented with meditation in the impressionistic fillips of *Kora in Hell* before he discovered the "variable foot" and the possibilities of raising environment not only to form but into the life of its inhabitants. Yet his poetry is not strictly inward. On the contrary, the inwardness of *Paterson* is the landscape's. Miss Moore came to write reflective poems, like "What Are Years?" or "In Distrust of Merits," that issue clearly as thoughts and relationships rather than discoveries—a poetry that is not inward at all, though the last named concludes, "There was never a war that was/ not inward."[16] For these two, meditation followed description or grew out of it. Basically, "No ideas but in things," or at the outside, a few ideas about things. But things first, "real toads." Or there is Miss Moore's technique of montage, a few things to substantiate a few reflections or generate a thought—the analogy between mind and apteryx-awl, for example. "The accuracy of the vernacular," she told Donald Hall in the *Paris Review* interview, was her interest, and if but a half-truth it is revealing.[17] For Stevens, on the other hand, description was revelation, not of things but of self. There are no things, no forms, without the self: "This is nothing until in a single man contained,/ Nothing until this named thing nameless is/ And is destroyed" (CP 416). Here, in the transformations of imagination, in the exchanges between self and world, the generation of new forms out of old ones transforms the self likewise.

The way a poet feels when he is writing, or after he has written, a poem that completely accomplishes his purpose is evidence of the personal nature of his activity. To describe it by exaggerating it, he shares the transformation, not to say apotheosis, accomplished by the poem. It must be this experience that makes him think of poetry as possibly a phase of metaphysics; and it must be this experience that teases him with that sense of the possibility of a remote, a mystical *vis* or *noeud vital*. . . . We are interested in this transformation primarily on the part of the poet. Yet it is a thing that communicates itself to the reader. Anyone who has read a long poem day after day as, for example, *The Faerie Queene,* knows how the poem comes to possess the reader and how it naturalizes him in its own imagination and liberates him there. (NA 49–50)

Stevens' satisfaction with the scannable measure, always an irritation to Williams, and his preoccupation with metaphor and analogy—these manifest the inwardness of Stevens' poetry, just as Miss Moore's craftily stylized *vers libre* and Williams' "variable foot" reveal their attempts to bring their idiom to precise description of thing or thought or emotion. The essential difference is this: language for Williams must be made to work upon the world, bringing that world to form while preserving its diversity even within the perceiver; language for Stevens is the form into which the incessant exchanges of self and world flow, the syntax of inwardness or fiction. It does not describe the world, much less effect changes in the world; it describes the world in the mind. Stevens accepts the conventions of external form (his basic iambic pentameter, his penchant, especially in his late verse, for unrhymed triplets) not because this was the way poetry traditionally had been written, but because this was the rhythm of his imagination as it moved from perception to form. Metaphor, not the line, was his concern, and stanzas existed to be dissolved: set forms to remind the poet of the set limits of language. (One recalls Frost's claim that iambic is the basic rhythm of English and that set forms are commitments, as against Pound's and Williams' argument that the formal measure distorts the idiom and hence distorts reality.[18] Stevens would find this argument academic in either case, and irrelevant.) But more than that, the traditional forms and even the language of early Stevens become in the later simply a framework which is the essential form of all acts of mind, while within the framework, like the bed of a river, there flows the ever-changing, ever-various process of reality. The structure of a poem, for Stevens, becomes the action of metaphors. The landscape of his poems, whether it be "Sea Surface Full of Clouds" or "Credences of Summer," is in the mind. His subject is the activity of this mind, the act of creation, to which the reader is witness and in which he is involved. It was Stevens' faith that by being true to himself, by exercising his own imagination upon the world (whether external or internal), he could manifest the possibilities of every mind, and hence create for his time the idiom of man. For him the poet was born with his sense of the world, and that sense "dictates his subjects to him." Moreover, "The measure of the poet is the measure of his sense of the world and of the extent to which it involves the sense of other people" (NA 122–24). He believed no less than Williams that the poem had a social function, but Stevens would have it speak for, as well as to, the community of minds.

This ambition bespeaks Stevens' limitations. We know them well enough: abstractness, impersonality, a poetry without people and drama, a world without passion in which suffering is academic and tragedy non-existent, a solipsistic poetry. Even Eliot's poetry is more densely and variously populated. Ironically, Stevens seems to have achieved by plunging into the self that impersonality which Eliot sought in an escape from self. But this is to mistake Stevens' intention and, I believe, his achievement. The movement from the personal voice of *Harmonium* to the impersonal, vatic "I" of the later poems evidences Stevens' attempt to hypostatize his humanity, not transcend it—a development from what Emerson called "mean egotism" to a human state of "Man Thinking," or to what Thoreau described as his cabin on the frontiers of thought. One has but to give himself up to the activity as well as the idea of Stevens' last poems to discover the intense passion there, a passion seeking form. What his fellow poets, especially Williams, felt to be a decline of *brio* in his late poems was for Stevens an essential sacrifice of one kind of idiom for another (a sacrifice demanded by internal changes of his poetic self). It was the necessary result of his desire to write the great poem of Man or earth, now that the great poems of Heaven and Hell had been written, and Heaven and Hell had proved to be of man's making (see NA 142).

To reject the abstractness, the narrowness of theme or intellectual posture of Stevens' poetry is to reject a kind of poetry once regarded as supreme. The eighteenth century, for example, could not entertain a percept without a concept, an experience without a form, an act without an idea, or a poem without a moral. On the other hand, to accuse him of departing from the life of sensation, or passion, to entertain empty abstractions is to evoke a dogma of poetic value equally stifling. Stevens links his poetry with past traditions, the continuity of human minds or imaginations. But in that very act he extends it to the frontiers of modernism, offering us acts of mind rather than the mind's finished formal products. It redounds, this mind, in forms ever so much alike, but we will be mistaken if we take Stevens' apparent repetitions of thought and form as repetitions alone. He never feels "twice the same about the flecked river" that is his ambience.

Accepting the challenge to prove the being of man in a secular age, stripped of his divinity and left an impoverished animal, Stevens pursued the human with an energy and intrepidity unequalled in our time. Whether or not he asked too much of poetry, history will judge. It is my task in the chapters ahead to present not only what he asked of it, but what he realized in it. But first it is necessary to look more carefully at the particulars of his development and at the theory (or lack of it) of imagination which lies at the heart of that development.

chapter 1

Virile Poet and Necessary Angel

The imperfect is our paradise.
The Poems of Our Climate

This endlessly elaborating poem
Displays the theory of poetry
As the life of poetry. A more severe,

More harassing master would extemporize
Subtler, more urgent proof that the theory
Of poetry is the theory of life . . .
An Ordinary Evening in New Haven

*P*aul Valéry has offered a provocatively germane observation on the knottiest of questions about modern poetry:

"Every true poet is much more capable than is generally known of right reasoning and abstract thought.

"But one must not look for his real philosophy in his more or less philosophical utterances. In my opinion, the most authentic philosophy lies not so much in the objects of our reflection as in the very act of thought and in its handling." [1] Valéry's position is appropriately modern and representative of an age when the poet discounts any pretense to systematic thinking (knowing the failures of system), disdains the abstractions of reason which separate mind from the swarm of vital life, and assumes that the *Weltanshauung* of his age, as well as its symbology, reflects chaos rather than cosmos. For Valéry, post-symbolist and in the truest sense a humanist, locates cosmos in the self, in the activity of mind contemplating itself, and thus creating order (and itself) out of nothingness. Valéry again:

17

Our poetic pendulum travels from our sensation toward some idea or some sentiment, and returns toward some memory of the sensation and toward the potential act which could reproduce the sensation. Now, whatever is sensation is essentially *present*. There is no other definition of the present except sensation itself, which includes, perhaps, the impulse to action that would modify that sensation. On the other hand, whatever is properly thought, image, sentiment, is always, in some way, *a production of absent things*. Memory is the substance of all thought. Anticipation and its gropings, desire, planning, the projection of our hopes, of our fears, are the main interior activity of our being.[2]

Beyond Valéry's remarks the question of poet as philosopher tends to become academic. Is Archibald MacLeish, for example, presuming in a work like "Einstein" to write the poem of astrophysical vision, more philosophical than one intent on limning the immediate world and man's relation to it? Is T. S. Eliot, reflecting his formal philosophical training in a poetry stuffed with learned allusions and philosophical echoes, more philosophical than one who plays with ideas by way of exploiting their poetic qualities? Does Eliot's use of knowledge, his fidelity of objective reference, his systematic evaluation of ideas, betoken the equipment of the philosophical poet—as against, say, Hart Crane's use of pseudo-science to bridge the actual and ideal? Not according to Eliot himself, who in his undogmatic commentaries measured accurately the difference between the word and the deed, and knew very well that poetry was the deed of the total self, not the word of reason. The dogma of our century has separated reason from feeling, and the Imagist renaissance and all the strenuous theorizing of Eliot and the New Criticism has not resolved it.

The restlessness of Nietzsche still broods over our poets—if not always his nihilism, then his exasperation with the limits of reason, with Apollonian fatigue and the desire for normalcy it breeds. Henri Bergson confirms the loss of a closed and closeted universe, yet finds that the artist's intuitive way to reality succeeds where Newton's reason failed. Alfred North Whitehead, pursuing Coleridge's end in a different context, praised poets as arbiters of the diverse and discoverers of rational man's misplaced concreteness. George Santayana, who should have been the philosopher of the modern and somehow failed (perhaps because of his assurance that the forms of animal faith were adequate to explain reason's simplifications), never ceased to insist that reason died without imagination. Each contributes, if not a convincing metaphysics for his age, a powerful apology for the poet and his way to "truth." The modern poet, too self-conscious to be anything else, must in Valéry's terms be "philosophical." The reality he confronts is in no sense to be endured passively nor (omitting possibly Cummings) celebrated without qualification as a world of pure possibility. "Sensation" demands "sentiment," as Valéry said; or oppositely, according to Eliot, an idea must be felt as immediately as the odor of a rose. Stevens called the opposites of the pendulum reality and imagination, but his concern was with the swing of the pendulum itself—the poetry which connected the two and in which the poet realized his being.

Valéry's distinction, stressing as it does his preoccupation with the processes rather than the forms of thought, presents a stern challenge to humanists. For if authentic philosophy is the "act of thought," what objective measure, what norm of correctness beyond the pragmatic test is there? What then are the philosopher's hard-earned truths but images of his own concoction, and hence examples of sentimental error? Thus positivism reads metaphysics as poetry, another form of pseudostatement. The solution has been to divorce the poet from the philosopher, to justify his world of feeling by denying him access to the world of thought. Critic-poets like John Crowe Ransom, who would ionize (or ironize?) Cartesian opposites, are harshly dealt with as philosophical interlopers, wishful monists masking as neo-Kantians. Critic-poets like Yvor Winters, who would moralize them, become dogmatic about the limits of feeling and of poetry. But the problem for criticism has been poets like Stevens, who seem to enjoy the dualism, even to the point of making riot of it, and in their fun stealthily suggesting that they have resolved it. Nothing discomfits the old humanist so much as E. E. Cummings insisting that "all ignorance toboggans into know" only to trudge back up the slope (toward the heights, ironically enough) to ignorance again. Or Stevens mocking Professor Eucalyptus, seeker after the source of things in New Haven, for doing what a plant or a poet naturally does and thinking it special. And when Stevens writes his essay on philosophy with a student's handbook for reference, to prove that philosophy is an analogue of poetry rather than its opposite, critics groan and philosophers return the paper without comment.

II

It is in Stevens that this vexed (and perhaps irrelevant) question of philosophical poetry in our time is most clearly focussed—in Stevens who began as an unremitting antirationalist and ended by aspiring to write the great poem of earth, a great philosophical poem. But the problem presents itself in Stevens in more obvious ways: in his aspiration toward a "theory of poetry" that would be nothing less than a "theory of life"; in his longing for a complete *Ars Poetica,* and his realization in his prose of something less; in his obsession with making his poems account for the reality of poetry and thus become commentaries on themselves. Yet it is not Stevens the theorist who is a philosopher, any more than Stevens the poet who wears the mask of philosopher and creates metaphors on the subject of creating metaphors. It is rather the poet who, as Valéry said, manifests his real philosophy in his acts of poetry, in the activity of his imagination swinging free between sensation and sentiment, feeling and form, fact and memory, and creating in that process a self as well as a poem.

There remains, nevertheless, the question of Stevens' own theorizing, and the attention he repeatedly called to the imagination as at once the source and subject of his poetry. The influence of his own commentary, as it proliferated in the 1940's, had the effect of isolating this implicit subject of the poems, of the earlier ones as well as those just appearing. The results were, on the one hand, a crystalization of the themes which had preoccupied Stevens from the beginning, and on the other, a revelation of their abstractness. After the publication of *The Necessary Angel* (1951), it became necessary to account for Stevens' theory of imagination and to define its obvious sources. Moreover, the volume, as a kind of *vade mecum,* could only raise the issue (pro or con) of romanticism in our time. Stevens' preoccupation with his formula reminded too many critics that if romantic poets made extravagant claims for the imagination, they need not limit themselves to commemorating it in every utterance. Ranging between reasoned argument and commentary that sounded like offhand Coleridge, like Stéphane Mallarmé's Tuesdays, or Valéry studying his *moi,* the essays nonetheless insisted that the poet's business was with the "contemporaneous" and not transcendence.[3] As a gloss on his poems, Stevens' essays had the effect of reducing the earlier eloquence and *joie de vivre* to a core of statement about the nature of things. But the essays themselves, more intractable than Coleridge's *Biographia Literaria* because at once less personal and more casual, would not submit to formal analysis.

The most famous of them, "The Noble Rider and the Sound of Words," is a typical example (NA 3). Designed for oral delivery at an academic symposium which included papers by I. A. Richards, Cleanth Brooks, and Philip Wheelwright, it plays brilliantly upon a few *aperçus* illuminated by a number of casual and often incongruous examples. But three quarters of the way through the paper, beginning the last of five parts, Stevens can remark: "Here I am, well-advanced in my paper, with everything of interest that I started out to say remaining to be said." It so happens, however, that what he has to say *has* been said, in the play of his mind upon the examples. He had begun with the metaphor from Plato's *Phaedrus* of the two-horsed chariot, concluding that this figure no longer engages the mind since it no longer is attached to a reality shared by all men. The imaginative tension between our earth- and heaven-bound self no longer exists; mythology, stripped of belief, becomes a form. Stevens continues, in perhaps the most famous sequence in the essays, by describing two statues. One, of Bartolommeo Colleoni by Verrocchio, which stands in Venice and is described no doubt from reproductions, strikes him as a remarkable example of imaginative power, capturing in its rhythms the spirit of its subject and his age. Yet in a prosaic time, our time, this classic of imagination is out of place. "No longer quite the appropriate thing outdoors," it clashes with the pure prose of this age; it is "a little overpowering, a little magnificent." On the other hand, Stevens refers to Clark Mills's statue of General Jackson that stands in Washington, D.C. This is, contrary to Verrocchio's Colleoni, a work of fancy, a pastiche of nationalistic aspiration and vulgarity. "Fancy is an activity of the mind which puts things together of choice, *not* the will . . . striving to realize itself in knowing itself." The terms fancy and imagination, of course, are Coleridge's, borrowed as Stevens indicates from I. A. Richards' study of the Coleridgean imagination as a "principle of the mind's being" rather than of some transcendent source. Stevens then offers a third example, *Wooden Horses,* a reproduction of a painting of an American carnival scene, a merry-go-round of motion and earthy life, created in the proportion of today's reality, attending to nothing but this world, yet, unlike General Jackson, importing into its world no facile desire. Thus having finished two parts of his essay, Stevens launches more directly into his discourse on art today and the "pressures of reality," referring in the course of his exposition to F. W. Bateson, Locke, Hobbes, Wordsworth, Joyce, Boileau, Descartes, Freud, Georges Braque, Picasso, Arnold Schönberg, Croce, Friedrich Schlegel, I. A. Richards, Robert Wolseley, Coleridge, Sir Walter Scott, Jane Austen, Virginia Woolf, Hitler, Horatio, Dr. Joad, Bergson, and others, all in a few pages.

By the time he gets to his explicit subject, the role of the poet in the contemporaneous, what remains to be said only begs the question: the role of the poet "is to help people to live their lives." The substance of the argument has come earlier. Plato's parable is wrong for our time because it no longer attaches to reality—that is, no longer accounts for imaginatively, nor animates, any fundamental conception we have of ourselves as men. Similarly, Verrocchio's statue depicts a nobility, appropriate for its age, which is out of touch with an antiheroic time. Mills's, on the other hand, projects the wishes and the vulgarities of a country without custom, in which an arrangement of superficial gestures satisfies the appetite for nobility. There remains only the painting of *Wooden Horses,* created in the idiom of modern reality, imbued with a life whose coherence is its naturalness, its spontaneity, its attachment to the vitality of the commonplace. These are illustrations only, but this indeed is the way of Stevens' prose. Even the more orthodox discourses, essaying an argument, develop by example and illustration rather than through closely reasoned exposition.

This is not to say, however, that the essays reveal nothing but themselves. On the contrary, they reveal everything, including the mind in the act of seeking order. These opening illustrations from "The Noble Rider," for example, contain nearly everything he would have to say about the relations of imagination to reality and about the role of the poet in the contemporaneous. It begins by denying the transcendent and the myth of the Platonic soul, which is to say, man's ability today to indulge in the "dear, gorgeous nonsense" of myth. Modern man as noble rider is an attenuation of Plato's, caught in an alien and violent world that will not allow him to soar. The poet as noble rider, in contrast to Plato's, is not simply a spirit snagged between body and soul; he is man confronting the only reality he can presume, the contemporaneous, with words for his mode of transport. But his are not magical words. No longer able like Verrocchio to conceive of man in neo-Platonic terms, as power manifest in form, the modern poet is condemned to live in the present and the actual, which challenges both his power and his form. On the one hand, he is bade not to turn away, not to reduce reality to wish or fancy; on the other, his role is defined as a kind of escapism, a resistance to the external event or events—like, say, the picture of *Wooden Horses* which, while it acknowledges the incoherence of the commonplace, discovers the vital patterns that inhere there. Stevens had written a poem on the theme, "The Pleasures of Merely Circulating." *Wooden Horses* acknowledges life as motion, and does not wish to suspend time. Discovering the balance between the contemporary and the ideal, Stevens defines the eloquence of the ordinary and fixes the role of the poet in terms of a marginal (but necessary) angelism. The imagination he invokes, if a metaphysical power, is subsumed by no metaphysics. It is an aspect of mind bound by its ambience. While universal—that is, the common denominator of men, of mind—it exists as a function of man's being only in relation to the external contingencies of his being. If it resists the pressures of the actual, it is only because it has first admitted them. It helps us "to live our lives" not by altering nature, but by altering the self. Or to put it another way, it affords a continuity of the self through a world that is discontinuous, even while it helps one adjust to the necessities of circumstance. The imagination, in this context at least, is both psychological and metaphysical.

What remains in this essay, the tissue of learned references, merely amplifies. Wordsworth's "Preface" to the *Lyrical Ballads* serves to define the proper idiom, the language which honors the ordinary; James Joyce demonstrates the possibilities of extending this idiom in the direction of connotation, extending the particular into idea (form) yet retaining its facticity. Freud's *Future of an Illusion* exemplifies the modern demand that the mind submit fully to reality. (This seems a deliberate misreading of Freud as a kind of positivist; an earlier essay had heralded him for giving authority to the irrational.) But Croce's theory of intuition-expression indicates to the contrary the kinds and degrees of self-transformation possible in the life of the mind, the perpetual creation of the self in its acts of the mind. And so on. The sifting of contraries is as felicitous as in the poems, and that indeed is Stevens' mode. Like his later meditations, though with a greater illusion of rigorous thinking, the essays move from imagery to idea and back again, from illustration to condensed epigram and beyond. His most effective strategy is to begin with the illustration (like a sensation) and proceed inductively and indirectly, with startling shifts and returns that distill the sentiment. The procedure is deliberately repetitious, wrapping a thought in qualifications and exempla, until, as in meditation, one arrives at the epigrams or capsule ideas that are a kind of order—a balance of the real and the imagined.

This is as true of the other essays as of "The Noble Rider." A more obvious example is "Three Academic Pieces," which begins as a rigorous examination of levels of resemblance (between thing and thing, thing and image, image and image, and even idea and idea), but two thirds of which consists of poems about metaphor exemplifying a *"gradus ad Metaphoram."* One is struck by the occasional clarity of definition and example, but the clarity (it is usually epigrammatic) will not render anything like a metaphysical theory of imagination. There is no essay of Stevens which quite escapes these limits, nor is any intended to. Even that presumptuous attempt to write something for a philosophical journal, "A Collect of Philosophy," building as it does on notes from friends, poetic marginalia, and the basic summaries of *A Student's History of Philosophy,* is a work of illustration in its own right. And given its assumption, it is irrefutable—given the assumption, that is, that the old distinctions between reason and imagination are no more valid than faculty psychology, that any conception of reality (cosmic or otherwise) which issues in the descriptive form of words, whether it be Leibniz' *Monads* or the idea of God, has a touch of the poet in it. The need to affirm this truth was, of course, Stevens' old need: to make a place for poetry at the center of our lives. And how better do it than insist, as Kant and Berkeley and Santayana and Whitehead and Bergson had done, that imagination lies at the origins rather than the end of reality?

Stevens' arguments, though relaxed and amateurish, exist to a very real degree at the center of modernism. He seems to begin with F. H. Bradley, who shocked professionals with the assertion that "metaphysics is the finding of bad reasons for what we believe on instinct." With the disappearance of all but the vestiges of adequate metaphysical systems of explanation, the retrenchment of modern literature in self-examination, its obsession with epistemological relativism rather than metaphysical coherence, has become commonplace. Stevens' poetics, to put it all too simply, begins with the very real problem of a self that is no longer a soul. Perhaps we do not always recognize this in Stevens because we do not find in him the expected forms of anguish. But Stevens' imagination is nonetheless involved in the deadly game of being modern. There is no clearer evidence of this than in essays like "The Noble Rider," which ask the question of whether the artist (as representative self) should face the world of violence or withdraw from it, and answer that he has no alternative. Stevens' commitment to his mortality is evident in the limitations of his noble rider, by no means the bard or hero of old. But the testimony of his choice is the poetry: from the adventures of Crispin in "The Comedian as the Letter C," discovering the minuscule self in a world that rejects the old definitions of man, to the poet of "Esthétique du Mal," assessing the causes of man's reduction as a forfeiture of the imagination that provided those definitions. Crispin's posturings are parodies of the old beliefs in an orderly universe; the poet of "Esthétique du Mal" confronts that loss realistically. The thing that distinguishes Stevens is that which superficially separates him from the existential dilemma: his "passion for yes." That passion is, quite simply, his retention of the imagination and thus the will to act joyfully in the face of absurdity. If it is risky to extract a systematic theory from Stevens' prose, it is equally risky to avoid that prose or deny its relevance. For what Stevens has to say of the imagination provides more than a gloss on his poetry and the development of his self in poetry; it provides a tenable explanation of the imagination in an age which can make every claim for it that Coleridge made, except one: that it may be more than human in origin.

III

Stevens began writing prose in the thirties, a decade after *Harmonium* had manifest his poetics. Characteristically, this early prose, though it does not use the later terminology, is preoccupied with the challenge of the contemporaneous and, secondarily, with the significance of romanticism in our time. Neither is deeply probed, perhaps because of the nature of the occasion, but more obviously because analysis is not strictly possible. Idealist metaphysics are no longer tenable, and the imagination as an aspect of psychology has proved the perilous future of illusions. In any event, Stevens was concerned with the poetry of two peers, both romantics like him because they had powerful feelings about their worlds. The first of these essays, an introduction to a collection of Williams' verse, produced a lasting irritation between the two poets because it called Williams a devotee of the "anti-poetic" (OP 254).[4] The second, a review of Marianne Moore's *Selected Poems,* attends more dutifully to individual poems, while offering some tentative asides on two distinctive kinds of romantic poetry (OP 247). A third and longer essay, written a short time after (*ca.,* 1937), presumably as commentary on the reading of some of his own poems, fills out a thin sheaf of reflections that preceded Stevens' major efforts in the next decade to outline an *Ars Poetica.*

They do, however, offer some points of departure for speculation. The Williams essay, in all its innocence of terminology, is indispensable, with its talk of modern reality as antipoetic and the poet's feeling for his world as sentiment. It not only says something about Williams—his "sentimental side"—but about Stevens, especially his sense of the ordinary, of a nature no longer alive with its own meaning. What he calls the antipoetic is nothing more than the texture of the commonplace, of ordinary things and events. (Stevens never attempts to specify "reality" as anything beyond ordinary appearance, commonplace events, or the texture of social reality. His is a perceiver's reality, not an ontologist's or metaphysician's.) His remarks about the poet as romantic ("All poets are, to some extent, romantic poets") assume likewise that sentiment is a "blood passion," not the divine light of self. Stevens' romantic poet—defining himself as well as Williams—is a man on the dump, "one who still dwells in an ivory tower, but who insists that life would be intolerable except for the fact that one has, from the top, such an exceptional view of the public dump."

This early obsession with fact and facticity, with the inescapable "thinginess" of the material, yet the need to resist the pressure of fact—this governs his remarks on Miss Moore, too, especially his effort to isolate two kinds of romanticism. The essay provides likewise an early instance of Stevens' reading and reflects the putative early influence of Irving Babbitt whose courses in French literature (in translation!) Stevens had attended many years previously. Stevens' two kinds of romanticism are elementary: the one an "obsolescence" because it imputes to the world a vitality of transcendent origins; the other something "living" because it incorporates ("hybridizes"), in a kind of symbiosis, fact and feeling. This is clearly the minimum definition—as in the later essays, definition by exemplum. The review tells us, however, a little about Stevens' thinking if not about his reasoning. His allusion to Babbitt offers no evidence of the lasting impression of academic humanism; his reference to A. E. Powell's *The Romantic Theory of Poetry*, on the other hand, might indeed reveal the particular kind of romantic Stevens wishes to isolate as "true." For Miss Powell's (Mrs. E. R. Dodds's) book reads the English Romantic poets through the eyes of Croce, rejecting explicitly their claim of mystical or transcendental origins of the imagination and at the same time modifying Croce's theory of expression to make it account for the materiality of the world on which it is dependent. One cannot, of course, presume further than the direct reference to this book. But we can understand from it, and from Stevens' preoccupation with Miss Moore's and Williams' kind of romanticism, Stevens' attempt to define the imagination in humanistic terms, or in terms of its obligation to a given world of vital matter—a world of Darwin and not of Plato, as he put it years later (OP 246).

This is not so evident in the third essay, "The Irrational Element in Poetry" (OP 216), though again it is dedicated to defining the poet's struggle with the contemporaneous (this time the violent pressures of history *entre deux guerres*), and his attempt above all to preserve his sensibility amid that reality. "One of the motives of writing is renewal," he concludes, anticipating that later conviction, supported by Bergson, that the projection of imagination upon the matter-of-fact was the struggle of maintaining and extending the self (its duration) in time and space. In one very real sense, this was the challenge to the new poetry of the century's earliest years, which not only found it imperative to voice a new idiom, but to do so by way of defining what it is to be a self, a consciousness, in a world that promised no coherence between mind and matter. The more precise Imagist exercises, projecting consciousness into objective forms, manifest one aspect of this literature attempting to survive a failed romanticism.[5] Stevens, whose early poetry especially shares many affinities with Imagism, indicates nevertheless a revealingly opposite strategy: relating himself to his world by ingesting its flow of appearances and transforming sensation into the rhythms and forms of his own sensibility. He seeks identity (and a duration of self) in conjunction with a vital, not a static, world. One has only to compare the spontaneity of his early style, his extravagant images which flow into the motions and forms of a continuing experience, with Pound's emphasis on sculptured verse or Eliot's attempt to relate the self to a fixed time, to see two responses to the romantic dilemma. Both kinds of form, as Stevens accurately discerned in his essay on Miss Moore, are indeed romantic in nature. Poetry is an epistemological adventure for Stevens because life is. The disappearance from the modern mind of metaphysical assurances, including even Kant's *a priori*, leaves the self and its formal imagination with only a tenuous identity. The imagination, or that power of mind which appears to be involved actively as opposed to passively in human experience, becomes the sole reliable *a priori*. Through it alone does one achieve identity and continuity in relation to his world and its pressures. The image, for Stevens as well as for Eliot and Pound, is a gesture of the self in search of order.

A corollary of this in Stevens' poetics is his alleged and at times militantly professed antirationalism. The history of Stevens' attitude toward reason as the enemy of imagination follows a line of moderation, from the almost absolute separation of the two in his early poetry to an attempt in later writings to define them as integral and complementary.[6] The history may in fact describe no more than Stevens' maturity and his full involvement in the temper of his time. Surely his disrespect for reason is not unique, nor his misprize of it so extreme as that of many of his contemporaries. The moderation of his antirationalism is to be explained in one way as an education in epistemology, exposure to philosophers like Santayana and Whitehead who wrote compellingly of the congenial activity of imagination and reason. In another sense, it is the product of Stevens' own discoveries, through poetry, that the fragmentation of things, of purposes, and of the self was the result of man's willfully dividing his inherent capacities of mind into various activities and designating some of them as true, to the exclusion of others. Reason, as an official view of being, was arrogant in its exclusiveness, and Stevens' early poetry, offering its intuitions and perceptions, freely criticized this arrogance with its own. His discovery later that poetry was of the whole being brought about the moderation in a grand succession of remarks on the subject. He concluded finally with the observation, many times repeated, that if the poet and philosopher had different modes, their objective of truth was the same, and that, indeed, the imagination was the "sum of our faculties." The graduated change is evident in his poetry, beginning in *Harmonium* with the sense of an imagination which affords the self a unique sense of the world (and hence defines a unique self) as opposed to the reason's conventional and ordinary apprehension of the real. In the later poetry, to the contrary, the imagination becomes a part of total consciousness, operative not only in the discovery of novelty, but in realizing one's continuous identity within the flow of ordinary events. In short, Stevens' changing attitude toward imagination (for that is what his changing attitude toward the reason is) reveals his own growing sense of composure, his discovery of full identity and the community of consciousness shared by all men. It manifests likewise his difficulty in offering a coherent theory of imagination without the foundation of an idealist metaphysics. Fortunately, congenial philosophers like Bergson and Santayana had shown him the way.

IV

If Stevens did not formulate a metaphysics of imagination, however, it was not that he lacked the theoretical equipment. He distrusted theory, it is true; but he knew also that any talk of imagination must be descriptive and analogical, and that any theory depended on a larger schema—a metaphysics or a faculty psychology—which subsumed poetry even as it made poetry magical and apocalyptic. Like a good realist of the imagination, he wrote only of what he experienced. Imagination was manifestly a part of the poet's experience—evident in his feelings, in his language, in his forms. And though he had experienced that feeling of transport, of ecstasy, which so often gives the poet a sense of being possessed by a divine power, he could never quite believe in the miraculous.

Stevens' ex cathedra theorizing, however, is neither wholly derivative nor thoughtless. It is a deliberate, and at times perfectly cogent, attempt to define the modern imagination—the secular imagination—without such appeals to the mystical as characterize Graves's *White Goddess,* Yeats's *Vision,* or Hart Crane's "logic of metaphor." His language may echo Coleridge—it could hardly do anything else—but the fact is that Stevens is alert to the distinctions between his account of the imagination and Coleridge's. Whatever else can be said against the vagueness of his terminology, he cannot be accused of parroting transcendental idealism. The same caution must be advanced against those who find in his poetry not only the characteristic moods of Romantic poetry but the forms and images of *Symbolisme*. These forms, images, attitudes are there, as several responsible and discerning commentators have attested;[7] but their significance lies, as I hope to demonstrate subsequently, in Stevens' variations upon them. In almost every essay Stevens admits the challenges of the modern and makes claims for the imagination in terms which reflect the disintegration, from Coleridge to the present, of the romantic vision. It is necessary to make this point, and reinforce it, not simply because Stevens has so often been compared with Coleridge, but because it is essential to the understanding of Stevens' contribution to (not theory but) poetry. If his explicit description of Coleridge as "a man who may be said to have been defining poetry all his life in definitions that are valid enough but which no longer impress us primarily by their validity" (NA 41) were not enough, there is the reservation, concerning Shelley's definition of divine poesy, that definitions are "approximations," reflective of the vision and need of the time which offers them.

But more important are two separate instances in which Stevens reveals the particular stresses on the poet trying to define his power in an age that suspects the arcane and has no common metaphysics. The first, appropriately, is in the essay "Imagination as Value" (NA 133), where he attempts, with the aid of Ernst Cassirer, to distinguish "between the imagination as metaphysics and as a power of the mind over external objects." The one, as he allows the neo-Kantian Cassirer to explain for him, derives from a sense of the transcendental, in which the universe itself is conceived as a work of art continuously realizing its divine author. The second is the work of the artist every day, or even of the self every conscious moment. The truth of the first ("romantic thought"), he adds, is not necessarily proof of a metaphysical or transcendent reality, but only a manifestation of the wonder the poet feels in possessing imagination. And he suggests that we must somehow "cleanse the imagination of the romantic." The modern poet's metaphysics must be of another kind, centering in the mind and honoring the mind's attachment to an ambience of things and forces.

In still another essay, "Effects of Analogy" (NA 107), he says that the poet is "constantly concerned with two theories." In one sense, the poet feels his imagination "may be part of a much larger, much more potent imagination," like Coleridge's, or Emerson's. In another, the imagination is a "power within him to have such insights into reality as will make it possible for him to be sufficient as a poet at the very center of consciousness." He goes on to distinguish the one from the other, "adherents of the imagination" as against "adherents of the central," saying that "the adherents of the imagination are mystics to begin with and pass from one mysticism to the other. The adherents of the central are also mystics to begin with. But all their desire and all their ambition is to press away from mysticism toward the ultimate good sense we term civilization." This poetry of the central is, indeed, the crux of Stevens' theory, his concern with abstraction, and his development. I will return to it later. For now it suffices to distinguish the two kinds as (1) a poetry which implies a metaphysical relation between man and the universe and (2) a poetry which implies only the poet's relation with his world and his centrality in that world. This does not quite afford a complete poetics, because, once again, the theory of poetry seems to imply a theory of life that is not completely sketched. But the negative side of it is clear enough; repudiating the romantic, it repudiates the transcendental and makes poetry central in the struggle of the self to know its world.

One has to allow Stevens a great deal of latitude in these essays. Moreover, he must resist the temptation to grasp at the seedling ideas and residual thoughts that seem to echo more considerable and ambitious theories of poetry. For one thing, the opaqueness of terminology, along with the effusiveness of those passages which are heralds to the manna of the word, allow easy and illuminating comparisons with Coleridgean and Symbolist poetics. The imagination Stevens describes is an "esemplastic" power. Its function is a corollary of Coleridge's primary imagination, or creative principle of mind. Its end, "reconciling opposite or discordant qualities," is pleasure. Similarly, Stevens' casual remarks on metaphor and image suggest something like a theory of "correspondences," though more typically his terms are resemblance and analogy. Occasionally, he identifies the transformations of the poetic act as a "metamorphosis," with all the implications that it effects changes in reality, though he knows very well the transformation is in his way of seeing reality.[8] A careful scrutiny of the terminology, however, reveals that it is usually something less than imprecise, and nearly always qualified. Whatever else one can say of Stevens' debts to Coleridge, the fact that he finds the source of imaginative light—light is a basic metaphor of imagination for both—to be wholly human is a signal difference (see NA 61–62).[9] He advocates no meta-physics of imagination, except that which accounts for the refraction of perception into arrangements of value, causing in its transformations a transformation of the self.

The evidence of the poetry bears out this resistance to what must be called the transcendental origins of imaginative light—from that set exercise "Sea Surface Full of Clouds," with its attempt to define the activity of imagination in the several unique moods it yields, through "An Idea of Order at Key West," which discreetly rejects the implication that the imagination has any causal effect on the material, to "The Rock," which defines the life of the mind as a world of reality existing in analogy with, yet independent of, the indifferent materiality of things. Stevens' kind of poetics, in other words, is missing one of the essential romantic coordinates. One recognizes, for example, some characteristic symbols: the moon, blue, light, the many women (usually either fertile or ordinary, never ideal or veiled maidens). But the symbols do not function in a fixed and predictable fashion, are not, in other words, archetypal. There is evidence in his poetry of the thirties and in his essay "The Irrational Element in Poetry" that he at one time gave some thought to the universality of the imagination's forms, the source of which was some kind of "subman" or primitive self. But neither Jungianism nor primitivism had any real attraction for him. For the most part Stevens' images, like his allusions, do not depend on their external reference but are defined in their relationships within the poem, or within the total world of the poems. The images exist to relate the self to its world, not to any greater self or any transcendent world, and in their existence manifest the *durée* of mind.

Stevens' remarks on images and resemblances underscore this. There is nothing in them to suggest either an Emersonian or Baudelairean theory of correspondences. The concern is exclusively with language as it intervenes between the self and the particulars of its world. The poetic image is an analogy, or what Stevens calls a "praeter-nature," symbolic in the sense that all forms are symbolic. The act of imagination imports "the unreal into what is real." Which is to say, it creates what did not before exist, an image or analogy which is in itself real—not simply as an image, or poem, or metaphor, but as a quality of the poet's world, his self. All of this, suggestive as it is of the mystique of imagination, is descriptive of something like a phenomenology of mind and, as one commentator has remarked, has certain associations with Sartrean and Husserlean intentionality.[10] Stevens' penchant for simplification and broad generalization—e.g., that poetry manifests the poet's "sense of the world" or that an image expresses an attitude on the part of the maker and an intervention in terms of style—does invite a number of comparisons with various epistemologies, existential as well as neo-Kantian. But Stevens' concern is not simply to describe the process by which the poet apprehends nature; it is with the process by which he apprehends his own. And thus he is concerned with verifying the poet's "third world" (see "Esthétique du Mal," xii) as a reality, a reality not so much in the substantive sense as in the sense of a manifest consciousness, manifest sensibility, or a manifest self.

Two passages will suffice, each coming at the conclusion of an essay. The first is from "Effects of Analogy":

[The poet's] words have made a world that transcends the world and a life livable in that transcendence. It is a transcendence achieved by means of the minor effects of figurations and the major effects of the poet's sense of the world and of the motive music of his poems and it is the imaginative dynamism of all these analogies together. Thus poetry becomes and is a transcendent analogue composed of the particulars of reality, created by the poet's sense of the world, that is to say, his attitude, as he intervenes and interposes the appearances of that sense. (NA 130)

The word "transcendence" as used here is a kind of abstraction from the flow of particulars, which becomes an analogue of the poet's sensibility, his own continuous and dynamic sense of things projected in a dynamic form, the poem. The life of transcendence is a life of the mind, or imagination, the self achieving duration not in its consciousness of things (images) so much as in its "imaginative dynamism" (flow of images). The second passage is from "Three Academic Pieces":

In the fewest possible words since, as between resemblances, one is always a little more nearly perfect than another and since, from this, it is easy for perfectionism of a sort to evolve, it is not too extravagant to think of resemblances and of the repetitions of resemblances as a source of the ideal. In short, metaphor has its aspect of the ideal. This aspect of it cannot be dismissed merely because we think that we have long since outlived the ideal. The truth is that we are constantly outliving it and yet the ideal itself remains alive with an enormous life. (NA 81–82)

Once more, the "ideal" is abstraction from the incessant flux of the natural; or in Bergson's paradox, the ideal is real, but a real illusion. The search for the perfect resemblance, an "ascent to any of the abstractions that interest us importantly, an ascent through illusion," it is suggested, is the normal activity of mind. This ideal does not so much deny the natural, as transform it figuratively into relationships of value. Stevens' is the voice of an age which no longer accepts the illusion generated by the human tendency to project the ideal beyond the self (either Plato's forms or God) and then attribute to it creative power. The ideal he seeks lies in the "central" of the self. Or as he puts it in a context I noted earlier, "poetry is a process of the personality of the poet," but it is of his "whole personality," including that which he shares with other men. Theoretically, this is as far as Stevens could go, or needed to, in asserting as he did at the conclusion of "Notes toward a Supreme Fiction" that the irrational is rational.

V

There are two other aspects of Stevens' poetics which need comment, because they call for comparison between his and Symbolist poetics, yet distinguish his modernism. One is his professed disregard for inspiration, so like Valéry's. The other is the impersonality of his poetry, especially the later, which not only does not include other people but abstracts even the poet's voice into an impersonal idiom. To take the last first, Stevens' poetry develops generally from a poetry filled with individual feeling and singular (if abstract) personae to an abstract voice of the poet as any man, or everyman, the poet as imagination itself. One result of this, which relates to Stevens' particular development of style and his quest for the central, I will treat later. Another, that quality of introspection which makes so many of his poems either dramatic dialogues (especially such early works as "Sunday Morning" or "Le Monocle de Mon Oncle") or meditations of the self upon itself (later poems like "The Auroras of Autumn" or "The Course of a Particular") manifests his assumptions about the role of poetry in life. These poems, of which the contemplative situation of "The House Was Quiet and the World Was Calm" is an excellent shorter example, are exercises in intensive abstraction, of the mind reading itself. This mind seeks within itself those forms (fictions) by which imagination arrests the incessant flow of things, including memory, and through which it accomplishes its own duration. It is not just that

Stevens, eschewing the personal, hopes like the Symbolist to discover the duration of the soul, its oneness with the ideal, in this almost perfect moment of contemplation. On the contrary, the process of contemplation is an act of abstracting from the clutter of one's particular mind inward to what is the essence of mind. It is an attempt, in the act of imagination, to discover the common denominator of the human rather than his common ambience, a search within the common and the ordinary for the "substance in us that prevails."

Stevens' impersonality is the result of abstracting from the particulars to the forms of mind, in order to discover what he shares with the human— the forms by which man apprehends the world and the dependence of these forms on the world. His poems, however impersonal, are never devoid of the flowing masses of material things, the ordinary from which consciousness draws its stimulus and to which it is married. The physical world of the earlier poems is, in a general sense, a continuing reality in the later poems, a world of process, only now mixed with memory and a new kind of desire. It is a world experienced not in and for itself but as the projection (the *durée*) of the self. In a late poem like "An Ordinary Evening in New Haven," a voice speaks from a place, but it is the remembered as much as the actual place that moves him. The images in Stevens' later poems are transcendent analogues of the life of the mind, not of a single, separate self but potentially every self if it will but realize its potentiality. Stevens' impersonality is not Bradleyan, nor Eliotic. Having no metaphysics on which to hang imagination, he makes of imagination a pure metaphysics, an activity of process analogous to the vital process of the material, which perpetuates the self as a part of, yet apart from, "things as they are." Accused of pursuing one kind of abstraction, Stevens would point out that he was doing no more than the great poems of Heaven and Hell, which projected the drama of self into the spheres, creating the illusion that there was a drama of immortal souls. For him the self contained within itself the wherewithal of transcendence. It is to this end of defining the limits of imagination, the common ground the poet shares with his auditors, that Stevens devotes a large part of his essay "The Figure of the Youth as Virile Poet." If poetry is a manifestation of the personality of the poet, it is not a "direct" but an "indirect egotism." He would be Emerson's representative man, but only after achieving Eliot's impersonality.

Similarly, his indifference to inspiration. The crucial passage appears in the essay "The Relations between Poetry and Painting," and like everything else in these essays seems more an aside than the center of an argument:

The mind retains experience, so that long after the experience . . . that faculty within us of which I have spoken makes its own constructions out of that experience. If it merely reconstructed the experience or repeated for us our sensations in the face of it, it would be the memory. What it really does is to use it as material with which it does whatever it wills. This is the typical function of the imagination which always makes use of the familiar to produce the unfamiliar. What these remarks seem to involve is the substitution for the idea of inspiration of the idea of an effort of the mind not dependent on the vicissitudes of the sensibility. It is so completely possible to sit at one's table and without the help of the agitation of the feelings to write plays of incomparable enhancement that that is precisely what Shakespeare did. He was not dependent on the fortuities of inspiration. It is not the least part of his glory that one can say of him, the greater the thinker the greater the poet. It would come nearer the mark to say the greater the mind the greater the poet, because the evil of thinking as poetry is not the same thing as the good of thinking in poetry. The point is that the poet does his job by virtue of an effort of the mind. (NA 164–65)

One thinks in contrast of the claims made for Shakespeare by the Romantics. Stevens, like Valéry, denies that the poet is visited by any power but his own. The activity of poetry, far from being a special or exceptional activity, different in kind from the ordinary acts of the mind, is different only in degree, intensity, or effort. Perhaps Stevens came upon this fortuitously, but it coincides with his sense of poetry as a normative, and central, human activity. It may very well explain Stevens' tendency, especially in his later years, to publish poems that appear to be no more than exercises, or poems which cluster about familiar themes with familiar images, playing variations ever so slight in keys ever so like. Surely it helps to explain the naturalness with which he developed the long poem, not as a form describing its own inner logic, but as a concerted "effort of the mind" in the process of realizing itself, achieving duration of self through evolving forms: "the sense of being changes as we talk/ . . . talk shifts the cycle of the scenes of kings" (OP 109).

But there is still another aspect of this rejection of inspiration relevant to an understanding of Stevens. Poetry becomes an everyday activity, not special, a part of the normal life of the mind, as almost every paragraph of Stevens' prose attests. Indeed, it is the conception of the poetic activity, its centrality in our lives, that best explains the philosophical ambitions of Stevens' prose. He wants, needs, to establish poetry at the center of our lives. It is difficult, being confronted by a poet who insists that the "irrational is rational," to make a case for his "philosophical" poetry; it is equally hard to concede that his habits of reading could have had an indelible influence on his sense of the world. The evidence of Stevens' prose reveals that he had read in almost every modern philosopher and, except in a very general sense, understood almost none. This may very well be true, but as an amateur of ideas Stevens knew whereof he borrowed. The clusters of philosophical reference in his essays testify, if not to the profound absorption of philosophy, then to his judgment of the pertinancy of modern ideas to his poetics. Even a partial listing of these thinkers indicates a distinctive pattern: Berkeley, Leibniz, Kant, and more particularly Nietzsche, Schopenhauer, Whitehead, Croce, Bergson, Santayana, Jean Wahl, Ernst Cassirer, and aestheticians like Henri Focillon and Ramon Fernandez. Within the variety there is the concentrated preoccupation with the primacy of the mind, not only as form-giving but as a vital, generative energy which in its activity transforms the whole being. One can, it is true, trace Stevens' poetics to any number of philosophical, as well as aesthetic, origins. But the characteristic quality of each of these presumed sources is the stress on the ordering center of mind.

If there were a culture hero for Stevens' imagination, it should perhaps have been Nietzsche, with his radical optimism of will, his arrogant championing of the irrational, and his herald of the power of mind over the ordinary. For Nietzsche best satisfies the modern artistic temperament, more so than Kant's fixed grammar of mind. Yet for all the affinities with Nietzsche, who turns up in Stevens' poems and prose of the late thirties and early forties, as seeker after the innate idea of reality, it is with the more clearly epistemological and vitalistic philosophies of Santayana and Bergson that Stevens' poetics must be identified. Frank Kermode has said that it is as much through the influence of Santayana and Bergson as through direct exposure to French poetics that Stevens is linked to the Symbolist tradition.[11] Yet one may interpret the evidence oppositely. The vitalistic materialism of the two—their stress on the primacy of immediate experience, the dangers of conceptualism, and the duration of the self in consciousness—offers a gloss on Stevens' resistance to the transcendental appetite of symbolism.

The evidence of influence is abundant, though the degree of direct influence remains, especially in the case of Bergson, problematic. Bergson's theory of comedy, as Samuel French Morse has convincingly shown, found its way into the forms as well as the conception of Stevens' early poetry, and may even serve to explain Stevens' comic strategies.[12] The possibilities opened up by Bergson's theory that in seeing the world we project ourselves upon it were, as Stevens could infer, as various and as unpredictable as the imagination. But they were likewise dangerous to be indulged unless accompanied by a critical sense of how one's view of the world mocked one's limitations. For Bergson the comic was the gesture of the human, and it offered a dramatic way of projecting the little vices of human egocentrism into a form that might free one from those vices. It might offer the hedonist a way out of the cul de sac of self-indulgence. It might offer him, that is, detachment from himself and return him, as it would return Stevens' Crispin (and perhaps even Stevens), to his full social, and human, nature (see Chapter 2). But the ultimate philosophical import of Stevens' affinities with Bergson is the way Stevens' poetry, especially that written after 1940, realizes in its own intrinsic style Bergson's theory of the duration of the self in time, the continual and continuing self-creation which takes place in the act of imagination, in the intercourse of consciousness and flux. (That particular style, and its significance for modern poetry and poetics, I treat in the Afterword as the distinctive quality of Stevens' modernism.)

The influence of Santayana is, on the other hand, more immediate and probably more direct; for the most part, his influence is more evident in the poetics and later poetry than in the early writings. More than any other modern thinker, more certainly than Walter Pater, Santayana exemplified not only an aesthetic in which imagination and art were central, but a life lived in the imagination (see NA 147–48; CP 508). Just when Santayana's attraction to Stevens began is uncertain, though unquestionably it goes back to Harvard days and the early writings (see Chapter 2, pp. 53–54). And it is very obviously an enduring influence, expressed more as a sympathy of minds than in direct debts. What is important is the brotherhood of sensibilities, which is confirmed by Stevens in the way he absorbs and translates Santayana's thought into poetic act. It is Santayana who offers the clearest focus on the ground of Stevens' poetics (as contrasted with the techniques and strategies of his poetry), just as Bergson offers the best metaphysical perspective on the implications of his later meditative style. As more than one of Stevens' critics has remarked, Santayana's enlargement of poetry's moral and religious nature, combined with his unremitting secularism, made its early impression on Stevens. For Santayana, the possibilities of transcendence were the possibilities of mind; the fullfillment was Form, the inner life of the human projected into the matter of the world. Erecting a humanist system of value out of the fragments of idealist thought, Santayana has been somewhat disregarded by poets and suspected by humanists for at once failing to place enough faith in the irrational (which is a part of Reason) and allowing it too much. It is interesting that Stevens' expressed admiration for formalist and neo-Kantian aestheticians—like Ramon Fernandez, Henri Focillon, or Ernst Cassirer—emphasizes in them what is basically present in Santayana's thought. Santayana's animal faith, like Bergson's intuition, continued the Kantian tradition by seriously qualifying its idealist dimensions and returning the life of forms to its wholly human source.

The points of reference between Stevens' poetics and Santayana's early writings on aesthetics and art are numerous. But more need be said about the epistemological ground of the affinity, as well as something about Stevens' emphasis on the "good," his poetics of "pleasure," and his poetry of "order." A theory of poetry may begin right here with Santayana: "Perception is a stretching forth of intent beyond intuition; it is an exercise of the intelligence." [13] Or, as a corollary to Bergson, it is an extending of the self into time-space through consciousness. In the act of apprehending reality, one realizes himself in respect to his world, and not beyond it:

By a substance I understand what modern philosophers often call an "independent object"—a most unfortunate phrase, because precisely at the moment when a substance or an essence becomes my object, by becoming the theme of my discourse, it ceases to be independent of me in that capacity: and when this happens, before the cognitive relation between me and my object is established, a dynamic relation has probably arisen between the substance of that object and the substance of myself. . . . When a thing becomes my object it becomes dependent on me ideally, for being known, and I am probably, directly, or indirectly, dependent on it materially, for having been led to know. What is independent of knowledge is substance, in that it has place, movement, origin, and a destiny of its own, no matter what I may feel or fail to think about it.[14]

Stevens' poetics substantially agree to every point. But this is the barest structure of an epistemology, upon which the drama of consciousness rings extraordinary changes; it is hypothesis clearly, but it approves the independence of the self from the monistic origins which had finally suffocated the Romantic imagination. It is here that Santayana's example lends intellectual respectability to Stevens' shifting of the relations between imagination and reality:

> If all data are symbols and all experience comes in poetic terms, it follows that the human mind, both in its existence and its quality, is a free development out of nature, a language or music the terms of which are arbitrary, like the rules or counters of a game. It follows also that the mind has no capacity and no obligation to copy the world of matter nor to survey it impartially. At the same time, it follows that the mind affords a true expression of the world, rendered in vital perspectives and in human terms, since this mind arises and changes symptomatically at certain foci of animal life.[15]

That "all experience comes in poetic terms" is Stevens' beginning; thus symbol is reality, a form of the marriage of self and world, a phenomenon of mind. For him, experience, like poetry, is a "transcendent analogue composed of the particulars of reality." Experience is symbolic, but only of itself. Other particulars of Santayana's thought are equally relevant: mind is an activity of the total self, not causally effective (and Stevens' poetry, critics like Winters notwithstanding, never commits the romantic fallacy of thinking mind is causally effective upon matter); mind entertains qualities, creates values and, in its highest moments, works of ultimate value, represented in the forms of art, religion, morality; in search of value, desiring to contemplate beauty, the mind generates the highest forms of animal existence in its artistic and moral visions; above all, imagination needs the discerning judgments of reason to distinguish and direct the various forms in their proper relations.[16] If Stevens' poetics stop short of the moralistic dimensions of Santayana's philosophy, it is just as we would suspect. But his essay "Imagination as Value" is a virtual testimony to Santayana.

Stevens evaluates the normal life of the mind and the creation of poems proper as different in degree, not in kind. Imagination lies at the center of the self and becomes *a* (not *the*) source of reality, even if it "adds nothing, except itself" to reality (NA 61). Hence poetry is an essential and integral human activity. How else justify its "pleasure" as anything but the meanest self-indulgence unless it were intrinsic to the needs of the mind? how else embrace a "good" that is not God's? how else approve man? Imagination is an energy of the intensest creative life, which can free man not by giving him dominion over matter but by sparing him from matter's dominion. Stevens' poetry is a grand example of that struggle with matter and with time.

VI

Philosophy may illuminate aspects of Stevens' poetics. But only his poetry illuminates philosophy. This is not to confuse either poetry or poetics with philosophy. Indeed, the only contribution Stevens' poetics makes to modern thought is the perspectives it offers on his poems. Unlike Eliot's or even James's essays, Stevens' provide but few valid reflections on the essential nature of the artist's practice, or on the cultural phenomenon of his art. Here and there appear a few tacit suggestions on poetic form or style, on language, on the temper of the modern. But the essays in conjunction with the poems form a part of Stevens' Grand Poem. They illuminate, moreover, his development.

Whatever else one may say of *Harmonium,* it was not a poetry given unconsciously to hedonistic pursuits, but contains within itself a criticism of how far the imagination can go in interpreting itself. There is a crucial passage in "Le Monocle de Mon Oncle" (CP 15) which begins:

> If men at forty will be painting lakes
> The ephemeral blues must merge for them in one,
> The basic slate, the universal hue.

The uncle, a mask of the poet, laconically suffering the wisdom of age and loss, tries hard to believe that "there is a substance in us that prevails." He knows the power of our desire for transcendence, our need to know the one (the basic slate) within the many (the ephemeral blues). But he knows too that the one kind of experience is different from the other:

> When amorists grow bald, then amours shrink
> Into the compass and curriculum
> Of introspective exiles, lecturing.

Like the lady of "Sunday Morning," though more alert to the paradox, the uncle longs for permanence, but finds all of paradise in change. His problem is a problem of the modern: how to retain amours in a world of sensibility which shrinks more and more everyday; how to retain them even as an introspective exile. The answer is not to embrace fixed forms of belief, but to find one's truths in forms of poetry which relate one to reality and change, yet provide whatever transcendence is possible within the real.

There is every indication that Stevens' poetry develops according to this early discovery. "When one is young," he wrote later, "everything is physical; when one is old everything is psychic" (OP 167). If an imperfect epigram, it nevertheless confirms his own sense of the way one comes at last to live in the mind rather than at the tip of the senses. But there is little enough in *Harmonium,* despite claims to the contrary, of direct, sensuous experience; rather there is a questioning of that experience, and of the uncertainty attendant on committing oneself wholly to it. For every poem of pure delight there is one, like "Domination of Black," equally absorbed by the perils of self-consciousness, the domination of time. And the volume's most ambitious poems—"Sunday Morning," "Le Monocle de Mon Oncle," "Peter Quince at the Clavier," "The Comedian as the Letter C"—as well as the finest of the minor exercises, achieve their greatness just to the degree that they honestly confirm the uncle's dilemma: not by making a leap of faith, but by discovering the pleasures of time and change to be dependent on time and change. While it is as commonplace to call this a hedonist poetry as to call it symbolist, neither term adequately takes its measure, any more than facile comparisons with imagist qualities define its style. *Harmonium* is, as I have claimed, essentially an inward poetry, a poetry of spontaneous celebrations of pleasure and delight, but spontaneous celebrations of doubt and uncertainty and searching as well. The two are fused, most often in dramatic or pseudo-dramatic antitheses which confront a persona with a vital landscape. The result is a volume of poetry in no way guilty of slighting the intellect or neglecting the commonplace.

That much-abused little exercise, "Anecdote of the Jar," is a case in point, because it submits so readily, in terms of the title, to allegory. The most famous of its commentators, Yvor Winters, has read it in severely moral terms, with the jar representing intellect set over against the wilderness, or nature—a conflict which ends to nature's disadvantage.[17] According to Winters, this fear of reigning intellect is just another example of romantic error. Here is the poem:

> I placed a jar in Tennessee,
> And round it was, upon a hill.
> It made the slovenly wilderness
> Surround that hill.
>
> The wilderness rose up to it,
> And sprawled around, no longer wild.
> The jar was round upon the ground
> And tall and of a port in air.
>
> It took dominion everywhere.
> The jar was gray and bare.
> It did not give of bird or bush,
> Like nothing else in Tennessee. (CP 76)

The thing that troubles Winters is not really romantic dogma; it is the ambiguity, the indecision, what he called in Frost, the spiritual drifting. Like Stevens' other anecdotes, this is a kind of aesthetic joke, a part of the incongruity of self-consciousness. Just how the jar, an artifact, comes to represent intellect is not clear. That it is an artifact, shaped in the kiln of mind out of the stuff of nature, would seem a basic clue. There is something ambiguous about its shape: a barrenness yet portliness. In any event, jar clashes with "slovenly wilderness" and, finally, draws all attention to itself, at the expense of distracting from all the naturalness (whose beauty is its own and not recognized by the poet until after his act). But if the voice of the final stanza repudiates this "dominion" of jar, the poem fails to decide between art and nature. It is as incongruous as displaying a still-life in the wilderness. But in terms of the unresolved anecdote, man's desire for wholeness, or roundness, leads in one way toward sur-roundness, and in the other toward the freedom of chaos. The poet (any conscious self) is caught between: he *places,* arranging here and there, seeking what will suffice to reduce his world to his forms and finding, most often, that the struggle between the self and its matrix is at once necessary and unresolvable. Like the jar, the imagination's forms invariably leave something out of account. Later poems would first intensify the opposites—city and jungle, statue and Africa—before rejoining then in a completer harmony—abstraction and change, self and rock. The binding landscape of Tennessee (like Crispin's Carolina) is a virgin and vulgar land to be explored and tested by the man of imagination seeking how far he can go in reducing the world to his own proportions. The whole of *Harmonium* is summed up, not resolved, in the tension between two opposites which do not submit easy answers about the "dominion" of man or nature, imagination or reality. (The pun on *see*-ing is obvious.)

Harmonium is a physical poetry only in a sense relative to Stevens' later introspective mode; it is a poetry of balding amorists (not necessarily Stevens, but the poet as modern self, *l'homme moyen imaginatif*) readjusting himself to a world which is not, as it formerly was, his plum. The world of *Harmonium* might be summed up as the opposition between two personae: between Hoon of "Tea at the Palaz of Hoon," who believes that he contains all of his world within him, and Crispin, who at the end of "The Comedian as the Letter C" discovers how much of himself is contained in the world. A more revealing poem, because less obvious, is "Sea Surface Full of Clouds," which is not, as it first appeared, an imagist or symbolist poem so much as an epistemological exercise. It is that in the sense that it consists of five still-lifes (seascapes) exemplifying one man's attempt to fathom the shifting surfaces of a world at once changing and constant. It is a poem at once "pure" (a series of unique perceptions which exist in and for themselves) and a revelation of the process of perception.

"Sea Surface" (CP 98) offers one of the rare examples in Stevens of a set form, each poem consisting of eighteen lines in six tercets, each developing according to an inner law of perception. The set form, representing the complete sequence of an experience, represents similarly the form of imagining which does not lead to transcendence but only to momentary composure; the different textures of each of the five poems suggest the possible variety within the form. It is an open-ended poem, its five sections arbitrarily limited to five distinct impressions out of a potentially infinite number. Having assumed the constancy of the imagination as process, Stevens can then introduce the variables of change, not only in the mood of the perceiver but in the modality of what is perceived. The boundless, apparently formless sea is a place apart from the human. Stevens' use of the ship as perspective is more than the accident of its occasion—a vacation poem?—for the ship like the self is afloat in indifferent waters, without which it has no being and in which its place is provisional. That each section opens with a conflation of sky and deck, modulating into a conscious self-sea drama, suggests something of the passive nature of the self as it awakes to its place apart. Being stimulated to "think," the imagination is moved to resistance, generating what Valéry called "sentiment," forcing the "machine/ Of ocean" to unclothe an animate being which is then redressed with the light of imagination. The key twelfth line, so aptly a thing apart, is, moreover, an act of the imagination assuming its full identity. And in this discovery of its own power, the self transforms the uncertainty of the initial perception into "fresh transfigurings." What follows line twelve is resolution, those transfigurings which are accompanied by a sense of renewal within the self. In every instance, no matter what the poet's attitude toward his gift, no matter how he questions its discovery of animate or malevolent sea blooms, the poem dissolves into an order and the experience is made whole. It is not alone a phase of the imagination that has passed, but a phase of the life of the mind.

The resolution of each poem is a curious and important event; for the various poems prove the imagination's action to be not only formally constant, but humanly inconsistent in the quality of its products. Only poem one is without conflict, the imagination—"C'était mon enfant, mon bijou, mon âme"—moving from the hesitancy of that first impression of morning into a tranquil delight that is just slightly perplexed by the polychrome and many-masked sea. The question the self asks of its imagination in lines seven through eleven adduces no tension, only a sanguine, ambrosial confidence, and the precious imagination of line twelve casts an assuring radiance upon the fertile sea "blooms" in the concluding six lines. Not so any of the other poems. In each other case, the self's initiation into morning brings a challenge to imagination and an uneasy pleasure to the perceiver: something "sham" and "malevolent" in poem two, tense and still like a "prelude" in three, overwhelmingly malicious and suffocating in four, and deceptively antic in five. But even when the imagination is perplexed, or finds in the cloud-pregnant waters not delight so much as an ominous dark, it redeems fear by the very act of asserting itself in the face of the object and thereby discovers its proper proportions.

Poem two deserves scrutiny in this respect, not only for its remarkably precise imagery, but also for its metamorphosis of fear into faith:

> In that November off Tehuantepec
> The slopping of the sea grew still one night.
> At breakfast jelly yellow streaked the deck
>
> And made one think of chop-house chocolate
> And sham umbrellas. And a sham-like green
> Capped summer-seeming on the tense machine
>
> Of ocean, which in sinister flatness lay.
> Who, then, beheld the rising of the clouds
> That strode submerged in that malevolent sheen,
>
> Who saw the mortal massives of the blooms
> Of water moving on the water-floor?
> *C'était mon frère du ciel, ma vie, mon or.*
>
> The gongs rang loudly as the windy booms
> Hoo-hooed it in the darkened ocean-blooms.
> The gongs grew still. And then blue heaven spread
>
> Its crystalline pendentives on the sea
> And the macabre of the water-glooms
> In an enormous undulation fled.

The rayed decks which remind the poet of "chop-house chocolate/ And sham umbrellas" are, imagistically, an uncertain perception; the imagination is baffled by the expressionless surface. Not knowing his imagination, one might say, the observer is victimized by it, seeing only the world's "malevolent sheen" in which fecund "blooms" are ominous, not procreative—or if procreative, shivering with mortality. More than in any other except the fifth poem, the self in poem two is shocked into recognition that the imagination can produce fear as well as faith. And knowing this, it can then draw a faith out of fear. (Note the predominance of liquid sounds in the section, a constant flowing away even to the final phrase of renewal.) Similarly in poem five, in some ways the most engaging, the imagination is caught in its antic phase, disengaged from reality and submissive to its own private dawdlings. Detached from reality, brought into doubt—"*C'était mon esprit bâtard, l'ignominie*"— it nevertheless discovers itself to be self-corrective, and hence can refocus the "conch/ Of loyal conjuration" upon the surface of the real. Repairing the tension between itself and the sea, the self can compel the "fresh trans-figurings" which distinguish the conclusion of each separate experience.

"Sea Surface," like "Anecdote of the Jar," presents rather than resolves, and in the sense that it captures a totally unique series of impressions does obtain to a kind of purity. More appropriately for early Stevens, however, it sustains the opposition of self and reality and emphasizes the imagina-tion as that which distinguishes as well as reconciles opposites, by way of achieving an identity for the self. But this was not altogether satisfac-tory, this endless engagement of surfaces, this relating of the self to the husk rather than the core of things. It was even somewhat of an impasse: a drama in isolation, the experience of the effete rather than the common self. Clearly it could not satisfy one fully cognizant of his own changing needs, even as it reaffirms Crispin's discovery of how much his soil is his intelligence.

Writing many years later of John Crowe Ransom's regional conscious-ness, Stevens offered some observations on the poet's attachment to his soil: "This is a vital affair, not an affair of the heart (as it may be in one's first poems), but an affair of the whole being (as in one's last poems)" (OP 260). The passage may fairly describe his own sense of development. The changes in Stevens' poetry in the thirties and forties manifest a graduating inwardness. The changes in style are obvious, but not abrupt: the expressed relation of self to reality first becomes talk about the nature of reality (rather than about the sensing of it) and then about the nature of one's knowledge of reality—which is to say, about poetry as it comes to be that knowledge. For Stevens, who resists any suggestion that poetry is related to formal discourse, knows very well that the "poem of the act of the mind" (CP 240) consists of talk about reality—that it involves not only feeling, or heart, but the whole being, including the forms of the mind.

Stevens' development toward a poetry of the whole being, or what he elsewhere called a central poetry, constitutes a gradual evolution of self. His poetry of the thirties, responsive as it is to the conditions of social reality in the decade, is nothing less than a prolonged apology for poetry —at times labored and tendentious, at others eloquent and lyrical, but al-most always aware that the way to defend poetry is to attend to the busi-ness of poetry. Its focus upon reality—not that off Tehuantepec but that of a world less opulent, more northern, more filled with social pressures

—is testimony that Stevens never quit looking directly at his world. But the mode of this poetry, and that which was to follow, grows progressively more discursive and contemplative. It is in two senses of the word a "philosophical" poetry: aspiring like the essays to make statements about the nature of poetry and the man who makes it; and realizing in the style what Valéry called the "act of thought."

Stevens' later mode begins in the thirties in long poems like "Owl's Clover" and "The Man with the Blue Guitar," seeking to establish poetry at the center of experience and man at the center of reality; continues in the forties with ambitious examinations of the supreme possibilities of poetry in realizing the human aspiration to know beyond his world and yet to live within its vulgarity and violence; and concludes in the quiet eloquence of an almost purely contemplative poetry that illustrates how introspective exiles not only exist in the mind but create themselves there. This generalization, to be filled out in the subsequent chapters, is intended only to suggest the relation between the later poetry and the poetics Stevens derived in the forties. From the poems in the late thirties, which aspired to express the "idea of man" as creator of reality, to the very last ones, which seek not the surface but the very "rock" of reality, the direction of Stevens' poetry is inward.

But it is inward in a sense that must be more exactly defined. Stevens in his late poetry becomes, in terms set forth in "Effects of Analogy," an adherent of the central as opposed to an adherent of the imagination. Which is to say, he has passed from an adherent of the imagination (one who is satisfied that the imagination, as part of a larger imagination, provides him with transcendent world enough and time) to an adherent of the central (a poet satisfied to live in the "very center of consciousness," who exercises this consciousness by attending to what it can create within reality, what Stevens calls, quoting Whitehead, the "ultimate good sense which we term civilization"). This is general enough, but it has little to do, clearly, with Shelley's poetic legislator. Rather, it applies in Stevens' poetry to the discovery of what it is to be human, to rest at the center of reality.

"A Primitive Like an Orb" (CP 440) is a relevant text here. It is a poem about poetry—about the joy of language, about imaginative discovery, and above all, about the "essential poem at the centre of things." The central poem conceived here is one of a number of metaphors for a kind of ultimate reality evolved by Stevens in his late poetry. The "first idea," the "rock," the "supreme fiction," and the "thing itself" are others. The terminology is ambitious, and tempts one to large speculations. But each of these figures, posited as something like the ground or substratum of reality which manifests the human desire for ultimate knowledge, represents the ultimate creative potential of man. In trying to get at the ultimate or essential, in seeking for the central, the mind creates the forms by which it lives, and in that act "celebrate[s] the central poem." That is, poems, or man's created forms, testify to his desire to know the essential, the central poem.

"A Primitive Like an Orb" develops as a meditation, feeding upon the images and ideas of the mind rather than of the senses; it is casual and digressive, rhetorical yet insouciant, moving between satisfaction with its "lesser poems" (one's immediate sense of the world) and a desire to achieve the "central poem." The lesser poems, the poet says, are celebrations of the central, and in themselves so satisfying, so filled with images of the world, that the "central poem [becomes] the world,/ And the world the central poem. . . ." Denying that the central lies in some transcendent world—"it is not a light apart, up-hill"—the poet discovers that it lies in himself. The central poem, then, is the totality of all possible poems about reality. But the poet learns that it is also the begetter of lesser poems, that it is not a source beyond the self, but within: "a principle or, it may be,/ The meditation of a principle," and "a nature to its natives all/Beneficence, a repose. . . ." This act of meditation, assaying the ultimate, issues instead in a revelation of the poetic self. It is not only that the poet discovers that if man makes one abstraction he makes them all, including the ultimate to which he attributes ultimate power; more important, he discovers in his own activity another dimension of his being. The poem he creates, his act of mind, is a part of himself married with reality, projected forth here as the "giant." And the giant, this "abstraction given head," far from being the end of reality, the ultimate, is the source, "patron of origins," very like the primitive of the title. Which is to say, the poet discovers the central within himself, that which gives birth to the orb of reality. (One is tempted to see in Stevens' use of the giant a conscious response to Wordsworth's in Book Eight of *The Prelude*. Wordsworth's imaginative scrutiny of nature has discovered, albeit refracted through the mist, the sublime and divine figure of man, "like an ariel cross" atop the mountains, at the meeting point of the physical and the spiritual. Stevens' giant, at the "centre of the horizon," is the image of man at the center of his world, which is to say, of himself perusing the "nothingness" beyond). And so the poem ends not in apocalypse but in discovery, affirming the good of simply imagining, of living in the time-space of the mind and creating the poems which are not only *about* the world but *are* the world of the self.

Another very late poem, attempting to extend imagination into reality, puts it this way: "What self, for example, did he contain that had not yet been loosed,/ Snarling in him for discovery as his attentions spread. . . ." It goes on to speak of the fresh universe created out of nothingness by the addition of the self, the mind (CP 516–17).

So Stevens moves in his last poems to an activity of the mind, a "never-ending meditation," that feeds upon the earlier poetry of sensation, now in the repository of memory. The self perpetuates and sustains itself, in the continuous creation of mind. This is as much argument for Stevens' development as need be made. The pages ahead take up each particular of that development. I offer the theory as only one way of understanding Stevens' growth, and the particular contribution he has to make not only to poetry but to the conception of the modern imagination. What follows is an effort to read Stevens' poems not in the light of a thesis, but individually, stressing those incessant lesser poems by which he celebrated his being and his world's, and considering the transformations achieved in those lesser poems, a transformation of the self that is continuously being loosed until there is achieved what I regard as, however imperfect, Stevens' Grand Poem.

chapter 2

Disguised Pronunciamento — *Harmonium*

The honey of heaven may or may not come,
But that of earth both comes and goes at once.
Le Monocle de Mon Oncle

*H*arriet Monroe tells the story of the occasion when she and her associates, while preparing a special "War Number" for *Poetry* magazine, received unexpectedly a parcel of verses called "Phases" from an unknown young poet.[1] The contents of the edition had been decided, but these poems were so impressive, Miss Monroe recalled with some pride, that the editors decided to make a place for some of them. And so, she says, Wallace Stevens received his first publication. This is not quite so. Even excluding his published juvenilia, two separate groups of his poems, ten in number, had appeared in consecutive issues of the *Trend* (September and November, 1914) before the "War Number" of *Poetry*.[2] With the exception of one poem from the "Phases," none of these were reprinted in Stevens' lifetime. But in the next nine years, more than ninety of his poems and two verse plays appeared in the journals. Wallace Stevens had a considerable coterie reputation when, in his forty-fourth year, he published his first book.

The reputation, however, did not adequately prepare readers for the cumulative impact of *Harmonium*.[3] Stevens, it is true, had been the subject of some earlier controversy over the new poetry and a major figure in a minor literary quarrel between Louis Untermeyer and Conrad Aiken.[4] Untermeyer, a tireless promoter of a new "American" (that is, nativist vernacular) poetry, was a constant detractor throughout most of Stevens' early career, and more than anyone else is responsible for the prevalent view that Stevens' kind of "impressionism" was out of touch with the mainstream of the new poetry, as well as with reality. While Stevens found his champions, he remained, at least in the influential reviews, a poet of the avant-garde, associated with the experimental "French" poetry of *Others* and *Rogue*—a poetry which reflected neither the nativist vigor of the Chicago Poets nor the revolutionary modernism of Eliot, Pound, and the Imagist confederacy. Indeed, the striking quality of Stevens' poetry was that it reflected all the new vogues, and no single one of them. But Untermeyer's version of the impressionist interested only in "sound values" and the color of words prevailed, even when the critic, like Aiken, meant this as praise. The point is, however, that *Harmonium* upon its appearance superficially resembled so much other new verse that even the praise for it took the form of quizzical blandishments.[5] Stevens, it was agreed, was an impeccable and singular craftsman; the question of whether this poetry was alive, whether it reflected life, would vex Stevens critics for the remainder of his career.

When we recall that *Harmonium* appeared in the year of Cummings' *Tulips and Chimneys,* Frost's *New Hampshire,* and Williams' *Spring and All;* the year following *The Waste Land* and Edna St. Vincent Millay's Pulitzer Prize-winning *The Harp Weaver;* a year before the *Observations* of Marianne Moore, John Crowe Ransom's *Chills and Fever,* and MacLeish's *The Happy Marriage*—when we recall the abundance and variety of the new poetry appearing at this time, it is no surprise that Stevens' volume was considered hardly more than a novelty of style, perfect in its way, but "hermetic," a "revival of aestheticism." [6] *Harmonium* was to its time just what a new poetry should be, a refreshingly personal idiom not easily assessed. But looking back at it from present perspective we can see really how much it was a poetry of its time: self-consciously in search of a style; affirmative and enthusiastic, yet with shadows of despair and world-weariness; filled with masks and personae, none of which suffice for more than its occasion; at once nativist and international; and above all acutely aware of the crisis of its age, if only in its dramatic gestures of defiance. The literary renaissance that came to full flourish in the early twenties produced what has aptly been called a "dogma of style." [7] Style was not only the man but his last refuge, veritably his identity, a way of relating himself to the world by isolating himself from its disastrous chaos. The various experiments in style—Eliot's complex strategies for achieving impersonality, Hemingway's sentences seeking a purity of line for the self, Cummings' syntax of pure feeling and lower case identity, to name only a few—become strategies in the quest for coherence, in the search for moral forms in a world for which the old forms, including literary, had failed miserably and dramatically. The variety of Stevens' world, its *brio,* is no less a manifestation of such "strategems/ Of the spirit" (CP 376), a result of the imperative that "Poetry// . . . must take the place/Of empty heaven" (CP 167). It demanded, at first, a return to innocence, a beginning over as Stevens would repeat again and again. And where best begin but with the old language (making the world new in words which, used in a new way, are renewed) and with new eyes (personae like Peter Quince, the Emersonian Hoon, or Crispin, the parody of innocence who ends by accepting the world outside Eden)?

Stevens' personal idiom so overwhelmed its auditors that it tempted them to describe it as a fetish. But if it sounded like an echo of *Others* poetry, of Alfred Kreymborg and Maxwell Bodenheim—like Verlaine in the vernacular and Laforgue in translation—there was nevertheless evidence that it was a very traditional poetry and a rhetorical poetry in its own right. For Stevens' idiom, however much stimulated by the freedom of the New York avant-garde and by the vogue of Imagism, has its roots in an earlier time. There is little enough information about Stevens' years between the time he left Harvard in 1900 and the beginning of his mature poetry in 1914. And there is little enough in his undergraduate writing to warrant a clear judgment about early influences and sources. There are by present accounting some forty-six separate pieces of juvenilia known to be Stevens', several of which are no more than filler editorials written during his brief tenure as president of the *Harvard Advocate* in 1900.[8] Most of his poems were "Songs" and "Sonnets," exercises of a formal nature he would religiously eschew later, and poems so patently *fin de siècle* that one shares Stevens' professed embarrassment over them.[9] One sonnet, a lightly turned, irreligious piece beginning "Cathedrals are not built along the sea . . . ," is notable for provoking a response from Santayana, whose "Cathedrals by the Sea" reminded Stevens that the course of civilization was marked by the development of human forms, including religious, as a stay against the great eternal flux.[10] (Stevens had written the poem expressly for Santayana and delivered it to his house one evening; the philosopher, so the story as told to me by Stevens' daughter Holly goes, wrote his response over the course of a long night.)

Robert Buttel, who has made a careful study of the juvenilia, finds some continuity in theme and style across the fourteen-year interval, especially in the personae of some of the stories.[11] But for the most part this juvenilia was either stylishly effete, like the poem entitled "Ballade of the Pink Parasol," which with a premature irony yearns futilely for the romantic past, or patently ironic, like this stanza from "Outside the Hospital":

> See the blind and the lame at play,
>   There on a summer lawn—
> She with her graceless eyes of clay,
>   Quick as a frightened fawn,
> Running and tripping into his way
>   Whose legs are gone.[12]

This is not a personal but a public style, a supercilious irony which owes more to the desire to shock than to honest feeling. It exploits rather than renders the pathos of its subject. On the other hand, Stevens was capable of such sentiments as these, the sestet of a sonnet on youth's first sense of time:

> Even in that pure hour I heard the tone
> Of grievous music stir in memory,
> Telling me of the time already flown
> From my first youth. It sounded like the rise
> Of distant echo from deadly melody,
> Soft as a song heard far in Paradise.[13]

Looking forward to "Le Monocle de Mon Oncle," this not only confronts us with the mannerism of youth but also invites us to imagine how the same theme can become great poetry by being subjected to the gentle irony of an aging man.

Though there is only the slightest echo in this verse of the poets who dominated the Harvard literary world at this time, one is left with the sense that these poets were in Stevens' mind when he began to write his mature poetry. By that time, of course, the renaissance was in full flower, and the Harvard Poets, traditionalists all, seemed rather out of than in the swim of things. On the other hand, the poems of Stevens' maturity, while reflecting definitely the early Imagist influence and rather less the spirit of Chicago, are engaged directly with that perennial theme of time and transcendence that is a mark of the Harvard Poets.[14] And they reflect alike the world of Josiah Royce and William James, the spiritual idealism of the one and the sense of the other that the mind is an alien in the world and must make of reality what it can. This is not to say there is a direct influence here of Royce or James. But the mood in "Phases," in "Madame Ste Ursule, et Les Unze Mille Vierges," in "The Silver Plough-Boy" and "Peter Quince at the Clavier," of the ideal struggling with time, is, if exceedingly more spirited, very much the mood that one finds in Trumbull Stickney's "The Soul of Time" or William Vaughan Moody's sonnets. "So in this great disaster of our birth," one of Santayana's sonnets muses, "We can be happy and forget our doom." His theme is the fortunate fall into mind; his resolution is to reject Emerson's Adamic innocence, to accept "Despair." Sentiments like these of Moody's would be the stuff, if not the style, of Stevens' earliest relations with his world:

> This earth is not the steadfast place
> We landsmen build upon;
> From deep to deep she varies pace,
> And while she comes is gone. ("Gloucester Moors")

But in "Peter Quince at the Clavier," I would suggest, the first poem truly in his personal idiom, Stevens resolves this mood of loss in affirmation, freeing himself from time by accepting it wholly. Its concluding section, offering the forms of art for the old religious or Platonic forms, provides Stevens' earliest metaphor for the creative self committed to time, yet playing a tune beyond. And having accepted this role, Stevens accepts it without reservation. Time and change, as in "Sunday Morning," become the mother of beauty. The poet's forms, eschewing transcendence, are substituted for fitful tracings of the heavenly portals. Here Stevens does in poetry what Santayana would in his philosophy, but not his poetry.

Harmonium performs the ritualistic service of introducing the self to time and change, in which it is to discover its instruments. The texture of the volume, however, is not the texture of the world's body so much as that body as perceived, "flicked with feeling" and re-formed in language. Yet, because Stevens is not quite certain of that percipient self—witness the recurrent motif, as in "To the One of Fictive Music," of the fall into consciousness, and thus selfhood—because the self remains tenuous and unsure, the poet in search of himself dons many masks and speaks in a medley of voices. He looks at the world first as almost pure object, then in his own subjective image, pretends it is all his making only to discover that he is all its making. Utterances range from the serious to the non-sensical, from the muscular to the fragile, and from incisive irony to bad jokes, in which language is used against itself rather than against its object. But more than anything else, Stevens' masks and poses in their self-consciousness manifest the poet's wish to relate himself to this world —there being no other—and, in discovering that relation, to discover what privilege he holds over reality.

Stevens' masks, though characteristic of the poetry of their time, re-sulted from a comic self-consciousness, not like Eliot's from a dogmatic certainty of the inadequacy of self. His clownishness, whether purely verbal or projected in a persona, is the very opposite of Eliot's, and of Laforgue's which is supposed to have influenced it most.[15] Stevens never wears his melancholy for long. Indeed, it is just that indifference to the tragic in *Harmonium* which caused so much unfavorable criticism. Stevens' severest early critics were, as might be expected, the humanists who found his manner, in opposition to early Eliot, beyond seriousness, uncommitted, devoted to verbal legerdemain and to self-aggrandizement. As an ironist Stevens appeared to be more like James Branch Cabell than Eliot or Ransom, seeking a world apart, exploiting his own private feel-ings. But that Stevens never created a dramatic metaphor for his age, like *The Waste Land,* does not alter the fact that his world was the same as Eliot's. His way of confronting it is different, and his style is the method of confrontation. The sensitive, even hyper-sensitive, man thrown back upon his diminishing resources is a twentieth-century type. The comedian as ironist knows self-consciously that his disdain of the world is no less a disdain of self. He pays a high price for his anger and an equally high price for commitment. But even in his most impoverished masks (as in "The Man Whose Pharynx Was Bad"), Stevens will not be overwhelmed by negation, any more than he will allow Crispin the comfortable self-deception that one can conquer the world by will or idea. Hence Stevens' alternative to all the sad young men of the twenties, his avuncular alternative, takes its life from a continuous assertion of ego that knows its own limitations. By the time he had collected the volume and written what is apparently its *summa* in "The Comedian as the Letter C," Stevens had discovered something of what the humanist meant about the dangers of living by imagination alone. But having nothing else, he found that more than adequate.

Looking at *Harmonium* retrospectively, we can see that it is a poetry more traditional than modern. We can see it, too, as a *vade mecum* for the later work. There are, for example, poems almost exclusively of the imagination, and oppositely, poems exalting the sensuous world (a geopoetical America, a virgin land of imagination) which in its vitality (and vulgarity) overwhelms the imagination or defies it. On the other hand, the major poems are reflective, meditations upon the meaning of the self's isolation in reality, upon time and transience. Or they are dramatic, presenting the intercourse between mind and world in all its comic variety. In the largest sense, these are poems about poetry, about the poet in search of how far he can go in re-creating the world in feelings and words, and how much he is held by reality to the world as it is. They are poems of a sensitive, alienated self, the poet as outsider seeking to be an insider, trying heroically to find his way through the world rather than beyond it. Looking briefly at his early verse plays, before turning to the poetry proper, we can see this motif unveiled; for in the weakness of Stevens' dramatic sense, his early aesthetic becomes manifestly clear.

II

Stevens' two plays, *Three Travelers Watch a Sunrise* (1916) and *Carlos among the Candles* (1917), have added nothing to his reputation. A third, Samuel French Morse reveals, was so unsatisfactory that it still remains in manuscript, though it did have a performance (see OP xxvi–xxvii). Even the two which have been collected, posthumously, lead one to wonder whether he is reading an uneven lyric or an exercise in symbolic action. In either event, they are deliberately, pointedly, dramatizations of the imagination in action, not dramas, and, as Stevens commented on *Three Travelers,* intended to illuminate the mutual interrelations of self and world (OP xxvii). Moreover, as experiments in creating personae, they demonstrate that Stevens is much more at home in the lyrical context, where his protagonist can remain a voice (as in "Sunday Morning") or where the action is internal (as in "Le Monocle de Mon Oncle") rather than external. But the projection of the aesthetic is just what allows us to see it so clearly in the plays.

Three Travelers Watch a Sunrise (OP 127) had the auspicious beginning of winning the *Poetry* prize for 1916,[16] a view not shared, it should be added, by audience and critics who saw it performed at the Provincetown Playhouse. The first-night audience, even if charitable, must certainly have puzzled over a performance which is less dramatic than Dylan Thomas reading his own poems. Hi Simons was many years afterward to call it an "allegory,"[17] which is perhaps close enough to indicate its relation to symbolist drama. *Three Travelers,* moreover, is a singular variation on the theme of art-in-life. Its substance is nothing but Stevens' constant symbols. The Pennsylvania landscape, for instance, might well have been an authentic backdrop, the remembered world of Stevens' youth. But it is simply an impression. The conceit of Three Chinese talking there of poetry is elegant and gratuitous. But what they talk of and the terms they use are familiar to any reader of *Harmonium.*

The abrupt intrusion of three Chinese into the forested hills of *"eastern Pennsylvania"* is a symbolic passage of sensitive man into a vital but alien world. Stevens' choice of Chinese to represent epistemological attitudes seems to owe little to any respect for the Mandarin, more to his desire for mood. The various responses of the three Chinese to the scene are kinds and degrees of response possible within an aesthetic scale. Very simply, the Chinese represent three abstract attitudes one may take vis-à-vis otherness: the First Chinese is a devotee of objective, tangible reality, including necessarily its rude violence; the Third Chinese is purely subjective, speaking only as he feels; while the Second Chinese, the theoretician, is a realist between two extremes. The girl and her suicidal lover are the most extreme forms of reality—beauty and death—which confront the sensibilities of the three Chinese and challenge their dogmas.

The opening scenes are essentially definitions of the stance each Chinese will assume. The First and Third Chinese debate fundamentally over the place of the actual in their experience: the First insists on the primacy of things themselves, grasped in their physicalness, while the Third refutes his deference to "melons" and decrees a world subjectively centered—around his porcelain jar which, recalling the jar in Tennessee, "fetches its own water" like a self-perpetuating imagination. The argument is mediated by the Second Chinese whose "maxims," both real and ideal, rule this world of thought:

> This candle is the sun;
> This bottle is earth:
> It is an illustration
> Used by generations of hermits.
> The point of difference from reality
> Is this:
> That, in this illustration,
> The earth remains of one color—
> It remains red,
> It remains what it is.
> But when the sun shines on the earth,
> In reality
> It does not shine on a thing that remains
> What it was yesterday.
> The sun rises
> On whatever the earth happens to be.

His theory is firm and axiomatic. The shifting relation of imagination and reality is further complicated by an ever-changing reality and the fluctuating temperament and intensity of the individual imagination: a formula more successfully demonstrated in the proper lyrical setting of "Sea Surface Full of Clouds." For the Second Chinese, neither the pure self nor the physical world is real: "It is the invasion of humanity/ That counts."

But the First Chinese insists that the romantic's "light" could never suffice to illuminate—give order to—a vital and a violent reality: "The light of the most tranquil candle/ Would shudder on a bloody salver." The fateful appearance of real violence soon lifts the drama beyond academic theory, but even this violence comes in the impressionistic mood of a ballad strangely realized upon the stage, attended by two Negro mimes. The story of Anna and her suicidal lover, however, can provoke in the

Chinese only the responses native to their sensibilities. It remains for the Third Chinese to sum up the experience of death; neither the devotee of reality nor the man of ideas, so caught up in the immediate action (they are helping Anna from the scene, are personally involved in the pathos), has the perspective afforded the man of pure mind, who, not being undone by the violence, finds appropriate order in a kind of poetics:

> Red is not only
> The color of blood,
> Or
> . . . . . .
> Of a man's eyes,
> Or
> . . . . . .
> Of a girl's.
> And as the red of the sun
> Is one thing to me
> And one thing to another,
> So it is the green of one tree
> . . . . . .
> And the green of another,
> Without which it would all be black.
> Sunrise is multiplied,
> Like the earth on which it shines,
> By the eyes that open on it,
> Even dead eyes,
> As red is multiplied by the leaves of trees.

And one is left to wonder if the violence is not what the sun brings every day, bringing time, from which only imagination can save the self. Still, the mask of the Third Chinese, who triumphs here, is not the ultimate ego which evolves in *Harmonium*. The scale of personae between this Chinese and Crispin is a measure of Stevens' early poetic adventures. The impressionistic conclusion—a Negro both responding to and ordering nature on his drum—evokes the presence of the subjective in any sense of reality, though there is no triumph over the startling "dead eyes" which command the scene. Death, the "hermit" as he is called by the Second Chinese, has his residence in the world of people and things and is ever the price one pays for imagination. But the mood of the play remains the poetry of its poetry, not the poetry of its drama, and therein it fails.

Carlos among the Candles (OP 144) is even more impressionistic and esoteric, and focussed intensely on the maxim of the Third Chinese: that reality is relative to person, place, and imagination. Or as Stevens said of it: "The play is intended to illustrate the theory that people are affected by what is around them." [18] And oppositely, we need add. The action of *Carlos*, beginning as it does in a birth of consciousness and ending in the dark, describes the narrow circle of man's creative possibility. Beneath the aesthete's exterior, Carlos is ironically the embodiment of the mauve decade, a frail imagination entrapped within all-too-mortal flesh. Stevens seems to sense his fragility, but unfortunately the very preciosity which should expose Carlos' inadequate sense of self turns out to be the substance of the "play."

Carlos is no more than a dramatic monologue with illustrating dance. The lone character, an *"eccentric pedant of about forty,"* a dandy in black who is *"over-nice in sounding his words,"* performs what is essentially a poetic ballet. As he speaks, Carlos goes through a ritualized act of lighting the thin black candles which fill his room, and as he lights each candle the tone of his discourse describes the changing tones of the room. His leap into the room (from the right) is a leap into consciousness. He becomes a part of that which he enters, as it in turn takes character from his presence: "I become a part of the solitude of the candle . . . of the darkness flowing over the house and into it. . . . This room . . . and the profound room outside. . . . Just to go through a door, and the change . . . the becoming a part instantly, of that profounder room." The play is an elaboration of Stevens' favorite metaphor for the imagination, light, and the manner in which light qualifies and arranges experience: "The light of two candles has a meaning different from the light of one . . . and an effect different from the effect of one. . . . And the proof that that is so, is that I feel the difference. . . . The associations have drifted a little and changed, and I have followed in this change."

Each candle that Carlos lights lends a distinct quality to his world: solitary, respectable, stately (cold), humorous, elegant, luxurious, magnificent, splendored. With exotic grace, he lights twelve candles on one table, then proceeds to the twelve more nearby. Opening the curtains which shade the room, he emits his light upon a narrow limit of the outside world, changing its texture. He has moved beyond solitude, but the light he casts is neither out far nor in deep. The wind comes, extinguishing some of the candles—man's ripeness of imagination, too, is transient. There then follows a gradual extinction of the light and closing of curtains, each candle accompanied by a simile, each simile changing with the number of candles remaining. As the last light dies, he leaves as he has entered, springing out the door to his left just as he had leaped in from the right. The cycle of entry and exit parallels the span of light, of imagination, which we are to assume is analogous to a single, intense experience. Carlos the pedant has invented the world within his narrow room of self, but the dark beyond the doors remains "matter beyond invention." His exit is ordered and rhythmic, imaginatively controlled, but it is nonetheless inevitable. He conditions his fate momentarily but does not dominate it.

The pithiness of Carlos' tale anticipates Crispin's, for Carlos represents in perhaps its most elementary form the romantic's experience in an atmosphere which is at once his creation and his fate. In Carlos' case the pose is diverting, affected, and unreal. But even in his almost complete detachment from any readily identifiable world and in his almost pure aestheticism, Carlos remains an extreme type, a mask which Stevens would wear occasionally in *Harmonium,* but finally discard. He is the beginning, not the end, of Stevens' examination of the solipsistic imagination, and an inadequate beginning at that.

III

To categorize poems in *Harmonium* as poems of the imagination is to see them in retrospect. There is so little explicit anguish in *Harmonium* that one is tempted to discount the dark and ominous sense of isolation which is everywhere. And similarly, one tends to overlook the anxious plea for imagination by which alone, these early poems seem to say, man finds a home in a world he can never quite know. There are at least five explicit references to "imagination" in the volume: one in "Another Weeping Woman," a second in "Colloquy with a Polish Aunt," two others in "The Comedian as the Letter C," and the famous lament for man's forfeited power which concludes "To the One of Fictive Music." The "violet light" of self, however, dominates the moods of the volume, and more than once creates its own private haven from disorder.

There is hardly a minor exercise without its celebration of subjective *élan,* of the imagination which is variously the "will of things," lifting man beyond the "common drudge," affording exotic pleasure; except those like "Anecdote of the Jar" which measure the expense of "will." The imagination is free, youthful, and not always dependable: it may be skittish or bizarre, as in "Disillusionment of Ten O'Clock," or a frail epicure tasting its honeyed world, as in "Hibiscus on the Sleeping Shores." "The Virgin Carrying a Lantern" (CP 71), with its virgin beauty and suspicious Negress, pure sensuousness as it were agitating an ascetic conscience, sets the tone of a poetry that is at once precise and precious. These poems almost shiver of their own frailty, but they leave no doubt that the slightest expenditure of imagination is a remaking of the world. There is nothing, surprisingly, so fragile or feminine in Marianne Moore. It is little wonder that Williams snorted about Stevens' lack of objectivism. "Hibiscus on the Sleeping Shores" (CP 22) is an interesting example, with its deliberately contrived simile of the "moth" as "mind," roaming the fragrant shore, turning away from the "blather" of the sea toward the certain food of the hibiscus, "the flaming red// Dabbled with yellow pollen. . . ." This mind is surely the pure imagination, decorated in innocence. It is as if Stevens were deliberately beginning anew, with the unformed self and a world as virgin and sensuous as mind can savor it.

More commonly, however, the world of *Harmonium* is pierced by a doubt, by shadows which lengthen over the imagination, accentuating the poet's isolation from things. Or, there are the deliberately theoretical poems, exercises in the definition of this "light" of self without which nature is too often dark. "Valley Candle" is perhaps the volume's purest expression of this near solipsistic imagination, and a revealing metaphor of early Stevens:

> My candle burned alone in an immense valley.
> Beams of the huge night converged upon it,
> Until the wind blew.
> Then beams of the huge night
> Converged upon its image,
> Until the wind blew. (CP 51)

The candle, like the romantic ego, stands amid process, and while it brings the world to order around it, this is anything but permanent. Read as a minor allegory, the poem becomes an apology for the imagination's slanted light, but it will not sustain a heavy burden, as will "Tea at the

Palaz of Hoon" (CP 65) with its Emersonian "I" in turn-of-the-century dress. The mythical Hoon is one of Stevens' first successful masks, and one of those which will have to give way before Crispin's reductive experience. But Hoon is the self in all its potential, the imagination as it were at the height of its powers, eloquent and commanding:

> I was myself the compass of that sea:
> I was the world in which I walked, and what I saw
> Or heard or felt came not but from myself;
> And there I found myself more truly and more strange.

Hoon's "Palaz" and his garments Stevens had to earn, by proving the role of poetry in life. The proof begins, very often, in the most innocent experience. The characteristic poem displays a very delicate balance, and occasionally a light ironic sweep, as in the mood piece, "Disillusionment of Ten O'Clock" (CP 66). This latter poem is a veritable spectrum of images, an exercise in color, beginning with the emptiness of houses "haunted/ By white night-gowns" and modulating into the one authentic dream of an old sailor who "Drunk and asleep in his boots,/ Catches tigers/ In red weather." Concealed in the poem is Stevens' symbolic world of color in its earliest form: ranging from the blue of mind to the green of nature, from the purple-violet of total subjectivity to the violent reds of nature's rawness. The poem is a plea for the very real pleasures of merely thinking, of subjective escape, even if delightfully oblivious to any conditions surrounding drunken sailors and their dreams. A more elaborate extension of this theme is found in "The Ordinary Women" (CP 10), a poem which develops almost exclusively through exaggerated tonal effects. The anecdote of the ordinary women's bizarre experience is related with gusto, a minor tour de force at the expense of the commonplace. Progressing through a cluster of sensuous and vocal images which bear the women beyond monotony into a whirling world of variety, the poem becomes an elegant sport with religious imagery, turning a ritual of asceticism into a ritual of epicureanism. Its movement, from the life of "dry catarrhs" to the sensual strum of guitars back to the vulgarity of catarrhs, is obvious enough. That the movement is perhaps inevitable, that the intensity of imaginative flights must be brief, can only be inferred from the body of *Harmonium*. It becomes increasingly obvious in viewing these early pieces that very few are thematically complete; rather they contain an intense moment of feeling, the sum of which is the life of imagination. Heavily imagistic, the minor poems are of a sensibility rather than a self.

Still, the major poems of *Harmonium* argue against the exclusiveness of the subjective life, and more than once evince uneasiness at withdrawal into a Hoon-like egocentrism. In this regard, Stevens seems to have profited from the experiments of Imagism, even as he found it natural to move beyond the Imagists, to extend the static image into a metaphor of the mind acting upon things. For his subject was not the world-as-seen so much as the process of seeing it, exercises in creative perception. Even in their purity, these poems surreptitiously imply a theory of poetry. "The Curtains in the House of the Metaphysician" (CP 62) is an example, beginning with the image of swaying curtains and leading out from that motion toward a recognition of the incessant motion that is the constant of the cosmos. The mind alone is capable of that discovery, and that delight. "Domination of Black" (CP 8), however, is the richest of these poems, and not alone because Stevens once designated it as his best.[19] It is not convincingly that, but it is a remarkable demonstration of his debt to Romantic poetry, and particularly to the Coleridge of the Conversation Poems. Less dramatic than, say, "Frost at Midnight," and obviously a slighter poem, "Domination of Black" is powerfully evocative. Enthralled by the dark mood of his isolation ("At night, by the fire, . . ."), the poet finds that the ominous spirit of blackness without provokes a spirit of blackness within. The images of the poem are subjective images, but images in motion. "Turning" is the poem's dominant verb, and the direction of the turning is constantly downward toward darkness, as at the end of "Sunday Morning." This tension between the still self and the turning world (interestingly, an inversion of Eliot's later metaphor) provides the major oppositions of Stevens' early poetry, which comes to discover, as in "Fabliau of Florida" (CP 23), that if the imagination can bear one enchantingly "outward into heaven," there will, nonetheless, "never be an end/ To this droning of the surf."

What Stevens adds to the image is first the "flick" of feeling that reduces object to nuance, and then, strangely enough, an intellectual or symbolic quality that places thing in a flowing relation of things—in a form. Stevens was ever a reflective poet, even in the purer experiences of *Harmonium;* this accounts, I think, for the omnipresence of the "I," and particularly for the self who not only feels but comments on his feelings. This is true, as I have maintained, of a poem as supremely imagistic as "Sea Surface Full of Clouds," and it is true collectively of the whole volume: that even the most unique perceptions, if defensive of the authority of imagination, repeatedly bring that authority into question. "The Public Square" (CP 108) is an instance of oblique demonstration, an almost purely imagistic poem. But it is not simply of things-perceived. "Homunculus et la Belle Étoile" (CP 25), on the other hand, leaves little doubt of its argumentative stance. "The Public Square" might well remind one of T. E. Hulme's exercises:

> A slash of angular blacks
> Like a fractured edifice
> That was buttressed by blue slants
> In a coma of the moon.

The qualities of the scene are radically modified by the changing quality of light, reinforced in stanza three by the simile of a "languid janitor" bearing his lantern through the streets. In the coming and going of his light, the "architecture swoons":

> It turned cold and silent. Then
> The square began to clear.
> The bijou of Atlas, the moon,
> Was last with its porcelain leer.

Curiously enough, the subjective light of the moon congeals reality, even as it supplies a buttress for the angular blacks of the scene. We might well wonder about the motivations of the poem, whether of direct observation or inner anxiety. But there is little question that the ambiguous mood which dominates "Anecdote of the Jar" is operative here, where light distorts and brings into question that which it dominates. Hulme could never have abided the nonobjective tone, the critical ambiguity.

The poet of "Homunculus et la Belle Étoile" knows better than to suspect the imagination; indeed, the very opposite. But the poem is no less critical and preeminently assertive. Who else but Stevens would offer a prinking star—which is "Good light for drunkards, poets, widows,/ And ladies soon to be married"? Who else would offer this light as corrective to philosophers, and not only as corrective but as the very charm of philosophy itself? Santayana, of course, who like Stevens would not separate the philosopher's imaginative quest too far from the poet's. This "later moonlight" of a unique sensibility is "good light, then, for those"

> That know the ultimate Plato,
> Tranquillizing with this jewel
> The torments of confusion.

The ultimate Plato is early Stevens, who would soon aspire to be an ultimate Socrates. In the meanwhile, the defense of a troubled self meant defense of imagination, even when that imagination brought itself into doubt. "Homunculus" will not bear the weight of the later meditations, but it anticipates their curious philosophical ambitions to redact a theory of poetry as a theory of life. As in "Stars at Tallapoosa" (CP 71), there is no distortion in that mindless firmament beyond the human where the "lines are straight and swift between the stars"; but man lives in a world where lines are not straight and has only his own "light" to still the "torments of confusion." The struggle of the poet, the imagination, is to attain that purity of line between the stars, but by taking the angular lines of earth into the self and straightening them in metaphor. This is the plea of the volume's most obviously programmatic poem, "To the One of Fictive Music," in which Stevens sets forth very clearly, and almost dogmatically, the authority of imagination over reality.

"To the One of Fictive Music" (CP 87) is one of a number of poems in *Harmonium* which metamorphose Christian imagery and traditional form into a personal, un-Christian aesthetic. Similarly, it almost mocks the old tradition from which it derives. The conventional homage to the muse, once a devotional exercise, has become a tired gambit. Stevens like Robert Graves revives it, though unlike Graves's, his goddess does not possess him. For Stevens' muse is no unearthly mother, no mystical patroness. Rather, she is very like the body of the world itself, on which the imagination dotes. Mocking an old tradition, Stevens refreshes it and thereby relocates poetry in man's daily adventures without conceding anything to the mythological archetype. She is "mother" and "queen"; yet, strangely enough, the poet addresses her in the very words he uses to describe nature's perfections. She "of the clearest bloom,/ And of the fragrant mothers the most dear" is at once, like nature, immortal and vital, mother of man and his "diviner love." In sum, the muse, though an ideal of beauty, would seem to be mirrored in the world's body, the mother from which man is removed, the ideal of whole being he worships. The lyricism of the opening invocation modulates into statement in the second stanza, as if to explain the attraction of muse to poet in terms of man's separation from her.

> Now, of the music summoned by the birth
> That separates us from the wind and sea,
> Yet leaves us in them, until earth becomes,
> By being so much of the things we are,
> Gross effigy and simulacrum, none
> Gives motion to perfection more serene
> Than yours, out of our imperfections wrought,
> Most rare, or ever of more kindred air
> In the laborious weaving that you wear.

This separation of man from nature, this birth of consciousness that isolates him from his world, is a basic metaphor for Stevens. Roy Harvey Pearce, talking of another poem, has called it Stevens' "secular version of *felix culpa*" [20]—fortunate because this fall into selfhood gives man the privilege to redeem himself. It gives him imagination. The muse in her perfection (like the order of nature) reminds us of our imperfections, summoning from us songs of order; for the muse too is ideal, a creation by poets who, knowing their imperfections, are inspired by what is not theirs.

The last two stanzas turn more firmly to the explicit theme, the relation of self to world. It is no less a theory of poetry, considering that poetry at this stage is for Stevens man's way back to the world.

> And of all vigils musing the obscure,
> That apprehends the most which sees and names,
> As in your name, an image that is sure,
> Among the arrant spices of the sun,
> O bough and bush and scented vine, in whom
> We give ourselves our likest issuance.

No golden "bough" this, but things as they are, to which man must first attend if he is to muse the obscure. (Note the pun on "musing" in this stanza.) In the elementary terms of his aesthetic, Stevens is pointing to the pole of reality, to the physical world on which the imagination must focus; for mind must reclaim that world if it is to discover itself. But the verbal echoes which describe this world—the "near, the clear," and the "clearest bloom"—summon up once again the muse of the first stanza. Hence reality, or man's awareness of his separation from it, has given birth to the muse. In seeing and naming "an image that is sure," the poet sees and names the muse, and celebrates her in that act.

There remains only the final variation on that naming, in which is created the poem of reality:

> Yet not too like, yet not so like to be
> Too near, too clear, saving a little to endow
> Our feigning with the strange unlike, whence springs
> The difference that heavenly pity brings.

"An image that is sure," "Yet not too like"—this is the "fictive music" of early Stevens. This, too, is the enchantress muse, the "Unreal" who inspires our affection for the earth and for the life we live there, even if we live apart. The rich texture of "To the One of Fictive Music" does not belie its urgency; neither does the mixture of Christian and pagan imagery obscure the secular plea. It is a poem Stevens needed very much, to reaffirm the importance of poetry in a time when the muse had become anachronistic, not to say unreal.

IV

The third stanza of "To the One of Fictive Music" was no principium to be dismissed by Stevens, even if Williams found his talk about reality so much nonsense. What Williams meant by reality was something more clearly commonsensical than Stevens', something *objective*. For Stevens, even if he had not heard of Bergson yet, the object stood still only in the imagination, in the forms of fictive music. There was no geography without man-forms, mind-forms. Still, *Harmonium* is not without celebrations of a physical world that even Williams could honor; moreover, it is not without its crucial examinations of the expenses of living in a physical world. Nature, clearly, is not reality, but an aspect of reality, and mind is not nature. Yet, nature has her gifts and her order. She is not to be violated at will or by reason. Winters, stumbling over this truism in Stevens and taking it for Romantic doctrine, misses the point that in

Stevens' early poetry it is not so much the bogus fear that mind may sterilize nature as the more honest fear that it may try to transcend her, may choose to live apart in ivory towers of the self or project upon her empty naves and haunted heavens. To talk about Stevens' investigations of reality is to talk of his search for forms, for the dramatic interrelations and balances of the ordering imagination with its living world. The adjustments of this drama are not simply academic; they are the very stuff of life thrust upon an acutely disturbed conscience, but one equally capable of pleasure.

The vitality of nature everywhere challenges the formal demands of the imagination, and out of this challenge, infinitely various, came Stevens' little dramas: the dance of Bonnie and Josie, in "Life Is Motion," or the clash of buck and firecat, in "Earthy Anecdote," or the rhythmic movements of the fan, in "Infanta Marina." And from this challenge also came the major dramas, Crispin's voyage and the lady's anxious Sunday morning. "Ploughing on Sunday," as one of his curious titles has it, would come to be the poet's role, ploughing always without rest even when the world rested on its unploughed beliefs (CP 20). North and America, he would eventually admit, were alien worlds for a poet in search of the congenial: vulgar and cold yet enticingly virgin, unploughed and—to pick up another of the poem's strange allusions—in need of a "Remus." (Does Stevens mean here the old American mythmaker, or the mythical founder of cities, or both?) Working toward Crispin's discovery that "his soil is man's intelligence," Stevens had first to sample the ingredients of that soil, before he could make it yield to his remaking. As early as *Harmonium,* he seemed to know that he must leave the overwhelming naturalness offered by worlds like Florida if he were to preserve the distinctive humanity that the imagination afforded.

Harmonium ranges between Floridian lushness and Northern cold, stretching over a continent to which Stevens, caught in a relatively provincial New England world, was only beginning to awaken. The Florida climes are richly present in the volumes, but have been overstressed by critics, and the reader is sometimes at pains to determine whether Florida is the world as it is, or the world as seen through the most exquisite eye: whether, indeed, the metaphor of the South is not a metaphor for an inward voyage. The apostrophe in "O Florida, Venereal Soil" (CP 47) is a case in point, in which the texture of things becomes real only in the texture of imagination. Florida seen in its parts—"A few things for themselves"—becomes venereal to the lover, and under imaginative scrutiny the "dreadful sundry of the world" is dressed "in indigo gown." The early Williams would have seen the "dreadful sundry" with an acute eye, but never the "Donna, donna, dark,/ Stooping in indigo gown." But then Williams would not have troubled over the incipient decay that Stevens came to discover in the ripeness of earthly paradise—or never with Stevens' intensity.

Harmonium is simply not consistent about the delights of living in a physical world. There may be "Depression before Spring" and delight after; or as the "lilacs wither in the Carolinas" the poet may discover this consummation of spring to bring him the "honey" of earth's "Timeless mother," who once had shown only "aspic nipples" (CP 4). But thrown into nature, the imagination is confronted by numerous contradictions, as in the somber lesson of "Anatomy of Monotony" (CP 107). Here is a finished two-part lyric on disillusionment, of man born of nature and left "naked in the sun," condemned to grow old in the monotony of unrequited want:

> Yet the spaciousness and light
> In which the body walks and is deceived,
> Falls from that fatal and that barer sky,
> And this the spirit sees and is aggrieved.

There is grievance, too, in "Banal Sojourn," and disquietude in "Lunar Paraphrase." Interestingly, two of the last three poems were not included in *Harmonium* until the later edition, though the first two were among Stevens' earliest, when the world yet remained open and spring eternal. The most notable of these very early poems is "The Paltry Nude Starts on a Spring Voyage." Set beside the objectivist exercises of Williams, it reveals not only a difference of sensibility but also why Stevens would eventually have to introduce the principle of evil into his imagination.

Nature's vital rhythms are potentially the lure of imagination and may deceive even as they delight. Stevens' symbolic geography stretches from Tehuantepec and Africa to Hartford, from Tallapoosa to Minnesota, and back again from the harsh abstractions of the North to the jungles of Southern flora. Similarly, reason is Northern, imagination Southern—or so it is in the early poems. Reason resists change, abstracting absolutely;

imagination dotes on it, abstracting proximately. Reason reduces to form; imagination discovers the life of forms. Associated with the frigid North are the personae of rationalist and religionist who, along with the ascetic, are the early anti-selves of Stevens' world. The rationalist, for instance— he of "square hats" in "Six Significant Landscapes" (CP 73)—is variously the contemptible modern and the devotee of inflexible tradition. He is post-Renaissance man and "The Doctor of Geneva" (CP 24), who lives within the certainties of Racine or Bossuet, a figure who anticipates the "logical lunatics" of "Esthétique du Mal" and the official life of the Canon Aspirin in "Notes toward a Supreme Fiction." One of his faces is the symbolic caliper of "Last Looks at the Lilacs" (CP 48), who represents the extreme consequences of the rational mind which, like Wordsworth's botanizing intellect or Cummings' "prurient philosophers," prods nature illicitly. Indeed, caliper is such a standard figure of minor romantic poetry that he does no credit to Stevens' inventiveness; surely he has done little more than remind critics that *Harmonium* is militantly anti-intellectual. The rhetoric of "Last Looks at the Lilacs," for example, indicates the as- sertiveness of Stevens on the defense, but it lacks the subtle turn of wit which makes Cummings' satires so poignant. That caliper can turn the bloom of lilacs into "The bloom of soap" and their fragrance into "the fragrance of vegetal" is almost a cliché. Still, the poem's opening stanza has an appropriate wit, though it comes to minor grief in the serious, if eloquent, conclusion.

A firmer, indeed the firmest, expression of the theme lies in the subtle irony of "A High-Toned Old Christian Woman" (CP 59), where elegance and rhetoric disport together at the expense of dreary asceticism. The short lyric, affecting the style of a one-sided debate or monologue, is Stevens at the top of his early rhetorical style, which he directs most characteristically against religious abstraction and self-denial. As in "Sunday Morning" and "To the One of Fictive Music," he twists the formidable imagery of religious convention against itself, but not simply to deny; in the fusion of argument and evocation, the heresy is qualified by the very conventions it seems to be upsetting, and the riot of sensuality takes on the order without which it would be chaos. The poem's dogmatic tone, along with an unorthodox imagery in an almost conventional blank verse, gives the speaker just the right stance. Out of the argument, of which we hear only one side, there emerges not so much a denunciation of old Christian women as a defense of poetry.

The poet's opening gambit—"Poetry is the supreme fiction, madame"—looks forward to the fictive "wink" of the final lines, while the middle proves just how fictive things wink by an elaborate play on basic metaphors: the architectural figures of religion's airy nave in opposition to solid peristyle of the realist; and the complementary musical figures of archaic citherns against the jazzy vitality of "Squiggling . . . saxophones." Likewise, the clever extension of the ceremonial palm, beyond its obvious association with the martyred Christ, allows Stevens the kind of ambiguity Eliot manipulated so well, but to different purpose, in "Journey of the Magi." The poet's argument assumes the conventions of the old woman's belief in order to refute; in fact, it is a kind of traditional body-soul debate, with the moral reversed. For just as the stridency deflates the old woman's haunted heaven, so does it affirm an ordered, restrained hedonism, a "jovial hullabaloo among the spheres," affirmations set firmly upon the solid peristyle of this world.

The quality that spares "A High-Toned Old Christian Woman" from tendentiousness is its wit, but even with that it lacks the grace (and consequent harmony) of a supreme fiction. "Peter Quince at the Clavier" (CP 89), avoiding defensiveness, is at once a more characteristic and more rewarding expression of Stevens' early faith in poetry-in-life. As a major thematic chord, however, "Peter Quince" is to be seen as an introduction, and not alone because it was Stevens' first really noteworthy poem. His themes would not significantly change. But his forms would become less obviously experimental, and his exposition of ideas would for the time being be put aside for an exploration of the world as it is. Most pertinently, "Peter Quince" is a poem about poetry, and particularly about form as it comes to be an imperative in a world of flux. As such, it parallels "Sunday Morning," which appeared barely two months later. But whereas the latter poem is a full embrace of an orderly vitalism, "Peter Quince" is devoted to the essential form which preserves art from the transience of life. The musical analogy suggested by the title is sensitively developed, though not explicitly: the four parts of the poem are stretched casually upon the three-part sonatina framework of exposition, development, and recapitulation with coda. The two-part development, with its strikingly divergent style, is Stevens at his lyrical best, while the opening and closing sections reveal his ability to shift keys without violating the basic chords. And then there is Shakespeare's Peter Quince, whether for the harmony of his name or for his role as director of comedy in *A Midsummer-Night's Dream,* who becomes in his lyric voice an eminently proper mask of the poet.[21] In his role of *improvisatore* he turns a myth into idea; which is to say, he gives back to the myth its reality, including its violence, and then shapes it in the enduring forms of music (Stevens' equivalent for poetry).

Part I is a simple expository movement, establishing the primary and secondary metaphors—the one stating the theme, the other restating it as a parable. The theme assumes simply that feeling has its form; that is, feeling is a music, is imaginative:

> Just as my fingers on these keys
> Make music, so the selfsame sounds
> On my spirit make a music, too.
>
> Music is feeling, then, not sound;
> And thus it is that what I feel,
> Here in this room, desiring you,
>
> Thinking of your blue-shadowed silk,
> Is music.

Blue here does not have to bear an arbitrary symbolic load. The equation of music and feeling is given dimension in the Apocrypha story of Susanna and the elders; for the experience of the elders before Susanna's nude lure is a feeling of alien passion and thus a pizzicati. Against the warm and fertile tones of her "green evening, clear and warm," against the composed ambience of her "still garden" (non-Eliotic certainly), the vibrations of the elders grate, feeling as they do,

> The basses of their beings throb
> In witching chords, and their thin blood
> Pulse pizzicati of Hosanna.

Insensitively reducing feeling into restrictive as opposed to imaginative (lyrical) form, the elders confuse flesh and spirit in a timbre of perversions.

The lyric softness which opens Part II—with its subtly varied short lines, soothing liquids, and subdued imagery—is a striking break from the similes of Part I. Susanna's liquid sensuality is a perfectly attuned natural response to her world, indulgent but discreetly ordered. In one of Stevens' finest extensions of Imagist limitations, the rhythm of Susanna in her garden modulates into a picture of graceful, controlled action. But the dissonant intrusion of crashing cymbal and roaring horns that closes the passage succinctly fixes the attempted rape as a violation of beauty by an unnatural sense: the intrusion of man's appetitive energy into the natural. Part III continues the dramatization of violence, as the naturally harmonious world of Susanna is reduced to the severe moral judgments of her "attendant Byzantines." These attendants receive her violated purity under the moral, not the aesthetic law, committing a further ravishment of beauty. Stevens' clever shift to self-consciously formal couplets manifests this additional rape of Susanna's naturalness; likewise, the similes of disturbed and chaotic activity, a "noise like tambourines," clashes with Peter Quince's earlier lyricism.

The recapitulation returns, then, from parable to idea, from the dissonance of mortal passion to the pure form of art, and Part IV becomes, in part, a variation of Stevens' enduring theme:

> Beauty is momentary in the mind—
> The fitful tracing of a portal;
> But in the flesh it is immortal.
> The body dies; the body's beauty lives.

Not only the "ultimate Plato," this is Plato stood on his head or Stevens leaning close to the Platonism of Santayana. "Beauty is momentary in the mind," it says, in that any pure abstraction is not enduring unless manifest in some sensuous form. The bare idea is the "fitful tracing of a portal," which in Stevens' usual sense of "portal" would suggest a horizon, beyond which is only pure idea, or nothingness. "In the flesh it is immortal," not because the flesh endures but because beauty once embodied is realized as only it can be, in a form. (Cf., the climactic line of John Crowe Ransom's remarkable "Painted Head," a poem somewhat later than "Peter Quince": "Beauty is of body.") This is, of course, an aesthetic, improvised not deduced. The extraordinary metaphoric elaboration of this premise focusses on an old paradox: the ideal must take body, and thus become less than ideal, before man can know it. The paradox of the maiden's choral as at once the end and fullest realization of maidenhood is eminently precise. The coda thus reaffirms the opening. The truth of the parable is distilled (given aesthetic form) in the music of feeling, whereas "Death's ironic scraping" has possessed the recreant passions of the elders. Peter Quince's controlled tonalities preserve what first was immortal in that it was mortal:

> Now, in its [beauty's] immortality, it plays
> On the clear viol of her memory [her being remembered],
> And makes a constant sacrament of praise.

As Fred Stocking has pertinently commented, "A sacrament is a physical act; but it is holy and it is ritualistic: it is an act of art." [22] The forms of poetry, accounting like music for change, create and preserve beauty; the blind laws of moral convention, the Puritan distortions of the elders, leave it spent and dissipated. It was the discovery that made "Sunday Morning" possible—that death is the mother of beauty because death is the end toward which life grows; it inheres in the process of all living things. But in this poem, immortality is form, the constant sacrament of art. More than any other of Stevens' poems, "Peter Quince" pays homage to the problems of the poet in a post-transcendental world, to the problems of adjusting poetic vision to the world's incoherent but sensuous body. For in this poetry, if transcendence is impossible, art itself is the only refuge from time. Perhaps this explains the imagistic quality of the poem, as well as its *fin de siècle* tang.

V

That Stevens should meditate so intently upon death has troubled the critics who dote on the gaiety and "essential gaudiness" of *Harmonium*. But for the poet of the physical world, this must be so. There are no transcendental promises, no "passage" as Whitman envisioned it. The question remains, however, of how much the First World War and its aftermath altered the traditions of response to violence and death. Clearly the times were new, the age demanding, and the literature very often tied to a crisis mentality. Professor Frederick Hoffman concludes his informative study of the twenties by suggesting that the literary renaissance of that decade must be seen in close relation to the enigma of violence and death. The imperative to create weighs heavily upon the artist in a secular wasteland, when the guideposts of the past are blurred and each day brings challenges to which tradition has no comforting answers:

"The moment of one's death," says Hoffman, "is of such primary importance that the history of an entire culture can be relevant to it. The crisis in human experience requires all moral strength to meet it. But no one has sufficiently explored the role form plays at such a time." [23] Literary experimentalism in the 1920's cannot be separated from the search for moral forms. In a time which lacks the assurances of tradition, the place of the self in a naturalistic cosmos is highly problematical, and the meaning of death, once absorbed in the metaphysics of transcendence, becomes increasingly the sensitive man's obsession. For Stevens, there were only the forms of art to replace the lost forms of belief, a romantic formula that the previous century had disproved. But he was not alone in a time that was rapidly discovering that art for art's sake had become art for life's sake.

Stevens' great poems of death have little direct relation to war, or even violence. The breath of war, however, blows through several minor ones, though Stevens' response to the distant nastiness offers meager proof that the tooth and claw of war was other than a peripheral concern. His poems touching directly upon the soldier treat him as a warrior in reality, not one in France; later poems, of World War II, recreate him as the prototype of the actor in modern reality. The scene of war is a metaphor of the modern world and the modern consciousness, the conflict of selves and things. That *Harmonium's* exuberance and its comedy are not unrelated to this crisis of the limited self in an alien world may be taken as a truth if not a truism. Morbidity was not of Stevens' nature. Even the whimsical could be affirmative, shallow though it occasionally is. Without death the world of change had no meaning; with it meaning came at great price, but the purchase was individuality.

The impact of death and violence as realities at once denying and confirming the self are most revealing of the spiritual role of Stevens' early imagination. He can be jocular, grotesque, ironic, dogmatic, wistful or somber, even humble. Both the very early "Phases" (1914) and a later series, "Lettres d'un Soldat" (1918), neither of which ever saw print in its planned entirety, reveal Stevens as a poet of war somewhat behind the scene. There is this early instance, for example, called "Fallen Winkle"—from the "Phases"—which is almost more of a stylistic exercise than an observation, and further, is strangely Eliotic in its deliberate irony:

> Death's nobility again
> Beautified the simplest men.
> Fallen Winkle felt the pride
> Of Agamemnon
> When he died.
> What could London's
> Work and waste
> Give him—
> To that salty, sacrificial taste? (OP 4)

Similarly, "Lettres d'un Soldat" presents war as a metaphor for alienation and the soldier as representative of the modern alienated ego. This series has a fascinating history. It appears never to have been published complete nor even finished to Stevens' satisfaction. Hence there is the question of whether Stevens' subject is war, which the poems ostensibly treat, or his almost academic fascination with man in the face of violence and death. Characteristically, the variations were inspired not by the war but by a book—letters by a French soldier, from which Stevens took his epigraphs.[24] In the initial printing the first poem, beginning, "The spirit wakes in the night wind—is naked" (OP 11), is only impressionistically of the battlefield (its ancestor is Rimbaud's "Le Dormeur du val"), while one of those which remained unpublished for many years, and now entitled "Common Soldier," treats of a soldier who is a curious relative of Frost's defender of fences:

> I take all things as stated—so and so
> Of men and earth: I quote the line and page,
> I quote the very phrase my masters used.
>
> If I should fall, as soldier, I know well
> The final pulse of blood from this good heart
> Would taste, precisely, as they said it would. (OP 11)

Though this anticipates the later "Dutch Graves in Bucks County," it is not, obviously, the mode of *Harmonium,* and Stevens knew it when he omitted the series from his selections. Yet he did detach three poems and preserve them independently in his first volume.[25] At least one proves him a deft self-critic, fully attentive to the "world" of *Harmonium.* "The Death of a Soldier" (CP 97) offers a succinct example of the early powers, not at all those of a detached observer of violence, but rather of one engaged totally with a world in which violence, like change, is the given.

Life contracts and death is expected,
As in a season of autumn.
The soldier falls.

He does not become a three-days personage,
Imposing his separation,
Calling for pomp.

Death is absolute and without memorial,
As in a season of autumn,
When the wind stops,

When the wind stops and, over the heavens,
The clouds go, nevertheless,
In their direction.

There is nothing else in the series to equal it, nothing else so artistically precise: the marmoreal tone, the carefully chiseled rhythm which falls with controlled dignity through each triplet, and the pertinent imagery of natural as opposed to sacramental death, unaccompanied by ceremony or apotheosis, something as constant and continuous as the mysteriously driven clouds. This is not only Stevens in the sureness of his mature style, but in the true mood of *Harmonium,* where death is absolute and all the poet's joys and sorrows come from that revelation. As a poet of death-in-life, Stevens is ever the poet of his favorite theme: poetry-in-life.

"Sunday Morning" (CP 66) in this respect is a central poem, though once again, like "Peter Quince at the Clavier," an introduction rather than a climax. It is to "Sunday Morning" that Stevens owes his early reputation, and anthology purviews until very recently tended to present him as the poet of this one great piece and a limited number of others. Perhaps Yvor Winters is responsible for the poem's inordinate but deserved fame. He once called it one of the "few great poems of the twentieth century in America" and has never recanted, though there is little of Stevens' subsequent work that has pleased him.[26] But Winters notwithstanding, "Sunday Morning" in all its greatness is reflective of the whole uneasiness of *Harmonium,* and its eloquent "yea-saying" for life-as-it-is should not be misinterpreted as a pretty and detached hedonism. It is a rhetorical poem and even, as Winters insists, "discreetly didactic," a foreboding of the later Stevens in his assertive, meditative style; but more centrally here, it is a moment of true discovery for a poet who was willing to chance all the mistakes of his romantic heritage. Neither experimental in form nor exceptionally complex in idea, "Sunday Morning" presents the usual difficulties of early Stevens in its overlay of rococo diction and hyperbole. J. V. Cunningham's contention that the Christian imagery and traditional form moderate the poem's antitraditionalism is instructive.[27] Cunningham notes the Wordsworthean style and tone, which is at once antithetical to Wordsworth's spiritual meditations and similar to his sentiments of the creative life amid nature. Stevens, indeed, stands Wordsworth on his head and severely tests the tradition from which the poem seems to derive.

"Sunday Morning" is of Stevens' early esthete phase, and despite the attempt of critics to read it in strictly modern terms, it reaches back to the last part of the nineteenth century and to Stevens' formative years. This is not to say, in fact, that it is not a modern poem, for it is as certainly of its age as are Eliot's early poems. And that, indeed, is the point. "Sunday Morning" is vaguely reminiscent of Walter Pater's world in that it subtly weaves Christian imagery into purely aesthetic forms; but perhaps the influence is more generally Santayana's distinction between physical and aesthetic pleasure in *The Sense of Beauty*. Stevens would have argued that the imagery was aesthetic (imaginative) before it was Christian. Even so, Stevens has carefully defended himself from *fin de siècle* escapism, on one side, and on the other from the kind of orthodoxy which Pater's world view entails. Moreover, Stevens is absorbed by existential challenges much more characteristic of American literature, most simply the need for personal rather than institutional ceremonies of order. Death, ever morbid and ominously present in the esthete's world, becomes a vigorous part of Stevens' affirmations. Among the poem's predecessors, Emily Dickinson's "Death sets a thing significant/ The eye had hurried by" is a most remarkable anticipation, though the two poets are decades if not worlds apart. It is significant, too, that Miss Dickinson personifies, in various poems, her figure as a father-lover-gentleman and in more personal and dramatic terms than Stevens' "mother of beauty." But a more revealing contrast would be with Whitman's *"Dark mother,"* from whose womb one is born into cosmic oneness.[28]

In its final form "Sunday Morning" is a moderately long poem of eight fifteen-line stanzas, developing as a meditative argument in which the poet assumes the role of his lady-subject's conscience, both presenting and interpreting her drama of self. Once again, Stevens appears to have modified the old body-soul debate, by giving the body a role equal and sanctified. Thus the opening stanza, with its panoply of sensuousness, the lady settled at home, flouting the "holy hush of ancient sacrifice" which nevertheless troubles her deeply. But the encrustations of rhetoric and the solemn, dark intrusion of religious imagery suggest the very opposite of "Complacencies." Hence the "dark/ Encroachment of that old catastrophe" (Christ's, no doubt) which comes to disturb her world of "green freedom"; hence the poem's developing tensions:

> The pungent oranges and bright, green wings
> Seem things in some procession of the dead,
> Winding across wide water, without sound.
> The day is like wide water, without sound,
> Stilled for the passing of her dreaming feet
> Over the seas, to silent Palestine,
> Dominion of the blood and sepulchre.

The lady, caught between desires, would like to transmute ephemeral pleasures into eternal ones. Death, however, disallows easy consolations and forces a mortal choice. The flow of things here is from color to shade, sound to silence.

It is clearly presented alternatives, not a paradox, which open stanza two with a rejection of sacrifice. The poet's voice becomes rhetorical, denying the "ancient sacrifice," denying what is promise for what is. The lady's dilemma, indeed, becomes the poet's *parti pris:* "Divinity must live within herself," a latter-day Emersonianism without its transcendental rationale. It is at once a discovery and a premise, entailing a full acceptance of the contradictions of living in a physical world.

> Passions of rain, or moods in falling snow;
> Grievings in loneliness, or unsubdued
> Elations when the forest blooms; gusty
> Emotions on wet roads on autumn nights . . .

"These," says the speaker, like the apocalyptic spokesman for a new order, "are the measures destined for her soul." Here the physical landscape, as an extension of self, becomes likewise an antagonist. No pantheism this, but life deliberately measured to include all pleasures, all pains. The price is sacrifice of the comforting myth of immortality.

The apparent shift of theme in stanza three must be seen as a brilliant *divertissement,* but eminently apropos of the theme. Altering the imagery from Christian to pagan mythology, Stevens in effect plays a variation on the theme that "Divinity must live within herself." And an interesting variation it is. For this Jove of inhuman birth, the old god who "moved among us, as a muttering king," is dead, victim of time and his own gaudy munificence. That is, Jove is dead, and likewise Christ, all gods perhaps, because the history of gods is the history of their death; they become anachronistic when their role becomes familiar and formal, and reason refutes their magic. Stevens is anticipating in this stanza his later speculations on the gods as aesthetic creations who disappear when their aesthetic becomes apparent, when we know them as gods in myths, being unable any longer to embrace them as truth.[29] This is not to say that Stevens achieves here a credible theory of mythology, however, for the stanza presumes only to underscore the previous one: the inevitable centering of divinity until it comes to live in the self. From Jove to Christ, it seems to say, was a centering, a humanizing of divinity; and now the Christian myth is in its throes, leaving us once more with ultimate questions.

> Shall our blood fail? Or shall it come be
> The blood of paradise? And shall the earth
> Seem all of paradise that we shall know?
> The sky will be much friendlier then than now,
> A part of labor and a part of pain,
> And next in glory to enduring love,
> Not this dividing and indifferent blue.

Neither heaven's indifferent blue nor Mallarmé's oppressive "azur," this sky is the horizon of the self—beyond which is nothingness. No longer will the Pascal-like fear of silent spaces haunt one, for there will be full knowledge that our senses scan the only horizons and self is the last divinity.

Therefore, stanza four can confront directly the *non*-sense of a transcendent paradise. This stanza is a minor reprise of "Peter Quince at the Clavier," rejecting the unembodied beauty, embracing the world of nature which is regenerative of itself, though not of man. This, the lady is forewarned, is her choice: remote paradise or fullfillment of the senses, future *or* present. And the extremes of her choice become a vivid paradox in the transformation of Christian and pagan imagery. The sensuous world of wakened birds and swallow's wings takes on the qualities of paradise, which the lady's orthodoxy has always reserved for that "isle/ Melodious," or "visionary south," or "cloudy palm/ Remote on heaven's hill." The poet, presenting the lady with her choice between heaven and earth, subtly manages his imagery to conceive that earth as paradise.

The shocking, and pivotal, rejoinder to the lady's wish for "some imperishable bliss," which opens stanza five, is not at all gratuitous then. "Death is the mother of beauty," and the poet has proven it; or what is better, has bedeviled the lady into discovering it. For it is consciousness of death which has forced her to embrace her contentment so intensely, to sustain her Sunday morning even when harried by the "dark/ Encroachment" of conscience. Indeed, nothing is unearned in this poem, not even the poet's metaphorical proofs that it is death which makes us grasp things of the world with *élan*. This is not simply psychology, but awareness that life is change and growth and diversity, the fruit of growing into death. But the poem says it better:

> Although she strews the leaves
> Of sure obliteration on our paths,
> The path sick sorrow took . . .
> 　　• • • • • •
> She makes the willow shiver in the sun
> For maidens who were wont to sit and gaze
> Upon the grass, relinquished to their feet.
> She causes boys to pile new plums and pears
> On disregarded plate. The maidens taste
> And stray impassioned in the littering leaves.

And stanza six can reinforce the truth with a succinct metaphorical contrast between the ponderous ennui of a paradise without change and the light, spicy sensuousness that is our reward for embracing the "earthly mothers." (The "happy boughs" of Keats's "Grecian Urn" are denied, and with them the metaphysical agony. Here is true negative capability; likewise the following strophe, which rewrites the "Ode on Melancholy" in a comic idiom.)

Released at last from negation, the poem bursts forth in stanza seven with a dazzling paganism, yet a paganism that has its own incipient order. Its ritualistic chant has a Whitmanesque breadth, though formally contained in a discreet pentameter. Accordingly, the imagery of the sun generates life and motion, and hence death. It is shocking, this "boisterous devotion to the sun," but not without restraint or order; it is an aesthetic, not a physical orgy of pleasure. In at least one printing of the poem this was the concluding stanza; but as it now stands, more deliberately tempered by the still darkness of stanza eight, it offers a climax of sensuous enthusiasm—the "bough of summer"—before the final resolution—the "winter branch"—anticipated in stanza two. Once again, however, the paganism is flooded with Christian imagery, and the worship of reality is not without its price. For the price of this boisterous devotion is the mature recognition of the concluding stanza, in which death and life are married. (Cf., for example, the affirmative dance which Whitman, in section 14 of "When Lilacs Last in the Dooryard Bloom'd," sets against death's *Dark Mother.*")

The resolution turns to the secular adaptation of Christian forms of value. The opening line of stanza eight returns us to stanza one, to the "wide water, without sound" that bore the lady's conscience first to "silent Palestine." Only now Palestine is the world of a secular Christ, man himself and not the Martyr, the divinity of self caught in the existential insularity of an "unsponsored" world.

> We live in an old chaos of the sun,
> Or old dependency of day and night,
> Or island solitude, unsponsored, free,
> Of that wide water, inescapable.

Within this ironic paradise of impermanence, nature's casual harmonies enact the only permanence. And like a totally conceived poem, the life cycle resolves the pathos of man's self-awareness; life comes to fruition and passes into nothingness in a constant rhythm that provides a secular metaphor for man's cosmic (or is it comic?) existence. Nature is complete, but man? He shares only death, which lies at center of all motion —the still point:

> Deer walk upon our mountains, and the quail
> Whistle about us their spontaneous cries;
> Sweet berries ripen in the wilderness;

And, in the isolation of the sky,
At evening, casual flocks of pigeons make
Ambiguous undulations as they sink,
Downward to darkness, on extended wings.

The deathless beauty of "Sunday Morning" lies not in its shocking ironies, nor alone in its almost perfect decorum of style, but in its extraordinary sense of dialectical form. When first published in *Poetry* magazine, it consisted of five stanzas now placed as follows in the long version: i, viii, iv, vi, vii. But the poem as it now stands was the original poem, the earlier version having been shortened for *Poetry* at the request of Harriet Monroe.[30] That Stevens could so arbitrarily rearrange the poem and still maintain its unity—for the shorter version has its order—attests to his sense of meditative form and looks forward to the later poems. The shorter poem, ending on the high note of pagan ceremony, is more affirmatively hedonistic than the longer, and Stevens' keying-down in the later stanza has caused William Carlos Williams, among others, some discomfort. In the shorter version Stevens used the remarkable last stanza to the finished poem simply to extend the imagery of the opening strophe; not being climactic, the present stanza eight served to amplify but not extend the first stanza, and it lost its thematic impact. The present second stanza is missing from the short version, and along with it the necessary expression of the woman's developing conflict. Of the three strophes, only stanza six may be in excess, yet who would dispense with the richness it lends to the full poem? And the presence of stanza three expands the poem's import by including a new perspective on the modern crisis of a spirit bereft of its consoling mythologies and isolated beneath the pure blue of a physical sky. The final triumph, however, is the dignity of the concluding stanza, which, in picking up the metaphors of the opening, restrains the "orgy" of stanza seven and supplies the proper diminuendo into stillness. These "ambiguous undulations" of the vital world around the dark center bring the poem into gentle focus. For this has been a poem of undulations, of fluid and flowing images moving about one ominous thought. Thus the triumph of form—and in the concluding tableau, the elementary tension of life and death.

Extraordinary as it is, "Sunday Morning" is only the initial statement from which Stevens was to launch quest after imaginative quest into the nature of being and the self. The enigma of death (and of beauty) is elaborated but not resolved, and the orgy of stanza seven set against the darkness of stanza eight leads directly to the questions of "Le Monocle de Mon Oncle," where self-consciousness dares to forfeit the pleasant truth found in "Sunday Morning" and elsewhere: that "Life Is Motion." The intensity of life, Stevens discovers, takes its value from the intensity of death, whose imminent certainty is felt in the bone, not as a chill but as a warm marrow, as a part of living and growing in a world that is living and growing. Death as a grotesque is laid, though it will return to *Harmonium* in other masks than the mother of beauty. But Stevens has made a signal gesture toward endorsing reality, and thus transience, facing it with a style of life rather than capitulating to melancholy. He will take what he has as blessing enough. His gesture, indeed, anticipates the Camus who came to offer the individual style in life, as in art, as a lone recourse against the absurd.[31] Worshiping the sun was a return to first things.

"Sunday Morning," however, did not permanently allay the anxiety of that "old catastrophe." [32] There is a brooding presence throughout *Harmonium* of the futile "combat with the sun" that inspires the misery of Don Joost (CP 46), or the "malady of the quotidian" of "The Man Whose Pharynx Was Bad" (CP 96). There is anger, rather than ridicule, directed at the old promises of transcendence, as in "The Bird with the Coppery, Keen Claws" (CP 82), in which Paraclete is reduced in a withering rhetoric to a "parakeet of parakeets," a "pip of life amid a mort of tails." The puns on parakeet and mort cannot be denied, but the poem will not be satisfied with irony alone. This parakeet is blind, as he is in the even more rhetorical "Negation" (CP 97) which begins, "Hi! the creator too is blind," and ends by ironically accepting our will to "endure brief lives." Death is the "Domination of Black" (CP 8), felt in the cry of the peacocks which haunts the mind of the lonely, isolated poet. In this poem a discreet blend of meditative style, imagistic precision, and impressionistic tone (a remarkably suggestive chiaroscuro) portend ominous metaphysical consequences to the isolated mind. There are few modern poems which better evoke the experience of cosmic fright. The turning world, caught in the motion of leaves (and through an ominous anaphora), enshrouds the poet in fear, and the refrain of the crying peacocks echoes through the "color of heavy hemlocks" to catch a melancholic struggle of the self with its fate. Likewise, several of the "Thirteen

Ways of Looking at a Blackbird" (CP 92), an epistemological tour de
force, acquaint one with death's ever-presence in a mixture of wit and
preciosity. Just as the blackbird is a part of man's reality (iv), it is also the
symbol of his horizons (ix), of flux (xii), and in essence the piercing reminder of human mortality (xi):

> He rode over Connecticut
> In a glass coach.
> Once, a fear pierced him,
> In that he mistook
> The shadow of his equipage
> For blackbirds.

Few poets so delightfully attentive to the life of color have paused at
such length over black. Stevens knew all the delights and fears of casting
a shadow. Dominating life, spelling annihilation, death is strangely
creative, and at last the mother of poetry. Richard Ellmann's contrast of
"The Emperor of Ice-Cream" (CP 64) and "Cortège for Rosenbloom"
(CP 79) as two antithetical ceremonies of death is to the point: the
former the "right way" to conduct a funeral, the latter the "wrong way";
the former hortatory and defiant in its ritual of living, the latter ironically
ceremonial and mournful in its negations.[33] "The Emperor of Ice-Cream"
has achieved a fame somewhat disproportionate to its virtues; exhaustive
analyses of ice-cream, its transient but irresistible sensuousness, and the
improbable nature of "concupiscent curds," have tended to obscure Ellmann's most pertinent remark that the emperor is neither life nor death
alone but the "force of being understood as including life, death, and
imagination." [34] Death's role in the natural continuum is at once commonplace, grotesque, vital, and reassuring: "be" is "finale of seem," because
being is what we have, good or bad, and seeming can only be some empty
imitation or idealization of being. The ceremonies for Rosenbloom, in contrast, are deathly conventional, much like those mimicked in Williams'
forceful "Tract." To act and live in a scene where death is natural—that is,
as in "The Emperor of Ice-Cream"—would quiet the anxieties which
haunt Rosenbloom's mourners, who turn away from the world in wishful ascension. It is this discovery—not at all a dogma—that allowed the
next mature step in Stevens' contemplation of death, or death-in-life.

"Le Monocle de Mon Oncle" (CP 13) is a masterful if deceptively obscure poem, and, in its way, an exemplum of Stevens' early style. Comic lightness modulates into irony, and finally precipitates seriousness. But it is the comic, and with it life, that triumphs. Stevens' assumption of the avuncular mask, in contrast to the more familiar youthful masks of his early poems, supports a double-edged irony which at once brings the whole of *Harmonium* into question and justifies it. In places, particularly in the opening stanzas, there is an excess of flippant diction and high-handed rhetoric which almost overwhelms the Prufrockian ironies that lie at the poem's center. But even hyperbole comes to be a norm of the poem's ironic manner. The uncle-poet *is* Stevens' own Prufrock, whose self-consciousness provokes the tragi-comic reflex of his meditations, but with the difference (from Eliot's mask) that anxiety releases his imagination rather than paralyzes his soul.[35] And this basically is Stevens' point of departure from Eliot, even as he finds his own "agèd eagle" suffering from the modern dilemma.[36] Death lies heavily upon the middle-age consciousness, and it forces Stevens' uncle into curious retorts. The uncle's vision is narrow, even peremptory, pathos unrelenting, but he is never paralyzed by the Laforguean helplessness of his own self-consciousness. That, in effect, is the source of the poem's vitality.

One critic has suggested cleverly that the title contains the poem, that the "monocle" is a reductive spectacle of man's once vital self left with empty abstractions—deeds of love reduced to words or "mon oncle" elided into "monocle" by the "clashed edges of two words that kill." [37] The angle of vision has everything to do with the aging self as he moves from a life primarily physical to one primarily reflective. Moreover, his new love, which he must celebrate in poems or parables, confronts him with the paradox of words, which in giving form and order to emotion also kill the true feeling. Here Stevens for the first time investigates "the motive for metaphor," and the paradox of the fictive truth. Stevens may once have considered calling the poem "The Naked Eye of the Aunt"— or perhaps he was planning to play a set of variations on the original (OP xix). Happily he abandoned both ideas. The discarded stanzas which Samuel French Morse collected in *Opus Posthumous* indicate how deliberately Stevens culled excesses and framed a tautly developed meditation. The single, limited, sad, self-mocking, ironic, wistful, searching "eye" of the finished poem justifies Stevens' mask; for here is the comic self-portrait of man undone by his own notions of romance, and, in the words of John Crowe Ransom, "instructed of much mortality." "Le Monocle" is about the necessary retreat into poetry, by way of searching for the "substance in us that prevails."

Perhaps the poem is best approached through a summation of theme: (i) stanza one opens with a mock invocation to some faded muse (or love), an invocation born of loss and the cognizance of mortal loneliness; (ii) the second strophe thus initiates a series of ironic "thoughts" on loss, and on man's longing for immortality, his "anecdotal bliss"; (iii) doubt leads beyond the personal hurt to a skepticism of all formalized conceptions of truth and beauty, and especially of all longings for permanence; (iv) the fading of youthful passion forewarns him of his fate, the clash of youth and age in the single body, except that it is the aging man who suffers limply the erasures of time; (v) and mature self-consciousness intensifies the twilight awareness of "crickets," "dust," and time's pace; (vi) the contrast is extended, the aging man's concerns turn inward as "amorists grow bald" and the longing for absolutes (the "basic slate") replaces the pleasures of sensation; (vii) the conflict is partially resolved by the acceptance of mortal and ephemeral consolations and the rejection of dubious "heaven"; (viii) this acceptance is realized in a mature but self-conscious and somewhat grotesque consideration of love which is now no longer physical, but only memorable, and hence comic in its nostalgia; (ix) poetry, then, not religion, becomes a surrogate "oblation" of the middle-aged man who is thrust upon his fate without either the old pleasures or the consolations of immortality; (x) consequently, the poet turning to poetry for consolations of necessity turns to ceremony to recoup the losses of age, but a ceremony of reality, not the chants of "fops of fancy," not to singers of an ideal of romantic or divine love; (xi) thus, the spiritual life of man is to be realized in living fully our "anguishing hour!" but living it in the eloquence of a realistic, an earthy poetry; (xii) the final strophe returns to the fundamental clash of youth and age, and the poet's discovery of the continuity between his youthful appetite for love and his mature hunger for "the origin and course" of things, the one looking back, the other forward, but meeting in the present where the self now rather helplessly finds itself.

Though loosely constructed, the poem gives evidence of a carefully designed inner dialectic of mood, as the uncle's meandering discoveries progress hesitantly from the shock of recognition toward some tentative acceptance. Having lost the physical life (his love), the uncle will take no pleasure in transcendental chants, but in poetry will make a new kind of love out of the love he has had. In this respect two lines in stanza five sum up what was (what is?) lost, and intimate the expense of man's devotions to a physical world: "The measure of the intensity of love/ Is measure, also, of the verve of earth." The uncle may well be Prufrockian; but more important, he is an earlier Crispin, perfunctorily clipped by life, yet tenaciously intent on retaining his measure of selfhood. Thus the comic pose, the hierophantic tone, the quizzical self-consciousness, all of which tend to dilute and disperse the seriousness which might have fettered the poem with morbidity. The avuncular ironies play two ways: against the uncle's once blossoming love and against the uncle himself, whose posturing is nonetheless comic in its uncertainty. The deficiencies of vital but unconscious youth are counterbalanced by those of a conscious but aging man. The desire for a problematical heaven is negated by a lust for life, as in "Sunday Morning." These contradictions haunt the uncle into seriousness, but only momentarily. There is no tragedy for aging lovers. Between the uncle's laconic acceptance of his age and his ironic lament, "We hang like warty squashes, streaked and rayed" (viii), Stevens achieves sentiment without sentimentality, and an emotional variety which is rare throughout his canon.

The poem has its moments of strategic obscurity, or better, opacity. But this is consonant with the speaker's mind and his unsettling discovery. The self-mockery of the invocation—the futility of words—has its origin in the comic self-consciousness that motivates the poem (i). The uncle's memory of his passionate youth and young love—she almost Venus-like in the "spuming thought" of his recollections—cannot deny the "saltier" awareness that passion and love and youth are ephemeral. But love is now a dream, a memory. And man like the red bird seeks his secure place in an orderly nature only to discover that, unlike the bird, he is an alien in the world: "These choirs of welcome choir for me farewell" (ii). It is doubly ironic that the uncle, sardonically aware that Heaven is make-believe, an "anecdotal bliss," is himself a man of parables, and must resolve his dilemma in a parable, or in poetics. Caught between the desire for permanence and the certain beauties of change, he opts for this life (vii):

The mules that angels ride come slowly down
The blazing passes, from beyond the sun.
Descensions of their tinkling bells arrive.
These muleteers are dainty of their way.
Meantime, centurions guffaw and beat
Their shrilling tankards on the table-boards.
This parable, in sense, amounts to this:
The honey of heaven may or may not come,
But that of earth both comes and goes at once.

The parable of the mules—one to which he will return with variation in "Mrs. Alfred Uruguay"—offers the same alternatives as "Sunday Morning," and implies a similar choice. Thirsty men want their thirst quenched; yet man as "centurion"—Stevens' inversion of Eliot's "Gerontion"—cannot live beyond himself. Deliberately artificial, this is simply a parable of the imagination returning to reality, embracing what little of the honey of earth may come, rather than wishing for the airy honey of heaven. To have loved is inevitably to have lost, except in memory (in poetry), where one may embrace "A damsel heightened by eternal bloom." And so the uncle comes to live in the mind, in memory, by imagination. Is this not a gloss on stanza six, the pivotal strophe?

If men at forty will be painting lakes
The ephemeral blues must merge for them in one,
The basic slate, the universal hue.
There is a substance in us that prevails.
But in our amours amorists discern
Such fluctuations that their scrivening
Is breathless to attend each quirky turn.
When amorists grow bald, then amours shrink
Into the compass and curriculum
Of introspective exiles, lecturing.
It is a theme for Hyacinth alone.

I have already made claims for this as the most prophetic stanza in early Stevens. This is the crux of his development, the discovery I submit that led eventually to Crispin's voyage and directly to the composed "I" of the later poems: the self who can meditate the basic slate, or as Stevens would come to call it, the "first idea." Here, however, he celebrates the life-preserving imagination, the "substance in us that prevails," by which the tragedy of amorists, like that of Hyacinth, is transmuted into beauty's enduring form. Hence, to recall the final stanza, the uncle discovers the truth of his growth from dark rabbi to rose rabbi, from the youth of infinite vistas to the introspective exile whose bloom is gone. Between man's pursuit of the "origin and course/ Of love"—universals—and his need to cherish "fluttering things"—vital particulars—Stevens' avuncular persona realizes with tragic humor that the honey of earth "both comes and goes at once." The dull scholar of stanza eight survives as poet of reality, or is it as poet of memory? In any event, he is a poet of earth, of fluttering things and not of golden boughs (x). And more than anything else, the uncle has discovered, even in the composition of his own poem, the self's power to act and thus to escape the inundation of reality that drowned Prufrock.

> I quiz all sounds, all thoughts, all everything
> For the music and manner of the paladins
> To make oblation fit. Where shall I find
> Bravura adequate to this great hymn? (ix)

It is "Le Monocle" rather than "The Man Whose Pharynx Was Bad"— Marius Bewley's choice[38]—that I would nominate as Stevens' dejection ode, were it not for the uncle's remarkable recovery, his discovery of affirmation in the comedy of loss.

So much beauty emanating from darkness, so great an affirmation of life in the presence of death—this indeed is the essential *Harmonium,* in which gaiety is born in decay. "Life," as Stevens later put it, "is the elimination of what is dead" (OP 169). Stevens' poems of death are clearly poems of life, without dark rhetoric, without morbidity or despair. But the gaiety of *Harmonium* comes not without the excises of self. The most carefree and precious of poems must end with an evocation of the ultimate Plato to tranquillize the torments of confusion, and in the ripe world of "Banal Sojourn" there is imminent decay: "One has a malady, here, a malady." The malady is reassessed but not relieved in "The Man Whose Pharynx Was Bad" as the "malady of the quotidian" which does not relent, and even the glittering seascapes of "Sea Surface Full of Clouds," that "pure poem," are rayed by ominous shadows. Mutability like ripeness is all.

VI

All the themes of *Harmonium* culminate in "The Comedian as the Letter C" (CP 27), a poem which despite its unevenness must take its significant place in that favorite genre of American literature, the symbolic voyage. For it is a quest poem, a voyage of experience, and, in another sense, a parable of the modern poet. Its theme, put simply, is the quest of the self-conscious modern, disabused of his romantic "mythology of self," for something other than mythology. In asking questions about the reality of self, it manufactures a curiously reduced persona who is the very opposite of the all-encompassing, Emersonian Hoon.

The history of Stevens' publications leading up to "The Comedian as the Letter C" does not indicate any consistent evolution either of style or idea, but it does anticipate the onset of some uncertainty. In 1921, for instance, he published along with several other poems in *Poetry* magazine, "From the Misery of Don Joost" and "Tea at the Palaz of Hoon," two lyrics of incompatible theme. At nearly the same time, "The Man Whose Pharynx Was Bad" was published in the *New Republic*. A year later appeared "To the One of Fictive Music," with its almost desperate plea for the return of imagination. Despite Hoon's assurances that he was the sovereign of his world, the edge was rubbing off Stevens' gaiety. The horizons of the "I" had ceased to dilate.

A long poem, Stevens' first really long poem, "Comedian" is an engaging tour de force which has baffled more critics than it has satisfied. Its 570 lines include a panache of language in a most orthodox blank verse, another of the obvious paradoxes of Stevens' early style. And through his familiar device of double perspective, of protagonist and commentator, Stevens achieves a range of speculation—ironic, self-mocking, yet self-creating—which elevates the anecdote of Crispin into an incisive commentary on man's dimensions in a secular world. Crispin's voyage, which Stevens once thought of entitling "From the Journal of Crispin," is symbolic surely, but to what end it is not always easy to say. If the poem is intensely personal, as many have justly observed, it is nonetheless a comedy of the imagination's manners. Without question it is Stevens come full upon the incipient contradictions of *Harmonium*, in which devotion to the physical world began to crowd the self into the corner of its mortality.

Whether parable or allegory (the last is certainly too strong),

"Comedian" is convincingly what the late Hi Simons called an auto-biographical generalization.[39] That it is a poem about poetry in the largest sense there can be little doubt, but that its main concern is with the poetry of living more clearly accounts for its comic design. The humbling of Crispin hardly implies the undoing of Stevens. For Crispin is a version of the modern ego in the comic process of confronting its isolation. In this regard, Stevens has offered a significant clue: "The central figure is an every-day man who lives a life without the slightest adventure except that he lives it in a poetic atmosphere as we all do." [40] Hence, he says, the poem is "anti-mythological." This "every-day" man (the poet is "any man of imagination") is secular man, man with only definitions of himself. Possibly Stevens meant by antimythological that the poem, contrary to the contemporary trend (e.g., *The Waste Land*), depended on no allusive strategy and on no structure of history that affords man mythological or trans-human definition. More likely, he is denying that the history of Crispin has archetypal or metaphysical meaning. Furthermore, it is antimythological in the same sense as Stevens' later rejection of all mythologies and ideologies, in the sense that he rejects any final synthesis, any ultimate fictions, knowing that one's moment-by-moment experience is always destroying the old by way of discovering the new. It is perhaps this simple—but the remark probably refers also to the experience of man in a world of change, of man whose history may be instructive (parabolic) without being cosmic (mythological). Like many another writer in the modernist tradition, Stevens comes dramatically upon that unflattering quality of his own being which impedes rather than assists his growth. Yet Crispin, unlike even Pound's Mauberley, is not finally to be exorcised. He is assimilated rather, "clipped" and humbled, then turned back to the dull quotidian where he must live as the author of whatever coherence his life may achieve.

This is not to say, however, that the poem is autobiographical, except in the sense that Stevens can assume all poems to be autobiographical: ". . . it cannot be otherwise, even though it may be totally without reference to himself" (NA 121). Crispin is the self as representative sensibility, an aspect of the failure of man to confront reality and in that act to know himself in true comic dimensions. Crispin as persona has many sources, not one as most commentators insist. He has been variously identified with the valet Crispin of late seventeenth-century French comedy, with the third-century Saint Crispin, with Candide, Figaro, the Pierrot of Laforgue, and with the several types of harlequin in the Italian and later the French comic traditions.[41] Stevens, it is known, had a more than casual interest in harlequinade.[42] His association, in the late 1910's especially, with Alfred Kreymborg's *Others* would have brought him into direct contact with Laforguean enthusiasts, particularly Walter Arensberg, who translated some of the Pierrot poems, and Maxwell Bodenheim. Still, Crispin is not related intimately to the Pierrot, any more than he is a modern Candide. He owes the name of Crispin and perhaps little else to the French comic valet, and similarly to Saint Crispin.[43] He has many qualities, but no distinctive ones, of the many-masked harlequins of *Commedia dell'Arte*. The point is, however, that Stevens deliberately refrained from specific allusions, making his figure a composite which borrows from a heterogeneous tradition. Crispin has his own modern gestures, his own pathos, and his own destiny, free of traditions. Using an idea in general, Stevens is indebted to no specific mask, in keeping with his antimythlogical intentions; moreover, his range of allusiveness, including hints which associate Crispin with Figaro and Candide, offer comic as well as philosophical perspective on this "every-day man" without binding him to a type. Indeed, the poem's excesses may well be the result of this failure to draw Crispin more definitively. But Stevens' purpose was to create a sensibility, not a protagonist, and to chart the evolution of a seedling self, not a character.

Crispin's experience is essentially that dilemma precipitated by Hoon's confidence, which previously had been undercut by the discovery of "mon oncle" that life exacts its pound. As poet, he is first the hapless champion of idle fancy, and then, once disabused of precious ego, a humble slave to a voluble reality. But before the violence of Yucatan's portentous thunder—the illimitable sublime—he makes a compromising adjustment, aesthetic rather than moral, between two extremes. The poem's loose and rambling narrative orders this drama primarily in two ways: through the qualitative change of images which describe a symbolic geography, both east-west and north-south; and by a number of thematically shifting epigrams. The poem's changing landscape is the extended metaphor of Stevens' private geography as it developed in the whole of *Harmonium*. The epigrams compose the structure of ideas which Crispin's journey dramatizes step by step and make pronouncements on the significance of his acts. The double structure allows an excessive freedom which Stevens occasionally abuses with his buoyant anecdotes and verbal repetitions. Undoubtedly the most aspiring and least economical poem in *Harmonium,* it is a most interesting example of the conflict between language and meaning, or between language and the man who creates it.

Crispin's experience is a *reductio* of romanticism (and even may be seen as a comic history of the evolution of modernist poetry). It is likewise an inward quest to a discovery of the secular self: its needs, its limitations, in a cosmos which no longer feeds the romantic-transcendentalist appetite for self-definition. The comic valet, who is in the beginning an extremely pompous "Socrates/ Of snails," is a decadent, but no less a child of the Enlightenment (i). His dilettante's manner exposes the deficiencies of his closed world which has shut out the "terrestrial" for a "snug hibernal" escape into the "lex" of a closed mind. He is a poet of neatly defined things in a "World without Imagination." Stevens' opening epigram is both thesis and prophecy; Crispin's subjective cloak is an almost naively prim "mythology of self," and Crispin himself an untidy mélange of masks, without a country and thus without definition.

> The lutanist of fleas, the knave, the thane,
> The ribboned stick, the bellowing breeches, cloak
> Of China, cap of Spain, imperative haw
> Of hum, inquisitorial botanist,
> And general lexicographer of mute
> And maidenly greenhorns . . .

As the presumed intelligence of his soil, Crispin, like the doctor at Geneva, is a carryover from a simpler time when the world seemed to be man's plum and not a turnip. He will grow beyond his foppishness into the wiser Fool, altering his masks by necessity and according to his maturity. But first the fabricated self must be "washed away by magnitude," by the discomfiting floodtide of reality that Emerson called the not-me.

The first condition of Crispin's undoing is the exposure to "polyphony beyond his baton's thrust." Characteristically, there is no motivation for Crispin's fall into experience, no reason for his exposure to the not-me, and hence no real drama. There is only an awakening of sensibility, followed by the flood of an "inscrutable world" rushing in upon the hapless "short-shanks." The sea as "watery realist" dissolves the old Triton, refuses to be defined by its old mythological forms, leaving Crispin without familiar understanding, forcing him out upon alien waters. And Crispin is to suffer a sea change. Crispin "dissolved" is Crispin bereft of his tradition-oriented consciousness, cast out from the sophisticated order of continental Bordeaux toward peninsular Yucatan and its disordered welter of reality, thence to Carolina, a provincial compromise between two extremes. His voyage has more drift than direction, but the inevitable compromise must be read in terms of his aesthetic. Bordeaux and Yucatan form the poles of Crispin's world (form and vitality), and his western voyage, if introspective, has something of the American experience in it. Confronted by the enigmatic "ding an sich," Crispin is reminded of the attenuation of self:

>   Severance
> Was clear. The last distortion of romance
> Forsook the insatiable egotist. The sea
> Severs not only lands but also selves.
> Here was no help before reality.
> Crispin beheld and Crispin was made new.

He was made new, however, by being unmade, and thrust most rudely into the intensity of the "Carribean amphitheatre." The second section is a curious landscape, lush and overwhelming, yet with an incipient order all its own. In contrast to Bordeaux, Yucatan drives its inhabitants into withdrawal from experience, as with the Maya sonneteers who evade the barbarous in worship of the mystical night-bird. Not so Crispin, who rushed to embrace the "green barbarism," forfeiting his prudish aesthetic for one more appropriate to a young Rousseau: "an aesthetic tough, diverse, untamed,/ Incredible to prudes," an aesthetic, one notes, in which the soil not only dominates but overwhelms the intelligence. Yet Crispin is not ready for revelation; his sensibility is no compass for the immensities of Yucatan. The thunderstorms west of Mexico dissipate this new illusion of self, driving him to the cathedral, an experience not unknown in the history of Romanticism. Crispin's confrontation of the gigantic Andean breath is Stevens' first audience with the giant of reality, and like Crispin, Stevens will have to grow up to what it means. Like

Crispin, too, he will have to find a soil to accommodate the self, which is to say, a "Carolina" of discreet but rude reality. Put in terms of the later Stevens, one comes to understand the mountainous giant of reality by first understanding the plain over which he broods; or, one comes to know reality by first knowing the physical world, and hence measuring truly the capacity of the self to know and to make. Romanticism reaches out to its obverse and its complement, Naturalism.

"Approaching Carolina," then, is a compromise, but not without its gains; for the poet who is, as Eliot said of all poets, the most civilized and primitive of men must mediate in effect between Bordeaux and Yucatan.

> How many poems he denied himself
> In his observant progress, lesser things
> Than the relentless contact he desired;
> How many sea-masks he ignored . . .

He denied, too, the evasions of moonlight. Hence is developed the dialectic of early Stevens, or perhaps new Crispin: the "up and down" between subjective moon and objective sun, between two elements which, like the self and winter in "The Snow Man," are nothing in themselves. He has not denied imagination, but simply turned it outward, upon the flourishing tropic, finding in that act just what priority the mind has over things:

> He came. The poetic hero without palms
> Or jugglery, without regalia.
> And as he came he saw that it was spring,
> A time abhorrent to the nihilist
> Or searcher for the fecund minimum.

Exorcising the moonlight fiction, he does not exorcise the imagination; rather, he embraces the essential prose, the physical world, as the "one integrity . . . the one/ Discovery still possible to make,/ To which all poems were incident. . . ." Hoon departs his Palaz and descends toward the "Fat girl" of earth. But that is another, and a later, poetry.

Discovering the "essential prose" to be the ground of an essential poetry, Crispin has come at last upon the true aesthetic ratio: "Nota: his soil is man's intelligence." And the last three parts of the poem proceed to investigate the expense of this discovery. Crispin's comic reduction is both beginning and end of a western voyage, an attempt to define the role of poet as everyday man within the narrows of a world which demands mythologies but rejects the imagination. Crispin's regional aesthetic is in one sense existential, in another a return to the primitive, innocent consciousness with its deference to the "ding an sich." Beginning again, in a world unnamed, he begins like Emerson, in the "Language" section of *Nature*, with the word that literally contains the thing. He would out-Williams Williams. Projecting a colony, Crispin in effect projects an aesthetic, of smart detail, "veracious page on page, exact"—not unlike the plea of Ezra Pound to "make it new," yet worlds apart. For Crispin has learned to serve "grotesque apprenticeship to chance event," not as Pound might insist, to preferred event. A colony is limited in its history, and history is the enormous present with all its clutter— America with its provinces of rude reality and tenuous tradition.

This limit, indeed, is what Crispin learns in "A Nice Shady Home," that a colony must honor the quotidian:

> He first, as realist, admitted that
> Whoever hunts a matinal continent
> May, after all, stop short before a plum
> And be content and still be realist.
> The words of things entangle and confuse.
> The plum survives its poems.

It is a sober lesson, and one that Stevens could valuably unlearn, but not until it was clearly learned. This education in reality, in the "is," is an education in the ratio of mind to its world, a rediscovery of self confined in its matinal continent. For the poet, Crispin learns, must always begin in a matinal continent and build cabins before he plans "Loquacious columns by the ructive sea." It is the cabin, indeed, that is his life, that houses his marriage with the prismy blonde (of earth? a "Fat girl"?), a humble marriage in a humble house, made in the knowledge that "what is is what should be." Is this not an analogue of the modern poet, trapped in his mortality and jigging earthly rather than ideal "chits"? Is it not, at last, the price for cultivating, like a latter-day Candide, one's own gardens?

> While he poured out upon the lips of her
> That lay beside him, the quotidian

> Like this, saps like the sun, true fortuner.
> For all it takes it gives a humped return
> Exchequering from piebald fiscs unkeyed.

No "tragedian's testament" for Crispin, but no heroics either. The economic metaphor becomes an extended pun on continence. There is no tragedy for selves of Crispin's stature. But in the grotesque experience of loss, there is some slight "humped [!]" return—the lover's knowledge of what the world is to him, and he to it.

Crispin's return to social nature ends his reductive voyage, and in an ironic exuberance that puts his anecdote in critical perspective. His "Daughters with Curls" become the plausible issue of a clown whose very name, as has been remarked, predicts his offspring:[44] the man of curls produces curls just as the man of Georgia must be pine-spokesman, and the melon have apposite ritual. The indulgent fatalist finds himself trapped by the conditions of his own limited nature, his "chits" representing the cost of living an everyday life. Desiring divine progeny, like the bard of old no doubt, he produces a human progeny and finds himself "sharply stopped/ In the door-yard by his own capacious bloom" (possibly a hidden thrust at Whitman's cosmic prophecy when lilacs last in the dooryard bloomed). This is his "disguised pronunciamento," an apt metaphor for the journey of a "stiffest realist" in a world that insists on remaining materially itself, that offers but little comfort to the "seraphic proclamations" of a man with a limited, or secular, imagination. What, then, is this nondoctrinal anecdote of Crispin? What is this plea to seize the day, when the day exacts more than the humped return it gives? And what are the implications of his return to social nature?

"The Comedian as the Letter C" is neither a comforting nor a clear poem; the pith of Crispin's anecdote, however, brings the evolving self of *Harmonium* to a provisional wholeness by stripping that self of everything but its elemental energy. These curious chits of his making, these human progeny, exemplify the heart of the poem's ambiguity. Are they human issue, and analogously imaginative issue? Are they both children and poems? Both perhaps, but they are unquestionably out of the imagination's spectrum: "As buffo, yet divers, four mirrors blue/ That should be silver, . . ./ That spread chromatics in hilarious dark." The dark, too, haunts Crispin, and is illuminated only by the chromatics of his own self. Frank Kermode's suggestion that the chits are the faces of nature's four seasons is fruitful,[45] for the chits also teach Crispin that the soil is his intelligence. But are they not also his bloom, his own produce, self-mocking, delimiting, instructive, engaging, and above all vital—which is to say, human and reductive? (One of the root meanings of chit, interestingly, is sprout or shoot; another, primarily British, is letter, memorandum, or, more relevant here, a voucher for debts incurred. Stevens' way with multiple levels of suggestion would imply an extensive pun.) The relation of Crispin to chits is an original, and amusing, relation of creator to creation:

> Autumn's compendium, strident in itself
> But muted, mused, and perfectly revolved
> In those portentous accents, syllables,
> And sounds of music coming to accord
> Upon his lap . . .

They are his voice, his limited range. "So may the relation of each man be clipped"—thus the saga ends. Is not the pun here on relation, as well as on clipped? [46] For Crispin's own narrative, his relation, has come "benignly, to its end," humanly, comically, without the greater consolations. Similarly, his relations—the chits, and thus his relations with and to the world—have left him with only the form, the thin letter, of his pretensions to a fuller identity. But even Crispin must know that curls require clipping if they are to mature, to flourish. So is each relation (relating) of the imagination, each synthesis, completed, then clipped. And the self grows on.

"The Comedian as the Letter C" is a profuse and eloquent extension of a theme Stevens had presented shortly before in the verbal disguises of "Bantams in Pine-Woods" (CP 75). This latter poem, with its strident tone and opaque rhetoric, is a playful but resentful protest against the "ten-foot poet" whose exaggerated (mythological?) "hoos" pay no heed to the particulars of his world. At least it is this among other things, as Marius Bewley has shown at some length.[47] But Stevens is no more the ironically pathetic inchling of that poem than he is the rather ineffectual Crispin, whose bafflement is the initial lesson for one who has lost everything but ego and finds that ego barely adequate. It is this uncertainty, partly shared by Stevens, which accounts for the poem's excesses, and may account for the strange consistency of style which William York Tindall insists fails to convey the changes in Crispin's sensibility.[48] There is merit in Tindall's criticism, though it tends to overlook that the texture of images does change even as the lush eloquence is consistent. Imitative style, however, should not be a question with this poem, since the style is in substance indicative of the commentator's detachment; it is a contrived narrative style, consciously anecdotal. And if the exuberance is unfortunately excessive at times, the failure would seem to be the narrator's forced detachment from Crispin's follies. Crispin's voyage is never seen in true focus, and its ambiguity in the end seems to bemuse Stevens. Wanting to be affirmative—and Roy Harvey Pearce's suggestion that the poem may have been an answer, even a deliberate one, to *The Waste Land* cannot be disregarded [49]—wanting to be affirmative, Stevens could not in the end measure the degree of his negation. Nonetheless, the purging of the Crispin persona appeared to be necessary, even if the consequences of that purging were not immediately realized. Crispin assimilated the various masks of *Harmonium* and neatly trimmed them into a discreet and humble ego. How necessary this pruning of self was to later maturity, subsequent volumes would reveal. But its immediate importance was that it brought the celebrant of the physical world back to that world and freed him from the drift toward solipsism.

With all the emphasis on *Harmonium*'s gaudiness, it is necessary to reiterate again and again the essential seriousness. The sensuous surface cannot be stressed at the expense of the shadow which falls across the glass coach of self in Connecticut, or of the sense of inadequacy which propels Crispin, or even of the ominous dark which spreads over the fertile sea blooms of "Sea Surface Full of Clouds." "Sea Surface" was one of Stevens' last before the interlude of half a decade in which he ceased to write or, more likely, to publish poetry. Already Crispin had regained some of Hoon's aplomb, while refusing his dangerous isolation. To be gay is to be mortal, and Stevens was the gayest of poets. Students of Laforgue can readily account for the contemporaneity of this pessimism in gaiety, except that Stevens' irony is the very thing that spares him from Laforgue's impasse. The Laforguean manner, nevertheless, carries over into *Harmonium,* to be redressed in affirmation: at the center of the volume stand the discoveries of "Le Monocle de Mon Oncle," and at the end, the hoisting of Crispin with his own petard. These "Preliminary Minutiae" must be seen in all their rich ambiguity as a poetry in search of its author. Stevens knew very well that Crispin's "cabin" (like Thoreau's perhaps) need not be the poet's final dwelling, and accordingly that the American experience had its inevitable roots in an organic, a changing self.

chapter 3

Poets' Politics

If ploughman, peacocks, doves, alike
In vast disorder live in the ruins, free,
The charts destroyed, even disorder may,
So seen, have an order of its own, a peace
Not now to be perceived yet order's own.
Owl's Clover

In the late summer of 1924, Stevens published in *The Measure* a poem called "Red Loves Kit," a minor variation on the harmonium. He did not, it appears, publish again until the spring of 1930, when "The Sun This March" appeared in the April 16 issue of the *New Republic*.[1] It was a strange silence for one who needed poetry, particularly for one who so recently had discovered America and all that it demanded of the poet. Whatever the reasons, the new Stevens imago, like the somber advent of the decade, had come upon its own cruelest month:

> The exceeding brightness of this early sun
> Makes me conceive how dark I have become,
>
> And re-illumines things that used to turn
> To gold in broadest blue, and be a part
>
> Of a turning spirit in an earlier self. (CP 133)

The landscape was different; the light of an earlier self was dimmed and shone upon a less opulent world:

Cold is our element and winter's air
Brings voices as of lions coming down.
Oh! Rabbi, rabbi, fend my soul for me
And true savant of this dark nature be.

There is a sharp change of tone in Stevens' poetry of the 1930's, but no distinct break in theme. In 1931 he reissued *Harmonium* to the pleasure of many, though in a time not given to the old pleasures the gay tones were anachronistic. Four years later he tantalized the politically conscious with his own *Ideas of Order,* at best a maverick response to an "epic of disbelief." Whereas his cavalier approach to order in the 1920's could be understood in the idiom of that decade, the poetry of *Ideas of Order* appeared to be nothing less than morally irresponsible. In the act of abandoning the rich flora of the South, as the volume hesitantly announced, Stevens refused to abandon the imagination; he continued to talk of order outside the context of politics or religion, though with a more pressing sense of social crisis.

William Carlos Williams, reviewing *The Man with the Blue Guitar and Other Poems,* began by stating that Stevens "has turned of late definitely to the left." [2] That he had not turned far enough for the advocates of the left is most dramatically revealed in the now-famous Stanley Burnshaw review of *Ideas of Order,* which attacked Stevens for his indifference to the confusions and evils of his time, calling the volume a "record of a man who, having lost his footing, now scrambles to stand up and keep his balance." [3] Stevens had lost his footing, it seems, in the "subjective emotions" of *Harmonium,* "the kind of verse that people concerned with the murderous world collapse can hardly swallow today except in tiny doses." Stevens listened, even when he wished to ignore, and he stopped to argue with his antagonists, only to learn that the defense of self has its price. *Ideas of Order* suffered in comparison to *Harmonium,* in its removes from gaiety. And so did much of Stevens' writing in this decade, perhaps the most revealing single period in his career.

Stevens' controversial introduction to Williams' *Collected Poems, 1921–1931,* published in 1934, may well explain his own preoccupations at the time better than it explains Williams'. Calling Williams a romantic poet, and defining that term in a strictly modern, nonidealistic sense,

Stevens also called Williams the poet of the "anti-poetic" (see OP 254–57). What he meant, in effect, was that Williams was a devotee of a world so drab and actual that it virtually repelled the imagination and resisted the poet's effort, as he later put it, "to move in the direction of fact as we want it to be." The world of "The Sun This March" was distinctly antipoetic, and times would worsen. Such a world brought new challenges, not only to the poet's belief but to his style. Yet Stevens' changes of style in the thirties are not alone attributable to the changing world. Politically, Stevens was of the far right; but the pressures of the age did have the effect of pushing him, as he later admitted, toward the left.[4] He meant the left, however, in terms of poetry—in the sense that he wanted his poetry to speak for man rather than for the isolated mind. Stevens' development in the thirties, I think, can be explained largely in terms of these pressures, which produced a gradual metamorphosis of his poetic self: of how he conceived of man, of himself as poet, and of the reality in which he was condemned to live and play his guitar.[5] Crispin is left to another time; the "I" who speaks in this verse is becoming distinctly impersonal—"*any* man of imagination."

The relation of Stevens' poetry to politics is an interesting footnote in the history of modern poetry's struggle to survive as a humanity. It is not without cause that Stevens was assailed for continuing the trend of the twenties to make the individual style a private retreat from reality, to make poetry a mode of escape. Stevens was not, like Cummings, a poet who could willfully avoid the shoals of political and social reality; nor one like MacLeish, susceptible to radical changes of belief and commitment. Hence it is perhaps in his development that we can best see the enormous pressures of the decade on the forms as well as the matter of poetic discourse. For Stevens in his early poetry is readily identified with a kind of experimentalism which assumed that its purpose was more than making a poem *be:* the *being* of the poem constituted a search for, and at times the discovery of, new forms to replace the old outmoded forms. Form itself implies something larger than the specific forms of art; even the art for art's sake of the twenties was more often than not a struggle toward some surrogate moral or spiritual order, some personal chart in a world in which the charts have been destroyed. Crispin's reductive voyage and his colony manifest one response to the crisis. But in the thirties, Stevens like many another poet woke up to a new and startling reality—one that challenged his very being and denied his art. If a great deal of the literature of the twenties had been devoted to personal revolt against the old order, or nostalgically to willing a return to it, or even to erecting a new tradition out of old fragments, the artist in the thirties found himself confronted by conditions which brought the individualism and irrationalism of the earlier decade into grave question. More important, he found himself caught in a war of monolithic ideologies which offered new forms to replace dead ones, but only at the price of giving everything to the new "faith." The question for poetry was not whether it could save man, as I. A. Richards phrased it, but whether man could save it by way of saving himself. Indeed, Stevens' work in the thirties seems almost exclusively to be motivated by this effort to save poetry from ideology—"to isolate poetry" as he said—and to establish it as an essential human activity.

In this sense, Stevens is fully engaged in the strife and the polemics. But residually he is still the poet of *Harmonium,* facing middle age in a world of change. The great difference is that the poetry speaks less often through the private mask, more through that of the poet as representative man. His subject is "to play man number one" (CP 166), to reveal man in his root being. It is no surprise that Stevens finds the universal characteristic of this root being to be his "rage for order," and hence his need for poetry. The rationalization goes back to *Harmonium,* in which Stevens had discovered that we live in poetry because we live in perception. The problem facing him as poet, however, was that he had now to assert this belief to angry and alien ears.

Stevens' defense of poetry at this time is not historically unique. Ransom and Tate, along with their fellow Agrarians, had almost concurrently taken a chapter from Eliot's traditionalism to argue for the essential role of poetry in the human economy—as a form of ceremony, of discipline, that related man to his community and gave him identity in the greater, ordered social whole. Even the more sophisticated Marxists, like Christopher Caudwell, finding that the arts would not be reduced to the handmaiden of propaganda, offered rationalizations that made poetry central to the development of community. Caudwell, in particular, stressed in terms not altogether different from Ransom's the mythopoeic role of poetry in human history. Poetry, he claimed, was historically a manifestation of the "emotional, social and collective complex" of a society, and should retain that nature even in today's industrial world.[6] The means, like Ransom's, were to help men live their lives; the ends, however, the kinds of community each envisioned, could not have been more different. But Stevens was almost alone in defending the romantic, the individual, against the decade's demands for collective commitment, for community. Cummings had, but simply by ignoring the external challenges (or as in *Eimi* and some satiric poems, brilliantly disposing of them with non-argument). Frost had, but by his personal kind of democratic mysticism.

Stevens, however, is in many ways the characteristic American poet of this generation. Without taking Frost's mode of political attack through witty reassertion of the old democratic values, he managed to engage the realities of the decade and maintain his own integrity as poet. Moreover, he learned to change when change was mandatory. Compared to W. H. Auden's, of course, Stevens' political poetry gives little overt indication of political acumen—there is nothing in it of Auden's skill in capturing simultaneously the social and individual dimensions of man in his relations with the state. And that is just the point. Stevens' poems of this time seem less experiences of man in a social environment than what he calls "ideas"—by which he means perceptions, imaginative clarifications of what it is to be a poet, a man of imagination who cherishes his selfhood, in an antipoetic age. He never forgot that he was writing of the poet: that is, of what any man of imagination *could be,* not what he is. This is why Stevens' poetry is often so limited. It is also why he spares us the kind of sentimental apologetic that spills over into so much proletarian poetry of the time, why he wrote but few lines like these by MacLeish:

> There's nothing good in the world but the rich will buy it.
> Everything sticks to the grease of a gold note—
> Even a continent—even a new sky! ("Burying Ground by the Tie")

These are lines in which the argot of social protest and its extension into some hazy cosmic truth bring together two distinctive faults of style.

But this is not to suggest that Stevens' poetry escaped the taint of the age. *Ideas of Order* is too spare a poetry. And the long poems, "Owl's Clover" and "The Man with the Blue Guitar," pose questions of style and organization. Dr. Williams' attack on the pentameter line of the former, that it makes the poet "think he wants to think," cannot be dismissed.[7] For it is in "Owl's Clover" that Stevens most clearly reveals the burden of his poetry at this time. Faced with the claims of ideologies (particularly Marxism) that they can provide men with spiritual as well as physical succor, Stevens felt it necessary to counter promise with promise. Offering poetry (or "poets' politics") instead of politics, he protested all too urgently that not only was poetry previous to politics, but that the one common thing shared by all men—the thing which made them men—was the imagination. For the moment he found himself embarrassingly in defense of the century's newest apology for romanticism —the belief in a collective or racial imagination, the communal self within. He promoted a universal, collective imagination in opposition to a universal, collective ideology. The results for poetry were predictable. It is a measure of the time that it could do such violence to Stevens' resistance to grand abstractions; and a measure of him that he could survive, at least in parts of "The Man with the Blue Guitar," to write a spontaneous poetry once again. For Stevens' purpose, as we see it in retrospect, was first to save poetry—which is to say, provide a rationale for man as creator of the order within which he lived, for good or for bad, rather than as the creation of that order. Order is imagined before it is real—an "idea" before it becomes congealed like the many statues in this poetry, which stand variously for the human struggle to impose form upon a world of change. What we see happening in these three volumes is Stevens seeking for a definition of the aesthetic order, which "includes all other orders but is not limited to them" (OP 166). The rudimentary human urge for order in effect proves that poetry is basic to all human activity of mind.

II

Ideas of Order is a slim, modest volume, with thirty-three poems in first printing, thirty-six in final form. As the title suggests, it does not lend itself to any one thematic approach, even though the historical epoch constantly challenges, and even taunts, the poet to face it and still be himself. In style, a most striking reduction of sensuous detail is accompanied by a less ironic tone, which is even more indicative of the new reality. For in his deliberate shift from the ironies of "The Comedian as the Letter C" or "A High-Toned Old Christian Woman," Stevens admits to forces more dehumanizing than those which assaulted Crispin. Insisting that the poet should (even must) be concerned with the political and social changes of his time, Stevens nonetheless argued that the volume was primarily "ideas of order of a different nature," of

the dependence of the individual, confronting the elimination of established ideas, on the general sense of order; the idea of order created by individual concepts, as of the poet, in "The Idea of Order at Key West"; the idea of order arising from the practice of any art, as the poetry in "Sailing after Lunch."

The book is essentially a book of pure poetry. I believe that, in my society, the poet should be the exponent of the imagination of that society. *Ideas of Order* attempts to illustrate the role of the imagination in life, and particularly in life at present. The more realistic life may be, the more it needs the stimulus of the imagination.[8]

Ideas of Order is not pure poetry in any usual sense, i.e., poetry which is language emptied of rhetoric or of generally restricted meanings.[9] Though there are instances of the almost "pure," such as several of the short, evocative ideas of "Like Decorations in a Nigger Cemetery" (CP 150), it is assertion more than evocation that characterizes the volume. In any event, the verbal music which reminded *Harmonium*'s critics of Verlaine is largely diminished. Statement and metaphoric nuance rather than the quality of image become the stylistic norm, and the poetic eye begins to scan a world of men as well as a world of things. This does not preclude a substantial poetry. "Sad Strains of a Gay Waltz" and "The Idea of Order at Key West" are first-rate. It does, however, limit the range. *Ideas of Order* is at best a transitional poetry, modestly successful in its own right but important primarily for its place in the greater canon.

The tone of the volume appears to change according to whether "Sailing after Lunch" or "Farewell to Florida" leads off.[10] The former is a tour de force on the place of the romantic sensibility in "an unpropitious time"; the latter, an active reengagement of Crispin's problem, though with a deeper and more serious concern for the poet's responsibility to man rather than to his private "colony." One may better approach the volume, however, through a poem which first appeared during the *Harmonium* period, "Academic Discourse at Havana" (CP 142),[11] in which the contrasts of jungle and city offer the antitheses of order (intuitive vs. rational) from which Stevens' simplistic ideas spring. Stevens examines here an old theme, an American theme: the vital self against the rigid institution. And he makes the Emersonian choice, attacking the restrictive ordering of the reason, the kind of "thought" which evokes "a peace eccentric to/ The eye and tinkling to the ear." It is a plea for the "function of the poet" whose hymns will resolve all contradictions.

There is nothing new here. Just why the poem is preserved for *Ideas of Order* is uncertain, unless for the attack on politic man who "ordained/ Imagination as the fateful sin." For politic man is synonymous with rational, ascetic, institutional man—any man who legislates rather than discovers. The poet, naturally, is his opposite.

> As part of nature he is part of us.
> His rarities are ours: may they be fit
> And reconcile us to our selves in those
> True reconcilings, dark, pacific words,
> And the adroiter harmonies of their fall.

Despite the pronouncement in "Farewell to Florida," the volume's emphasis does not generally affirm more than the need to reconcile us to our selves. Politic man remains the inhuman abstraction, with his several obvious masks: of Marx, the "Founder of the State," or the fixed and spiritless statue of General Jackson in "The American Sublime." The statue will later be modified into the reigning symbol of "Owl's Clover," a symbol of order that allows for a range of speculation on the necessary balances between abstraction and change. *Ideas of Order,* however, is more various than its statues. Its themes, which grow out of *Harmonium* and are continuous with it, are familiar: (1) the responsibility of the poet to reality; (2) the dirty, formless reality of modernity which both demands and refutes ordering; (3) the primordial will or rage for order which all men share; (4) natural as opposed to artificial order; (5) personal as opposed to collective order; and (6) the prevailing theme of death, as it modifies and conditions "ideas" of order. All of these take us back to the early aesthetic, except that the world of Hoon is in *déshabillé* and the poetic self less sure of its privileges: whether, as in "Sad Strains of a Gay Waltz," it is the failure of the human to adjust to time and change; or, as in "Farewell to Florida," it is because the old order changeth; or, as in "The Idea of Order at Key West," there is a transformation of hope into belief. The old faiths of *Harmonium,* so alien to the times, cannot be discarded, but only modified: as witness the "Re-statement of Romance" (CP 146), in which man is "So much alone, . . . //That night is only the background of our selves,/Supremely true each to its separate self."

"Sailing after Lunch" (CP 120), which opened the first edition, is the plight of Crispin ten years after, the comic lament of "A most inappropriate man/ In a most unpropitious place." What begins as a serious attempt to celebrate the romantic develops into an uneasy tour de force, deflating the romantic's pretensions even as it makes the single, separate self the only center in an otherwise "vertiginous" world. The poem's basic tensions lie between the self's boat (hardly a *bateau ivre*) and the pressures of the "heavy historical sail," which suggest, however obliquely, the larger problems of the time. The comedy here is lightly turned against the poet, but the lusty vigor of the younger Crispin is absent. What emerges, nevertheless, is the voice of *Harmonium* hesitantly raised against the forces of history:

> To expunge all people and be a pupil
> Of the gorgeous wheel and so to give
> That slight transcendence to the dirty sail,
> By light, the way one feels, sharp white,
> And then rush brightly through the summer air.

But even this forced insistence was not to last; the slightest transcendence would soon become problematical, the "gorgeous wheel" of earth, a detritus.

A year later, the issues are more starkly defined; the self undergoes a sea change as announced in the "Farewell to Florida" (CP 117). This poem clearly displays Stevens' shift to the rhetorical key of the late 1930's. "The past is dead," the voice of *Harmonium* stilled in the leafless and wintry slime of the North. The poem's four very precise movements are outspokenly programmatic: a repudiation of the past (i); a review of that past, that South he is leaving (ii); but nevertheless a refusal to deny the old belief in the self, or the old world now gone (iii); and finally, a tentative commitment to his new role, to seek order in a northern and a social world (iv). It is a step from an individual to a social conscience, from the world of vivid sensuousness to the society of these men, whose needs "will bind/ Me round." It is not, however, a break with the past so much as a realignment of the self to the swiftly changing landscape of historical reality, to time the "snake." A pall descends upon the enchantments of imagination, and the once confident poet who masked as Hoon rejects the moon and turns realist in a way Crispin never anticipated.

The volume provides an extensive chart for this symbolic homecoming, northward into the wintry slime, into a "smutted semi-world hacked out// Of dirt" (CP 119). Such images proliferate, evoking a North that is more a world of reason than imagination, more dead than alive. It is a world of mickey mockers and plated pairs, haggard, constructed of gray stones and gray churches, where the sun, "that brave man," comes seldom and with little warmth. There is only a hesitant, last hurrah for Hoon, whose "forms have vanished" (CP 121). "A Fading of the Sun" one poem is entitled. Yet, there is sun and motion and the South, as in the poem which pays oblique homage to Whitman as a kind of "sun" of man, the source of the vital (CP 150). But Whitman's democratic vistas too rarely open upon the drab muck of this alien land.

Ideas of Order, however, is no mirror of the age, but a transformation of imagination and of the poetic self. If the North is a vicious and omnipresent reality, it is uncharted, unexplored, and it lends to man neither comfort nor certitude. The quest motif dramatized earlier by Crispin is explored in a soberer, less ironic, mood. One poem, "How To Live. What To Do" (CP 125), echoes the symbolic journeys of Auden and Day Lewis to the ideological frontiers of the decade, though Stevens' search for the salient rock is something other than Audenesque. Departure, yes—from the muck of the past and from the isolated, private self. But there is no collective commitment. The poet is called upon to play his traditional role in a time that has obviated tradition, to "play the present" in a world of "envious cachinnation." It is indeed a responsibility unknown to the poet of *Harmonium:*

> If they throw stones upon the roof
> While you practice arpeggios,
> It is because they carry down the stairs
> A body in rags.
> Be seated at the piano. (CP 131)

This is his "Mozart, 1935," compelled to "be thou/ The voice of angry fear," to embrace the jazz discordance of his age and supply the softening but not evasive tones of imagination.

In one poem, "Sad Strains of a Gay Waltz" (CP 121), Stevens manages to capture and subdue this cachinnation by the very act of holding it at a metaphorical distance. The gay waltz is the rapidly exhausting rhythm of a traditional order, and likewise of a traditional art, no longer relevant to the present. The chaos of the age is projected in the metaphors of music and motion now overwhelmed by cacophony. The comfortable solitude of Hoon collapses in the din, and the ghost of Emerson is laid. Even the severely formal tercets assert themselves as the remains of coherence, the order of honest perception. Hemingway might have honored these lines:

> There is order in neither sea nor sun.
> The shapes have lost their glistening.
> There are these sudden mobs of men.

"Too many waltzes have ended"—the line echoes like a refrain, but it is a music and music is order. The poet proves himself and the imagination; or better, he wills order and meaning through imaginative *will*ing:

> The epic of disbelief
> Blares oftener and soon, will soon be constant.
> Some harmonious skeptic soon in a skeptical music
>
> Will unite these figures of men and their shapes
> Will glisten again with motion, the music
> Will be motion and full of shadows.

Still, this affirmation following upon Hoon's dissolution is impertinent in a time which punishes romantic heterodoxy in artists as well as in unimaginative citizens. It is easy enough to understand Burnshaw's despair with so naive an indifference to the "murderous world collapse." But Stevens is consistent, knowing as he does that poetry dies in the service of politics or morals—knowing, that is, that the role of imagination precedes either and is fundamentally the origin of both. Or, as he puts it in two related poems of identical titles, "Botanist on Alp" (Nos. 1 and 2), the choice for his time is not between Christ and Marx but Claude and Marx: between imaginative (personal) or political (collective) order, both of which have implications transcending the present scene (CP 134). The choice, clearly, is not simple, but it is aesthetic: Claude's mannered world is dead; Marx's is not yet born and cannot be. One is reminded of Yeats's horrifying but beautiful prediction for our age in "The Second Coming," or even more, of Matthew Arnold's lament for the sensitive man "Wandering between two worlds, one dead/ The other powerless to be born." But Stevens will struggle to bring the residue of Claude's discreet vision to bear on the present:

> The pillars are prostrate, the arches are haggard,
> The hotel is boarded and bare.
> Yet the panorama of despair
> Cannot be the specialty
> Of this ecstatic air.

The spare, precise images, the falling rhythm and deliberate rhyme—it is not Claude's world, not nostalgic but realistic. In the second poem, he begins the redemption of despair by rejecting the promise of any future, religious or political:

> And what's above is in the past
> As sure as all the angels are.
> Why should the future leap the clouds
> The bays of heaven, brighted, blued?

Death, which in *Harmonium* forced the individual back upon the essential pleasures because the world is change and death, remains the dominant force in a landscape of violence. It is neither a bourgeois nor a proletarian fact, but like the imagination democratic and universal, vital. His hero in "Anglais Mort à Florence" (CP 148) is a victim of the self-deception that ideological promise of either Church or State can defend one against this last overwhelming reality. He is the artist who, finding his art inadequate to the pressures of the time, sacrifices his self to "God" and the "police," church or state. Collective sanctions become another kind of death, the sacrifice of imagination, and thus one's identity, for the security of living with comforting forms of belief. In a manner consistent with all of Stevens' poetry, the volume becomes an extensive critique of poetry itself in a time which makes egregious demands on its art.

Poetry touching the bass of our being, can still the "pizzicati" of living in a violent time—a theme which goes back to "Peter Quince." But the clavier is ever so passé, and the self flung out into the whirl. "The Pleasures of Merely Circulating" (CP 149), like the earlier "Life Is Motion," offers the modest but firm recourse of living in time and change:

> The garden flew round with the angel,
> The angel flew round with the clouds,
> And the clouds flew round and the clouds flew round
> And the clouds flew round with the clouds.
>
> Is there any secret in skulls,
> The cattle skulls in the woods?
> Do the drummers in black hoods
> Rumble anything out of their drums?
>
> Mrs. Anderson's Swedish baby
> Might well have been German or Spanish,
> Yet that things go round and again go round
> Has rather a classical sound.

All is motion—and motion in its repetitions is a kind of cosmos within chaos, the creation myth itself. The second stanza, however, introduces its antithesis, death, also an elemental truth, the enigmatic stillness around which life circulates. The pull of the poem's circular motion is centrifugal, yet the whirl is always related to the ominous dark of the central stanza. Note the driving rhythms of stanza one, the verbs of motion, the continuity between real and imagined—as against the curt, sharp images and abruptly stopped questions of the second. The concluding strophe suggests that beneath the particularities or contingencies of life (what might be or might have been) is one certainty: a roundness, a circularity, an orderly motion. Life is process; all particulars are subsumed under this first law, this "classical sound." Elemental, it is true! and that is exactly the point. The poem like life issues from the mysterious center and returns to it. We need no cosmic myths to explain it, nor ideologies to promise more.

When looked at through Marxist eyes, Stevens' aesthetic order is not only irresponsible and bourgeois, but imminently dangerous: not, of course, as an opposing ideology, but as an individual revolt against the massive commitment ideology demands. Stevens like Thoreau does not deny institutional order so much as insist that its origins are in the self.

This is clear in the volume's most typically Stevensian poem, "The Idea of Order at Key West," in which he turns back from the hortatory to the lyrical statements of *Harmonium*. There is a certain Emersonian quality about "The Idea of Order at Key West" (CP 128), as if Stevens had suddenly rid himself of naturalistic bonds and revived Hoon. The Emersonian tone, however, that suggested communion with nature which echoes in the lady's song, is simply the old duality once more in dramatic form—the duality of self and world from which comes man's "rage for order."

The poet has not yet departed Florida, but he no longer enjoys the comfortable isolation off Tehuantepec. His experience is a shared experience; his discovery an urgent need to feed a rage for order. The anxieties of the decade are subdued momentarily: man and nature stand once more nakedly face to face, not in angry opposition but in lyrical antiphony. The performer on the edge of nature is like Peter Quince before Susanna's legendary beauty, but here the relation has implications beyond the fastidious mood of *Harmonium*. "The Idea of Order at Key West" is a prelude to "The Man with the Blue Guitar"; the relation of man and world is not played out on the traditional and fashionable chords of the harmonium, but is improvised in the maiden's discreetly controlled lyrics. Even here improvisation bows lightly to tradition, the flow of metaphor overrides even as it remains within the strict pentameter.

Perhaps Stevens himself has suggested the meaning of the epistemological experience through his appeal, in the final stanzas, to Ramon Fernandez. Asked once about the name he replied with characteristic indirection: "I used two everyday names. As I might have expected, they turned out to be an actual name." [12] If Fernandez is unknown to Stevens, then we are witness to the most astounding instance of critical telepathy in literature, though Fernandez' criticism shares much with Santayana's aesthetic of perception. Fernandez was no minor critic; his theory, in a general sense, is a precursor of recent phenomenological criticism. He called it "philosophical" criticism and his favorite term was "impressionism," which for him meant something close to the intentionalism of Edmund Husserl. In any event, it is a theory which is remarkably parallel to Stevens'. A single quotation from Fernandez' essay, "Of Philosophical Criticism," should reveal something about Stevens' allusion, even if it was a happy coincidence:

Impressionism sets us afloat, suppresses the artificial intermediaries between reality and ourselves, and by maintaining us constantly in the presence of life makes us forearmed against the sophism of cause and fact. Further, because it brings us back to the hither side of common-sense perception, and as it were to its source, it invites us to a revision of the ideas guiding us; but this latter task becomes possible only if first this world of sensibility with its mirror-like facets is integrated by intelligence. Note that the required effort is not super-human. The state of anarchy is not so serious as one would be tempted to believe. In spite of our worst extravagance we are moving towards unity: I mean that in us the unity of the dislocated and scattered object is remade, *this time in a purely sentimental form.* . . . Thus are formed in us *psychic equivalents* of things containing within themselves the principle of their elucidation. Through the concentration of impressionism reality is translated into human tendencies and these in turn have to be treated by analysis.[13]

"The Idea of Order at Key West" might have been written to confirm this passage. The lady's song is the lyric modulation of the sea's impersonal, even cosmic, rhythms, a modulation which allows the sea its immensity and vitality but nevertheless brings it within sensible proportions. The song, indeed, is an impression; it becomes an "idea of order" when it brings the intelligence of the poet into unity with his world, from which nevertheless he is separate. As with the major exercises of *Harmonium,* Stevens retains the double perspective of actor and commentator; the drama is played out between the lady and the sea and is properly analyzed by the two onlookers, or at least by the poet with deference to his friend. What begins as an observation turns into a realized moment of order, an idea or abstraction of felt order; the poem, strangely enough, is not *about* but *is* the experience of this order. If the lady's song is heard at all, it is in that lyric echo of the poet's commentary. "A poet's words," as Stevens insisted in "The Noble Rider and the Sound of Words," are "of things that do not exist without the words" (NA 32). The poet receives the impression of a drama, and translates song into the sound of words, which become at once a projection of and comment on an experience. (Note that the poem is three removes from the girl's sense of order; it has become an "idea.") The poet's analysis realizes, in a psychic equivalent, the poem of the mind in the act of seeking what will suffice.

The opening two stanzas recreate the drama of *Harmonium* in the choric exchanges of animated sea and the lady's song: the one an inviolable reality, the other a separate distinct self. "The sea was not a mask. No more was she." Nor are the blending tones an imitation of one by the other—they are "not medleyed." There is the suggestion here of three realities: sea, song, and the higher synthesis of the two, another repetition of Stevens' secular trinity. The self nevertheless dominates: "But it was she and not the sea we heard."

The poet's subsequent questioning is an attempt to define the exact nature of the relationship, a rhetorical analysis which essentially repeats the opening stanzas. And it is this reflection which takes us beyond *Harmonium*. If the song were only a verbal imitation of reality it would be sound alone; were it only her voice, it would be an empty subjectivity. The answer obviously is an impressionistic marriage of subject and object, a "sentimental form." The poem's statement is academic, almost formulistic. But the incantatory tone, with its impressionistic echoes of liquid "plungings" and mounting heaves of sound, transforms formula into theory and theory into perception, that is, into experience:

> If it was only the dark voice of the sea
> That rose, or even colored by many waves;
> If it was only the outer voice of sky
> And cloud, of the sunken coral water-walled,
> However clear, it would have been deep air,
> The heaving speech of air, a summer sound
> Repeated in a summer without end
> And sound alone. But it was more than that,
> More even than her voice, and ours, among
> The meaningless plungings of water and the wind,
> Theatrical distances, bronze shadows heaped
> On high horizons, mountainous atmospheres
> Of sky and sea.

As "the single artificer of the world/ In which she sang," the lady achieves the moment of psychic order—of taking the thing impressionistically into the self and maintaining it there in sentimental unity—that Fernandez says is the essence of art. The observers hear and feel, redeeming their faith in poetry and the creative self. Heaven and earth, abstraction and reality, are collapsed in the order of aesthetic vision:

> Oh! Blessed rage for order, pale Ramon,
> The maker's rage to order words of the sea,

> Words of the fragrant portals, dimly-starred,
> And of ourselves and of our origins,
> In ghostlier demarcations, keener sounds.

Poetry, which emerges from the animal rage, is the containment of experience in the order of words, or in the order of an imaginative self whose words attach to the world but are forms of his mind. If poetry searches the fragrant portals of the ineffable, extending our horizons and creating our ideas of order, or our heavens, the outline or abstraction of those portals is blooded by things of this world. Fragrance, we know, is a quality of this world and no other—and so, implies Stevens, are the roots of heaven. The portal at last is a mirror in which we view our own rage for order. The poem has been compared to Wordsworth's "The Solitary Reaper"; it is more aptly a modern answer to "Dover Beach."

Whatever the break announced in "Farewell to Florida," it has nothing at all to do with abandoning the discoveries of *Harmonium*. For *Harmonium* above all had proved the dangers of isolation. There is only the slightest difference between Yucatan and Key West; there is very little more between the agonies of Crispin's reductive experience and Stevens' insistence that we live by poets' politics. When he reasserts, in a poem like "Evening without Angels," the man-made center of our religious life, when he champions the vital mind against the closeted and studied abstractions of civilization, Stevens is writing but another variation on the theme that "death is the mother of beauty." Only, in the wintry slime of the 1930's he does not talk of beauty but of politics and the ugly. "The babble of generations magnifies/ A mot into a dictum" (OP 34). The poems of *Ideas of Order* are anxious to communicate. Thus their capitulation to the age—but if the age demands dictum, it will be the dictum of poetry that Stevens offers. The realities of ideologies, unlike those of Florida, are not to be indulged and enjoyed; they are militant, coercive, and bring death to the spirit if not the body.

III

Ironically, Stevens found himself under attack by the decade's idealists for his own idealism. His order was not practical; his ethic not social or economic. Burnshaw, having despaired of finding an idea consonant with the social crisis, ended his review by asking if Stevens would "sweep his contradictory notions into a valid Idea of Order?"[14] At nearly the same time, F. O. Matthiessen, reviewing concurrently *Ideas of Order* and Burnshaw's volume of poetry, *The Iron Land,* found the latter a study of a mill town which is "not portrayed with the felt detail that would take it out of the realm of political theory and make its anguish seem as real as it is." Stevens' new volume, on the other hand, was more "robustly integrated" than *Harmonium* and the year's only book of poetry "that would lend great distinction to the Pulitzer prize."[15] Despite such receptions, however, Stevens himself, not always above the battle, found it imperative to make his case more firmly and openly—not to say, tendentiously—in his next poem, "Owl's Clover."

"Owl's Clover" is hardly a political poem, though it is involved with politics. Almost as soon as it was published Stevens showed dissatisfaction with its excessive rhetoric, and even after extensively cutting and revising it for a later edition (1937) he refused to include it in his *Collected Poems.* William Van O'Connor, calling it Stevens' finest long poem and one of the best in English during the first half of the century,[16] enthusiastically praises Stevens' "Politics of Order" as a sane conservatism as well as a convincing defense of poetry. But O'Connor conveniently disregards what Stevens later came to condemn, the rhetoric which resulted when he tried to argue rather than create, when he attacked false myths by offering his own. Stevens himself has said that although the poem reflected the political and social furor of the decade, its main intention was "to emphasize the opposition between things as they are and things imagined; in short, to isolate poetry."[17] The two judgments are apt: it is not his finest long poem and its intention, as we assess its place in the canon, is to defend poetry.

Stevens' distraction by Marxist criticism and radical ideology, however, is as much poetic strategy as individual pique. The Marxist program becomes for him only the most recent of a long line of conceptual failures to provide a rationally ordered society. Though Stevens understood the dangers of putting poetry at the service of politics, he was not so alert to the consequences of trying to subsume the practical in the ideal. It was he, not his critics, who made the error of deserting a defensible position to contend with the enemy on its own terms. Cummings had more wisely ignored the argument; Frost had consistently avoided "ideas." Neither did Stevens have the political acumen of an Auden, who knew full well how far poetry could go in the service of a cause, and to what degree it had to be impersonal, aloof from causes and action. But Stevens was faced with two challenges: to his vocation as poet, and to his convictions of democratic freedom, the *laissez faire* of self and its economy. He said specifically of "Owl's Clover" that it concerned "the effect of the depression on the interest in art," that

I wanted a confronting of the world as it had been imagined in art and as it was then in fact. If I dropped into a gallery I found that I had no interest in what I saw. The air was charged with anxieties and tensions. To look at pictures there was the same thing as to play the piano in Madrid this afternoon. I was as capable of making observations and of jotting them down as anyone else; and if that is what I had wished to do, I could have done it. I wanted to deal with exactly such a subject and I chose that as a bit of reality, actuality, the contemporaneous. But I wanted the result to be poetry so far as I was able to write poetry. To be specific, I wanted to apply my own sensibility to something perfectly matter-of-fact. (OP 219)

"Owl's Clover," in its original form, is Stevens' longest poem, more than 860 lines divided into five separate, but thematically continuous, poems. Its dialetical, rather than narrative or lyrical, progression realizes a major step from Stevens' early to his late style. But more revealing is Stevens' own urgent sense of being a man with a program. Behind his rhetorical mode is the assumption that rational ideas of order are no more than forced and congealed manifestations of man's primitive will for order. Tradition in art and law as in religion is a hardening of ideas, and thus a violation of the everchanging, fluid rage. The Marxian faith, for instance, translates "need" as biological, denying the total self. Ideas of order are molded into ideologies, fixed and final forms which rule the men who evolved them. Politics is Stevens' ostensible subject, but the self remains his true source of authority. A poem dedicated to defending what can only be called anarchy, in the kindest words of rationalism, is destined for hard times in an age of disorder. But Stevens' greatest heresy in "Owl's Clover" was his offering the imagination as the one universally shared quality of all men. It is the rage for order, the "subman" within, that distinguishes man, the poem pleaded. It is this need for order, and the imaginative creation of it, that precedes politics—a theme unlikely to attract many converts.

A loose and rambling poem, enormous in its purport, "Owl's Clover" has only the order of its *idée fixe* and the urgency which compelled Stevens to write it. The statue is his controlling symbol; the subman is his subject. Speaking specifically of the first poem of the series, he remarked that the "old woman is a symbol of those who suffered during the depression and the statue is a symbol of art, although in several poems of which *Owl's Clover* . . . consists, the statue is a variable symbol" (OP 219). Throughout "The Old Woman and the Statue" it stands for the art (the imagination) of an anachronistic tradition. In subsequent poems, as it submits to Stevens' imaginative remodeling, it comes to stand for the one kind of form (organic, I suppose, in contrast to fixed) which Stevens later called the "abstraction blooded." An analogy of this form is the poem of reality. The statue, then, is an idea of order, and in the largest sense, was the binding symbol for what all men shared —a rage for order and an imagination which could satisfy that rage. "Owl's Clover," in a sense, offers a range of speculation on the relation of form to flux, and a number of possibilities for their marriage—as a poetry of course. The "supreme fiction," which was finally to evolve out of Stevens' search for order in the 1930's, necessarily takes a form, but not at the expense of change. At this point, however, Stevens seemed content, perhaps out of necessity, to examine the intercourse of abstraction and change without much pleasure. For the first and only time in his career he boldly, and uncompromisingly, took up the argot of the enemy and twisted it into poets' politics. Crispin's colony had opened upon the social state.

"Owl's Clover" is a rather drab piece beside "The Man with the Blue Guitar." But it can be dismissed only at the risk of misunderstanding Stevens' development. If we do not find it the comforting balm suggested in the title, we may discover in it Stevens' reason for seeking that balm. Its posture of attack exposes the poet in crisis, not only of craft but of self. The challenge of politics in the thirties was a challenge to the right to be. Stevens could no longer feign indifference even as he had no genius for being political (or politic when the self was at stake). "Owl's Clover" is a poem almost unique in Stevens' canon in the sense that it extends his familiar themes beyond their familiar world. A poem of ideas, it is perhaps Stevens' first explicitly intellectual lyric. Its curious lines of argument demand close attention. To this end the first version of the poem is essential (OP 43).

In "The Old Woman and the Statue" Stevens moves directly to the imminent challenges of his time: the statue of the past caught in the turmoil, the ugliness and poverty of the present. The question, clearly, is as relevant to poetry as to politics, and Stevens exploits the parallel throughout. The statue is of "another evening," a more tranquil time, its design an investment of imagination that repudiates change. And this, the poet remarks with ironic nuance, is just the problem. If it is art —and more than the artist's "muddy hand" is in it, the whole conscience of his age is in it—it now stands isolate among the rotten leaves of the present. How conventional the symbolism it is unnecessary to remark; a contrast with Tate's "Ode to the Confederate Dead," however, is indicative. That the statue is meaningless to an old woman, "the bitter mind/ In a flapping cloak," is poignantly obvious. Thus the failure of tradition, as of poetry, to account for change: that is, tradition's assumption that the age molds the man and that man is essentially unchanging. Like a topical poetry, the statue exists in sentiment and not in reality. Enter, then, the old woman, and with her the elemental opposites of Stevens' poetry—she "So destitute that nothing but herself/ Remained." Hence, "The mass of stone collapsed to marble hulk" before her. This tableau of woman and statue reminds us that the past is only prologue, that there is no eternal time, that reality is change and death, and that order involves the constant activity of self in its adjustments to both. Reality in the guise of the old woman becomes another domination of black, and the past is dissolved into her dark mood. The old woman's appetite transforms the hulk into the shape of her need: it becomes a "manner of the mind, a mind in a night/ That was whatever the mind might make of it." Poetic rhetoric has seldom been more intense, or more labored.

The poem's concluding section hardly relaxes that intensity. The old woman has profoundly modified the present, a present less "brilliant" than its past (the past of the budding yew which must recall the ancient sacrifice of "Sunday Morning"). For the "harradin self and ever-maladive fate" is the utter poverty of a world which has lost the old brilliance, and the old beliefs. Like a dark Medusa, the old woman paralyzes the scene, in which desolate syllables drowned out old hymns. The stanza, indeed, is another of Stevens' concentrated views of historical change, decrying here an idealized past that remains "Untroubled by suffering, which fate assigns/ To the moment." The new imagination cannot be untroubled by suffering. Thus the stanza's concluding metaphor: of the statue revived into a vital, soaring Pegasus of the imagination, facing the Medusa, and transforming her dark presence into a life. It is Stevens' old solution, but the somber mood is telling—yet Pegasus against the Gorgon is an apt figure for the opposition of imagination and reality in an ugly time. The impoverished owl's clover of the present provokes its own cure, just as reality challenges the imagination to act. But the order desired by the present world, which the poem heavy-handedly prescribes, cannot be the old order, or old myths.

"The Old Woman and the Statue" is a poem in its own right, a rhetorical critique of the traditional past which is not to be absolved for its failures, no more than its glory is to be regained. But in the context of "Owl's Clover," the poem becomes a prologue of modern need, and initiates the quest to which the greater poem is dedicated. The past, Stevens speculates hesitantly, belongs to us and not to itself, is a part of a human (imaginative) continuum, or else it is a relic set futilely against change. Stevens found his working metaphor in a decade in which the failure of the past was most acute. Art, religion, politics, memory—whatever the statue is, it is too abstract, too formal, too much codified, and too unimaginative.

"Mr. Burnshaw and the Statue" picks up this failure of the past and explores the possibilities of a revitalized order, generated out of the individual and his imagination. But before it can affirm, the poem must contend with contemporary ideologies and thus enter a controversy where poetry is not always at ease. Though predication of the future is not a part of Stevens' hope for poetry (poetry is an act of being, not apocalyptic for him), he must deal with futures as well as pasts, and in terms other than political. Called "The Statue at the World's End" in later editions, the second poem was undoubtedly first titled as an answer to Burnshaw's criticism. Later Burnshaw dropped out altogether from both poem and title, a casualty of Stevens' self-criticism and no great loss. For the subject of this poem is change, not ideology, and to promote an idea of organic and thereby imaginative order (poets' politics) is its burden.

The opening stanza is a shock gambit—establishing the poet's defensive tone:

> The thing is dead . . . Everything is dead
> Except the future. Always everything
> That is is dead except what ought to be.
> All things destroy themselves or are destroyed.

No Marxian cry for the future this!—but a mocking restatement of the natural law of change, intended to irritate dialecticians. The statue returns, once again as a failure of imagination, the horses "made to affect a dream they never had." It is indeed a toy ("a thing from Schwarz's"), with a toy's relevance to the present.[18] The horses are as rigid and "ugly as an idea," or an ideology, sheer fancy in formal dress, violating life by denying death. To this point, however, the poem is repeating itself.

An expected change of pace in the second section relieves the rhetoric, but only for another kind, which is at pains to generate some hope for a new order. Out of the death of tradition, and the "sibilant requiems for this effigy," the poet heralds a new day, contrived in a metaphorical dance of opposites: the celestial paramours of individual imagination and world's body. Not a preconceived order, this day is a present made continuous in the act of imagination, a dance of creation which evolves out of the death of the past. But the boisterousness of the orgy in "Sunday Morning" has subsided into prose. "New" here is an equivalent of "vital" (Bergson's continuous creation). The metaphor of the dance set against the statue's gawky plaster must recall that romantic image of timeless, vital motion. Denying Shelleyan flights, the poem celebrates the sentient body of nature elevated into forms of belief, thereby rejecting the future: "the apple in the orchard" "will not be redder, rounder then/ Than now." (This is a good example of Stevens' antimythological imagery; the apple is not in Eden but only itself.) But still, Stevens' rhetoric appears to be defending *Harmonium,* not *Ideas of Order,* from Burnshaw, trying to mend fences before making another effort at colonizing the aesthetic.

His new order, then, begins with his old:

> *"The Mass*
> *Appoints These Marbles Of Itself To Be*
> *Itself."*

"No subterfuge" in this devotion, "no memorable muffing"—only simple homage to the "bare and blunt." Rejecting the illusion of a fixed and final order, either Christ's or Marx's, he opts for an ideology of imagination, the poets' politics which rule only in the poets' world: politics (that is, order) which are intuitional rather than reasoned, ritualistic but not formal, natural rather than abstract, poetry rather than prose. Rejecting the bardic unhappiness of those transcendental or nostalgic poets who "are never of the world in which they live," Stevens insists on his heresy of the natural, of the order within organic disorder, which he was later to espouse as a "connoisseur of chaos." The double view of Shelley in these stanzas reveals Stevens' conscious and ambiguous sense of his romantic heritage, especially in a world he must legislate with poetry but cannot transcend.

Burnshaw and his social commitment are to be met on the elemental ground of life; the reality of death set against ideological promise. Thus section five. Stevens' death-in-life theme furnishes its own rhetorical opposition, for death has no categories. Rich and poor alike must submit to this resolution of change, a truth untouched by ideology. And the finality of death makes materialistic optimism absurd; likewise the dream of futures. The law of change foretells the "immense detritus" of things; ideas of progress lead "from waste/ To waste, out of the hopeless waste of the past/ Into a hopeful waste to come." It is necessary to remind oneself repeatedly that Stevens is arguing on nonpolitical grounds, or on prepolitical grounds, that he has misunderstood Burnshaw just as Burnshaw has confused poetry with politics. Otherwise, Stevens' indifference to immediate "detritus" is callous (or as the Marxist would say, bourgeois). Unfortunately, the exuberant vitality of *Harmonium* is dulled, but argument here must be seen in the context of the whole: as a defense of poetry which managed, almost miraculously, to survive the time in a way Burnshaw's poetics did not. Like Auden, Stevens knew that poetry "makes nothing happen" except within the self.

But if an order which lies in some ideal future will not suffice, he continues, neither is it enough to hold to belief which is soon to be swept into the past. The temple, or final order, "is never quite composed," leaving one to worship that whirling world outside: "It is only enough/ To live incessantly in change." "So great a change/ Is constant"—the order of cosmos over chaos, the order of nature, that "moving chaos that never ends": "... change composes, too, and chaos comes/ To momentary calm." Man, evolving a "drastic community" from the "whirling, slowly and by trial," becomes Stevens' still-point, though not without some expense to his style. For the conclusion of "Mr. Burnshaw and the Statue," resolving into a dance like that former "boisterous devotion to the sun," is rhetorically drab. But its argument is clear. Fearing ideology's history of error, Stevens is left with only the beleaguered self and its elemental relation to the world. He embraces change and thus chaos, and hesitates to prophesy. Like Thoreau before him Stevens must make the present do for all futures; unlike Thoreau's nature, however, Stevens' is devoid of spirit, its order alien to man. His ritualistic dance of the self amid chaos is a little grotesque, not to say frenetic. But it makes its point bluntly.

Having established the basis of his order in the elemental, Stevens turns in "The Greenest Continent" to the form that order must take and to its origins in imagination. Against the statue and the chaos which surrounds it, he opposes a symbolic Africa, that realm of innocence where the rule of the blood is law. (Stevens may well have drawn his symbolism from Jules Laforgue's excited writings on *"l'Afrique intérieure,"* a phrase Laforgue picked up from the German Romantic Johann Richter and expanded into an extensive metaphor of the unconscious self, a world of rich decor where Laforgue prefers to reside.[19]) Africa against Europe —it is for Stevens vitality against form, the natural against the civilized, the irrational against the rational. Above all, the poem is Stevens' initial excursion into the jungle of the Jungian unconscious, there to discover man's constant rage for order as "Fatal Ananke," the "final god" and author of that "aesthetic order" which lies behind all other orders.

The poem opens with a short rhetorical question: what god-form prevails in Africa? None, of course, except the jungle law of order within chaos. Africa defies abstraction, just as Europe has sold its freedom for a heap of archaic statues. Stevens' genius of sharp juxtapositions is never more keen than in this poem: the question about Africa, left unanswered, and then the abrupt shift to Europe whose "heaven" is "empty, like a Schloss/ Abandoned because of taxes." Section two of the poem is as good as anything Stevens did in "Owl's Clover," even though in the revision he eliminated all but a half-line. As a preview of the spiritual decline and fall of the West, it is acutely of its time, and powerfully compact. The shell of Europe is a civilization gone to spiritual pot. Once alive, filled with pomp and circumstance, it is now culturally bankrupt, a relic on the altar of progress. Stevens' tropes marking its historical decay are topically pertinent: "Verhaeren in his grave," "the Daimlers that/ Dissolved the woods." (The aptness of the Verhaeren reference speaks for Stevens' accuracy of allusion as well as for his grasp of French poetry. Émile Verhaeren, a symbolist but no less a realist than the brothers Goncourt, was the poet-prophet of the industrial wasteland. See his "Vers le futur," which includes the appropriate image, "L'usine rouge éclat òu seuls brillaient les champs. . . .") This is a precise and timely lament: art gives way to the motor car, nature to petrol, something out of E. M. Forster and the Bloomsbury Group, not to say Agrarian Nashville. "Everything did it at last," the failure of order to ascribe to change destroyed Europe: static culture and the Church, science and finally war, that "fatal farce." This is Stevens' wasteland, 1930's version, but a self remains intact if in tatters; it explains, surely, Crispin's earlier departure from Bordeaux.

Thus section three, which takes up the failure of religion:

> There was a heaven once,
> But not that Salzburg of the skies. It was
> The spirit's episcopate, hallowed and high,
> To which the spirit ascended, to increase
> Itself . . .

A radical protestantism, this is no less an appeal to the origin and source of spiritual order in primitive feeling. It was, the section says ruefully, a religion of "each man" who "beheld the truth and knew it to be true." But it makes a dour poetry, a tired pleading. The verse, however, regains its lyrical quality in section four, with the shift to Africa where no god rules, where serpent and elephant range freely with death as the lone herdsman. Here at last, in the tension between death's omnipresence and the lion's roaring protest, Stevens returns to the elemental law that governs his ideas of order and his theory of poetry-in-life. Here death-in-life is change-in-life; variety is vitality and incipient death.

There follow three sections of variations on the theme of statue against Africa, including a *divertissement* on the contemporaneous and topical. More or less as an aside, Stevens introduces into Africa the missionary with his radical devotion to order. Dedicated to saving souls, he comes as emissary of death, bringing his false messianic order. His forms "slay" in Africa: the "Seraphim of Europe" are "cuirassiers against/ The milkiest bowman." Stevens' vigorous attack leaves no question that the old wit directed against high-toned old Christian women is not etched deeply enough to score off these men of ill-purpose. The occasion demands rhetoric and a sustained offensive: hence the succeeding section which transports the statue to Africa, another version of the intrusive missionary with his Northern forms. Still another shift in key (vii) returns to the topical and the negations of intellectualism. The missionaries destroy by zeal; the coffee-house intellectuals by abstractions without blood. Denying gods, these latter deny the human; devoid of belief, they have murdered passion. They have rejected the statue and the "cavernous past" without being able to "feel the sun." Theirs is an empty ritual of "Champagne/ On a hot night and a long cigar and talk," a nihilistic game without imagination.

One resolution remains, one source of order: "Fatal Ananke," the god of necessity, which possesses every man and kindles his rage for order. Having swept away the false orders and returned to naked reality, Stevens is ready now to admit a need of an essential form which will contain reality without suffocating it. Ananke, more Jungian than Greek, is Stevens' "angel in the nigger's mind," the final, the inner god, "who ordains/ For races, not for men"; that is, he is the human constant, the elemental need. As always when he toys with personification, Stevens is neither dramatic nor prophetic, and the personification exists only for its occasion, personal and rhetorical. Personification is for him a mode of imaginative conception, used here to identify man's inner rage for order as the changeless element that makes him man, and thus a creature who needs statues. But at this point, Stevens has succumbed to his own necessity, of countering ideology with an ideal of man. Moreover, uneasy of self, he hesitantly offers his own kind of collectivism.

"A Duck for Dinner" proceeds to investigate the possibilities of order by opposing Ananke to ideological promise. But the voice grows more urgent, not less; Stevens is caught up in the immediacy of the moment and its shrillness. He had mused, in the second poem, on the dream of a future developing gradually out of the present, from hopeless waste to hopeful waste, but had denied the hope of Burnshaw. Now he had to engage the more immediate politics of crisis, of which the Marxist promise was most eminent. Though the debate is significant, it is almost fatal to poetry. While one is treated to some suggestive variations, he enjoys no discovery, and what is more, must suffer some turgid repetitions of the preceding poem.

The first three sections of "A Duck for Dinner" form an interesting if curious tour de force on the vagaries of American history (i.e., a democratic, individualistic saga of self in embryo), with special reference to the proletarian self-consciousness of the present. The first and third sections concentrate on the figure of the "Bulgar," a composite mask of the immigrant, while the second counterpoints this rising self against the ideal of the buckskin, "crosser of snowy divides." The buckskin symbolizes the spirit of the American adventurer, or more generally the spirit of the democratic secular self, free at last of "cadaverous Eden." Though not altogether successful, the Bulgar figure is a creation which reveals much of Stevens' problem in the poem. For he is the voice of the anti-ideologist who sees the rise of the workers not as a revolutionary leap into the future but as the gradual and continuous evolution of sensibility, whose rise is "only an inch, but an inch at a time," like that of the foam-born Venus out of a self-creating imagination. His is no solution to the decade's chaos certainly. But his faith is linked to an ideal of the democratic spirit, to a hope for recovering the energy of the buckskin from the industrial "wrick-a-wrack." The buckskin on the other hand is the old spirit of Whitman's single, separate self, not simply American but the poet who lives and thrives and at last rises, as the Bulgar envisions, by his own will to be. Hence, a return to the Bulgar in the third section is a paean to the hope that imagination can release man from circumstance and the pandemic of materialistic despair, that ugly duck which satisfies physical but not spiritual appetites. The roots of this hope are in Emerson's "Fate."

Politically unsound as it must have appeared, the poem is nonetheless apolitical, an early exercise toward defining that radical humanism which was to culminate in a search for an idea of man to replace the idea of God. Section four, explicitly rejecting the "newest Soviet reclame" for the future, is absorbed by its own doctrine of imaginative, sub-historical order:

> What man of folk-lore shall rebuild the world,
> What lesser man shall measure sun and moon,
> What super-animal dictate our fates?
> As the man the state, not as the state the man,
> Perennial doctrine and most florid truth . . .

Hesitantly formulated here, this is the seedling idea for "The Man with the Blue Guitar," an idea of man become the poet-guitarist who confounds chaos in the sound of words:

> It may be the future depends on an orator,
> Some pebble-chewer practiced in Tyrian speech,

> An apparition, twanging instruments
> Within us hitherto unknown, he that
> Confounds all opposites and spins a sphere . . .

The final two sections return to this definition of the modern Demosthenes as politician of the self, as "Don Juan turned furious divinity/ Ethereal compounder, pater patriae," whose compounding must be this myth of man—the statue in the image of the self in opposition to the statue as myth of the state. The statue, of the poet's making (*any* man's making), has nothing to do with doctrine as such, except to deny doctrine:

> The civil fiction, the calico idea,
> The Johnsonian composition, abstract man,
> Are all evasions like a repeated phrase,
> Which, by its repetition, comes to bear
> A meaning without a meaning.

Rejecting theological recourse ("catastrophe/ For Isaac Watts") as he rejects the politico's "diverting of the dream/ Of heaven from heaven to the future," Stevens ends by fixing his own moral wasteland in appropriate images:

> How shall we face the edge of time? We walk
> In the park. We regret we have no nightingale.
> We must have the throstle on the gramophone.

"The pianola 'replaces'/ Sappho's barbatos," wrote Ezra Pound of his culture's postwar disintegration. Stevens' metaphors are no less severe and no less directed at the moral alluvium which has settled upon his age, offering a duck for dinner as appeasement to the gnawing hunger for order. Asking "Where shall we find more than derisive words?" Stevens will hardly wait for an answer.

The dark mood in the final lines of "A Duck for Dinner" points forward to "Somber Figuration" and its evocation of the provisional subman, the man below, a second self who is free of the chaos of reason. Forced to reject the logic of a future, Stevens seems to appeal, for the moment, to a vague composite of Jung and Bergson, the "imagining, anti-logician" who

> . . . was born within us as a second self,
> A self of parents who have never died,
> Whose lives return, simply, upon our lips,
> Their words and ours . . .

Just how far Stevens submits to the Jungian vogue is questionable. The subman is no more than the child of Ananke, an *élan vital* which amends the shoddy denials of the sterile rationalist, making him see "maidens in bloom, bulls under sea." In sum, the subman is our essential self, but a most arbitrary and unhappy figure for the mystique of imagination.

The strategy which created the subman is partially clarified in section three through the evocation of the "sprawling portent," a projection of the subman in divine perspective and thus a tentative personification of the poet's new idea of man. More urgently, however, he is a symbol here for the human continuum which affirms that "the future must bear within it every past." For the portent is time itself (all pasts and thus all futures) condensed in the image of man, without whom there is no time:

> The portent may itself be memory;
> And memory may itself be time to come
> And must be, when the portent, changed, takes on
> A mask up-gathered brilliantly from the dirt,
> And memory's lord is the lord of prophecy
> And steps forth, priestly in severity,
> Yet lord, a mask of flame, the sprawling form
> A wandering orb upon a path grown clear.

Portent against statue, then—this is Stevens' argument in cameo; and the concluding section turns to this opposition for a final review. In the previous section, the portent is identified as the "form/ Of a generation that does not know itself," the mask of a time without perspective. The statue in section four would appear to be the expression of community need, set over against the expression of self, the portent: two incommodious symbols that the subman in us has erected against chaos. I hesitate to suggest these allegorical equivalents, but something like this is suggested in the conclusion: something which implies that neither the "man-haggard" portent nor the statue which stands in "hum-drum space" is an adequate conception of the human need for order. They are proximate, yes, but our images, our imaginative conceptions of ourselves and our gods, are always proximate. And taking form, like the portent, they become man-haggard (e.g., the anthropomorphic God), threaten to suspend process in a fixed image, deny time and change, and thus grow unreal. It is a thesis clearly anticipated in stanza three of "Sunday Morning," and elaborated later in "Esthétique du Mal." Caught between his two images, Stevens returns to his subman not as creator of portents and statues, but as the vital being itself and chokes off his poem with a plea for the absolutely irrational, a commitment to the sheer "gaudium of being." *Harmonium* is re-envoked, but all figurations now are somber. And the imagination is identified with night, its paramour sun having vanished along with the spontaneity of the old gaudium. What Stevens suggests, albeit vaguely, is the imagination as universal unconscious. Struggling to will again the old mask of "Jocundus," Stevens wears instead the cloak of his black-blooded scholar. Or more clearly, he wears the cloak of the tendentious scholar who composed an essay in apology for "Owl's Clover." It was entitled "The Irrational Element in Poetry" (OP 216) and in it he insisted that even a poetry which explicitly undertakes politics serves only to "disclose the individuality of the poet," a sensibility. But in "Owl's Clover" we see most clearly that under pressure the individual has come to unveil a common self and a common need.

Within a year Stevens experienced dissatisfaction with his apologia of aesthetic order. When he released the poem once more, for publication in *The Man with the Blue Guitar and Other Poems* (1937), he had revised and cut it extensively. The original version remained out of print during Stevens' lifetime and until the publication of *Opus Posthumous*. The excisions, almost 200 lines in all, are significant. Aside from tightening up the poem's structure and omitting several repetitions, Stevens culled many of the topical allusions and somewhat qualified his own tendentiousness. References to Burnshaw were omitted completely, for the good reason that private allusion made little sense. Unfortunately, the poignant analysis of the decline of Europe was reduced to a sentence, and the section on the café intellectuals wholly excluded. But perhaps the most striking omission is that of the poets' politics and the poets' world. Stevens had bowed to the argot of the decade and found it costly. It is strange that no more of the rhetoric disappeared in revision, particularly the sections on the missionary's huckstering and Marxist posturing. In all, the omissions do not save the poem, but do unfortunately deprive it of many grandiose passages. At worst "Owl's Clover" is contentiously defensive, impenetrably opaque, and gracelessly hortatory. At best it represents a poet facing with candor and passion the ugliness of a time so real that it virtually paralyzed the imagination. One can see the failure of the poem in Stevens' inflated hope for it, his hope as he said that he could escape the anxieties of the decade by engaging "actuality, the contemporaneous," with "my own sensibility or individuality" (OP 219). That he failed is testimony to his courage as well as his innocence. But the value of the poem in Stevens' canon is what it made way for: poems which more clearly understand the capacity of the secular imagination to create order and hence a life of the mind.[20] In no other poem does Stevens come to grips with the topical as he does in "Owl's Clover," except possibly in "The Man with the Blue Guitar." The triumph of the later poem is its imaginative transvaluation of the topical.

IV

If "Owl's Clover" was designed to elaborate the "opposition between things as they are and things imagined," "The Man with the Blue Guitar," Stevens claimed, dealt with the "incessant conjunctioning of things as they are and things imagined."[21] The distinction implies the revived lyrical voice of the later poem. "Owl's Clover" is a struggling definition of poetic order in the face of grave contradictions of the poetic; "The Man with the Blue Guitar" is an effort to relate poetics to life lived in the ruins of modern society, not by rhetoric so much as by simple enthusiasm and imaginative energy. There is more to the two poems, however, than Stevens acknowledged, much more than a concern to purify the definition of poetry. In each, and especially in the second, Stevens begins his search for a new myth for the age, the myth of man to replace the myth of God; for this, as he asserts in "A Thought Revolved" (CP 184), is the "era of the idea of man." Seen in retrospect, such an ideal was dangerously ambiguous, and at the time, morally irresponsible. Yet, in the midst of the turmoil of that first Writers' Congress (1935), Kenneth Burke had confronted the literary left with a challenge that they must be artists before propagandists, and that the idea of the masses *must* for the artist be an idea of the people, and that the poet's symbol must not be proletarian but "man" who stands outside the diminutions of class.[22]

Stevens had been revolving this thought for some time, long enough for it to take shape as an idea: the idea of man which he needed if he were to write a major poetry. In the midst of an "epic of disbelief," the Ananke within needed justifying. Man as both creator and creation needed to be insisted upon:

> Happy rather than holy but happy-high,
> Day hymns instead of constellated rhymes,
> Hymns of the struggle of the idea of god
> And the idea of man, the mystic garden and
> The middling beast, the garden of paradise
> And he that created the garden and peopled it.

In this secular Genesis of "A Thought Revolved," the poet has created the garden; or as Stevens was to enforce it in an aphorism: "This happy creature—It is he that invented the Gods. It is he that put into their mouths the only words they have ever spoken!" (OP 167). "Owl's Clover" was a failure of style largely because it departed from Stevens' norm of comic irony or dramatic enlargement of ideas, to engage the contemporaneous directly, assertively. Thinking his way back into the imaginative mode —through "A Thought Revolved" and "The Men That Are Falling," the *Nation* prize poem for 1936—Stevens moved from the subman in us all to the poet as hero. He found renewed confidence in the poet singular as earthly leader, in contrast to the mystique of a universal self evoked in "Owl's Clover." Instead of the Jungian, Bergsonian subman, he took up once more the comic mask of poet, "striding among the cigar stores" of a vulgar world. In both these poems, however, the comic is focussed on a violence and death that is more actual than in the earlier poems: "The Men That Are Falling" is responsive to the Spanish Civil War, if only in a general way. Man in his happy finitude, caught in the landscape of violence, amid the "grinding ric-rac"—this was Stevens' familiar image of the thirties. That it excited rather than benumbed his imagination is indicative of his self-reliance.

"The Man with the Blue Guitar" (CP 165) reveals only brief stretches of the rhetoric for which Stevens rejected "Owl's Clover"; yet it probably owes its existence, and its quality, to the experience of "Owl's Clover." The one builds upon the other, learning from the mischances and excesses, and more than anything else, drawing upon the very belief which had urged, even at the expense of lyrical grace, that the individual need preceded politics and was realized in the act of poetry. "Blue Guitar" is a moderately long poem (402 lines), composed of thirty-three independent but thematically interrelated lyrics which vary from eight to sixteen lines of rhymed and unrhymed couplets. Less argument than improvisation, it forgoes the unities of the traditional long poem, even the loose dramatic continuity of "The Comedian as the Letter C," for the qualitative structure of the modern long poem. But it is less cerebrally designed than *The Waste Land,* less rigorously framed in mythological history than Crane's *The Bridge.* In this respect, it follows "Owl's Clover" and looks ahead to the several long poems of Stevens' last decade and a half, to poems whose structure is primarily the order of a man thinking. But even the later meditations are more deliberately ordered—particularly the dialectical trinity of "Notes toward a Supreme Fiction" or the thematically concentric "Esthétique du Mal." "Blue Guitar," like "The Comedian as the Letter C," and with nearly as much spontaneity, is an aesthetic anecdote, but the poet who sits in the center is more mature than Crispin.

The design of "Blue Guitar" is, most simply, the order of improvisation, or theme and variation. Moreover, there is some evidence of the kind of dialetical progression that Stevens was to perfect in "Notes toward a Supreme Fiction." There are, for example, enough standard guideposts— recurrent images, periodic aphorisms, or plain transitional statements— to alert the reader to shifts of theme and advances of thought. The poem is not circular, but spiral, moving from the initial situation of the poet playing imaginatively upon the world to his discovery of the meaning of what he plays and why, leading finally to the revelation of the role of poet in "Oxidia," the nonmythical, real, vulgar, toxic landscape of the present. The casualness of Stevens' organization is revealed in his experiments: his occasional but irregular rhymes, his casual introduction and just as casual dismissal of a dramatic motif, his elliptical if not abortive variations which simply stop when things seem to be going badly or become tiresome. The conversational interchange which takes place early in the poem, for example, is dropped without warning at the end of the sixth section, and one does not miss it at all. Indeed, it is hardly noticeable, for the poet's questioners are never really identified. Nor need they be, for this is not a dramatic poem. Its intention is to set the poet, a common self, at the center of the world.

One recourse for the reader baffled by the virtuoso performance is Stevens' own extensive commentary on his symbolism and general meaning as recorded by Renato Poggioli in *Mattino Domenicale ed Altre Poesie,* a selection of poems Poggioli translated into Italian. Though occasionally whimsical, Stevens is more objective than usual in response to Poggioli's questions, perhaps because he wished that the translations not distort his intentions. In any event, his notes clarify more than one obscurity, and provide at least one remark on the overall poem, which may be trusted or not as the reader wishes: the "general intention of the Blue Guitar was to say a few things that I felt impelled to say 1. about reality; 2. about the imagination; 3. their interrelations; and 4. principally, my attitude toward each of these things. This is the general scope of the poem, which is confined to the area of poetry and makes no pretense of going beyond that area." [23] "Poetry," as the guitarist divines, becomes "the subject of the poem," but in Stevens' especial sense that human experience, the marriage of imagination and reality, is by its very nature poetic. The blue guitar is Stevens' overt symbol for imagination, which at once recalls the old harmonium and emphasizes the distance from that too precious sensibility. No longer can the poet, like Hoon, subsume his world, or reduce reality to the measured forms of Peter Quince's clavier; he must now strum it out moment by moment in the folksy voice of his guitar, piece it together like Picasso's "hoard/ Of destructions." [24] For Stevens' "Oxidia," if not a Guernica, is the city whose productions rained down on Guernica. "Blue Guitar" entertains the extreme form of disintegration in Stevens' experience; in no other poem will the unity of the work be so tenuous, but seldom again will he achieve, or need to, the fine balance of wit, irony, and passion which, like Picasso's *Guernica,* imposes an aesthetic cosmos upon physical chaos. "Blue Guitar" is an awkward poem to treat as a totality, even if one accepts Stevens' intention of the four-part emphasis. The imagination's priority gives the poem the unity of free association, or the spontaneous unity that is captured so well in the figure of the clown, the performer on the edge of nature:

> He held the world upon his nose
> And this-a-way he gave a fling.
> His robes and symbols, ai-yi-yi—
> And that-a-way he twirled the thing. (CP 178)

The poem opens on a note of drama, the guitarist being implored to play both "things as they are" and a "tune beyond." The task is self-defeating —the need for the artist to be more than artist, to be the creator of magnificent proportions, to bring "a world quite round," bears the seeds of failure. There are several suggestions here. Stevens has begun by accepting the full responsibility of the poet as creator. Yet, the imagination is superbly secular and no more; the "shearsman," like Crispin, is one who experiences rather than transcends things as they are. His profession is self-limiting, but thus ever is life:

> I cannot bring a world quite round,
> Although I patch it as I can.
>
> I sing a hero's head, large eye
> And bearded bronze, but not a man,
>
> Although I patch him as I can
> And reach through him almost to man.
>
> If to serenade almost to man
> Is to miss, by that, things as they are,
>
> Say that it is the serenade
> Of a man that plays a blue guitar. (ii)

Stevens' own comments on the poem indicate that it is a nearly literal confession of the poet's frustrations in unlocking the enigma of man, and of himself as man.[25] The remainder of the poem offers a series of variations which celebrate the guitarist's victory in defeat, which is to say, his humanity. To sing the "hero's head," to reach almost to man if not to his essence, is to be poet and not prophet. "Things as they are" become here, clearly, not objects so much as the intrinsic nature of things, the essential as opposed to existential.

The guitarist's desire to "play man number one," to create the perfect abstract of man in what Stevens called, in a note, man's "happier normal," [26] is a godlike though fatuous desire to know the ultimate, a divine rather than human knowledge (iii). Thus ever is the poet's hope, and just as certainly his defeat. For to "strike his [man's] living" is to kill by abstracting—the old jar theme again—and an art that would catch life ultimately would kill that life it caught. This poem, which ends in an ellipsis, suggests the poet's defeat, even as the poem exercises the lively abandon with which he engages the world. Poem three voices an impassioned desire to know ultimately, to create perfectly, coming as it does after the failure in poem two to play man number one. And four delivers a corrective to three, intimating that the buzzing intercourse of blue guitar and things as they are, even to the very echo of their rhyme, is at best an imperfect thing, a happy, human act. Stevens comments on the drama of poem four: "In this poem reality changes into imagination (under one's very eyes) as one expresses it, by reason of one's feeling about it." [27] But this is the world of the "Fictive Music," and in its way, of *Harmonium*.

Accordingly, the poet is rebuffed by his auditors for playing old music. They wish to hear not of the "greatness of poetry" but of its reality. For they know poetry in this world is not charismatic, not "of the structure of vaults upon a point of light," but of a world "flat and bare," things as they are. And the poet willingly abides their flat contention: "Poetry," says the chorus,

> Exceeding music must take the place
> Of empty heaven and its hymns,
>
> Ourselves in poetry must take their place
> Even in the chattering of your guitar.

This is the second major declaration—and one of the most quoted passages of Stevens—a reiteration of the idea of man as a secular myth, and without doubt a major crest in the progress of Stevens' transition to his later aesthetic.

Rhetorically, then, the poem is ready for a new turn, picking up from the initial theme of playing things as they are while preserving their integrity as things. The pace of the rhythm increases, the guitarist hard at his business of substituting the sound of words for revelation. Things as they are, abstracted upon the blue guitar, assume the permanence of poetry, the abstraction blooded, in opposition to the permanence of empty heaven. For the artist works within space, composes within time, and records in spatial and temporal abstractions (vi). He does not, cannot, imitate the religious mind and transcend the physical (vii). And he must accept with humility the limited power of his imagination, which, like "reason in a storm," bends with the tumult but nevertheless "brings the storm to bear" (viii). This last poem is a startling achievement in the fusion of suggestive imagery and metaphorical statement, of the storm's reality and the imagination's "leaden twang" of ordered sound, reality caught in the rhythm of music. The imagination, in a phrase, is of its environment, and the poet wears an atmospheric cloak (ix). (Stevens' note on this last poem, defining the imagination as "not a free agent," offers some provocative hints about his use of blue, which he attributes in this poem to the "environment"—the "overcast blue"—as well as to the "blue guitar" of self: "The color of the weather is the robe of the actor, which, after all, is a large part of him. The imag. depends on reality." [28])

Out of dramatic weather—Stevens' poetry accentuates weather as it accentuates change—come a few peripheral questions, to be strummed as asides: the kind and nature of divinity within this very real world (x); the danger of a world without imagination (xi); the amorphousness and disorder of things as they are (xii); and oppositely, the empty purity of imagination which does not focus on reality (xiii). What Stevens appears to be offering in these four improvisations is a critique of his prescribed aesthetic, in an attempt to isolate the contradictions which arise when poetry's abstractions replace empty heaven and its hymns. If God is dead, as in poem ten, what of the man-hero who will take his place? Will he be politico or poet? The question posed, if Stevens' own commentary is to be trusted,[29] concerns the conditions of belief in a secular world, the problem of believing in that which one knows to be a fiction. But it also denounces the false gods, the old historical deities or heroes, who affront the imagination and provoke its derision. Rejecting the "pagan in a varnished car," the poet is left without a deity but not without the guitar. (Though I hesitate to offer it as an interpretation, I wonder if the evocation of "slick trombones" to "hoo" down the false gods does not recall Stevens' shriller rhetoric of defense in "Owl's Clover," as opposed to the more lyrical and synthetic guitar.) But it is not wholly the tinsel gods that the poet must "topple"; with only the self and his guitar, he must face the vortex of chaos that threatens the individual everywhere (xi). This anxious possibility—the petty gods of poem ten have bred, one supposes, a petty world in poem eleven—this possibility of the extinction of self is a nadir for the guitarsman and demands that he pick himself up by his own bootstraps, there being no others:

> Where
> Do I begin and end? And where,
> As I strum the thing, do I pick up
> That which momentously declares
> Itself not to be I and yet
> Must be.   (xii)

Poems thirteen and fourteen provide some reassurance in terms of the imagination's priority over things. Hesitant, evasive, poem thirteen

toys with the purity of imagination, the "amorist Adjective," and finds
the definition unsatisfactory if not abortive. Says Stevens, "The poem has
to do with pure imagination," [30] and in saying it he admits that the idea
of imagination without reality, a self without a world of otherness is a
fatuous belief of idealists. Fourteen is more successful, limiting the imagination to its role in the life of perception, the life of the existential mood:

> A candle is enough to light the world.
> It makes it clear. Even at noon
> It glistens in essential dark.
> At night, it lights the fruit and wine,
> The book and bread, things as they are,
> In a chiaroscuro where
> One sits and plays the blue guitar.

With this definition, the guitarsman moves on momentarily to the
world in which this candle must flicker, the greater world beyond the
"book and bread," those sacramental objects of the physical world. It is a
world of violence, Picasso's reality—"this 'hoard/ Of destructions,' a picture of ourselves"—a world in which "things as they are have been destroyed" and only the self remains to ask, "Have I?" Questioning again,
the moment of despair, and then comes the discovery that even asking
questions is an act and an affirmation. But the affirmative comes not
without its price; this world of poem sixteen is "not the mother"—as in
"To the One of Fictive Music" or even the death of "Sunday Morning"—
"but an oppressor." The combat of imagination and this violent world
issues in its own kind of violence, and produces a harshness rare in
Stevens' canon:

> To live in war, to live at war,
> To chop the sullen psaltery,
> To improve the sewers in Jerusalem,
> To electrify the nimbuses—

And the guitarsman experiences another moment of despair amid the
meretricious present: "Place honey on the altars and die,/ You lovers
that are bitter at heart." The mood is that of *Ideas of Order;* the impera-

tive is to play on or die. But the depression, if not before spring, is a turning point, a recovery.

Poem seventeen opens, as is customary in these variations, with a proposition and continues with a brief excursus on the dualistic self, on the soul (here "animal" or mind) which lives both in and beyond its "mould" of body. It is a metaphysical paradox, or potentially so—but Stevens prefers to treat it as an explicit dualism: as soul to body, so imagination to reality, or even, strangely, vice versa. And somewhere in his punning, the guitarsman discovers his guitar to be a mould, a supplier of shapes, a body or form for the soul of things as they are.[31] Poem eighteen underscores the theme in familiar terms, of the dream which is no longer a dream but things as they are—the perennial formula of imaginative reality, of the thing which emerges when the "blue guitar// After long strumming on certain nights/ Gives the touch of the senses, not of the hand. . . ." Things as they are, then, are things-as-seen, neither things in themselves nor ideas—they are poetry and they confirm the poet's *being* as creator.

There follow three poems on this familiar opposition, the first in terms of the guitarsman's desire to "reduce the monster" of earth "to myself," to be, as he jauntily puts it, the indomitable "lion in the lute/ Before the lion locked in stone." Stevens' particular affinity for animal imagery in his late poetry is caught most purely here. Strangely enough, the lion is hardly related to the animal in poem seventeen, which Stevens explained as a pun on "anima," the soul (Jungian?) being the body's animal. Here both self and world are animated (vital), the one locked in the lute of imagination, the other formed in the stone of matter. Such oppositions recur incessantly, most notably in "Notes toward a Supreme Fiction," as metaphor for the activity, the drama, of imagination. The lion of self and matter is not pantheism but poetics. Poem twenty, for instance, proceeds with a thematic variation, but the imagery changes, or better, disappears into statement. Hence the evocation of the "poor pale guitar," hardly the lion in the lute of the previous poem, which is summoned to believe (or as Stevens comments, to "search for a belief"[32]), to create certainty out of "good air." But twenty-one both cautions and reassures, denying belief in a "gold self aloft" and reaffirming the "Lord of the body" as "substitute for all the gods":

> One's self and the mountains of one's land,
> Without shadows, without magnificence,
> The flesh, the bone, the dirt, the stone.

This at last is the idea of man, more bold than Emerson's because less divine.

What the guitarsman has discovered once more, in essence, is a theory of poetry, that the act of poetry is a thing itself, that "things as they are" *are* only when contained in a mind, or married to mind in a poem:

> Poetry is the subject of the poem,
> From this the poem issues and
>
> To this returns. Between the two,
> Between issue and return, there is
>
> An absence in reality,
> Things as they are. Or so we say.
>
> But are these separate? Is it
> An absence for the poem, which acquires
>
> Its true appearances there, sun's green,
> Cloud's red, earth feeling, sky that thinks?
>
> From these it takes. Perhaps it gives,
> In the universal intercourse. (xxii)

This is both climax and resolution. Critics have regularly confused the aphorism of the first three couplets, accepting it as literal. The absence in poetry, however, is just what the poet is quick to deny. If poetry "takes" its matter from the world, it "gives" in exchange coherence. The push-pull of the aesthetic literally creates: if perception is a poetry, then poetry is the subject of the poem, for the poem is a perception. Lurking here also is the unasked question Stevens would soon have to ask, and answer: what of the absence, the unperceived, the nothingness we can know of but never know?

There remain, then, only "a few final solutions" (xxiii). The last third of the poem is concerned mainly with evolving this new poetry-in-life, and hence the self as center of the world it creates in poetry out of the many possible worlds. The duet of poem twenty-three is a start, and a norm, an expression of the never-ending exchange of clouds and earth. It is the act of continuous creation: "One keeps on playing year by year,/

Concerning the nature of things as they are." Poetry becomes a "missal" of reality, the book or form of a ritualistic act (xxiv); the poet becomes an agile clown juggling a reality that is ever vitality in motion, ever changing, but always around the "eternal" nose of the self (xxv). Thus,

> The world washed in his imagination,
> The world was a shore, whether sound or form
> Or light, the relic of farewells,
> Rock, of valedictory echoings,
>
> To which his imagination returned,
> From which it sped . . .

Coming and going again, "the swarm of dreams/ Of inaccessible Utopia" —the dialectic remains firm as strength flows back into the guitar. These three poems take life from verbs of motion; the self as actor, acting (imagining) in a world of continuous motion.

Not only, the poet avers, is poetry realized in the poet's chords, it sounds in the constant revolutions of nature (xxvii), is observed in the "sea that whitens the roof," in the constant (water) within the inconstant forms (snow, fog), in the order of natural change. Thus the guitarist, natural man, submits to the constancy of his world, becomes, unlike the archaic "Gesu," a "native in the world/ And like a native think[s] in it" (xxviii). Here, alone, the poet affirms his "I am," inhales "profounder strength," and can proclaim: "things are as I think they are/ And say they are on the blue guitar." He recovers from the doubt of poem twelve, and the despair of sixteen. The delights of this new aplomb, however, as poem twenty-nine reveals, come not without loss, not without departure from the cathedral of old faiths and the intellectual sedatives:

> "So it is to sit and to balance things
> To and to and to the point of still, . . ."

An apt inversion of Eliot's still-point—recalling the clown's nose of poem twenty-five. Circumspectly, it places man at the center, though his balance is eccentric: "'that the balance does not quite rest,/ That the mask is strange, however like.'" Balances are aesthetic, human, and the images of order no more than "like." Hence the poem's concluding figure, of the Franciscan don in the fertile glass, is an image of aesthetic balance, the vital contained in an abstraction, the mask which is strange but strangely beautiful.[33]

Having reaffirmed the self, the guitarist is willing at last to confront his reality, the violent, toxic "Oxidia" which is what we have today instead of mythological "Olympia" (xxx). Landscape alone would be enough to enforce Stevens' vision of the modern poet's trial; and the landscape is the man:

> From this I shall evolve a man.
> This is his essence: the old fantoche
> Hanging his shawl upon the wind,
> Like something on the stage, puffed out, . . .

A comic figure, a bitter world—this too has its balance, and man, like the Franciscan don of the previous poem, "was never more/ Himself" than when seen in comic dress. Oxidia is the world as it is, and the old fantoche man as he is. The remaining three poems make what they can of this discovery, though it is not always pretty. It is, indeed, a "combat," in which, as in poem thirty-one, nature's shrieks echo social confusion, and the guitarist is compelled to play his rhapsody there: compelled, as he indicates in thirty-two, to "Throw away the lights, the definitions,/ And say of what you see in the dark// That it is this or that it is that." This is veritably "The American Scholar" again, but with little of the bravado, more of the imperative to be rather than to transcend. Hence the conclusion, with its dexterous play on the Marxist and Christian failure to offer sustaining "bread." Committed to "Time in its final block, not time// To come," the guitar subdues jauntiness into a judicious affirmation: the world, it says, is a stone, "except"

> The moments when we choose to play
> The imagined pine, the imagined jay.

Thus ever is our life in this block of time, ugly and vulgar; but we can "choose." And the last note of the guitar gives back to man his freedom, setting him alone at the center, maker of himself though not yet of the world. What he can choose is not to live beyond the world but to live in it —choose, that is, to live in the imagination.

The guitarist has discovered, to turn one of Stevens' phrases, repetition to be master, the act of strumming itself to be a good. But Stevens' journey through the ideological wasteland, amid burnt out Oxidias and harridan selves, though made with heroic purpose, has not been repetition alone. Returning incessantly to his paradigm of imagination and reality, Stevens rings incessant changes, until he has evolved "a man," which is to say, a tentative idea of self as the only creator of order in this turmoil of a world. Crabbedly, fitfully, even willfully, Stevens herded his imagination (and his theory) through a world of broken statues and challenges which tempted him to self-caricature. "The Man with the Blue Guitar" displays the best and worst of his poetry at the time, but more than anything else it reveals that he had emerged from the trials of "Owl's Clover" with sensibility intact if somewhat shaken.

"Blue Guitar" is a peculiar poem, if not unprecedented. It has no apparent formal ancestor. Though its title suggests analogy to musical improvisation, the various poems are more nearly cameo impressions—more nearly the world of Picasso's guitarsman than Verlaine's.[34] One senses the distinct effect of post-Impressionist experimentation with tones and colors. Yet the work has its argument. The tetrameter couplets take every liberty with the couplet, and the guitarist is dour or animated as the occasion suits. Whatever there is of a total structure emerges in the progressive evolution of the poet's identity, of a man, from the parts of a world which threaten to blot out the self. The waves of gaiety, anxiety, depression, and joy are more smoothly integrated than is obvious, the guitarist commanding every shift of tone and maintaining his identity in that firm command. Even the recurrent and various symbols arrange themselves into a fairly predictable formula: guitar, shearsman, blue, moon, candle, mould, dream, and the term imagination on one side; blue again, world, man, things as they are, sun, stones, war, Oxidia, on the other. Out of the tension comes poetry, or balance: the hero's head, the tune in space, substitute for the gods, the missal, the Franciscan don in the fertile glass, the old fantoche, the idea of man. This is the union, as poem twenty-six anticipates, of the giant and the murderous alphabet, a marriage in which each gives up a part of itself in the "rhapsody of things as they are." Like "Sea Surface Full of Clouds," this poem is as various as the guitarist's moods and his tireless attention to "things." But this much has changed: Oxidia has replaced Tehauntepec as the landscape of the real, and the whole texture of the rhapsody takes on a different quality because of it.

With the freedom to choose, of the poem's final line, Stevens came to the crucial juncture of his new "idea," and to a new style. The texture of earth will hereafter be more remembered than felt; the physical world of *Harmonium* has disintegrated into Oxidia, and tropical Africa is only an idea. Reality, as Stevens so variously adapts it, will remain "things as they are," but with the developing sense that there is a thing-itself within the thing-as-seen. Moreover, reality is a thing of the mind. With his discovery that the idea of man is an idea of man as creator, Stevens had come upon a most fertile truth: that the imagination could perpetuate itself. Man's imaginings of the physical world create poems in the mind, abstractions, ideas, memories; and these poems in the mind, these abstractions, become in turn, like Bergson's creative memory, stimulants of the imagination. What follows in the late thirties may be seen as a dry interlude in Stevens' development; certainly the imagination would be asked to play all too often on "good air," more perhaps to keep itself in tune than to proceed in its investigations of reality. But Stevens had to define his idea of man as hero, as creator, and to consolidate his belief that the act of poetry was an act of life, of creating and sustaining oneself in a world that is otherwise nothingness. Coming upon reality without benefit of clergy, Stevens emerged at the frontiers of modernism: the self stripped of everything but its ability to act, to choose, and in that choosing to be.[35]

chapter 4

The Hero's Head

The prologues are over. It is a question, now,
Of final belief. So, say that final belief
Must be in a fiction.

Asides on the Oboe

The lean cats of the arches of the churches,
That's the old world. In the new, all men are priests.

Extracts from Addresses
to the Academy of Fine Ideas

S ince Emerson's famous address, our popular mythology has been mildly tolerant of the American "scholar," the "heroic mind." But the possibilities for this kind of heroism were never so forlorn as when Wallace Stevens came to that moment of choice in the "The Man with the Blue Guitar," which dictated that he either discover once and for all man in his "happier normal," the idea of man, or forego poetry altogether.[1] There is no evidence that Stevens ever considered the latter. That he found the former a baleful challenge is a fact of literary history. It is evident in the poetry of his next phase—a five-year period of transition that can in the kindest sense be called a period of personal transformation. But in the end it produced his major opus.[2]

Between the years 1937 and 1942, which culminated in the publication of *Parts of a World* and "Notes toward a Supreme Fiction" within a two-month period,[3] Stevens accomplished the transition from his early to his later style and outlined the preoccupations of his last great productive years. But whereas *Ideas of Order* had indicated an abrupt change of mode—if not ideas—*Parts of a World* seemed upon appearance not only

149

to move further toward abstraction, but to confirm a considerable loss of power. Style tailed off into mannerism; theme became academic. The world's body disappeared, leaving in its place a residuum of images more remembered than perceived. Music became monotone. Even when "Notes" appeared, there was no reason to alter the verdict, for this is not a poem to be grasped suddenly or easily. And above all, one poem does not justify another.

But this is precisely the way *Parts of a World* must be approached if one is to understand Stevens' reasons not only for publishing the book but also for writing the poems. For these are poems, more than anything else, of impeccable craftsmanship, finely polished gems that are all too often soft at the center. As a book, *Parts of a World* has a forbidding singleness of tone, of a world without variety and hence life. A reader coming upon the equally precise artistry and the richer diversity of Richard Wilbur's *Things of This World* may well ask why Wilbur's poems seem to be so much of the world he lives in, while Stevens' seem more the world of the art gallery. His answer, I think, would be that Stevens' "world" is a gallery, of the mind—that by "a world" Stevens implied an idea of wholeness, of order, toward which the act of imagination directed itself. He was later to call it the "first idea," and the "parts" were its fictions. It is in this sense that *Parts of a World* becomes a meaningful, even necessary volume—as an interlude in the development of the self in poetry.

To see *Parts of a World* as preparation for the "supreme fiction," however, is not to justify it. Neither does it explain the particular experiments, the modes of investigation, nor above all, the philosophical necessity of its parts. For the book is indeed Stevens' first step toward the formulation of a "philosophical" poetry, or a poetry intended to elucidate reality beyond the surfaces of a physical world and deeper than the psychological "rage" for order. Its purpose lay in the discovery of "The Man with the Blue Guitar," that the poet could not "play man number one," yet must; that is, Stevens had to pursue his idea of man, to make man the hero of his world, if he were to justify poetry and the poet, which is to say, any man of imagination.

There are two significant kinds of poems in *Parts of a World:* short, rather academic exercises, concentrated on an idea or a perception, usually dedicated to the question of metaphor or abstraction, or to the relation of language to reality and the poet's ability to effect transformations of his world in words; and more lengthy examinations of one particular "idea," the hero. But the two kinds are essentially one and continuous. To understand what Stevens means by the "hero," one has first to know what he means by "The Latest Freed Man," the man who tiring "of the old descriptions of the world" discovers that the only way to apprehend reality is to be "man without a doctrine" (CP 204). Or as another poem puts it: "It may be that the ignorant man, alone,/ Has any chance to mate his life with life" (CP 222). Ignorance, meaning not so much an escape from knowledge or a transcendence of it as the beginning of the right to know, is the starting point of the human, that moment when he is purely himself. These exercises are intended to strip man to his essential self, to reveal the "evilly compounded, vital I" (CP 193) at the beginning of its day, by way of defining man's ability to apprehend reality and to create anew. For until man is stripped of the "old descriptions," he cannot create, only perpetuate; not know himself but only the old descriptions of himself. But this is the argument of the volume. Its primary significance lies rather in its evolution of a style: a style of assertion, formulation, and exposition meant to get at the process or activity of perception and imagination instead of at the form of a perception, as he attempts to do in *Harmonium*.

It is, in short, the idiom of the mind, or sensibility. In *Parts of a World*, for the first time, because in a way different from the rhetoric of "Owl's Clover," Stevens' imagination appears to be playing on the reality of ideas rather than on the reality of a physical world. Experience has become psychic rather than physical, not feeling so much as reflection. The style displays that quality of abstraction tempered by sensuousness characteristic of the late poems, when Stevens exhibits fully the experience of a thought revolved and fully known (that is, felt and at the same time generated). But in *Parts of a World* the style is not yet natural, perhaps a bit over-refined, studied—it is seeking a personal idiom, yet hesitant to forego the idiom of *Harmonium*. (One might remark that the titles out-*Harmonium Harmonium,* and some of the poems strain and fail to do the same.) And this is perhaps why one is struck by the deliberate exercises, why the ideas seem to have such a design upon the reader. Between the formulations of thought—"By metaphor you paint/ A thing" (CP 219)—and the pretentious bursts of verbal puff—"Pipperoo, pippera, pipperum . . . The rest is rot" (CP 230)—there is as yet an uneasy marriage.

The concentration on the poet, on language, on the reality of metaphor, points very clearly to the larger concern for the "hero," and beyond to the major voice of *Transport to Summer*. Unfortunately, Stevens' hero poems are challenged by the antiheroic, antihumanist times—and hence probably motivated by them—as well as marred by urgent assertion. But the idea of the hero he very clearly needed. For the hero is simply his metaphor (not personification) for the actor in an alien reality, the poet whose idiom is the human idiom, whose will is man's will toward order. Ernst Cassirer once defined the hero of mythology, in symbolic terms, as the elevation of the human into the divine, the individual becoming in his hero an "active and suffering subject": "And with this discovery a last barrier between god and man falls away; the hero takes his place between them as an intermediary. Now the hero, the human personality, is raised to the divine sphere and the gods for their part are closely interwoven with human destiny, not as mere observers but as fellow warriors." [4] With proper regard for Stevens' problems in an antimythological age, we may see in this his purpose. For his poet has become the intermediary between man and reality (there being no god), and in his words the poet-hero rescues himself from absorption in things of this indifferent world. The poet as warrior, the poet as hero—there is in Stevens' figure just enough hyperbole to indicate man's possibilities of self-transcendence, and yet maintain his root being in the physical world. Clearly enough, Stevens' hero owes his image to Nietzsche (the philosopher of moment for Stevens in the later thirties). The return of God to the self is, as Nietzsche suggested in *The Birth of Tragedy,* the imperative reflex of "man stripped of myth, [who] stands famished among all his pasts and must dig frantically for roots."

The hero, in other words, is Stevens' subman of "Owl's Clover" projected outward, as the self is projected in its visions, its perceptions, or its poems of reality. And this indeed constitutes an advance beyond the previous volumes. [5] But the motivations behind Stevens' preoccupation with such a questionable figure are a bit more complex. To project into idea this essential man, to examine his idiom, was not merely to extend the traditions of mythology, nor to add one more god to the pantheon of dead or dying gods. It was rather to seek the origin (and source) of the gods, to isolate the imagination as what we have instead of god, and hence to define our image of the hero as our own ideal self, whose definition is its ability to create.[6] It is necessary to discover what man is before one can know what he can be. Or, to put it differently, it is necessary to pursue the origins of belief before one can explore the possibilities of belief. In this large sense, *Parts of a World* precedes "Notes toward a Supreme Fiction." In "Martial Cadenza" (CP 237) Stevens explores this longing of man for knowledge of the first idea, for the fixed and changeless "evening star," and in his meditations comes to discover that he alone has conceived and created it—not the star but the idea, "Not the symbol but that for which the symbol stands,/ The vivid thing in the air that never changes." When he examines the hero he looks similarly beyond symbol at his own changeless, representative self, and knows that the personal idiom is no longer a private idiom. It speaks, the poet's voice, for every man.

II

In the five years following "The Man with the Blue Guitar," Stevens issued at least three groups of poems whose collective titles reveal something of the concentration and the urgency that drove him to define poetry as more than a human pastime: *Canonica,* in the *Southern Review* (Autumn, 1938); *Illustrations of the Poetic as a Sense,* in *Poetry* (July, 1939); and *Two Theoretic Poems,* in *Hika* (May, 1940). The first group supplied the initial twelve poems for *Parts of a World,* establishing its mode of indirect examination of a theory of poetry; the last group is the volume's focal point, the world toward which the parts contribute. At the same time Stevens published the first of two sets of "Materia Poetica," epigrams on poetry and life, in *View* (September, 1940), and had turned directly to exposition of a kind in "The Noble Rider and the Sound of Words," an essay which remains one of the most eloquent apologies for poetry in this century.

. *Canonica,* more so than *Illustrations of the Poetic as a Sense,* presents Stevens in his mask of pedagogue. It is a poetry of imperatives and self-analysis, the poet caught in the act of defining what it is to be a poet in a world without the old charts. Here the self is, as one poem puts it, the author of the charts, a "Prelude to Objects":

> If he will be heaven after death,
> If, while he lives, he hears himself
> Sounded in music, if the sun,
> Stormer, is the color of a self
> As certainly as night is the color
> Of a self, if, without sentiment,
> He is what he hears and sees and if,
> Without pathos, he feels what he hears
> And sees, being nothing otherwise,
> Having nothing otherwise, he has not
> To go to the Louvre to behold himself. (CP 194)

Asserting this dominance of self, Stevens is committed to a rhetoric that is often drily academic, and an imagery that has lost touch with the physical world. The poems of *Illustrations of the Poetic as a Sense* are benign illustrations, minor portraits of things seen imaginatively; those of *Canonica* are intended to prove that the poetic is a sense, a sixth sense and the unifying one, through which the experience of apprehending the world becomes really the experience of knowing oneself as the creator of that world. "The Poems of Our Climate" and "The Glass of Water" are two significant examples, and furthermore, are two considerable poems. The former, opening with a stanza that recalls the *dix-huitième* quality of Imagist exercises, fixes the role of imagination in our "climate," which is no longer a world of orderly and fixed laws, a still life (CP 193). For man is his world, and it he; and in our own climate of chaos and change, no simple return to the past, to the neat and orderly sense of a world in which the self has its place, is possible: "one desires/ So much more than that." He rejects the still perfection, the "complete simplicity"—as earlier in "Sunday Morning" he had rejected paradise—for

> The imperfect is our paradise.
> Note that, in this bitterness, delight,
> Since the imperfect is so hot in us,
> Lies in flawed words and stubborn sounds.

This "vital I," the essential self seeking the essential reality, must be satisfied with the imperfect; but it is the imperfect which drives him to imagine, to create in flawed words those poems in which alone there is delight. "The Glass of Water" (CP 197), a favorite anthology piece, offers some innocent metaphysical play upon the theme. Not an allegory certainly, but nonetheless predicative, "The Glass of Water" is characteristic of these self-conscious exercises. Light, the lion (like the "lion in the lute"?) sips from the glass of earth, which includes the plural states of reality, the sustenance contained there. Here, in the image of light partaking of (thus isolating and illuming) one of the many possible forms of being, we have a figure of the imagination's several possibilities. But if the lion has satisfied its thirst by creating poems or forms, the poet as "Fat Jocundus" has not; for he is a seeker after the center, not the surface, the changeless not the flowing waters. The reality he seeks is at the "center of our lives"; yet as one of our climate he must pursue his ideas among the "dogs and dung." To read the poem thus is to abuse it mightily, but something like this is happening throughout these deliberate exercises which draw so heavily on academic propositions and aesthetic formula.

Fortunately for Stevens, the poetry of the idea usually saves him from the bare idea. The poet, self-consciously "The Man on the Dump" (CP 201), is plumped down amid distractions which threaten to drown his questions and avert his pursuit of "The the." This last poem is itself a perfect clutter of images, of time's dump heap which thwarts desire: that is, the world of parts thwarts one's wish to get near to the "the," and yet one cannot know the "the" until he knows the world and what the imagination can make of it. The exercises of *Canonica*—and to a degree those of *Illustrations of the Poetic as a Sense*—must be seen as tentative definitions of the self working toward an idea of man as hero. They are attempts to define "The Latest Freed Man" (CP 204) as a man free of "the old descriptions of the world." This deeply rooted Emersonian impulse, however, lacks at least one coordinate of "The American Scholar": belief in the greater coherence of things and selves. "To be without a description of to be" is the experience of a "moment on rising," that moment of consciousness when animal self and human self are one and vital. "Connoisseur of Chaos," a title which has become a metaphor for the Stevensian poet, is the major text (CP 215).

Beginning with the mock-serious premise that "A violent order is disorder; and/ . . . A great disorder is an order," it proceeds through three stanzas of non-proof to a poetic conclusion that satisfies connoisseurs but not logicians. Offering "pages of illustrations" as its opening gambit, the poem touches first upon the emblematic world of nature whose law of inherent opposites suggests an essential unity, a thought as pleasant as a Marchand brush-stroke; then it proceeds to reject the "pretty contrast of life and death" as one eternal continuum (a "theory, when bishop's books/ Resolved the world"), finding rather than teleological assurance the "small relation[s]" of nature which sustain the self within chaos. Having proved nothing, but felt much, the poet tenders his own cryptic "theory":

> A. Well, an old order is a violent one.
> This proves nothing. Just one more truth, one more
> Element in the immense disorder of truths.
> B. It is April as I write. The wind
> Is blowing after days of constant rain.
> All this, of course, will come to summer soon.

Rejecting truth in propositions, he discovers instead the felt order of nature, and thus the organic order of the natural self. For if nature chalks her portents "on the sidewalk," the "pensive man," reading imaginatively, may be motivated by those markings to imagine, to probe for the order within the chaos of motion. As connoisseur, the pensive man of the final tentative section has penetrated to the law underlying chaos, the single nest amid the intricate Alps of reality.

This is an assertive poem, perhaps too assertive, but its sensuous surface moderates proposition into perception. The mood of casual observation predominates—these sensations of order in great disorder are pleasant as port, a small relation casually "chalked/ On the sidewalk" where the pensive man strolls, not imposed by intellect as severe metaphysical truths. Formulas which resolve the world are violent, the grammar of a squamous mind. "Connoisseur of Chaos" convinces if at all by its own rhythmic evocation of order, by its own pleasantness, and by its tentative, which is to say human, resolutions. If more intellectual than Robert Herrick's "Delight in Disorder," it is no less expressive of a similar delight; and the taut playfulness of the one set against the fancifulness of the other provides a comment on their respective occasions, particularly on that of the modern poem. In pursuit of the changeless, the single nest, the poet of *Parts of a World,* somewhat like the earlier Crispin, very often stops "short before a plum," but he is not always content as Crispin learned to be. And clearly he is not Crispin's kind of realist. Stevens' search for the "the" admits repeatedly to its frustration, except as the poses of words or the penetrations of the pensive man evolve an order within disorder.

By far the larger number of poems in the volume are dedicated to this search through particulars for "The the," several of them in verbal still-lifes which recall Paul Klee's experiments in structural forms and re-lations,[7] as well as the Impressionists' use of the commonplace as landscape of an interior reality. Like Klee's motion of a line, the poems seem intent on expressing process as that which is permanent, as the life or being of forms. Titles become poems *manqué,* forming a minutiae of figurative observations and perceptions. From "Poem Written at Morning" (CP 219), which avers that "The truth must be/ That you do not see, you experience, you feel," to "Variations on a Summer Day" (CP 232), which displays that very truth, the volume is a remarkable gallery of "parts," fragments of perceptions constituting the perceived world of the self. The metaphorical implications of "parts" is aptly caught in "Land-scape with Boat" (CP 241), a suggestive variation on the painter's quest through form and hue for the "neutral center," the colorless which lies beneath his world of color, a "truth beyond all truths." Yet, even this is only a way to discover the identity of self, which *is* because it is necessary that there be a mind before the world of parts has any quality, any life:

> He never supposed
> That he might be truth, himself, or part of it,
> That the things that he rejected might be part
> And the irregular turquoise, part, the perceptible blue
> Grown denser, part, the eye so touched, so played
> Upon by clouds, the ear so magnified
> By thunder, parts, and all these things together,
> Parts, and more things, parts. He never supposed divine
> Things might not look divine, nor that if nothing
> Was divine then all things were, the world itself,
> And that if nothing was the truth, then all
> Things were the truth, the world itself was the truth.

The healthy tensions of *Parts of a World* lie between a longing for the "the" and the significance of parts of the world, between desire for the pure and what is available to the eye—and even more important, what is available in the hue of the poet's "words." The explicit poems of theory, of which "Man and Bottle" and "Of Modern Poetry" are notable examples, are poems about poetry only in the inclusive sense that poetry is an act of discovery, and more precisely, a gesture toward the recognition of self. "Man and Bottle" (CP 238), the lesser piece, may offer a gloss on the role of the poet as representative man:

> The mind is the great poem of winter, the man,
> Who, to find what will suffice,
> Destroys romantic tenements
> Of rose and ice . . .

Whether or not romantic tenements connote man's old poems of heaven and hell,[8] or simply the private dawdlings of fancy, the call is for a poem of earth. The identification of mind, man, and poem is another variation on the idea of poet as central man, who as in "Asides on the Oboe" is a transparence of his world. The "man at the centre of men," seeking "what will suffice," is the poet's self, the central self in whose mind decreation (the "mind destroys") precedes recreation ("what will suffice"). Thus "Man and Bottle," unlike "Anecdote of the Jar," marries artifice and actuality and makes of man the container of the world. It is solipsism, yes, but the launching point of Stevens' last poetry—which would give back to every self the privilege of creating the world he knows, the world of the mind.

"Of Modern Poetry," another favorite anthology piece, would appear not to be what many critics presume, an explicit commentary on modern poetry, but a celebration of poetry which realizes and satisfies the rage for order. The idea of a "modern" poetry is an idea of poetry in our time only in the sense that our time is self-consciously discontinuous with a traditional past. Rejecting the old script, seeking for what will suffice, Stevens' meditation is dedicated to the beleaguered modern who must turn away from the providential to the hazards and beauties of the commonplace, as entertained by a common self:

> The actor is
> A metaphysician in the dark, twanging
> An instrument, twanging a wiry string that gives
> Sounds passing through sudden rightnesses, wholly
> Containing the mind, below which it cannot descend,
> Beyond which it has no will to rise.

The stylized figure of the metaphysician recalls the blue guitar; it might also summon up the Romantics' Eolian Harp, except the imagination is not attuned to Nature, and the self rather than Spirit is the active agent. "The poem of the act of the mind," giving pleasure, is the creative act of meditation carried on *in* a physical world, a wholly human affair. Throughout "Of Modern Poetry" the poet is metaphorically an actor, in the dual sense of one playing a part (and apart) and one doing; his audience is himself, for he is the sum of his audience, simultaneously creating and requiting.[9] The actor must not only contend with a world of parts, he must find among the commonplaces what will suffice if not what is ultimate. In the total view, *Parts of a World,* pursuing the "the," comes to a more provisional resolution in "On the Road Home" (CP 203): that there is "no such thing as the truth." And discovering this, the poet is released into a purer sense of how the sum is in its every part. The act of the mind, however, is not a single thing, but a process; its creations "suffice" one by one, but the total life of the mind is an act of continuous creation, what Stevens would call later the "never-ending meditation."

III

At the conclusion of *Parts of a World,* Stevens appended a charactertistically ambiguous postscript on the subject of poetry and war. "The immense poetry of war and the poetry of a work of the imagination," he says almost redundantly, "are two different things."

In the presence of the violent reality of war, consciousness takes the place of imagination. And consciousness of an immense war is a consciousness of fact. If it is true, it follows that the poetry of war as a consciousness of the victories and defeats of nations, is a consciousness of fact, but of heroic fact, of fact on such a scale that the mere consciousness of it affects the scale of one's thinking and constitutes a participating in the heroic.[10]

He goes on to consider the violence of war as a received impression, as a fact we must adjust to our human dislike for violence. It is not surprising that the defense constitutes a theory of poetry: "The poetry of a work of the imagination constantly illustrates the fundamental and endless struggle with fact." The human impulse, he adds, is "to move in the direction of fact as we want it to be." This is escapism—but escapism in Stevens' particular sense of the human need to preserve the self against the "pressure of reality," not deny that reality (see NA 30–31).

The longer poems of *Parts of a World* are at best exercises in preparation for "Notes toward a Supreme Fiction." Without the organizing idea of the "The Man with the Blue Guitar," or the urgency of "Owl's Clover," clearly lacking the *brio* of "The Comedian as the Letter C," they are pale copies of the earlier works in search of the later. What brings them together is their singleness of purpose and the style this purpose demands. There is no better example of this than "Life on a Battleship" (OP 77), which though included in *Parts of a World* was excised from that section of the *Collected Poems*. There would be no great loss were it not for its belligerantly rhetorical posture which harks back to the shrillness of "Owl's Clover," and its obsession with an idea of man which looks forward to "Notes toward a Supreme Fiction." Commissioning his poet as Captain (of the ship of self?), falling back upon the old strategy of inverting ideology to his advantage, Stevens takes a first big step toward the designs of "Blue Guitar" to play man number one. With some mock-logic that is no help to poetry, he works toward a *"Regulae mundi"* of very unclear proportions, at the heart of which is the premise that "our fate is our own." He is a comic "apprentice of/ Descartes."

But he is no less a kind of modern "Man Thinking," working toward the grand simplifications of the Cartesian dilemma. He exists at the center of his world—the battleship *"Masculine"*—and thus at the "center of/ The divinity." Here is the hero in topical dress, self-mocking and yet serious. The poem's failure is indeed one of tone, for Stevens takes his sophism both seriously and casually, and falls between two chairs. The poem—arguing that the whole cannot exist without the parts—is too programmatic to take advantage of its obvious ironic possibilities. This failure of irony also harms "Extracts from Addresses to the Academy of Fine Ideas" (CP 252), but not so distractingly. "Extracts," too, is a rhetorical tour de force upon one idea, and in a familiar key: turning over and over in mind, like the old connoisseur, the discovery that a "law of chaos is a law of ideas," that "systematic thinking" is its own chaos, and that the war of ideas is a slaughter in which "assassins" destroy their partial selves in getting at the one truth which they severally obscure.[11]

"Extracts" is not so much a poem as a series of poetic asides, jotted down for presentation to one's own ear. It is, however, one more interesting attempt to define the difference "between the and an,/ The difference between himself and no man," the answer to which is Stevens' oft-repeated discovery:

>   What
> One believes is what matters. Ecstatic identities
> Between one's self and the weather and the things
> Of the weather are the belief in one's element,
> The casual reunions, the long-pondered
> Surrenders, the repeated sayings that
> There is nothing more and that it is enough
> To believe in the weather and in the things and men
> Of the weather and in one's self, as part of that
> And nothing more.

There is one noticeable advance in the poem, the consequences of which will be realized in "Esthétique du Mal." Discovering the war of ideas, the law of chaos, the poet has isolated evil in the irradiations of natural being, in the process of living in change. That is, evil emerges in the combat of self and weather, in the disorders of living here and not in a "subtle center"; in sum, evil like death is of the essence of vital things, of the imperfect which is our paradise. Not yet ready to meditate the idea of evil fully, much less to see it as a paradox in which man seeks for order by clinging to the physical world and thereby to an aesthetic of disorder (evil), Stevens has nonetheless made one more significant addition to his poetics.

"Montrachet-le-Jardin" and "Examination of the Hero in a Time of War" comprise the last two major blocks in the foundation of the supreme fiction. The former (CP 260) is the more satisfactory of the two, perhaps because it is less programmatic, certainly less pretentious. Still, it attracts one not so much for its intrinsic qualities as for those which anticipate the finished style of "Notes toward a Supreme Fiction," particularly the very definite experiment in unrhymed tercets with a freely rhetorical enjambment. But the style lacks the ease of later poems, such as "An Ordinary Evening in New Haven," in which Stevens' triplets dissolve into the free rhythms of meditation. Otherwise, the poem is little more than a tentative exposition of the idea of the hero, not examined but evoked, and thereby preparatory to the major solo in "Examination of the Hero in a Time of War." The identification of the hero—"Man must become the hero of his world"—with the noble figures of the old mythologies—"He hears the earliest poems of the world/ In which man is the hero"—indicates that Stevens was working along lines of analogy and opposition between his modern poetic idea (man) and the outmoded poetic ideas (the gods) of mythology. Unresolved as the poem stands, looking back nostalgically as it does to the fading "Terra Paradise," possibly the world of *Harmonium,* it is nevertheless a proclamation of the poet's will to build towers of his own, to "project the naked man in a state of fact," to touch the "auroral creature musing in the mind." But its final lines, along with its glaring uneasiness of tone, admits at last to the evasiveness of the truth it seeks. Stevens' pursuit of an idea takes a severe toll in style, perhaps because he is making a significant transition from a poetry of perception to a poetry of the act of the mind. Always dependent on the metaphor, he does not yet have full control of metaphor which will blood an abstraction or draw out the thread of an idea into a feeling. Hence, poems like "Montrachet-le-Jardin" seem to move uneasily between statement and lyrical floss. It is, in the best sense, a practice poem.

"Examination of the Hero in a Time of War" (CP 273) is even less successful, perhaps because Stevens was toying with an analogy so common and so topically immediate that his unique idea of the hero begs the question of heroics. Still, Stevens is not concerned with heroes or war, but with man in a world that denies heroes. Which is to say, Stevens exploits the present war as a metaphor of modern reality and examines the hero as the image of the minimal god who can save man from this chaos. Or, to put it another way, the hero under examination is the self, which alone can save itself, there being no other gods. The sixth stanza is an example of the imperative behind the poem, and the drift of its urgent idea and willed style:

> Unless we believe in the hero, what is there
> To believe? Incisive what, the fellow
> Of what good. Devise. Make him of mud,
> For every day. In a civiler manner,
> Devise, devise, and make him of winter's
> Iciest core, a north star, central
> In our oblivion, of summer's
> Imagination, the golden rescue:
> The bread and wine of the mind, . . .

Denying the hero form—"The marbles are pinchings of an idea"—and image—"It is a feeling./ There is no image of the hero"—Stevens would seem to evoke not a concept—"It is a part of his conception,/ That he be not conceived"—but a sense of his own self in action. Like the poet in "Of Modern Poetry," the hero is an actor who acts in his own utterances, and what he utters would appear to be the essence of himself, the common man as exemplum of the highest self. Something like this is implied: the expressed self of a common man, if fully expressed, is a highest self, because there is only the human self and no other. Or to quote from the penultimate stanza:

> The highest man with nothing higher
> Than himself, his self, the self that embraces
> The self of the hero, the solar single,
> Man-sun, man-moon, man-earth, man-ocean,
> Makes poems on the syllable *fa* or
> Jumps from the clouds or, from his window,
> Sees the petty gildings on February . . .
> The man-sun being hero rejects that
> False empire . . . These are the works and pastimes
> Of the highest self: he studies the paper
> On the wall, the lemons on the table.
> This is his day. With nothing lost, he
> Arrives at the man-man as he wanted.
> This is his night and meditation.

He has arrived, too, at a near solipsism, spared perhaps by an awareness that he is not only a man but a man acting in and for the world, out of the world's need.[12]

Coming as it did so close upon the writing of "Notes toward a Supreme Fiction," "Examination of the Hero in a Time of War" might be expected to introduce that major poem. Rather, it would appear to have a role of its own, an aside like the hundreds of asides to which Stevens incessantly turned by way of sustaining himself and his Grand Poem. In pursuit of the hero, Stevens was perhaps distracted if not overwhelmed by the pressures of violence without, which he presumed to resist as he had resisted Marxism, by conflating the popular myth with his aesthetic. What remains of "Examination" in the later "Notes" is barely significant, even though "Notes," evolving a "major man," is equally concerned with the hero as actor of the imagination. The best anticipation of "Notes," and one of the triumphs of *Parts of a World,* had come two years earlier in "Asides on the Oboe."

IV

Looking back at the opulence of *Harmonium,* to the "Terra Paradise" now grown cold, Stevens by 1940 had taken full measure of his changing self and of the imagination's new commitments—to what in "Mrs. Alfred Uruguay" he called the "imagined land." Stevens' progress through the seasons is not alone an analogy for man's aging, nor is it the conventional cycle-of-life motif. It details rather the constantly altering experiential relations of the self to its world, the imaginative adjustments of a man standing joyously in process, seeking "what will suffice." Put simply, if spring is the time of almost direct exposure to the physical (as one may see his early years), summer (like a maturing self) demands the concrescence of mind and reality in a richer mingling, man living fully in the idea of what it is to live; while autumn portends the decay of the physical leading toward the culmination of the cycle when one pursues the "first idea" through contemplation, there being nothing else or no other way. His last two independent volumes, *Transport to Summer* and *The Auroras of Autumn,* metaphorically outline the mature stages of that continual adjustment to change and death. The opening stanza of "Asides on the Oboe" (CP 250) records this crucial point in Stevens' poetic growth:

> The prologues are over. It is a question, now,
> Of final belief. So, say that final belief
> Must be in a fiction. It is time to choose.

Though hardly a personal confession, the poem is about the poet— about man for whom the poet is representative, central. Offering a choice, it offers alike an answer: to know that belief "must be in a fiction" is to deny belief, unless fiction is in itself a truth, or unless belief is that which demands uncertainty for its starting point. The "belief" of the poem, however, is belief in man—the "impossible possible philosophers' man," the "human globe"—man as the container and the voice of reality. Knowing the possibilities of evolving this man, this central man who will replace the old gods—"That obsolete fiction of the wide river in/ An empty land . . ."—Stevens knows that the search for belief can no longer be directed outward to the spheres but only inward to the origin, in man. For the poet-hero, having lived in the world, has become a voice of that world: "the transparence of the place." And now reality lies in his poems, in which alone he may believe because they were acts of belief. They are himself, the possible man, the central. The act of poetry is the act of getting at the central, not of the world but of the self, at the god unencumbered by false forms, at what it is to be. Or, as Stevens put it in an epigram, "It is the belief and not the god that counts" (OP 162).

"Notes toward a Supreme Fiction" (CP 380) brings Stevens fully into the late phase of "introspective exile," whose amours have shrunk into lecturing as he put it in "Le Monocle de Mon Oncle." Yet, "Notes" offers a reappraisal of love, as in its introduction; for it is the poet's devotion to life and man that stimulates his search for the "central of our being," that point at which all men are married in their humanity. "Notes" is an ambitious poem—intricately personal, obscure in parts, exasperating in others, unrelaxed, and probably great. Its synthesis of lyricism and statement, pure sound and aphoristic terseness, argument and anecdote, formal dialectic and exuberant illogic—this is something unique in modern poetry, and yet fully predictable from the experiments of *Parts of a World*. Everything that follows in Stevens' ensuing thirteen years is the refinement and subtilizing of "Notes" into a natural mode, into an "act" that is also a habit of mind. There will be nothing else so deliberately patterned, however. The poem's tripartite frame is no accident even if its structure does not support R. P. Blackmur's assertion that trinity is the only "tolerable form of unity." [13] The trinity of "Notes" is mockingly dialectical, as if exterior design alone could lend authority to ideas, but its key is freedom and variety within design, which may suggest just the unity of the creative sensibility its argument tries to affirm. The unity would appear to be more problematic than actual; the poem is nothing less than an act of the mind, nothing less than an attempt to evolve a man, in this case, a poet, out of an "ephebe."

Weighted by final questions, "Notes" is not apocalyptic, its tripled wholeness offering no dialectical advance from naive perception toward ultimate idea. And the supreme fiction which it evokes is never reached, but only suggested in those penetrating "notes" or partial "fictions" to which the man of words is restricted. Stevens' dialectic celebrates its own shortcomings, for there is no progress beyond pleasure, that final good for the man who takes life as it is. Yet, the poem is concerned with man's constant seeking for ultimate reality, his need of it, his ability to apprehend it, and his discovery, in the end, that it resides in his powers to create and meditate the supreme abstraction. Stevens' theoretical structure, like his recurrent imagination-reality exchanges, is the one permanent reality in a world of flux, the order within which man's experience is contained and the ground from which he can project his fictions. The dialectical interchange becomes as final, if not as absolute, for Stevens as the dialectic was for Hegel, as certain as the invariable patterns within the incessant changes of nature. This intercourse of abstraction and change is Stevens' metaphor for the mind in its "act of finding."

The poem's three divisions may be seen as a provocatively arbitrary triad, an abstraction of sorts which like all abstractions suggests more than it nominally contains. The first third of the poem, *"It Must Be Abstract,"* entertains an elementary postulate of knowledge which summons its vital complement, *"It Must Change,"* the two in synthesis being nothing until they touch upon the human, and resolve into the order of man's awareness of his humanity: *"It Must Give Pleasure."* Epistemologically, the opening section works a series of variations on the forms of experience which emerge when subject apprehends object, abstraction ranging from the level of bare perception to extensive abstraction, from the felt to the envisioned possible. Abstraction is a way to pure reality, a stripping away of the husk of things; yet abstraction also denies the reality of process. Assuming we live in a world that is essentially process, incapable of ascertaining anything more than that process is process, the poet can assume only his own consciousness, and Bergson's paradox of the knowledge that kills. We abstract by merely being conscious, abstraction being the given of experience. But the poet, the self-conscious modern man, not only lives by abstraction but knows he lives by abstraction. And thus he knows that although he lives at the edge of things, he lives in the center of himself where abstractions are created. It is as if in these first sections Stevens had placed Aristotle against Bergson deliberately.

One phase of the history of Stevens' development has been his jockeying of attitudes toward abstraction, the abstracting imagination, and the reality of language that is by definition abstract. Metaphor, for instance, evades and averts, and the poet finds evasion and averting both necessary and inadequate. Abstracting ultimately, man is capable of thinking a "first idea"—not a first cause, note—and thinking it, he can conceive it as possible (cf. that "impossible possible philosophers' man" of "Asides on the Oboe"). As Stevens might have learned from Whitehead, though more probably it is the result of his own sensitive self-questioning, to abstract ultimately is to lead beyond things to a point where reality is outside process: thus ultimately real, thus nothingness.[14] The first idea as ultimate abstraction is unknown, beyond attributes. Coming back to change, the poet by committing himself to the reality of process discovers two kinds of first ideas: the false kind that man creates to dominate and rule him (the "inventing mind as source") and the true kind (the everchanging ideas he creates because he needs to know beyond himself).

What this poem dramatizes, above all else, is the need for poetry, the need to know, and the possibilities of the mind attending to this prison of a world which offers minor pleasures but no "final belief." The poet's motive for creating is love, a higher or moral act of love, because the poet, acting not for himself but as man, the hero, acts for the common good, for order. He shows man the possibilities, and limitations, of his humanity. This is, I think, the explanation for Stevens' introductory stanza, in which love is satisfied when men meet at their common center, seeking the "single, certain truth" through what is their common power, the imagination. I offer this not as an explanation of what was in Stevens' mind, but what lies behind the poem, saving it from Winters' charge that Stevens' doctrine of pleasure is merely self-indulgence. Winters' strictures seem to me to reject the possibility of any long poem, past or present, as surely as do Poe's, for they demand the kind of sustained perfection we are not likely to find in any but the briefest human expressions. But of more point here, Stevens in this poem, and all the later ones for that matter, is trying to define hedonism in Santayana's terms: as a greater act of good, not one man's feeling.

"Notes toward a Supreme Fiction" is a moderately long poem, 659 lines neatly balanced in an eight-line lyrical introduction, thirty cantos of twenty-one lines each, and a coda of twenty-one lines, divided like all but the introduction into seven tercets. The three major divisions, consisting of ten cantos each, have their own inner development: the first three sketch out the basic problem, the fourth derives a major proposition, and the next five advance negative and positive variations leading toward a synthetic conclusion in the final canto. The coda serves to bridge the three sections which, despite the obvious trinity, are not convincingly absorbed in the third—and it further satisfies by linking the dialectic with contemporary reality, or chaos. And yet, like other of Stevens' long poems, "Notes" cannot be defined by external form. As an act of mind, it is by no means a logician's exercise.

A poem so complex, and at times so unremittingly obscure in its separate parts, can be intimidating. Grasping at its ideas, the critic may find himself stunned by their contradiction; looking for sources, he may find renderings (Eliot would say thefts) but seldom borrowings. In this respect, the caution of Frank Kermode, quoting Stevens, is instructive: "In such a poem 'the feeling of one man is communicated to another in words of the exquisite appositeness that takes away all their verbality.' Comment puts the 'verbality' back in; the clearer the explanations, the falser they are likely to be. . . . Sometimes what is being explained isn't even fully there; Stevens is always fantastic, and when he creates a nature, as he does in *Notes,* it is shown as if in continuous creation, changing and incomplete, so that an image or an idea may be seen like Milton's lion, pawing to get free his hinder parts." [15] There is a possibility that Kermode's claims for the romantic "fantastic" do Stevens' work more harm than to coax meaning from it. One must at last take the chance, play with the "verbality," if only to give the fantastic an opportunity to do its work. "Notes" is simply not a poem that will *be* without *meaning;* for if it is about the "ignorant man," it will not meet him on the grounds of his ignorance. Like James in his major phase, Stevens' involutions may evade us, but they are so happily complex and fertile that they will not be violated by analysis.

"It Must Be Abstract." Opening with an imperative, the initial poem makes its appeal to innocence by way of defining the human limits within which the poem develops. What we begin with are the elementary opposites—pure self and pure being, ephebe and sun. But neither can *be* in and for itself, especially in this world of less than perfect invention. To know, as the ephebe desires, is to abstract. And here develops the first complication: all our knowing is abstract, but there are abstractions and abstractions.[16] Man may abstract forward to the transcendent future, or backward to the origin and source. Above all, he must know that ab-

straction is at once truth and fiction. Looking at the sun not as a fixed idea
—not as a thing named and thus contained within its image—the poet
demands that each man begin again like the old Adam, by naming
what the sun *is* and not what generations have told him it is. And yet,
one begins with an awareness of the limits of naming, that a name evades
its object, averts the *Ding an sich*. There is a suggestion, not clearly borne
out, that in the return to the sun as ultimate idea and source of this invented world, we return also to the source of the self, the source of oneness, that first idea in which self and reality were one. An idea only, or
or *the* truth? Denied the consolations of an "inventing mind as source,"
however, we discover that man has invented this present world, that is,
has invented the abstractions by which he knows it. For invention is a
falling off from reality—just as it is often a pejorative word in Stevens'
lexicon, something which denies. Invention, in sum, is the opposite of discovery. By rejecting the name of *"Phoebus,"* the *ephebe* (like a son rejecting the source he bears within himself) must admit the limitations of
abstractions and thus the limitations of the knowing self, accepting at the
same time the sun's *being* in and of itself. "Perceiving the idea/ Of this
invention," the ephebe will perceive not the world as invented but the
ultimate idea itself, in which he and the world were one and from which
he has now fallen. By the end of "Notes" he will have discovered that
the life of knowing is a fiction, that the supreme for which he aspires is
not really available "except in crystal." Stevens' ephebe is thrust into a
world in which nature is itself, not an emanation of the divine, and the
imagination, like Santayana's spirit, is epiphenomenally of nature.[17] He
begins, in short, in the world of *Harmonium*. His next step is to ask
why and what we know, why and what we need—and hence why and
what we are; knowing and needing the first idea, the ephebe comes to
know likewise that he does not live within it, but rather that it lives
within him.

Canto two, beginning with the awareness of this naked idea, investigates the origins of our absolutes, which is to say, our needs. Necessity,
the poet adduces, is the mother of imagination:

> It is the celestial ennui of apartments
> That sends us back to the first idea, the quick
> Of this invention . . .

Stevens' figure is impeccable—"quick" connotes animal vitality, as well as the pain of self-consciousness which quickens our need for truth; the apartmented world, like the apartmented mind, gives birth to desires for greater knowledge. But the poet knows that man's knowing is slanted: "so poisonous"

> Are the ravishments of truth, so fatal to
> The truth itself, the first idea becomes
> The hermit in a poet's metaphors,
>
> Who comes and goes and comes and goes all day.

The push-pull of experience, the exchanges of self and reality, is prologue to the perceiving of a first idea; yet it is experience which stands between us and idea. Hence, men of "desire," imaginative seekers of order, turn of necessity to partial resolutions drawn from the physical world, the only world they have—resolutions which nature in her dumb but vital constancy confirms. (Note here Stevens' compounding of imaginative men from all men who live in the mind.) The first idea, unassailable and mysterious, felt rather than known, is known intimately only in change. (In a sense, I think, this passage is not unrelated to Whitehead's exposition of the creative principle of God—an "inventing mind"?—which is neither outside the world nor static, but primordially within and active.[18]) Hungering for truth, these men of desire hunger for abstraction, but one which at once explains and contains the world rather than explaining it away. The truth they seek is fictive. That is where the next section begins.

Having proclaimed metaphor as the poverty of truth, Stevens submits his proclamation to investigation (iii). And the initial step is to identify the poem with the holistic vision of the ignorant man. A poem, so the poet begins, contains the first idea, and the first idea is a poem—the act of poetry, or of imagination, is, hence, an experience of the first idea, a knowing of what it is "to be." It is an act of creating, not receiving knowledge, a movement through the many toward the apprehension of the one, the "candor" of things as they are undergoing transformation ("exhilaration") into some pure sense of reality: "thought/ Beating in the heart." Canto three is a superb meditative discourse, developing from proposition to evocation, discovering animation in the poetic "elixir" which is the thread between actuality and idea. The almost surrealistic anecdote of the Arabian bears the import of a poetry which refines for us the confusions of experience, showing how "life's nonsense pierces us with strange relation." Relation, one may recall, was Crispin's problem—but the connotation here realizes, even as it relates poetry's elixir, that "pure power" to evoke the "primitive astronomy" which we feel as the first idea. This state of innocence—this "ever-early candor"—is by its very nature the beginning and end but not the middle of reality.

Hence the proposition of canto four, the strange relation between first idea and poetry:

> The first idea was not our own. Adam
> In Eden was the father of Descartes
> And Eve made air the mirror of herself.

In Stevens' secularization of the Fall, the origin of consciousness was the birth of imagination; man grown conscious of himself wills to name the world, to possess it as it once possessed him. He wills the "I am" of poem one, and in willing it completes his fall into an alien world. The paradox is this: without self-consciousness there is no poetry, no need for the fiction which marries self with world. The fall (Adam's or Descartes', that is, our own) is fortunate:

> The clouds preceded us
> There was a muddy centre before we breathed.
> There was a myth before the myth began,
> Venerable and articulate and complete.
>
> From this the poem springs: that we live in a place
> That is not our own and, much more, not ourselves
> And hard it is in spite of blazoned days.

Significantly, this is a return to stanza two of "To the One of Fictive Music," in which the birth of self prompted the need of reunion, in poetry. Stevens reiterates Santayana's epiphenomenal tenet that "all origins lie in the realm of matter." [19] Men are "mimics"; "Clouds are pedagogues." In the tension between the two, we add our sweeping meanings, creating those fictions through which we live in the world by making it live in us.

The tension is given dramatic body in canto five, in the violent combat of animal and nature. This is, however, an elementary opposition, brute consciousness confronting brute matter and finding a mutual freedom and oneness. In the ephebe's world, the self is "cowed," not free like the lion or bear—yet freer. It is not free to roar self-assertion, but free to suffer the agony of self-consciousness, and hence to work toward a higher knowing. If I read this poem correctly, the poet who stands "as sigil and as ward" in the penultimate strophe, finds his restrictive world, the "roofs" which limit his vision, both intimidating and challenging: thus, poets ironically are the heroic children in the final strophe, who, trapped in a world not their own, see life's realities not like an animal as naked otherness, but imaginatively, humanly, as the source of good. "Rooms" are the limits of self, housing the agony of self-awareness; but therein, paradoxically, is the imagination's life, its painful bitter utterance, so different from the brute's snarl, which ultimately masters the world in an act of mind.

The poet's constricted vision, therefore, demands of him the most concentrated attentions toward that world which he can master (vi). What he sees, the fabric of nature, must be masterfully realized, not only imagined but "imagined well" and conceived like a delicate canvas of "Franz Hals." Poetic abstraction is an admitted "falseness close to kin," a false form, and the poet must proceed with humility to affirm his stewardship of reality. His partial perspectives, indeed, are the measures of his humanity, and he can define the degree of his invention as an aesthetic knowledge. Out of the imaginative intercourse between the "weather and the giant of the weather" comes the abstraction blooded, Stevens' principal figure for a vital idea and a poem. What is affirmed is the life of the mind, in which abstraction is reality.

Cantos seven and eight, starting at opposite points, develop the possibilities of this discovery. They are, so to speak, extended proofs of the abstraction blooded: the former investigating the natural harmonies of the external world for evidence of "balances," the latter beginning with the abstraction of a "major man," an idea of man, and attempting to satisfy the conclusion of canto six. Nature provides its own balances, notes the poet, not "balances/ That we achieve but balances that happen." Life reduced to its essential fraction—like Thoreau's, say—invariably adapts to nature's harmonies in order to achieve its own, those "incalculable" balances which provide the poet with some of his felicitous insights: "Perhaps," he muses, "The truth depends on a walk around a lake": ". . . a stop to watch/ A definition growing certain and// A wait within that certainty."

But man's balances?—they do not just "happen." The human balances are of imaginative birth, the common apotheosized: in Stevens' figures, the self as "MacCullough" is dilated into a major man beyond commonalty. As first idea, this "pensive giant" is also the "crystal hypothesis," man become "Logos," a humanistic extension of finite man into creator of the infinite idea. As a "Beau linguist" he is both poet and poet's creation. Major man, in brief, extends Stevens' search for the man-hero to replace the divine-hero, which makes *Parts of a World* so personal and abstract. The old problem remains: the rhetorical difficulty of defining something that is at once symbol and creator of the symbol, who is "crystal hypothesis,/ Incipit and a form to speak the word/ And every latent double in the word." For the commonplace MacCullough, being a man with an imagination, is capable of imagining a major man, just as he once could imagine God. But what is significant is that he can imagine at all, that is, can create. This image of the MacCullough as man imagining (a dramatic realization of Emerson's "Man Thinking" or Whitman lying on Paumanok's shores) symbolizes the proper intercourse, man become his world as the world becomes his, change flowing into an abstraction blooded: "As if the language suddenly, with ease,/ Said things it had laboriously spoken." Taking "habit" from the "wave," MacCullough is man in his act of imagining, taking the world into his self, there to give it order and meaning as it gives him body and sustenance. Canto eight, in sum, is a reworking of the hero myth, man taking on the dress of his world precisely as in "The Man with the Blue Guitar" (ix), and in that attire proving himself to be "Logos and logic" of the place where he resides.

The concluding figure of canto eight is a discovery through language of the reality that is in man—his possibility as creator. It leads predictably into canto nine:

> The romantic intoning, the declaimed clairvoyance
> Are parts of apotheosis, appropriate
> And of its nature, the idiom thereof.
> They differ from reason's click-clack, its applied
> Enflashings. But apotheosis is not
> The origin of the major man.

The definition of major man continues to perplex. He is, in effect, another version of the abstraction blooded, an image to replace the idea of God.

Yet he is not a form so much as sense of human possibility: "The hot of him is purest in the heart." Canto nine provides a reverie of faith in the poet's new confection, the major man in whom resides the powers of creation itself.

In sum, major man proves the argument for abstraction, the flesh become word rather than word become flesh (x). He is neither transcendent deity nor anthropomorphic symbol, but a transparence of the ephebe, the humanist myth made in man's comic image. As a major abstraction of the commoner he recalls Whitman's idyllic democrat, but Stevens sees his representative man not as a "literatus" but as a harlequin in the human comedy, with "his old coat,/ His slouching pantaloons, beyond the town,// Looking for what was, where it used to be." The poet's responsibility to "confect" this figure turns away from the god without, acknowledges the self within. He returns the service of imagination to the commonplace world, to its fecund beauty and tragedy and to his own activity as the MacCullough, the creator and creation. The poet is not to elevate man but to reinvigorate him, not turn him from the world but toward it, not offer him future but give him back a present—not "to console/ Nor sanctify, but plainly to propound." As both the creation of man and the object of man's search, he justifies Stevens' belief in the self-creative act of the poem, or what Valéry conceived of as the moment-by-moment process of creating oneself in the mind.

"It Must Change." The search for the abstraction blooded was to affirm the life of the imagination as the source of selfhood. In every instance, abstraction was rooted in perception, and perception in feeling: as if to prove Kant's maxim of concepts and percepts. Since the essence of the real is change, to affirm life is to affirm living in change, within the natural theater where every pleasure posits its pain, every act an end, every life a death. The cantos of Part Two shift the focus to nature's flux and the kinds of experience possible there. To live in change is to submit to its multiple ambiguities: its constant inconstancy. The poet seeks both to resist and embrace change; which is to say, he embraces that which contradicts the first idea and resists abstractions. Yet even change, the vital process of things, has its rhythms, its forms, its universality, in a "universe of inconstancy."

Canto one establishes the encompassing reality of change which comes to natural order in "repetition." The opening images, of the old seraph (unlike Eliot's "agèd eagle") looking out upon a fecund world of doves and violets and girls with jonquils in their hair, dramatize the reality of change, not in the artifice of reasonable "chronologies," but in the continuity of vital life. Between the poles of youth and age there is change and exchange, and the old seraph discovers the paradox of joy in mutability:

> The bees came booming as if they had never gone,
> As if hyacinths had never gone. We say
> This changes and that changes. Thus the constant
>
> Violets, doves, girls, bees and hyacinths
> Are inconstant objects of inconstant cause
> In a universe of inconstancy.

Recalling Eliot's "hyacinth girl," and her role in the wasteland, the passage pays its homage to Bergson and to the pleasures of merely circulating ("bees" as being). But circulation here is of much purport, at least to the old seraph, another figure of the man of imagination confronted by the withering of his flesh, bound by his inconstant body but freed by his vitally constant imagination. Becoming "satyr in Saturn, according to his thoughts," the old seraph creates in mind what Hoon has experienced in pure feeling. Indeed, Stevens is at pains to separate his constant inconstancy of change from natural symbology, that teleological view of change which ordains nature's cycle as a symbol of man's immortality, which finds, that is, human analogy in Spring's rebirth (ii). But Stevens' poem of Spring is just what it is, an invocation to change in which "beginning" is "not resuming." Things have life because they are dying, not because they are reborn.

"It Must Change" begins with the changes of nature and modulates into a consideration of the role of imagination amid these changes: that is, the inevitable human abstraction from change. Denying the legislation of immortality, and subsequently its pathetic expression in false forms of wish-fullfillment—canto three returns to Stevens' statue of "Owl's Clover" and Parts of a World, and makes reference to his essay "The Noble Rider and the Sound of Words"—viewing man's will to preserve the self against change as one of "our more vestigial states of mind," Stevens must nonetheless arbitrate man's role in nature. For if man cannot survive beyond nature and change, neither can he live fully within change. To this end, canto four delivers a tentative proposition, which imposes an aesthetic order on change: that is, change as it is known and experienced by a self, not change as an inherent law of nature. Change, then, begins to flow into abstraction, like a blood:

> Two things of opposite natures seem to depend
> On one another, as a man depends
> On a woman, day on night, the imagined
> On the real. This is the origin of change.

A most succinct theory—quite simply an aesthetic which finds the origin of change not in the creation myth but in the instant of human consciousness. So is Adam's self-consciousness father to Descartes'. Poetry begins in this moment, and returns to it. Ironically, and richly, the metaphor of marriage itself constitutes an abstraction from process—an abstraction which contains change, an expression not so much about what *is* as about how man experiences *is-ness:* "The partaker partakes of that which changes him." He partakes of death and not of immortality (v). After the analytics of canto four, the sensuousness of five brings contrapuntal relief. The rich color tones of tropical flora growing wildly but with an orderly naturalness amid the civilized ruins catch the vivid opposites of things as they are. The scene itself is a lush fusion of the artificial and the organic, of man's order and nature's. And if nature finds its immortality in recurrence, man must find his in his fictions. Man the "planter" —and the poem is lightly allegorical—leaves his plantations to a world, but in a world of change, old forms submit to time's transformations.

The discovery leads directly to an animated rejection of the myth of immortality, in a poem that mocks even as it celebrates things of this world. It mocks as it were the insistence of things of this world—as well as selves—to *be* beyond change: to be *bethoued.* Nature, if vital, is chaotic, each of its elements calling out for identity, chanting an "idiot minstrelsy" of bethous. If Stevens is punning on Shelley here, as some have claimed, he is mocking the demands of each thing, and each self, to experience apotheosis. This points back to the dependency of opposites in canto four, underscoring the discovery that immortality belongs not to the thing but to the form, not to the individual but to the race. Hence change in its constant inconstancy is immortal: "the first leaf is the tale/ Of leaves," the individual sparrow immortal in its species alone—and man, one may speculate, in his imagination. In seven, then, the futile dreams of individual immortality are forfeited for the "lustre of the moon," the beauty of an idea, an imagined order. It is not the paradise of a seducing hymn but an accessible bliss that man seeks, and that bliss is dependent on change:

> For easy passion and ever-ready love
> Are of our earthy birth and here and now
> And where we live and everywhere we live.

Inevitably, however, man must suffuse the vital with his forms; the statue is essential though changeless. And thus in canto eight "Nanzia Nunzio" confronts "Ozymandias," another marriage of opposites: spontaneity challenging permanence, "nakedness" before an "inflexible/ Order," the fertile woman of earth (see the "Fat girl" of the final canto, Part Three) espoused by the statue. In short, it celebrates a putting back of abstraction into change: a dialectical marriage the fruit of which is a "fictive covering," poetry-in-life. (And once more we have a pun on Shelley, "Ozymandias" as a barren form of the past—which pridefully assumed itself immortal—revived by a vital, "vestal" reality, given identity once more by that which can affirm "I am," even as the past represented by Ozymandias provides the speech to clothe the vital.) This most clearly is in praise of poetry—Ozymandias' speech is order, the fictive covering that clothes reality in "the spirit's diamond coronal." Hence canto nine: "The poem goes from the poet's gibberish to/ The gibberish of the vulgate and back again." Stevens repeats his discovery in "The Man with the Blue Guitar" that somewhere between the isolated self and its alien world the poem captures not an absence of reality but the only reality available to man, an "evasion" perhaps of the thing itself, yet all we have:

> He tries by a peculiar speech to speak
> The peculiar potency of the general,
> To compound the imagination's Latin with
> The lingua franca et jocundissima.

From change to order, from process to the "imagination's Latin"— the poem that reflects change must also be abstract, even as the abstraction must change. And the poet of canto ten, sitting in the "Theatre/ Of

Trope," is not unrelated to the major man of Part One, the "Logos and logic," the poet who voices the "commonal." Talking about human experience as abstraction, celebrating change, Stevens proves poetry to be the subject of the poem and the poem to be an act of life. The method of Stevens' incessant return to this theme would seem to bear out his curious role in what Professor Charles Feidelson has called the American symbolist tradition.[20] For if Stevens is not a symbolist in the sense of one seeking reality beyond the world—nor even in Feidelson's sense of the Transcendentalist whose language, like Emerson's, partakes of the Spirit in the world—he belongs to that modern symbolistic fringe for whom words and the world must marry into a reality that is likewise a fiction. Says Feidelson, touching upon the symbolist's habit of turning his own method into reality, of writing poetry about poetry: "When the symbolistic method becomes the theme of symbolism, the literary work is attaining the immediate reality of symbol by acknowledging that language, after all, is at the same time mediate." [21] Frustrated by his failure to catch the evanescent ideal, the symbolist turns upon his method (and even his own words) to question it for its failure or to celebrate it as a final truth: Melville in one instance, according to Feidelson, Valéry in the other. There is a danger here, adds Feidelson, of "intellectual suicide," of an utter denial of the viability of any profane reality, as in Mallarmé's most extreme aesthetic. Indeed, Stevens avoids symbolistic hermeticism by his embrace of change, even as he participates in the symbolist's preoccupation with his own method. But for Stevens, the self is Logos, and the poet's words, though ideal, are of the world. Life and its reality are "vagabond in metaphor." Stevens' triumph is his ability to take the short view, that is, the human view: to accept man's comic role, and at last to make his method (the "imagination's Latin") connect with the way things are (the "lingua franca"), not transcend them. If metaphor evades, if the fiction is false, it has its human truth nonetheless. Unlike Melville's Ahab, Stevens' poet is delighted in his humanities. As an observer in the "Theatre/ Of Trope," he can happily admit the artificial things of his imaginings (x); meanwhile, the inherent will to change outruns metaphors. Participating in change, oneself is changed; remaking the world, honoring the vital, one remakes one's mortal self, even if in a peculiar speech. Canto ten measures carefully what truth there is in trope, and what of the volatile world will not be contained in the "glass" of metaphor.

"It Must Give Pleasure." What we get as synthesis is neither proposition nor example, but realization, an attempt to give pleasure intensely by way of indicating not what should but what does obtain in the marriage of mind and reality. About poetry, Part Three is also about life—the life we live in poetry. But the cantos do not dispense with propositions. Those too remain, directed against the artificial, the imitative, the formal—the excessively abstract which violates man's "ignorant eye." Yet Stevens rises to a new eloquence in his late style, because propositions about pleasure are not enough. We must see, feel, the very thing.

Stevens begins, as with each section, by denying preconceptions, in this case the pleasure of traditional rituals, customs, celebrations (i). They are, he concludes, a "facile exercise," traditional and dogmatic, restrained rather than vital. And they provide a false security. The greater pleasures, on the other hand, are the "difficultest rigor," pleasures of the moment grasped without reference to past joys. These are, if anything beyond the crudest self-indulgence, the unexpected discoveries, and hence creations of order, rudimentary rituals rather than confirmed ones. The irrational, the unreasoning, which are the poet's terms of this joy, can only be conceived in what he calls a "later reason," a phrase suggestive of Coleridge and most certainly related to the poet's penetrating intuition. The pulsing world of nature perceived in its own ceremonies is once again a starting point, the order inherent in the "image of what we see."

Canto two begins to advance the motif, moving from "things" to one's sense of things: the thing intensely felt with "later reason," as canto one has it. The anecdote of the "blue woman" is another example of the poet's deference to things of his world, her imaginatively endowed surroundings growing out of the unreasoning rites advocated in canto one. Once again there is a departure from the poem's rhetorical norm; imagery describes a ritual of sensuousness that recalls the ripeness of *Harmonium,* though here the tones are cooler, the passions more restrained. The woman's world, in short, is of discreet and real and vital things, and her pleasures those of unadulterated perceptions: "Clear and, except for the eye, without intrusion." We know very well how much "except for the eye" excepts, and how much humanity it affirms. The poem projects the irrationalist's plea of canto one by moving from facile exercise to natural form, and from rhetoric to extended metaphor. It leads, likewise, into the richly effulgent world of innocence (and involvement) of the subsequent variation.

Three, however, is almost impenetrable, a poem almost spontaneous, pure, as if the imagination were released into a freedom bound only by that "eye" of canto two. One possible way into the poem is through the imagery of the "blue" woman's world; another, through the imagery of a later poem, "Study of Images I" (CP 463). Warren Carrier has suggested of this latter piece that its opening image of the big blue bush delineates man's richly veined body mirrored in the striations of the natural world, or another of Stevens' imaginative conflations of nature and man.[22] Here the poem springs from an interfusion of constellated images combining the cool blues of the previous section with the violent reds of reality: or most simply, imagination and reality again, self blent with world. Just what is implied by the "lasting visage in a lasting bush" is not clear, and I hazard only the suggestion that the metaphor is another rejection of the violence of willed immortality ("lasting visage"), contrasted with the fluid life of the blue woman.[23] (One recalls the "lion locked in stone" of poem nineteen, "The Man with the Blue Guitar.") This is a poem to make the exegete scream "help!" and yet he can be satisfied to say that it is an experience, of seeing so deeply that seer and seen become one and "lasting." It is the experience of unreasoning, only partly resolved in the final stanzas: "A dead shepherd brought tremendous chords from hell"

> And bade the sheep carouse. Or so they said.
> Children in love with them brought early flowers
> And scattered them about, no two alike.

This may faintly echo the Orpheus myth, but it is not allusive. Who, for instance, are "they" or "them"? And what do the children celebrate except their own naturalness, their own innocent at-oneness with nature? the flow of life in and out of death? The beginning of canto four would suggest no more than that the clash of reds and blues is as fundamental as the making of poetry, the bringing of music from the subjective to harmonize with the objective, or children finding pleasure in their very affection for the world:

> We reason of these things with a later reason
> And we make of what we see, what we see clearly
> And have seen, a place dependent on ourselves.

The return to later reason yields its own kind of pleasure, its own kind of clarity. The "mystic marriage" of a "great captain and the maiden Bawda," who solemnize their rites in "Catawba," returns the poem to the pleasure of balances: to the ceremony of order within change, and to the geography of Crispin's Carolina. Recalling the "captain" of "Life on a Battleship," Stevens dresses him out in the attire of lover rather than legislator, and consummates his love of Bawda in another antimythological poem. The marriage is a poem of earth and not of heaven or hell:

> Each must the other take as sign, short sign
> To stop the whirlwind, balk the elements.
>
> The great captain loved the ever-hill Catawba
> And therefore married Bawda, whom he found there,
> And Bawda loved the captain as she loved the sun.
>
> They married well because the marriage-place
> Was what they loved. It was neither heaven nor hell.
> They were love's characters come face to face.

Love, the poem cautions, is of this world and no other—certainly not divine, but a poetry of place, as simple as the children's of canto three. (Stevens' lovers may be, like Donne's, "sublunary," and their souls only sense, but they are not "Dull," even in Donne's special use of the phrase.) Subtly, Stevens introduces as counterpoint to the bawdy ceremony in Catawba the anecdote of the Canon Aspirin and his form of order. The three cantos of this group form another of his animated rejections of the religious or institutional abstractions, heralding instead the natural and primitive, in sum the vital that lies at the center of us all. The Canon and his sister delight in the sophisticated pleasures of a provident life: her "widow's gayety" a sharp restraint on the vital children, his "outline of a fugue/ Of praise" indicative of his solemn, restrained pleasures. But in sleep, the children escape from avuncular privation into pure imagination and with them goes the mother's true blessing:

> Yet when her children slept, his sister herself
> Demanded of sleep, in the excitements of silence
> Only the unmuddled self of sleep, for them.

And in canto six, the Canon experiences a similar freedom, an escape into the nothingness of the pure pleasure of sleep. Through the evanescent purity of dream, in the transports of imagination, the Canon escapes the corridors of reason into a realm "beyond which thought could not progress as thought." This is not at all the province of his usual experience, for his is the world of institutions, of capitols and corridors, the city of God filled with "statues of reasonable man." [24] A dreamer of angels, he has the capacity to live beyond his canonical law, to grasp the first idea. But when he has it he awakens to the world and makes his canonical choice —he submits his experience to the formal ordering of dogma. His order violates his experience: "But to impose is not/ To discover." The truest pleasure resides in a moment of order, or as Santayana conceived it, according to Willard Arnett, in a "method of seeing, a mental condition or activity which is realizable by a living animal, and actualized by a propensity to witness rather than control the revolutions in matter." [25] It is, as the poet implies, a search for the absolute in the full awareness that the search is a necessary fiction:

> To find the real,
> To be stripped of every fiction except one,
> The fiction of an absolute . . .

Cantos eight and nine pursue this discovery, this truth not to be known but to be pursued. "Majesty," finite man learns, "is a mirror of the self" (viii), the apotheosis of the "I am"—a happy discovery for a poem which began with an uneasy ephebe and a minatory world which would not mean but only "be." This proclamation of the "I" consummates the ephebe's marriage with earth, and makes those external regions for which he, like the Canon, yearns reflections of the self: regions filled with Cinderella longings and the escapades of death. Thus Stevens' answer to canto eight's trenchant beginning: "What am I to believe?" Thus too his subsequent meditation of the "I" who can do "all that angels can" and more, being man. He is the poet who discovers that his capacity to "enjoy" is a capacity to master the earth's "eccentric measure" (ix). To celebrate the earth's whirl is to live as poet, "he that of repetition is most master," to affirm that "merely going round is a final good" because it is change enjoyed, change contained in the self but not denied.

What Stevens has evolved is a self, and in that self an image of the world of which man is master, the man-hero who comes to accept what is humanly possible and desire no more. The ephebe becomes a poet, lover of the "Fat girl," the vital heart of the world, the procreative source, the world that is no longer a place "not our own." And like the old Adam he proclaims this world to be his because his names, if evasions, are all the humanity the world possesses: "the more than rational distortion,/ The fiction that results from feeling." Stevens' concluding lines are the faith of an aesthetic which would replace the old theology. Man, possessing the world in tropes, possesses finally and irreducibly himself:

> They will get it straight one day at the Sorbonne.
> We shall return at twilight from the lecture
> Pleased that the irrational is rational,
>
> Until flicked by feeling, in a gildered street,
> I call you by name, my green, my fluent mundo.
> You will have stopped revolving except in crystal.

"Except in crystal"—except in poetry, in the self whose names master but do not deny the fluent mundo. Stevens needed a coda not only to coalesce his trinity but to return the argument to poetry proper as the "bread" of our being. The soldier of the coda is the human warrior, the mask of man bound in change, living there without his poet, without imagination, but whose identity depends on the poet's words:

> How simply the fictive hero becomes the real;
> How gladly with proper words the soldier dies,
> If he must, or lives on the bread of faithful speech.

Is there not a pun here? Has not language become our host? and at this point of Stevens' career, very nearly the thing itself? "The Noble Rider and the Sound of Words" provides a gloss: "A poet's words are of things that do not exist without the words. . . . Poetry is a revelation in words by means of the words. Croce was not speaking of poetry in particular when he said that language is perpetual creation" (NA 32–33).

The conception of "Notes" signifies that it was meant to be that Grand Poem which took shape in *Harmonium,* except that Stevens knew by 1940 that a supreme fiction was the poetry of a lifetime, to be evolved and not suddenly realized. "Notes" is an extraordinary poem, modern in its abstractness and in its intellectual posture yet deeply wedded to the romantic tradition of the reflective poem. It moves toward the symbolistic, searches for its balances or still-points, but refuses to rest on any final order. At times it recalls *The Prelude* with narrative sections excised; but then again there is nothing like Wordsworth's identifiable personal history stringing it together and fixing it in a natural landscape. Stevens resorted to a dialectical trinity that is almost a modern cliché, as if to mock form or to show the possibilities of freedom within it. Still, the internal progress of the poem is tautly thematic as well as qualitative. It is neither patched together like the surface of a surrealistic canvas, nor is it an arbitrary composite of thirty-one poems. It is not modern in the sense, say, of Pound's *Cantos,* with the glue of fact holding together feeling, history's vortex whirling toward an ideal center. Each poem in its way develops out of the previous one, even when the interconnections are barely noticeable or when a group of poems—for example, the Canon Aspirin sequence— asserts itself as an isolated unit. Anthology publication indicates that several of the individual cantos will stand alone, but with little of the import they bear in tandem. What emerges at last from the mists of rhetoric and private nuance is a voice fully identifiable, a voice which begins as uninitiated ephebe and evolves through self-discovery into an "I." The movement of the poem recalls even the aesthetic trinity of Joyce's Stephen Dedalus, moving from the ephebe's desire for wholeness (the first idea) to his discovery of the essential harmony of diverse things (change) toward a final vision of radiance (pleasure) in the crystal of poetry. But the "crystal," the poem, resides within the self who by the end has outgrown the ephebe and come to know that the first idea, if he is to know it, must be his own creation.

"Notes" gives us a comic, not a cosmic "I," the act of discovery, not ecstasy or vision. We have a poem, that is, so deliberately cerebral that we may fail to see that it is also excitingly lyrical, and that the lyrical results from that release of emotion which man earns when he probes and discovers his world, his place in it, and its place in him. The verbality is there, though verbality as Kermode indicates is not exactly the poem. Still, one cannot jettison the structure of argument for the residue of feeling; in this poem things, words, and ideas become one as they are entertained in a mind, and at last become the landscape of a total self. Stevens, for instance, could associate Adam and Descartes not through the history of ideas but because each stands for the human act of self-discovery: that comic self-consciousness, as Kenneth Burke has called it, which paradoxically alienates us from the world and drives us back to it. Meditations formalized into poetry are not thoughts but the processes of thought in search of resolution—thus the pervasive images of man-thinking, thus the recurrent nuptials ("Notes" is a poem of many marriages) which are never final in themselves but launching points for another rhythm of separation and reunion. But most of all, "Notes" is a poem of the act, the "poem of the mind in the act of finding/ What will suffice" (CP 239). In the end, coming upon the eternal "war between the mind/ And sky," we discover that what suffices for the ephebe is his act which, feeding upon the actual, may arrive at the discovery that what he knows is his creation. What he can know is himself. Man, discovering himself, discovers that all men are ephebes, who must evolve an "I" in this world. To this end, life and poetry are one. And so Stevens enters his last and major phase.

chapter 5

The World as Fiction

To say more than human things with human voice,
That cannot be; to say human things with more
Than human voice, that, also, cannot be;
To speak humanly from the height or from the depth
Of human things, that is acutest speech.
Chocorua to Its Neighbors

*T*he question of Stevens' symbolism—that is, *symbolisme*—is vexed, and vexing. *Parts of a World* and "Notes toward a Supreme Fiction," introducing a new style, did little to clarify the problem that in *Harmonium* had seemed no problem at all. Stevens in the twenties was easily identified with Symbolist and post-Symbolist influences—with Verlaine's music of words, Mallarmé's pursuit of *l'azur* through a haze of impure colors, Laforgue's ironic world-weariness.[1] His expressed affinity for French poetics is as undeniable as the verbal tinge which seemed to create in his poetry a life apart. But no amount of resemblance can gainsay the fact that Stevens' imagery, his language, the habit of his mind were, unlike the symbolist's, directed back to the body of the world. *Harmonium* on every page deplored transcendence, even as it made extensive use of the stylistic devices the French had perfected by way of achieving a world apart. The publication of *Transport to Summer* (1947), however, could only raise the question again, if in another way, for it is this volume rather than *Harmonium* that contains Stevens' truest symbolic mode.

At best critics of Stevens' symbolism have been less than discriminating in filling out parallels between him and the French poets he expressly admired and, in many places, seemed to imitate; at worst they have forced him into the French mould while at the same time arguing for his Americanness. One exception is Michel Benamou who is still at work on the revisionary criticism that stresses the finer distinctions, as well as the larger identities, between Stevens and the various Symbolists and post-Symbolists whom allegedly he succeeds.[2] Benamou's method is phenomenological: by the poet's metaphors you shall know him, and know his world, which is to say, his world as it is limned by the processes of the mind and issues in the form and flow of metaphor. This kind of evidence —the metaphors which compose the landscape of the poet's world of self—reveals very much the same thing as does my argument for the development of Stevens from poet of sensation to poet of the act of the mind: that Stevens' imagination, wholly human in its source, is no less attached to a "fluent mundo," a vital and fecund and ever-changing world that one purifies by seeing freshly, not like the Symbolists by denying. "The difference between Stevens and the French tradition," says Benamou, "hinges on the metaphysical meaning of the word *pure*. It is a contrast between feeling purity in the world, and reaching purity out of this world by an angel's flight." [3] Benamou's evidence lies in demonstrable contrasts: Stevens' fecund girls of earth against the ubiquitous ideal woman of the various Symbolists (and one might add, English decadents); Stevens' metaphors of place, colored by earth as well as mind, against the symbolistic language which evokes essences and denies presences; Stevens' resemblances between man and nature against Charles Baudelaire's "correspondences" that in effect deny nature; Stevens' dandyism which is a refuge from easy commitment against Baudelaire's dandyism which is an escape from change into permanence.

If the substantive landscape of Stevens' metaphors suggests a metaphysics that inverts the primary assumptions of symbolism, it is equally true that the process or activity or movement of his individual poems does the same thing. It is a characteristic that needs to be discussed, especially in relation to Stevens' later style, since it accounts for the simultaneously rhetorical and symbolistic quality native to so much American literature.

The naturalness of the act of the mind gives to *Transport to Summer* a tone of profound inwardness lacking in *Parts of a World;* though at the same time it confirms the abstractness and the philosophical detachment which devotees of *Harmonium* deplored.[4] The assertion of "The Man with the Blue Guitar," that "Poetry is the subject of the poem," becomes virtually a dogma, to be explored and revised extensively. It is, indeed, the narrowness of this dogma—or the fact that it appears as doctrine— which lends credence to Stevens' symbolism but at the same time suggests a ruthless throttling of his lyrical voice. The earlier poems, if indirectly about poetry, grew out of direct experience; these late grow out of memory and reflection. Perception generates idea, the idea is explored and pursued, and the end would seem to be not so much resolution as some momentary discovery—some form, some purified world beyond the ordinary conceptions of it, but not otherwise beyond.

In the fundamental sense, these are not symbolist poems. But in a very important sense they are. The self-consciousness of the artist about his method, especially his concern over the kind of truth it affords him or its validity as a way of investigating reality, is one of the obvious consequences of an aesthetic which, short of brief moments of ecstasy or apocalypse, cannot deliver what it promises—transcendence. This is the astute observation of Professor Feidelson on the nativist tradition of American symbolism, which he finds developed concurrently with, but for the most part independently of, the French tradition.[5] Its appropriateness to the plight of the modern, who would put upon his poetry the burden once carried by the old mythologies and religions, is twofold: he recognizes the failure of the old modes of belief; and he knows (even Hart Crane knew) that his own method is equally problematic, except as it provides him that momentary sense of the "the" that may occur in his act of applying the method. When this develops, poetry may become the subject of the poem in an urgent way. This is to say, the act of imagination, of seeking what would suffice, may come to supplant the ideal end of that search. It has always been so for Stevens, for whom the choice between life and transcendence was made before poetry became a normal as well as necessary act.

The tensions in Stevens' poetry about poetry, however, are of another kind. For the seeker after reality had come to discover as early as "The Man Whose Pharynx Was Bad" that the voice of imagination might falter, that nature, though vital, was neither moral nor spiritual, and that the realities of mind were fictive. Trying to define man as hero, he had been brought face to face with the question of creation—not only man's need to define himself as creator, but also his need to define what he could create, or even know. It became a matter not simply of living in the imagination but of reifying imagination as the essence of the human. The confidence in the reality of metaphor voiced in *Parts of a World* becomes in the first poem of "Notes toward a Supreme Fiction" a skepticism; the desire to get beyond symbol to that which it symbolizes, as in "Martial Cadenza," poses an essential question of the limitations of the self which uses language, as well as of the limits of language. And in that question Stevens is confronted by another: what reality does man seek? what belief if you will, what and why? In a sense, the whole of *Transport to Summer* is devoted to the "motive for metaphor," to the paradox that one must depend on metaphor as a way to reality when metaphor is an evident evasion of the first idea. It is a poetry called forth by a constant questioning of the very devices it uses.

The ambitious long poems and the numerous shorter ones which cluster about them in this volume manifest a concentered activity that is less a systematic aesthetic than an evolution of a living aesthetic. "Notes toward a Supreme Fiction," which is usually assumed to be the final word of the volume, is really its introduction. Beginning with the ephebe, it evolves an idea and an idiom of man, of the poet, and defines the province and the limits of his heroic actions as seeker after the first idea. The second major poem, "Esthétique du Mal," reaffirms the place of poetry, and hence the men who make it, in the imperfect physical world. Accepting evil, it accepts the incomplete, the mortal, and hence the existential fate of the self which would be its own destiny; yet in fashioning an "esthétique," it prescribes the human drive toward wholeness (toward form) manifest in the act of imagination. "Credences of Summer" forms the volume's capstone, a poem less argumentative and more lyrical than the earlier two, which normalizes the act of imagination and gives voice to its natural and necessary role in man's spiritual economy. It is the first truly meditative exercise in what was to become the dominant mode of Stevens' last years—a poem, for all its perfections of style, that is a casual act of the mind, a process, a poem becoming, moving toward credence or form.

The increasing volume of Stevens' prose during this period (a prose that in refusing systematic thought becomes its own kind of act of the mind) evinces not only the theoretical turn of Stevens' interest but also his attempt to dissolve theory into experience. Investigating metaphor, or resemblance, or analogy, he strives to define a mode of thought (and hence, the "act" of poetry) rather than a theory of language or poetry. In the broadest sense, he accepts the full activity of mind as a poetry, no longer excluding reason. The essays, beginning in argument, settle willy-nilly into a kind of contemplative activity rather than philosophical discourse. One of these essays, perhaps the most revealing one, celebrates with extraordinary sophistication the euphony and harmony of the life of the mind, describing the poet's responsibility to "accomplish a poetry that satisfies both reason and imagination" (NA 42). He applauds this quality in the best philosophers, especially Bergson. Among other of his wide-ranging allusions and quotations is this from Henri Focillon's *The Life of Forms in Art* (see also NA 46): "Human consciousness is in perpetual pursuit of a language and a style. To assume consciousness is at once to assume form. Even at levels far below the zone of definition and clarity, forms, measures and relationships exist. The chief characteristic of the mind is to be constantly describing *itself*." [6] He might well have added the following, from a little farther on in the same book:

I may call attention once again to the profound difference that separates the life of forms from the life of ideas. Both have one point in common that sets them apart from the life of images and the life of recollections, *i.e.,* they are organized for action, they combine a special order of relationships. But it is clear that, if there is a technique of ideas and if it is impossible to separate ideas from their technique, this latter can be measured only in its own terms, and its relation to the outer world is still but an idea. Now the idea of the artist is form. His emotional life turns likewise to form: tenderness, nostalgia, desire, anger are in him, and so are many other impulses, more secret, oftentimes more rich, colorful, and subtle than those of other men, but not necessarily so. . . . But his special privilege is to imagine, to recollect, to think, and to feel in *forms*. [7]

The poems of *Transport to Summer* are well described in this sense of movement toward form, the act of the mind describing itself. Stevens might even have quoted Focillon again: "Forms are always tending toward realization; they do, in fact, realize themselves, and create a world which acts and reacts. The artist beholds his work with other eyes than we do . . . for his vision is from within the forms, so to speak, and from within himself. Forms never cease to live. . . . They are the creators of the universe, of the artist, and of man himself." [8] Stevens' essay is called "The Figure of the Youth as Virile Poet," and in it he rehearses the world of *Transport to Summer,* his transport of the ephebe into the world he must finally accept and come to believe. Summer is not physical; it is the world in the self, the forms of the mind realizing themselves and the world. "Few people realize that they are looking at the world of their own thoughts and the world of their own feelings," Stevens concludes (NA 66). And the few who do, like Stevens, know that the credences of summer have not come without grave and serious doubts; nor do they endure without serious challenge.

II

Transport to Summer is dominated by the long poem, and this sustained, discursive mode has tended to obscure many deserving shorter pieces, the skeletal "forms" which seem less like acts of the mind than rhetorical exercises: e.g., "The Motive for Metaphor," "Crude Foyer," "Paisant Chronicle," "Dutch Graves in Bucks County," "Holiday in Reality," or even the moderately long "Chocorua to Its Neighbor." It is true that these poems and their companions are, in the light of the longer poems, little more than footnotes.[9] But the volume is repetitious for good reason. It is commonplace to note that Stevens at this time had derived an idiom much less vital to express a theme much more abstract. Judged as a system of ideas, Stevens' are both irrational and inconsistent. But this is to see the poems, as Focillon warned, with different eyes from Stevens.' Moreover, it advocates a severe orthodoxy of what experience belongs to poetry, what to other kinds of discourse. The quality missing in *Transport* is drama of style as well as variety. For the poetic self which rises to great eloquence in physical delights, or in the face of death and violence, may lapse into less colorful idioms when the experience is mediate rather than direct, when the landscape is the world in the mind and not the world as contemplated by mind. These poems labor under two burdens, their single subject and their polished style in which even the inkhorn of the mind has only one shade. But it is nonetheless true that on the whole *Transport to Summer* is Stevens' first major volume after *Harmonium,* and its best poems spring from the minor exercises which appear to be not only repetitious but adventitious.

"Life consists/ Of propositions about life"—the title of the poem to which this line is central is itself propositional: "Men Made Out of Words" (CP 355). The words of the world, the poet's propositions, are just what Stevens had called them in "The Noble Rider and the Sound of Words": a manifestation of the violence from within resisting the violence without, turning man's "terrible incantations of defeats" into tolerable if not comfortable dreams. The imperative of *Transport to Summer* is to act, to imagine, to speak, and thus to arrange, to encounter appearance and ask questions of its "pediment." In this way one at last defines his self, realizes what Focillon called the forms of mind, or sustains the mind which exists only in the activity of defining itself. "Crude Foyer" and "The Motive for Metaphor" are two eminent poems of transport which bear one most fully into the climate of the volume. For they are poems which precede proposition and in a sense outline the journey to "summer." "Crude Foyer" (CP 305) in particular is a poem of first ideas, which carries us back to the opening of "Notes toward a Supreme Fiction":

> Thought is false happiness: the idea
> That merely by thinking one can,
> Or may, penetrate, not may,
> But can, that one is sure to be able—

The broken rhythm, the hesitancy, betrays the logic of thought, exposes the false happiness, by way of disabusing the mind of its preconceptions. It is as if Stevens must periodically renew his ideas, return to the innocence of his interior self, there to confirm his knowledge that "foyers" of belief are man's imaginings. Rejecting foyers of the spirit which reach outward into empty paradise, he dons "humanity's bleak crown"; but not without an appeal to his ubiquitous ignorant men, who are "incapable/ Of the least minor, vital metaphor." The "ignorant," primal self begins anew, without preconceptions, without hope, with only the given.

It is necessary to read these poems in perspective and to allow for necessary contradiction; for while Stevens evokes the ignorant man who is incapable of metaphor he must at the same time establish "The Motive for Metaphor" (CP 288). Stevens' ignorant man is the rudimentary self, his Emersonian mask in secular voice. He is the ephebe of "Notes" set out in the sun of reality which he desires to know in and for itself. But he can know it only within the limits of himself. The ignorant man—as in an earlier poem, "The Sense of the Sleight-of-Hand Man"—is man without designs upon the world, and thus man who discovers order and beauty and delight and pleasure because he can take things as they are. But he lives nonetheless in the mind, sees by metaphor, and must violate the sun, must name it, even if naming is a crude evasion. "The Motive for Metaphor" treats explicitly of this "must," this imperative of the supreme fiction to live in abstractions or forms of the mind:

> The motive for metaphor, shrinking from
> The weight of primary noon,
> The A B C of being,
>
> The ruddy temper, the hammer
> Of red and blue, the hard sound—
> Steel against intimation—the sharp flash,
> The vital, arrogant, fatal, dominant X.

The human world, as in the poem's opening stanzas, is of autumn and spring, those seasons when things are slanted and not overwhelmingly real, when things are known mediately, not directly as the "dominant X." And Stevens' journey to summer can be seen as some compromise between what the ignorant man can know and the unknowable X, between what man desires of the ultimate and what he can know in his language of the eye. The transport is indeed a sustained activity of imagination, in which the poems themselves are very often acts of creating words or forms on the subject of what it means to create words. Take, for example, the volume's opening poem, "God Is Good. It Is a Beautiful Night" (CP 285), a title which might be better translated as "the idea of God is man's idea of the Good, and the experience of the Good is an experience of the Beautiful." The metaphors of the poem suggest no transcendence, no good except within the activity of attending the "rotted rose of earth." The experience is an action suspended in words; the mind like the "brown moon, brown bird" is caught in a tableau of its own forms, which, suggesting action, achieves a permanence. More explicitly, these concluding lines of "Certain Phenomena of Sound" catch the gist of the previous poem's "venerable song":

> You were created of your name, the word
> Is that of which you were the personage.

> There is no life except in the word of it.
> I write Semiramide[10] and in the script
> I am and have a being and play a part. (CP 287)

The "I" creating itself in words, "A sound producing the things that are spoken"—this is the mode of *Transport,* even when it leads to those meditations upon evil, or upon that chaos of reality against which the self contends with words. The mask of the redwood Roamer in "Certain Phenomena of Sound" is this near-solipsistic ego living in its own activity, finding self-definition in the words it makes; or there is the embattled "I" of "Repetitions of a Young Captain" (CP 306), which sustains itself in the very activity of making sounds. Words re-form the roar of the world, that chaos which threatens to dissolve the "I" into the indistinct noise of nothingness, that is, the darkness outside the self:

> On a few words of what is real in the world
> I nourish myself. I defend myself against
> Whatever remains.
>
>   .   .   .   .   .   .
>
> A few words of what is real or may be
> Or of glistening reference to what is real,
> The universe that supplements the manqué . . .

Supplementing the *manqué* would seem to be the poet's task, and the *manqué* is the natural, the given, which is at once man's paramour and antagonist. Or the *manqué* may be that nothingness of a self which has not yet discovered the world around it. To arrive at summer is to fill the void, with words which give shape to the clutter of things, but more important establish the discreet primacy of mind over things—what Stevens called in "The Noble Rider," words with a "finality, a perfection, an unalterable vibration, which it is only within the power of the acutest poet to give them" (NA 32). Such is the role of the "sound of words," filling-in the ether between man and world.

Occasionally, Stevens' preoccupations lead him into unfortunate extremes from which neither his matchless sense of nuance nor his humor can rescue him. Having assumed that propositional metaphors are themselves real, and thus launching points for meditative excursions, he risks having his propositions examined for their logic, and he becomes another symbolist or nominalist living off the fat of his own words. Poems like "Late Hymn from the Myrrh-Mountain" or "Human Arrangement" or "Burghers of Petty Death" exasperate rather than please, and attest, if not to Stevens' occasional laxness of energy, to the dangers of depending so exclusively on the imagination's tireless repetitions. The unalterable vibration becomes a meditative drone. I mention these poems not so much to downgrade them as to suggest the kind of thing that has led to critical disaffection with the late Stevens. In another mode, the affectation of a poem like "So-and-So Reclining on Her Couch" fails because of the very humor which should sustain it.

"So-and-So" (CP 295) smacks of the classroom, in part because its tone is derisive of the classroom and thus rather heavily self-mocking. Still, its mockery is serious, or perhaps reflects so seriously of Stevens' preoccupations at the time that the intended irony is dissipated. In any event, this lecture on the way things are demands consideration, for it is a full-fledged summation of Stevens' poetics even with tongue-in-cheek. Stevens begins in his donnish as contrasted with his contemplative mode, expostulating we suppose upon a painting (a paltry nude?), the texture of which he severely abstracts into ideas: first pointing out "Projection A," the form in itself, and then "Projection B," the form as perceived, then offering his synthesis in "Projection C," the reality "Between the thing as idea and/ The idea as thing." The portrait, in sum, "is half who made her." But the pedagogue has performed just that anatomy for which Stevens is constantly abusing the non-ignorant man. The arch conclusion, his "Goodbye" to "Mrs. Pappadopoulos," does not really put the action in the comic perspective it suggests. Rather than irony at the expense of abstraction, we have Stevens' aesthetic in the abstract.

Transport may be said to communicate by attrition as well as pleasure, and if this is not the way we like our poetry it is nevertheless Stevens' way of sustaining the imagination through dry spells, until it finds its proper mood once more. There is enough evidence of this mood in the volume to justify the indifferent poems, to indicate that the exercises of imagination produce something more than casual pleasure. For the end toward which these forms reach is nothing less than the "dimension in which/ We believe without belief, beyond belief" (CP 336). Here is the high seriousness we find in "Paisant Chronicle" and "Sketch of the Ultimate Politician"—two more notes toward an idea of major man—or in

"The Lack of Repose," and "Continual Conversation with a Silent Man" —in which the human voice speaks most humanly of never-ending things and in that very act comes to accept its comic role between the "old brown hen and the old blue sky" (CP 359). It is in "A Word with José Rodríguez-Feo" that Stevens, addressing himself to a friend and correspondent, speaks passionately of our need to believe first in our self: "We must enter boldly that interior world/ To pick up relaxations of the known" (CP 333). But the clearest statement of the paradox haunting Stevens is in "The Pure Good of Theory," at the end of the third part:

> Yet to speak of the whole world as metaphor
> Is still to stick to the contents of the mind
> And the desire to believe in a metaphor.
> It is to stick to the nicer knowledge of
> Belief, that what it believes in is not true. (CP 332)

Returning to theory as a pure good, Stevens returns to what is human, the "final need/ Of final access to its element"—for Stevens uses "good" almost precisely as Santayana uses it, as that which attends only the highest moments of the human experience of pleasure and thus brings us to human repose, beyond vulgar appetite. It is the good which, at the conclusion of "The Lack of Repose" (CP 303), satisfies the poet that his activity of living without repose—without the comforts of the past, without belief except as it is known to be fictive, without having written his book of life and thus without having spelled finis to living—"will suffice." [11] The good, "a good" as Stevens would have it in "The Lack of Repose," is what man has instead of God (and tradition). It is the repose achieved in those instances when theory becomes act, as in the contemplative moment of "The House Was Quiet and the World Was Calm" (CP 358), where Stevens realizes in poetry what Santayana has described as the perfect communion of self and other: ". . . as in reading a book, the material book is forgotten, and the reader lives in rehearsing the author's thoughts without thinking of the author." [12]

The propositional poems of *Transport* must finally be read not as statements about life or theory so much as meditative acts evolving this "belief, beyond belief." They perpetuate the kind of "truth in a calm world,/ In which there is no other meaning," elucidated in "The House Was Quiet and the World Was Calm." At this moment in his career, Stevens had arrived at a conception of poetry that offers several parallels with Paul Valéry's for which he always showed admiration; and it may well be that Valéry motivated his fullest statement on theory, in "Description without Place." But of course Stevens did not need the example of Valéry, any more than he could follow Valéry into the ultimate world of abstraction. Nonetheless, very late in his life, Stevens contributed two prefaces (now collected in *Opus Posthumous*) to an edition of Valéry's *Dialogues,* translated by William McCausland Stewart. What he chose as Valéry's enduring ideas is revealing, particularly the extracts from Valéry's modern Socratic voice:

Nothing beautiful is separable from life, and life is that which dies.

• • • • • •

By dint of constructing . . . I truly believe that I have constructed myself. . . . To construct oneself, to know oneself—are these two distinct acts or not?

• • • • • •

Man . . . fabricates by abstraction.

• • • • • •

That which makes and that which is made are indivisible. (OP 272)

There must be natural adjustments when translating Valéry's "ideas" into Stevens' derivations—the symbolism of one for whom reality was an act of abstracting beyond nature against the symbolism of one for whom reality was an act of abstracting within nature. The following comment by Valéry, which Stevens might well have read, provides an interesting gloss on their mutual need to hypostatize poetry, even as that need was interpreted differently:

[Poetry] is productive of fiction, and note that fiction is our life. As we live, we are continually producing fictions. . . . We live only by fictions, which are our projects, hopes, memories, regrets, etc., and we are no more than a perpetual invention. . . . You are here, and later on you will no longer be here, and you know it. *What is not* corresponds in your mind to *what is.* That is because the power over you of *what is* produces the power in you of *what is not;* and the latter power changes into a feeling of impotence upon contact with *what is.* So we revolt against facts; we cannot admit a fact like death. Our hopes, our grudges, all this is a direct, instantaneous product of the conflict between *what is* and *what is not.*[13]

"Description without Place" (CP 339) is the fullest statement in *Trans-*

port on the problem sketched out in "The Pure Good of Theory": of man's urgent search in time for an order beyond the "battering" of time, even as he is aware that what he seeks is a fiction. As such, it is an extension of the first poem of "Notes," and a complement to "Esthétique du Mal" which engages the opposite problem of how to exist in time and savor its good, without denying time and its challenge to the good. But what is of greatest significance in "Description without Place" is its exhibition of Stevens' symbolist self-consciousness *in extremis:* of how the poet, contemplating his own method, sustains himself in his acts of discovery.[14] "Description without Place" is a self-contained tour de force of a very special kind, which is not likely to earn for Stevens many admirers. But it is a conspicuous example of the risks he had to take in order to arrive at the repose of "Credences of Summer."

This is the argument. Beginning with the premise that to seem is to be (i), it proceeds to examine degrees of seeming, and consequently degrees of being: the seeming of our direct perceptions and the "greater seeming of the major mind," the one a passive, the other an active imagination (ii). What follows are variations: there are "potential seemings" or poetic visions, like ideas of immortality which are seemings not of things as they are but as they possibly may be (iii); there are introspective seemings and logical seemings, Nietzsche's imagination and Lenin's reason being examples, the former exploring the fluid realities of the inner world, the latter sterilely fixing life in the "eye" of one collective seeming, a rigid abstraction (iv); "seeming is description without place,/ The spirit's universe," but it takes its reference from the reality of place, from "an expectation, a desire," that which creates the "difference that we make in what we see" (v); hence, "description is revelation," being neither the "thing described, nor false facsimile" but a synthesis, a symbolistic reality (vi); therefore, the poem fullfills the symbolist's need to justify his method —since the "word is the making of the world," metaphor become logos, "seeming" is being in a world where "nothing solid is its solid self" (vii). The argument circles back, as Stevens' meditations invariably do, to its beginning, and achieves an aesthetic whole. To seem is to be in the sense that poetry's seeming indeed *is* a reality in the mind of the beholder.

There is a dangerous aridity in poems of such calculated purpose and intellectual invention. Saving his method, indeed apotheosizing it, Stevens sharply reduces the *rapprochement* between proposition and style. The esoteric and arbitrary byways into which his allusions take the reader are not altogether fortunate. For the reader must first "see" before he can appreciate the "difference that we make in what we see." Indeed, "Description without Place" is one of the most private of Stevens' poems, even as it is one of the most assertive of a theory. It fullfills itself only in the characteristic circularity of its argument, in which the initial proposition is discovery: "It is possible that to seem—it is to be,/ As the sun is something seeming and it is." This is Stevens' belief "without belief, beyond belief," the belief that man can know reality as separate from appearance because man alone is the author of his "descriptions." What he knows is himself, for in his descriptions man has given the world the cast of his humanity. The final section of "Description without Place" is, in this sense, one of the most revealing of all Stevens' late poems, in which the random act of describing the remembered world becomes a "making," a creation of the world not by design but simply in the act of being oneself:

> Thus the theory of description matters most.
> It is the theory of the word for those
> For whom the word is the making of the world,
> The buzzing world and lisping firmament.
> It is a world of words to the end of it,
> In which nothing solid is its solid self . . .
>
> . . . .
>
> It matters, because everything we say
> Of the past is description without place, a cast
> Of the imagination, made in sound.

This is not, as it might appear, nominalism; the reality of this world is the matter of mind. The poem looks inward, not outward.

III

Nearing the conclusion of his short essay, "About One of Marianne Moore's Poems" (NA 93), Stevens turns aside to recall a visit he had recently made to his ancestral home, the "old Zeller house in the Tulpehocken, in Pennsylvania." It was like going home, he implied, to a past which could only have been for him a description without place, were it not for the forbidding antiquity of the scene itself. For if Stevens had changed, if he was of another time in which the past beat upon the present rather than receded from it, the natives of the Tulpehocken had not changed, and would not admit that their world had. The world of the Zellers, those Dutch ancestors of his mother's side, came home to him most forcefully: in the austere forms of belief which remained firmly planted in God's dominion. For Stevens, however, the lonely, barren landscape with its decaying churches and desolate graveyards was a sharp contrast to that same scene as felt by the solitary old men of the area. On his return to New York, he had gone to an art exhibition at the Morgan Library. His reaction is significant: "The brilliant pages from Poland, France, Finland and so on, books of tales, of poetry, of folk-lore, were as if the barren reality that I had just experienced had suddenly taken color, become alive and from a single thing become many things and people, vivid, active, intently trying out a thousand characters and illuminations" (NA 102). This is the experience which Louis Martz has called the meditative transmutation of the remembered into the real, the fragments of experience harmonized in the mind's forms.[15]

It is the order and effulgence of art which made of the past a living present, a description without place, and thus a revelation. That Stevens' reminiscence comes in an essay proclaiming the "affinity of art and religion" indicates more about the urgent demands he made of poetry than about his heritage. The world of the Zellers set against his own reveals more than history; it dramatizes the historical uses of imagination. The Zeller theme provided Stevens with a useful perspective, in which poetry supersedes religion as the modern imagination has superseded the traditional. It supersedes religion, that is, not by substituting one form for another, but by substituting the search itself for any "final finding." The Zeller theme likewise provided him with a subject matter. In "The Bed of Old John Zeller" (CP 326), Stevens explores his two worlds by way of marking his alienation from a tradition to which he was nevertheless linked by his humanity. For the Zeller faith in things as God-symbols had given way to the modern poet's sense of things as man-symbols:

> It is more difficult to evade
> That habit of wishing and to accept the structure
> Of things as the structure of ideas. It was the structure
> Of things at least that was thought of in the old peak of night.

In "Two Versions of the Same Poem" (CP 353), old John appears again as man trying to contain the heaving bosom of the sea which defies his traditional categories, a man disturbed by thoughts that the elements may not be "an undivided whole." This doubt in a closed and God-determined universe motivates the effective counterpoint of "Dutch Graves in Bucks County" (CP 290), in which the thunder of modern chaos batters against the lyrical refrain, the orderly world of the old Pennsylvania Dutch. This poem, with its honorific yet ironic bow to "my semblables," is a kind of prelude to "Esthétique du Mal"; moreover, it explores the theme of identity and continuity in an age which has broken violently with the past. In more respects than the obvious it begs comparison with Allen Tate's "Ode to the Confederate Dead," though it is by no means so tortured, so metapyhsical a poem as Tate's; nor is it Baudelairean as the modest allusion might suggest. And this is just the difference: Stevens is not concerned with the violent break between past and present but with the continuity of imagination in a discontinuous landscape. Man rather than being walled-out from the past partakes of its humanity, just as he constantly re-creates himself in the ceaseless whirl of his present:

> This is the pit of torment that placid end
> Should be illusion, that the mobs of birth
> Avoid our stale perfections, seeking out
> Their own, waiting until we go
> To picnic in the ruins that we leave.

Rejecting the past and its stale perfections, the marchers of the present, in a violence altogether new, adopt what is human and continuous, and thus fullfill the continuity of mankind, ever more human in its quest for order:

> These violent marchers of the present,
> Rumbling along the autumnal horizon,
> Under the arches, over the arches, in arcs
> Of a chaos composed in more than order,
> March toward a generation's centre.

The past is renewed but not repeated in the present: "Time was not wasted in your subtle temples [the ancestral forms]/ No: nor divergence made too steep to follow down." [16]

The omnipresence of violence in the early forties was evidence that could not be denied by an advocate of reality. Yet Stevens was not so much intrigued by the phenomenon of historical violence—he never had been —as with man's passion to escape from, avoid, or even deny this given of reality. The *mal* of his time was simply the intensified *mal* of all time; and man's struggle to contain it, to mitigate it, and finally to humanize it was the essential human act, the rage for order. But one thing had changed: metaphysical evil had disappeared with the old beliefs; like Satan, it had been victimized by an age of positivism, leaving man with his imperfections but no systematic or imaginative explanation of them. What modern man had was not imaginative forms of explanation, but imagination; not the old mythologies, but the human power that created them and gave them life. Whatever had passed, there remained the human and its commitment to order, to aesthetic. Thus "Esthétique du Mal" (CP 313). The problem for Stevens was as old as "Sunday Morning," but a glance at the textures of the two poems indicates clearly that changes in sensibility bring changes in the posture of reality. For the crisis which de- manded the later poem, this reaffirmation of life in the physical world, was the problem of belief in a world beyond belief. It is a poem of con- templation—on what the commitment made in "Sunday Morning" had meant.

Stevens chose his French title carefully, implying by *mal* something more than an abstract or theological evil and an academic response to it.[17] If he were calling attention to Baudelaire's *Les Fleurs de Mal,* as the title may suggest, he chose the French not to imitate his predecessor but to dis- tinguish "esthétique" from the traditional forms of belief against which his poem set itself. For whatever the debts to Baudelaire, Stevens' poem is an intellectual lyric, which analyzes the historical failures of imagina- tion to account for the essence of the human—imperfection. This is the poem's actual subject: the study of the anomalies and incongruities of living in the physical world, and the way these disturbances may be miti- gated without their destroying man or without his denying them, either instance being an abdication of one's humanity. *Mal* would appear to be a synonym for disorder, just as *esthétique* is synonymous with order. In this perspective, the poem is one more engagement of chaos by the con- noisseur. But the poem very clearly introduces to Stevens' aesthetic the moral dimension he always claimed for poetry: that aesthetic precedes the moral but is integral to it.

"Esthétique du Mal" is actually closer in conception to "Owl's Clover" than to "Sunday Morning," especially in the way it approaches varied but thematically related problems of contemporary life: the bankruptcy of traditional forms of belief; sentimentalism and self-pity as escapes from reality; the secularization of religion and its contemporary consequences; the inadequacy of reason as a mode of belief; the pressures of modern violence; the poverty of materialism and utilitarianism. Though a similar indictment of modern man, it begins in a different historical context from that of "Owl's Clover." But even more indicative of its difference is the degree of objectivity Stevens has attained, a detachment which softens the rhetoric of the earlier poem and affords the poet greater economy. On the other hand, this same lack of personal involvement produces a more abstract, discursive style. In "Owl's Clover," the war of ideologies provoked excessive rhetoric, yet did allow the poet a centrally developing symbol, the statue, against which conflicting positions were measured; in "Esthétique du Mal," the abstract problem is central and unwavering, but the poet's variations on it are annoyingly diverse and private at times. The reader can avail himself of few reliable guideposts to the developing argument.

There are, nevertheless, indications of an inner unity. The poem is neither narrative nor dramatic, though it has elements of both. The protagonist, if indeed there is one, is little more than a rhetorical convenience for establishing a concrete setting and initiating the theme: In fact, the poet as more than a voice is recognizable in only five of the fifteen poems: i, ii, iii, x, and xii. The majority of the cantos are intellectual lyrics and treat the theme variously: by example, parable, representative anecdote, or calculated dialectic. They are not connected sequentially, but there is a qualitative development of the argument which seems to fall into interrelated "blocks" of poems, examining negative and positive approaches to life in a world where evil and pain are preeminent because life is. The following outline, though arbitrary, indicates something of the qualitative nature of the argument:

Poems i–ii: establish a scene and introduce a protagonist, suggesting man's relation to nature in the modern world as a metaphysical separation unknown to previous men and hence not explained by the old forms of belief.

iii–v: present various negative responses to this modern evil or pain, responses which point up the danger in avoiding or denying their reality; each poem ends with a corrective, poem five being particularly didactic throughout.

vi–vii: offer two further correctives by celebrating the reality of human imperfections; they indicate that man's lone defense against evil is to absorb it into the normal process of experience or into the timeless framework of art.

viii–ix: analyze the disaster of negation, the denial of evil as a reality constituting a denial of the human, which leaves man defenseless against the ravages of time.

x–xiii: suggest four various approaches to the reality of evil, each based on the acknowledgment of man's imperfection; but man nevertheless has the imagination and its powerful metaphors to fend against the times.

xiv: is a rhetorical attack on reason, counterpointed against poem thirteen; the argument for comparative or relative and thus necessary evil is vindicated in its contrast with the ultimate lunacy of extreme logic which legislates all antitheses out of its world.

xv: affirms the vital life which is the only possible deduction from the foregoing argument; the world of process, however, denies nothing, and evil thus recognized becomes a necessary and acceptable part of life lived in the "paradise" of the imperfect.

The poem opens with the poet at Naples, involved paradoxically in activities both mundane and intellectual: "writing letters home" and "reading paragraphs/ On the sublime." He is modern man: uprooted, alienated, disabused of his faith, man seeking coherence in a world without spiritual coordinates. The setting corresponds to Crispin's Carolina, part way between the rational abstractions of the polar North and the chaotic but essentially real tropics. He is not, one notes, at Rome. Letters and the sublime, however inconsistent, indicate a concentered desire for order, the one seeking imaginative continuity with his past, the other a strategy for defining his place in an awesome cosmos. If "Vesuvius had groaned/ For a month," its voluble complaint is a violence contained in traditional expectancy: "He could describe/ The terror of the sound because the sound/ Was ancient." He can, that is, understand Vesuvius' "sultriest fulgurations" because he has a language for it— "paragraphs/ On the sublime."

The contrast of ordered past and atomic present recalls the opening tropes in "Of Modern Poetry"; the poet's desire for a comprehensible order is a search for an aesthetic, a human norm. The "sublime" to which he attends is, it would seem, a specific reference to Longinus' grand style— of a time when both man and nature had meaning and place, and style could transport the man. "The volcano trembled in another ether" and is understood in terms of the sublime. But "pain is human" hunger pangs warn the poet, and in this juxtaposition of the ridiculous and the sublime, Longinus' style, like the dignity of man, is found wanting for this modern condition. Pain defines the human. To deny it, or to attempt to transcend it, the poet had discovered, is to deny life. "Except for us" there is no pain; within the sublime the human is negligible, and so is pain and human history.

Picking up this motif, the second poem must reject the Longinian "paragraphs" for a meditation of despair. Pain is not to be rejected but embraced. Poem two opens with a basic paradox: pain and evil are essential flaws in an imperfect world; moreover, as causes of despair, they provoke man's quest for transcendence and hence provoke his rejection of the life he cherishes. Pain motivates, ironically, that which if achieved would destroy it. The poet, lying in the bosom of his ripe world, considers these paradoxes in quiet desperation. Resolutions, he discovers, either cancel themselves or are beyond reach:

> The moon rose up as if it had escaped
> His meditation. It evaded his mind.
> It was part of a supremacy always
> Above him.

The moon—here apparently not a stock symbol of imagination, but a sign of a purity beyond man's distorting eye, beyond the poet's *Angst,* free and thus a contrast to and measure of his pain—this moon, transcending the poet's despair, becomes the absolute for which he longs. Representing transcendence, it denies the human. To enjoy "acacias" we must despair of the purity of the moon. For acacias are mortal and remind us that life's *mal,* like our cosmic incertitude, is the gift of life itself, which makes us conscious of things of this world and our separation from them. To desire the supremacy of the moon is a kind of bad faith; and yet our longing for harmony with the greater cosmos is equally frustrated. The moon, beyond our world of despair, is indeed the measure of our despair. Meditation at this point threatens to become formula, just as paradox refuses to unbend into lyricism. But the form here—the intellectual lyric —adequately embodies the meditation of despair and brings the poet if not to resolution, then to another point of departure.

Poem three turns to a firmer dialectic, employing the more familiar discursive triplets of the late style. Equally deliberate are the poet's careful formulations of argument reflected in a series of "as if" clauses. The moon and acacias of poem two are replaced by the antithesis of heaven and hell. Here the poet's fictions (his "firm stanzas") discover heaven in hell, unity in diversity, and so resolve the pain of poem two, not in transcendence but in forms of the imagination. Poetry is contrasted with the sentimentalism of religions which have forfeited imagination for the "over-human god," offering pity rather than life—a criticism not far from John Crowe Ransom's in *God Without Thunder.* Modern man, left without assurance of either this world or the next, indulges in escapes of self-pity, for he is isolated in a universe which affords him no consolations of immortality. The poet, however, does not desire a return to the superstitions of a "reddest lord," or what Ransom called the wrathful God. He suggests instead indulgence in the "honey of common summer," from which pain is not excluded but is denied preternatural significance:

> As if hell, so modified, had disappeared,
> As if pain, no longer satanic mimicry,
> Could be borne, as if we were sure to find our way.

The first stage of the poet's searching leads him to embrace the imperfect but vital world of flux; it follows that he must reject man's sentimental denials of that world, including denial of pain (iv). The opening two lines of poem four, so startlingly isolated, demand consideration:

> Livre de Toutes Sortes de Fleurs d'après Nature.
> All sorts of flowers. That's the sentimentalist.

Here "d'après Nature" is the key phrase. "All sorts of flowers" suggests that the single flower is denied an identity, being subsumed under the generic abstraction of Nature. The sentimentalist like the Platonist negates evil by denying the significance of individual things of this world. The artist in contrast ("B." may suggest Bach, Beethoven, Baudelaire, any artist who discovers the one by honoring the many) avoids the generic abstraction and celebrates the world of broken shards: his "transparence," analogous to the crystal, repudiates "All sorts of flowers." Likewise, the imagination of "that Spaniard of the rose" who "rescued the rose/ From Nature," and gave the thing itself meaning in his "own especial eye." There is a pun here on the cultivation of idea out of change, like love out of passion, poetry out of experience. The two examples of artistic struggle, to transcend nature yet preserve the particular, enforce the poet's conclusion that evil is in the world and a part of life, that it must not be sentimentally wished away but preserved in the texture of our vision. Life like art is imperfection seeking order, but the order can never transcend the imperfection. But the poem concludes with an excruciating rhetoric, which virtually defies paraphrase: the "genius of/ The mind," or pure imagination, is wrong, not in itself real; no more so is the "genius of the body," things as they are. Each is nothing in isolation; and man, committed to either one as truth, spends (exhausts) himself "in the false engagements of the mind." The sentimentalist, that is, is tempted to abstract, or sentimentally wish away, evil, like the book of all sorts of flowers which denies the flower itself. Poetry is a true engagement, mind married to thing, nothing denied, everything hallowed, including the *mal* without which there is no "dark-blooded" rose. The Spaniard, in cultivating his hybrid, creates a new form which is neither pure nature nor abstract idea; he is a metaphor for the poet. "Esthétique du Mal" is a poem of flowers, and this hybrid in its mature beauty is form ripe with decay.

With caution, then, the poet works toward a meaningful synthesis of art and life, form and thing (v). The contrast here of "true sympathizers" with the sentimentalist of poem four counsels a return to the "actual, the warm, the near," to a world "without the inventions of sorrow." (Cf. the maternal echoes of the earth as bodying forth the muse in "To the One of Fictive Music.") This world also recalls the conclusion of poem three, an acceptance of our own imperfections in our love for the world's:

"These nebulous brilliancies in the smallest look/ Of the being's deepest darling." Having embraced the imperfect, we forego the tragic or the transcendental: the "ai-ai// Of parades in the obscurer selvages." The density of rhetoric conceals an old theme. A world without God, or gods, removes from man the consolations of tragedy; no longer victimized by sublime fate, we become our own, build our own worlds, imperfect and wholly human. Imperfections become the essence of being. They produce no "inventions of sorrow," but rather joyous affirmations. Thus the "in-bar" of our true self must replace the "ex-bar," those "golden forms" of the old gods into which ancient and primitive man projected his own ideal image. The human supplants the supernatural; the gesture of compassionate love replaces the devotion to golden forms. We must, he implies, reclaim our humanity as did pagan man, who projected "in-bar" into "ex-bar," not as Christian man, by separating them. But "ex-bar" will no longer serve. In sum, before we can be wholly human, we must replace the old and empty rites with affirmations of self, the old mythologies with their source, imagination. This is a difficult and tortuous poetry, in which idea hides itself more than idea should. But it is a poetry, nonetheless, which catches the heart of the dilemma that perplexes secular man in a world which forfeited the old inventions because it had to forfeit the old myth of evil.

The rhetoric of poem five is translated into the parable of poem six. The sun as both source of life and cosmic timepiece becomes Stevens' symbol for the world of process and thus for imperfection: it "brings the day to perfection and then fails"; it "still desires/ A further consummation." Its opposite, the moon, is wholeness, the perfection of the lunar cycle. And the opposites become one: no lunar month without the light of the sun; no unity without the processes of time; no imagination, perhaps, without reality. And yet from his knowledge of their interdependence, man can glean no single, certain truth. The world is never brought quite round, the destructive flux never transcended: "space is filled with his [the sun's, time's, reality's]/ Rejected years." In his "clownish yellow," he enlivens the world but leaves it forever short of total fruition. The obsession with time here relates to Stevens' embrace of change and his paradoxical view of time's ironic continuum, death-in-life. Thus the parable of the voracious bird pecking at the sun, which extends the theme in terms of man's gross appetite for life. Like the phoenix, man has risen from his imperfections, nourishing himself on that which at once sustains him and binds him in mortality: this is man in his imperfection, man with his "curious lapses." The parable is a vivid paradox of the relation of man to his world; the appetite for life is an appetite likewise for apotheosis, two hungers which can only be satisfied as one. And in a concluding metaphor, we return once more to "Sunday Morning": the ambulant figure of the bird revolving downward to earth yet resisting the inevitable absorption of life into the common center of nature. This tension between bird and earth is metaphorically man's own struggle with a world that is at the same time mother and tomb. Our desire for wholeness, for the "lunar month," is satisfied only in the imperfect consummations of a day in the sun. Sun illuminates moon, then yearns for her perfections; the anecdote might well be that of mind and first idea. But in this case the mind-bird is caught devouring its own source.

Poem seven offers lyrical counterpoint, evolving its own affirmative parable out of the combat of bird and sun. This is the central meditation, picking up the affirmation of life in poem five and the paradox of poem six and combining them in a vision of suffering as a meaningful aesthetic experience. The familiar opening refrain ("How red the rose . . ."), so unlike anything else in the poem, prefigures the resolution: the wound of life given meaning because it is universally shared. The soldier's wound, drawn from the context of a violent world, is transmuted into a symbol of man's humanity, the mark of his distinctiveness, his individuality, his fall. Grown "deathless in great size," he becomes a surrogate and secularized martyr to man's fate, not a Christ figure but another version of Stevens' hero, who does not absolve human evil but solemnizes its necessity. Hence we share in his wound sacramentally, for it is ours; it binds humanity in a mutual suffering and a mutual joy:

> The shadows of his fellows ring him round
> In the high night, the summer breathes for them
> Its fragrance, a heavy somnolence, and for him,
> For the soldier of time, it breathes a summer sleep,
>
> In which his wound is good because life was.
> No part of him was ever part of death.
> A woman smoothes her forehead with her hand
> And the soldier of time lies calm beneath that stroke.

Death thus conceived is necessary to the complete awareness of life; the woman's emotional gesture of acceptance suggests a universal sharing of the soldier's fate, which makes that suffering plausible without denying it. The commonplace gesture, so pregnant with compassion, becomes revelation.

The two succeeding poems change the emphasis to the sentimental tragedy of denying mortality and hence denying evil. It is, in both poems, a "tragedy/ For the imagination," this denial of Satan; for it has been a rejection of the human, Satan being the symbol of our will to be individual. Hence he is the patron of imagination. His death destroyed many "blue phenomena" in that it destroyed the sense of man free to be himself, free to create. He was destroyed by the age of reason; thus evil or imperfection becomes, like Josiah Royce's perhaps, something to be transcended, or worse, a form of ignorance which time will amend. What was destroyed was the need for belief, and the consequences for the imaginative man were a "mortal no" less thunderous and less tragic than Melville's. Yet the poet, the "realist," cannot accept sentimental negations:

> The tragedy, however, may have begun,
> Again, in the imagination's new beginning,
> In the yes of the realist spoken because he must
> Say yes, spoken because under every no
> Lay a passion for yes that had never been broken.

Stevens' tragedy, recalling Emerson's, is the tragedy of self-consciousness, the fall we redeem only in imagination, in the passion for yes.

Poem nine distills from the broader problem the more specific cause for the mortal no: "Panic in the face of the moon." For the moon, one recalls, is that supremacy above us, that perfection for which we futilely long. And the panic, it would seem, is man's inability to face that supremacy with the knowledge that we are not to reach it and that, indeed, it is the idea of perfection which gives our imperfect life meaning. Poem nine, then, is an analysis of our loss of imagination, and of the consequences of losing the magical world view which gives our lives transport. It is likewise an aggressive denial of self-pity—the chant of "indifferent crickets"—and an affirmation of life even in its modern poverty. For if we have lost the "folly of the moon," the "miraculous thrift" of an imagined "paradise of meaning," we can still make music. The voice of this poem cries, but not plaintively, for music, for a poetry of "primitive ecstasy" to fullfill that passion for yes of poem eight: "music/ That buffets the shapes of its possible halcyon/ Against the haggardie." Once again loss is transmuted into affirmation, a yes in which each man is responsible for making the music that once seemed to reside in the spheres.

Poems ten through thirteen accept the challenge and proceed to examine various responses of secular man to his mortality. In poem ten, as student of the nostalgias, those old lost beliefs, he is led finally to embrace the most authentic, the softest woman, who is "reality/ The gross, the fecund." This is, of course, a familiar Stevens motif, an embrace of the "Fat girl" once more, and thus an embrace of change and death and *mal*. It is the love of "anima for its animal," spirit for body, and man for his mortal being. (Is there not a pun here on ani-*mal*?) As student of the nostalgias, he is not nostalgic, and what he seeks is their source. For the nostalgias are those archaic forms of metaphysical explanation which have meaning for secular man only because they are of human origin. They have satisfied a need, that need of our birth. But the poet, left without belief, is not left without the need for it—what he must believe in is the "grossly maternal," not the "mauve/ *Maman*"; this world as against any possible next. And hence he rejects the nostalgias, except one—the belief in life:

> That he might suffer or that
> He might die was the innocence of living, if life
> Itself was innocent. To say that it was
> Disentangled him from sleek ensolacings.

Consequently, he can face the shocking truth which begins the next meditation: "Life is a bitter aspic. We are not/ At the centre of a diamond." Emerson's central man, like Hoon, has been displaced at the center of things. The disjunctive imagery of masses, of violence, and of utilitarian excesses combines to alienate man from nature and from himself, and provokes the poet's somber prophecy: "Natives of poverty, children of malheur,/ The gaiety of language is our seigneur." Poem eleven displays an interesting mutation of images, filtered through this central couplet which celebrates the reigning order of language. Paratroopers, ship, and steeple, which are combined in the opening stanza to elaborate the violence, materialistic abandon, and spiritual evasions that have led to the dehumanization of life, become in the final stanza images of a sham world. A vulgar materialism provides the sacramental objects of worship, all of which the "man of bitter appetite," the poet, despises. He despises the anti-life imaged by a culture where violence and utilitarianism find a mutual justification and religious abstractions explain away moral contradictions. But he "caresses these exacerbations" and savors the painful truth of a meretricious world which threatens to destroy him. In the curious syntax of the last three lines, beginning with a plural pronoun whose only antecedent must be "exacerbations," Stevens appears to be asserting that these painful realities, by denying the poet's "tongue" which would acknowledge them, in effect destroy themselves, that the vulgar world denies itself by wishing away the incipient evils. It is a variation on poem two, but more notably, an inversion of the prophecy in the coda of "Notes toward a Supreme Fiction."

One of his ways of savoring the dilemma is to turn it into a theoretical problem. But the tortuous abstractions of poem twelve are difficult to savor. The poem is a calculated piece of dialectic, examining the poet's relation to his world through the formula of the subject-object antithesis and synthesis. Rhetoric, however, finally overcomes the poetry, and the ultimate resolution is little more than a clever game. The method is not uncommon to Stevens, the metamorphosis of his "peopled" and "unpeopled" worlds being the familiar dialectic of objective and subjective reality. In this instance, he complicates argument with a dense excursus on the ambiguities of self-knowledge before proceeding to the familiar synthesis in a "third world without knowledge,/ In which no one peers." This third world is, no doubt, the poem or fiction, not what the Symbolists conceived in the ideal of their symbol. The composition of his world, in terms of the poem, suggests the experience of Stevens' "ignorant" man, who knows reality without preconception:

> It accepts whatever is as true,
> Including pain, which, otherwise, is false.
> In the third world, then, there is no pain.

However ambiguous, Stevens is not saying, "Whatever is, is right" but that whatever is is real, and consequently an object for imagination. Pain is not pain because it is also life, a rationalization not likely to be accepted in any realistic sense, but metaphysically obvious as an assertion of the pleasure-pain continuum. More than that, however, there is no pain because the third world is form. The condensation of the poem's final lines is overwhelming, suggesting possibly the inordinate difficulty of attaining the poet's designed third world. At best the poem displays the futility of a metaphysical rationalization of pain, though it reminds one of the ease with which Emerson and Whitman disposed of evil in their respective worlds. But the final lines, separating "lover" and "woman," accept more realistically the truth that in such rocks as this world of time, there is no third world without pain. Here, there is no marriage, except in poetry.

In poem thirteen, then, he falls back on the urgency of accepting the "fragmentary tragedy/ Within the universal whole," the unalterable necessity of the human which must repeat its unalterable failures. This is a reductive tragedy, one remembers, for in poem three the poet forfeited the "ai-ai" along with any cosmic view of human grandeur, and in poem ten he rejected the old nostalgias. Here, however, is a tone of fatalism which solemnly acknowledges the paradox of organic life: the "force of nature in action is the major/ Tragedy." But the poet again wills affirmation out of his fatal logic:

> And it may be
> That in his Mediterranean cloister a man,
> Reclining, eased of desire, establishes
> The visible, a zone of blue and orange
> Versicolorings, establishes a time
> To watch the fire-feinting sea and calls it good,
> The ultimate good.

The sensual ease here relates this poem to the initial setting; but what is more suggestive, it evokes the spirit of Santayana's life and therefore his "good," the envisioned harmony of a secular self meditating in a world it cannot transcend. "Evil in evil is/ Comparative," then, because *mal* is foremost a disturbance of the harmony of the good, as well as a necessary, and therefore relative, antithesis of the good: it is a "force" of life-death "moving in the blood." His concluding sigh for the paradox lived by finite man is nonetheless an embracing of Santayana's intrepid skepticism: the evil of life is "an adventure to be endured/ With the politest helplessness."

Canto fourteen follows as abrupt counterpoint: the irrationalist's lambent meditations juxtaposed with the rationalist's jejune logic. It is at once a familiar attack on rationalism and the strategic use of an ideology —a faith—which denies the reality of evil. The extremes of a Marxist faith do lead, as the poem blandly suggests, to "worlds of logic," to an ideal synthesis in which logic itself is denied. The logic of Marxism aspires to this self-negation, while at the same time motivating inhumanism out of a logical humanism. (Victor Serge is the author of *The Case of Comrade Tulayev,* an exposé of the Stalinist purges.) The poet's revolutionists sublimate a blind romanticism in an "intellectual structure," composing their visions within bounded "lakes" which the poet finds ironically to be "more reasonable than oceans." To live in the singular world of one idea is to submit chaos to an intellectual cosmos which, in the terms of an earlier poem, is a violent order. Stevens' amendment of rational order, though topical, is but another rejection of the inventions of sorrow. Political lunacy, nevertheless, is one of those evils with which the connoisseur of imperfections must live, for it is simply imaginative order out of touch with reality. Thus the poem ends in affirmation "beyond belief," by accepting what has always been man's even when he has denied it through dreams or logic, rationalization or eager faith:

> The greatest poverty is not to live
> In a physical world, to feel that one's desire
> Is too difficult to tell from despair.

In a physical world, we suffer all pains as well as all pleasures; desire and despair cancel each other in a mutual dependence. But it is not the tangle of dialectics that triumphs here. On the contrary, it is the simple return to what is, to the beginnings of faith when the world is what it is because man has not explained it away in false nostalgias. This beginning, in the ignorance of what it is to be, accepts the *mal* in the sense that it accepts the human: accepts, that is, the desire and despair of being an alien in nature. Out of desire and despair, however, man aesthetically reconstructs his world, discovering his metaphysical in the physical. This is the way it always has been—except in the case of modern man. What he makes of it, these "many sensuous worlds," are makings of himself:

Speech found the ear, for all the evil sound,
But the dark italics it could not propound.
And out of what one sees and hears and out
Of what one feels, who could have thought to make
So many selves, so many sensuous worlds,
As if the air, the mid-day air, was swarming
With the metaphysical changes that occur,
Merely in living as and where we live.

The metaphysical changes of the conclusion send one back to the title. "Esthétique du Mal" is a serious consideration of man's need to accept this world as it is, without the old metaphysical assurances. Evil stripped of its sublimity becomes once again, in a secular world, the cause of man's good. Like death, it is paradoxically the mother of beauty and the destructive element; and one must embrace it as one does death, as the price of merely living. It is a truth almost too obvious to insist on, until one recognizes that it originates out of secular man's intense need of metaphysical assurances. But Stevens can only offer, albeit hesitantly, aesthetic to replace the old nostalgias. "Esthétique du Mal" is a concentrated meditation on authentic and inauthentic modes of being, authentic and inauthentic modes of faith.

"Esthétique du Mal" is one of those poems which, to apply that striking proposition from "Man Carrying Thing" (CP 350), "resist[s] the intelligence" almost too successfully. It is unwieldy, intense but provisional, the compactness of the argument suggesting a thoroughness which is not altogether realized. Composing himself in meditation, Stevens does not allow the reader similar composure. It has neither Baudelaire's vitriolic spleen nor Stevens' usual ebullience to captivate the reader, or convince him that evil is more than academic. However even in tone— and poem seven is one of its few purely lyrical moments—it remains a too private voice, especially in its esoteric reference and involuted rhetoric. An ambitious poem, it is nevertheless overwhelmed by unrelenting seriousness, for its affirmations are made only by sweeping away the putative faiths which have historically stood between man and an embrace of the physical world. Its role in Stevens' canon is similar to that of "Chanting the Square Deific" in Whitman's, and Stevens by no means suffers in the comparison. Without Whitman's arbitrariness, Stevens reclaims Satan as a worthy of the imagination. Whitman's Satan is a metaphysical cornerstone which fuses together an unconvincing cosmos; Stevens' Satan is more naturally he who has given man his selfhood. He is our constant symbol of how far we fail in quest for perfection, and hence signifies our need of "blue phenomena." The yes of "Esthétique du Mal" lies in its denial of absolutes and consequently of resolutions. If Stevens offers the imagination as defense against chaos, he is forever committing himself to the imperfect, which, after all, he repeatedly celebrates as our paradise. This has been his "thesis scrivened in delight." To create heavens in the image of earth is not only a natural inversion of religious orthodoxy; for Stevens it is the very act of self-preservation without self-denial: "Resistance to the pressure of ominous and destructive circumstance consists of its conversion, so far as possible, into a different, an explicable, an amenable circumstance" (OP 225). *Mal* corrupts the good, but there is no good without *mal*—and the exchanges between the two, the metaphysical changes, constitute an aesthetic that obtains on every level of human existence: from the most elementary act of perception to the most exacting turn of metaphor. *Mal* above all is inextricable from our need of faith, our "esthétique."

IV

Turning from "Esthétique du Mal" to "Credences of Summer" is like turning from dogma to ritual. The one precedes the other not logically but as preparation for devotion precedes devotion proper. "Esthétique du Mal," as an act of reconstructing the self, leads Stevens to the edge of philosophical abstractions that will not be absorbed in the poem. Moreover, "Esthétique" assumes the added task of begging that perennial twentieth-century question—what are we to do now the old beliefs are gone, and the green fields, too? It is an American question, of what to make of a diminished thing. If the poem has all the uneasiness of an excessive self-consciousness, "Credences of Summer" has all the repose of one's confidence of self, the passion for yes. But "Esthétique" is nothing less than a major poem, marvelously of its time; and, moreover, it is another signal moment in Stevens' search for what will suffice. Hunting for the ground of reality, the secular imagination hunts in effect for the unity of mind and world, knowing full well that, as the questers in "The Pediment of Appearance" discover, "The world is myself, life is myself" (CP 361).

Transport to Summer, rather than bringing to a close Stevens' search for the major man, continues the explorations. Resolved to unlock the enigma of being, to touch the essentially human, by way of confirming just what privilege man holds over the world in which he lives, Stevens could never actually resolve his questions. For just as meditation came to sustain itself, so did the meditations on the hero, and after him the major man, come to be acts which justified themselves merely by being acts. "Paisant Chronicle" (CP 334) veritably affirms this: proclaiming in effect that man in his need to apotheosize something comes at last to create the "fictive man"—the "major"—out of the demonstrably common. All men become poets satisfying their dreams—that is, all men who are intent on understanding their humanity. Or as another poem has it: "The whole race is a poet that writes down/ The eccentric propositions of its fate" (CP 356).

"Chocorua to Its Neighbor" (CP 296) is the volume's most formidable effort to define this power of major man, which, being indefinable, is prologue to the great meditative poetry of the last years. For Stevens is no longer concerned that the figure, the collective being, be other than the poet in fullest knowledge: a representative man whose meditative intonings are not moral guideposts, but notes about reality which appease the human need for form and understanding. This is what we find tentatively asserted in "Chocorua," in which man grown large in idea speaks prophetically but within the human range of speech. Man as mountain, man within the world become a dominant voice—this is the situation of "Chocorua": mountains bulk above valleys, pointing not to a permanence beyond as romantic man might have it, but offering only the substance of their own form which rises triumphantly from the common below. The mountain, in sum, is the symbolic voice of all "true transfigurers," all men committed to speaking of those truths which man finds it necessary to speak of. And speaking of truths "of or beyond or within reality," the speaker speaks only of the human:

> To say more than human things with human voice,
> That cannot be; to say human things with more
> Than human voice, that, also, cannot be;
> To speak humanly from the height or from the depth
> Of human things, that is acutest speech.

I have chosen the above passage as an epigraph for this chapter because it defines succinctly the secular bounds of Stevens' symbolism. Speaking from the "common" self, the poet "creates and re-creates" the physical world of his birth and finds what permanence he can in "human realizings." Emerson, looking at the world through his "transparent eyeball," saw the universe as Spirit ever-radiating outward through mind; Stevens, speaking of the world with "human voice," celebrates the self, "interior fons" and "fond," as center. By the time he had come to the full "realizings" of summer, the "glubbal glub" of "Chocorua" had become the "credences" of a self fully composed, for whom meditation was at once an act of belief and an act of creation—a possessing of the world and a remaking of it to serve our human need for form.

"Credences of Summer" (CP 372) more than any other poem in the volume recalls Wordsworth's leisurely compositions among nature.[18] Its lambent periods relax the arguments common to his poems in *Transport,* and its carefully proportioned single poems (of three five-line stanzas each) develop toward a meditative wholeness, but not designedly toward a dialectical peak. Yet the familiar theme of the poem about poetry lies just under the surface. Vital experience, the life of imagination—what Stevens calls the movement of a self in the rock—proves once more to be not only the impetus for poetry but the very thing itself. Life becomes poetry, poetry life. The poem's specific achievement is to reaffirm Stevens' convictions that although we live in the mind, the source of our satisfactions is in the earth: not alone in its green appearance but in its essential rock, the "rock" being Stevens' figure for the irreducible reality of the world as the imagination can grasp and conceive it. The lazy periods of the opening stanza establish the poem's tone:

> Now in midsummer come and all fools slaughtered
> And spring's infuriations over and a long way
> To the first autumnal inhalations, young broods
> Are in the grass, the roses are heavy with a weight
> Of fragrance and the mind lays by its trouble.

There is a lingering nostalgia here, which will affirm itself later in "The Rock," but most important is the aura of ripeness, nature fully realized and hanging on the edge of decay. The rich texture of things pervades the heavy consonants and slow-paced multisyllabic phrases that

THE WORLD AS FICTION 219

set the poem's casualness. It is process come to pure form which, as the second stanza indicates, soothes the mind and draws attention to the immediacy of the real world.

His meditations take a familiar course in poem two. They do not transcend the established scene, but transmute it in the self, into form. Consequently, he arrives at his first tenet: "as/ The physical pine, the metaphysical pine." The density of the real resists abstraction. The preponderant vitality of nature demands that one know it "without evasion by a single metaphor," know it, that is, as the ultimate abstraction, the *Ding an sich*. The mood of poem two is pagan and ritualistic—recalling *Harmonium*—and the intensity of things themselves commands the observer's devotions: "Exile desire/ For what is not." The "barrenness/ Of the fertile thing" rejects an ethereal world.

This continuum of physical and metaphysical occupies the poet's attention in the two subsequent poems. In poem three, "green's green apogee," which is "more precious than the view beyond," becomes his totemic object, to which he dedicates imaginative supplications. The image of the old man on the tower—a Yeatsean figure, but standing in sun, not moonlight—evokes the magic of the imagination's rituals which absorb the "ruddy summer" and accept the mortal pleasures. Here, sun worship is life worship, enacted in all the dignity of one who is "capable of nothing more." And poem four continues the theme in terms of the pervasive ripeness of the world in "Oley" (a community in Bucks County, Pennsylvania, remembered of Stevens' past) which resists heavenly longings, and is "too ripe for enigmas." As the primary sounds of nature revolve into the "secondary senses of the ear," there is achieved the only metaphysical order man is certain of:

> Things stop in that direction and since they stop
> The direction stops and we accept what is
> As good. The utmost must be good and is
> And is our fortune and honey hived in the trees
> And mingling of colors at a festival.

The sequence of *ands* evokes a world of process which is both present and eternal. But what holds the reader is the echo of *Harmonium,* the marvelous control of tone and nuance. And yet there are striking differences from the earlier poetry, for "Credences" speaks in a style of the inner ear and eye rather than primary perception.

It is of the physical world become metaphysical, become good in the "clairvoyant eye." And poem five addresses itself to this metaphysical, to this discovery that the particular subsumes the general, the thing precedes form:

> The more than casual blue
> Contains the year and other years and hymns
> And people, without souvenir.

Hence, as in poem six, the rock is the truth in that it is the physical transmuted in imagination and raised to the vital form (metaphysical) of poetry. The rock is our worship, our belief:

> It is the visible rock, the audible
> The brilliant mercy of a sure repose,
> On this present ground, the vividest repose,
> Things certain sustaining us in certainty.
>
> It is the rock of summer . . .

The rock of summer is not things as they are, but things transformed to the point at which form itself is reality, at once substance and symbol: it is seen "half way in bloom," in its own texture, and "half way in the extremest light" of imagination, a rock most unlike Eliot's in that it lives in man rather than his living in it. It is the certainty of this "present ground" as against the uncertain "view beyond"—but it is *meta*physical.

Poem seven shifts its emphasis to the intercourse of perceiver and perceived, to this act of metaphysical creation. The tension between mind and thing is developed in the metaphor of man acting in the rock: acts of averting, the ritual of transfiguration which takes place between the imagination and its world. Here is a particularly successful dramatization of the act of mind, which should be compared with poem twelve of "Esthétique du Mal." The birth of forms—fictions—is caught in an activity that is at once passionately and savagely sexual, and as discreet as a devotional exercise:[19]

> Three times the concentred self takes hold, three times
> The thrice concentred self, having possessed

The object, grips it in a savage scrutiny,
Once to make captive, once to subjugate
Or yield to subjugation, once to proclaim
The meaning of the capture, this hard prize,
Fully made, fully apparent, fully found.

Possession is discovery, and a yielding of the self becomes essential to
re-creation. Or, in terms of poem eight, it is a primal creative act of
bringing light out of dark, a "trumpet" of new morning which heralds
the visible as opposed to the invisible:

This [the visible], in sight and memory,
Must take its [the invisible's] place, as what is possible
Replaces what is not.

And the poem continues by reviewing the elementary Cartesian birth
that has long fascinated Stevens—day or consciousness bringing us to
an awareness of being, of "division," and thus to selfhood. Hence "Credences of Summer" returns to the old task of affirming the self by affirming
its primacy in a world which without it is unreal. Like Santayana,
Stevens finds this mind living both in and beyond its world—which is to
say, the world has come to ripeness, to form, in the mind.

The metaphorical flight of the cock in poem nine is the poet's imaginative journey among the growth and decay of his earth, a physical world
no longer delightful in itself. It is among the "salacious weeds" rather
than spring's green that he must sing his "complex of emotions" in
response to the "fund of life and death." The final poem closes the
circle, as in "Description without Place." Each vital thing flaunts its
ripeness before the poet who, even in his act of accepting the world
as it is, creates in his words of acceptance the "personae of summer,"
the forms or poems of reality in which the world comes to human completeness. Here, in his "roseate characters," are the perceiver's credences,
his metaphysical world which is no more than the physical re-posed
in the order of mind, "complete in a completed scene."

The theme is "belief, beyond belief," and hence the life of the mind.
The tone is contemplative, the texture sensuous; the rhythm is meditative, but the devotion is at the same time hedonistic. "Credences of
Summer," in short, is another way of saying that belief begins in reality,
in momentary fictions, rituals of delight, which precede any supreme

fiction and are ultimately supreme themselves. The poem echoes "Notes toward a Supreme Fiction" in a lower key. But this is just its virtue: that the convictions examined so deliberately in the earlier poem have become habits, credences of a man who knows what he can know and who created that knowledge. There is little wonder that Stevens considered it a favorite and thought sections four and seven among his best realized short pieces.[20]

Transport to Summer and his next book, *The Auroras of Autumn,* are companion volumes, whose titles outline the poet's development. The movement from the rock of summer to the rock of autumn is a metaphorical shift inward to the full activity of a contemplative life. "Credences of Summer" is a transitional poem in this respect: that it anticipates the more subdued tone of the final years, a mellowness and an acceptance, a confidence in the repose of mind. "Esthétique du Mal" seems to have solved the last great threat to his one belief and to have ushered in a period of light if not exactly of sweetness. But *Transport to Summer* in itself is a major volume. If it disappointed those who longed for the vitality and freedom of *Harmonium,* it established Stevens' claim as a major poet. It also surprised a great many critics who had predicted that the vigor, the *brio,* of *Harmonium* had finally exhausted itself in the patent exercises of *Parts of a World.* Rhetoric and argument, of course, could not satisfy devotees of *Harmonium,* but they could have found, had they cared to look carefully, a continuity of development. In *Transport to Summer,* as Louis Martz has accurately observed, "recessive elements in his early poetry develop into dominance."[21]

One cannot deny, however, the narrowing interests of these recessive elements. They are the acts of a mind absorbed in its own processes, because, it has discovered, the mind is where reality happens, where one comes finally to live. Any legitimate criticism of the volume's most ambitious poems must acknowledge their prohibitive unity of purpose, their obsession with the one idea of poetry as reality. It is perhaps ironic that as they aspire to speak for modern man, the common man, they speak an uncommon language; as they engage the great human paradoxes of belief, they rub the distinction off paradox; and as they celebrate a "primitive ecstasy," they become academic. When critics protested that Stevens had lost the physical world, however, they were only accusing him of what he readily acknowledged must be. Even in

"Credences of Summer" the world has become fiction. For that is what Stevens' summer is—the time when self and world reach a crisis of maturity, an apogee; the time when each desires to be itself, to subdue the other. It is a time for marriages, for balances. That is what Stevens' poems of this period strive heroically to achieve, and the best of them do.

chapter 6

The World as Meditation

It makes so little difference, at so much more
Than seventy, where one looks, one has been there before.
Long and Sluggish Lines

Life is not people and scene but thought and feeling.
Adagia

*W*ith the "thrice concentred self" of "Credences of Summer," Stevens had uttered the first tentative "yes"—uttered it in a style that promised a new repose, and a new beginning. The issue of *The Auroras of Autumn* (1950) altogether failed to confirm either this yes or this new poetry. Or so was the opinion of the reviewers, bemused by the discursiveness and monotone of abstractions, irritated by a poet who, taking on the mask of his "Large Red Man Reading" (CP 423), proceeded to "read from the poem of life" rather than life itself. *The Auroras of Autumn* is at once the hardest of Stevens' books to grasp (in part or whole) and the hardest to defend. Almost anything said against it can be supported, including Randall Jarrell's wry comment that the poems sounded more like the musings of Bernard Berenson than the Old Adam, or like "G. E. Moore at the spinet." [1] Still, it is difficult to reconcile the consensus that some of Stevens' best work appeared both just before and just after *Auroras* with the conclusion that between 1947 and 1950 everything went sour.

The poems of "The Rock," that distinguished concluding section of

224

the *Collected Poems,* do not of course approve the earlier ones. On the other hand, they are not a poetry different in kind from that of *Auroras;* and in fact they achieve in style what the earlier poetry had made possible. For the critics' quarrel with *The Auroras of Autumn* is not simply against abstractness or creative fatigue. It is against the kind of thing Stevens would make poetry do, the audacity with which he would sit and muse, and publish those musings as poems because they came out iambic pentameter. Yet for all that, the poems are anything but involuntary acts, the musings anything but careless. Then perhaps the problem is that they are all form, that the life of the mind came to be a mindless habit? But to Stevens these were considerably more than exercises. In a very special sense, they are poems over-committed: not to being poems, but to seeing how far the mind can go through language to apprehend a reality beyond language. They are meditations intent on appropriating the reality which Stevens had discovered in *Transport to Summer* to be "of or within or beneath the surface of reality" (OP 213). Critics could dismiss this kind of poetry, for it is not after all what poetry is supposed to be unless that poetry is apocalyptic, or symbolistic; unless, that is, the poetry deals with transcendence rather than, as Stevens claimed, the human. In search of what Stevens calls the "ultimate poem," these poems were themselves almost ultimately abstract, the utterances of an almost total inwardness. I do not wish here to apologize for them, but only to say what they are, or were intended to be.

Indeed, the future course of Stevens' style is evident in *Transport to Summer,* in his insistent probings of the motive for metaphor. *The Auroras of Autumn,* a questionable poetry even by generous estimate, is a logical consequence of having asked what man can ultimately know, and finding the answer to be: forms of his own conceiving. In order to justify poetry, and hence the man who created it, Stevens was led to push even deeper into the self, to seek out the ultimate form or ultimate poem, by which he appears to mean not a transcendental "poem" of poems, but that paradigm of poems which precede all particular forms. Yet, to take this frighteningly esoteric idea as the idea formulated and stated in the poetry is to mistake the poems. For this is a poetry of meditation in the fullest sense, a poetry purely contemplative, issuing from a mind which is exploring itself, not a set of ideas.[2] It is by no means always interesting, this poetry, or mind. And often it fails to achieve more than the empty form of a meditation. But this is just as often the result of the impossible end it seeks—to express the sense of "mere being," the being that lies within finite forms and at the "end of the mind."

One way of getting a perspective on these poems is to see them in relation to the earlier discovery, that between the self and any first idea there intervened the forms of our knowledge, the metaphors or fictions or poems by which we conceive the world and in which we manifest, no less, our failure to know it ultimately. For the paradox of language, like other forms or abstractions, was that it made us conscious of our isolation from the thing itself; and yet only in this self-knowledge could we conceive a reality within reality. Or to put it another way, if we create the symbol, then we create alike our sense of a reality beyond symbol. Our natural need is for belief beyond belief, some ultimate knowledge; and it is this need that compels the poet, even one who has accepted his human limitations, to seek a reality beyond the object. Stevens' various and changing metaphors for this reality—from the first idea of "Notes toward a Supreme Fiction" to the rock of his last poems—reveal his struggle to peel away the husks of form by which the mind perceives reality, so as to arrive at the irreducible thing itself. Seen in terms of the metaphysician's search for the *Ding an sich,* this poetic quest seems to promise not only futility but disaster for poetry. As indeed it nearly did. And yet one has to ask whether Stevens' search for the ultimate has anything at all to do with an intellectual attempt to abstract ultimately from reality; whether, that is, these poems with their propositions and bold abstractions, their prosaic mimicry of the philosopher chopping his logic, are concerned at all with argument or proposition as such. Or whether they are not really something more inimical to the ordinary conception of poetry: processes rather than forms, manifestations of the process of the mind in the act of imagining, peeling away the layers of its own world, deliquescing the tissue of memory and thought by which we ordinarily know reality in an attempt to get at their source, the creative moment itself.[3] This is to say, are these poems not utterly solipsistic? Rather than inducing abstraction, are they not engaged in the pulverizing of forms?

The answer would seem to be yes, that they are poems of a world (a mind) all its own. And they are to be saved from solipsism, if at all, only by Stevens' dubious and romantic assumption that men share the community of imagination, and that by entering our own unique self we might abstract back to a common self of humanity. Indeed, this is the assumption (developed as early as the subman of "Owl's Clover") on which Stevens' romantic humanism rests most precariously. In other words, Stevens inverts Plato, as he always had, finding the paradigm of things in the mind. This, it seems to me, is the discovery of "A Primitive Like an Orb" (CP 440): that although we conceive of the ultimate as lying at the end of our search for reality, it resides instead at the beginning, "a nature to its natives all/ Beneficence." "The essential poem begets the others." It is the source rather than the sum of our finite poems, those forms in which we "espouse" the world. And it is this source (wholly human) we seek when we ask questions of the origin and end of things.

In "Imago," one of the minor poems of *The Auroras of Autumn,* Stevens conceives of the imagination as a child who is father of the man. In the poems of "The Rock" and in several posthumously published poems, the figure of the child, "asleep in its own life," appears regularly as the image of the primal creative urge—a variation of the ephebe and the ignorant man, but now a purer abstraction of the mind itself. The poet of "The Irish Cliffs of Moher" (CP 501) seeks his father in this world, the parent before thought, at the head of the past; and in "Long and Sluggish Lines" (CP 522), he seeks the "pre-personae" he was seventy years ago. To recapture the past, even as Marcel Proust sought, is at once impossible and inevitable; for the struggle is to find what one is as a pure being, rather than the composite of thoughts and memories and masks one has come to be. The ultimate expression of this is in "The Sail of Ulysses" (OP 99). Hungering for knowledge, it begins, the mind is a figurative Ulysses sailing a sea of symbols that is itself. But the mind desires more than the "litter of truths," desires to go "behind the symbols/ To that which they symbolized," to destroy the ancient symbols of old imaginings by way of attaining an essential truth. The meditation attempts just that: to peel away the formal layers of the world in the mind in search of a "new knowledge" of reality:

> Master of the world and of himself,
> He came to this by knowledge or
> Will come. His mind presents the world
> And in his mind the world revolves.

Seeking a "life beyond this present knowing," in some "distant away," Ulysses discovers it is "not to be reached but to be known." That is, it is contained in the mind:

> In the generations of thought, man's sons
> And heirs are powers of the mind,
> His only testament and estate.
> He has nothing but the truth to leave.
> How then shall the mind be less than free
> Since only to know is to be free?

Hence, in seeking the "sibyl" of reality, he seeks the "sibyl of the self,"

> The self as sibyl, whose diamond,
> Whose chiefest embracing of all wealth
> Is poverty, whose jewel found
> At the exactest central of the earth
> Is need.

The sibyl is that within man which generates knowledge, and hence precedes forms. The sibyl's shape is a "blind thing fumbling for its form," like a child asleep in its own life. And the forms issuing from her—like our poems of reality, or metaphors—though destitute and lame are all we have in our poverty. They are "categories of bleak necessity," our own creations of the world, and children of the sibyl who lives mysteriously within us.

In the image of the sibyl, and the child asleep in its own life, Stevens had peeled away reality as far as a poem could, peeled it back to the ultimate, to the paradigm of forms which precede the forms of our knowing. "Since knowing/ And being are one," as a related poem puts it, "—the right to know/ Is equal to the right to be" (OP 106). The unremitting abstractions of *The Auroras of Autumn,* I submit, are the results not of Stevens' forcing ideas or theories into verse, but of a meditative activity of the mind submitting itself to extensive abstraction. It is a poetry which derives almost wholly from propositions common to Stevens' earlier poems. Yet the purpose here is not, as in, say, "Notes," to evolve an idea. Rather it is to catch the activity of mind as it creates and dissolves (decreates) ideas or forms, creating others in the same process. This was the life of the mind, the "never-ending meditation"

(CP 465), and he came to accept it, for better or worse, as what men of imagination do every instant, as well as in formal poems.

The explicit example of this intention is the title poem, especially sections two, three, and four, which begin, "Farewell to an idea." For not only does the mind in its creative activity produce forms, it creates them out of the death of previous forms. The life of the mind is a perpetual (and self-perpetuating) process, issuing in poems that are to the ultimate poem what man's knowledge (forms) is to the child's innocence (first idea). This is to say, Stevens conceives of the life of meditation as at once a continuous act of self-creation and a struggle to achieve, to know, the ultimate ground of this self. Inevitably, the life we live in poetry, in that it is life itself, will return to this ultimate point—in death. But this is to see Stevens' theory as a fixed philosophical conception of life. The poems themselves exist in that mid-region of consciousness; in the act of seeking the origin and end of reality, we really seek "what will suffice." But not just for one self. The strict impersonality of these poems suggests that they come from a representative mind. And this is clearly Stevens' intention, his way out of solipsism and his modern answer to Emerson.

It is no wonder that *The Auroras of Autumn* earned so little approbation. For they are at once poems in the ordinary sense—thus, poems based on propositions or ideas of a commonplace and often self-contradictory nature—and poems which attempt to extend the boundaries of poetry in a way Proust and Joyce extended the novel form. They plunge into the self, into the mind, in search of man's root being, since reality begins in man rather than he in it. In this regard, as experimental poems going as far as they can, they do not need our approval; history may give or deny that as it wishes. But future critics must certainly ask if Stevens' attempt to establish poetry as the elementary experience of all our lives does not in the end damage his own poems, as well as make the poems themselves so esoteric or abstract as to be of no consequence to readers of poetry. Yet it is wrong to conclude that this apology is the dry, academic argument. Their true quality lies rather in the texture of meditations which, if not altogether satisfactory to our present tastes in poetry, deserve our consideration.

The distinct differences between *The Auroras of Autumn* and the poetry of "The Rock," I believe, are to be understood only in regard to what Stevens achieved in the earlier volume. The passion for life, the sense of human presence in these last poems, is the reward of discovering how far the mind can go, and thus its limits. There are two kinds of poems in "The Rock": poems like the earlier ones, intent on pushing beyond symbol to the very rock of reality itself; and poems which elucidate the human limits within which this desire is to be realized and embrace these limits with humility and dignity. The calm preparations for death, the negative capability of these poems, give the impression that Stevens had finally discarded the pastiche of ideas that had preoccupied him since the thirties. It is rather, I think, that he had finally satisfied himself that "God and the imagination are one" (CP 524), and thus that whatever is created, or whatever is believed, is man's making. Like Whitehead's God, Stevens' is immanent and primordial, but in man rather than nature. It is the child of the self. Having affirmed this, he could return to a meditative poetry which did not have to apologize for being poetry or self-consciously parade its "theory of life." His poems of the last years evince the composure of one like Santayana who, accepting his humanity, was ready to realize what he could within it. Stevens came back to the world as it is, even though he lived in the world of the mind. He would be content, as he puts it in "Prologues to What Is Possible," simply to be, and explore that being:

What self, for example, did he contain that had not yet been loosed,
Snarling in him for discovery as his attentions spread,
As if all his hereditary lights were suddenly increased
By an access of color, a new and unobserved, slight dithering,
The smallest lamp, which added its puissant flick, to which he gave
A name and privilege over the ordinary of his commonplace—
A flick which added to what was real and its vocabulary,
The way some first thing coming into Northern trees
Adds to them the whole vocabulary of the South,
The way the earliest single light in the evening sky, in spring,
Creates a fresh universe out of nothingness by adding itself,
The way a look or a touch reveals its unexpected magnitudes. (CP 516–17)

II

The Auroras of Autumn, like the preceding volume, is dominated by long poems, at once more obscure and more naturally meditations than the earlier ones. Even within the impersonal tone, a mind who has come flush upon the naked threshold of winter and life's final questions speaks with a tremor of personal uncertainty. The themes are what they always had been: the imagination and death, and the inevitable search for some final order or knowledge. But summer having given way to autumn, there follows a similar denuding of style. The tensions allow less freedom of imagination and produce the *frisson* of mortality. The self, as one poem meditates the problem, needs a "mythology of modern death" to redeem the loss of a traditional immortality (CP 435). The poetry of the final years is dedicated to this mythology which denies mythology; moreover, it is another phase in the imagination's resistance of chaos—the chaos of unbelief—before the self gives up to the dominant rock.

There is a relaxation of argument and a return to a dramatic mode of sorts—a drama, however, of the mind examining itself, exploring its own wealth of memories. "What We See Is What We Think" (CP 459) reflects this compressed life in compressed metaphors:

> At twelve, the disintegration of afternoon
> Began, the return to phantomerei, if not
> To phantoms. Till then, it had been the other way . . .

In the morning of youth the physical is primary; at noon, secondary; and the "first gray second after," only a form in the mind. The quality of changing images describes a progressive internalization of experience: his once vivid blue and green world gradually becomes "dog-eared," a "tawny caricature and tawny life." Experience changes to thought and memory, "since what we think is never what we see." This concluding line inverts the title as process inverts things and imagination trans-values perception. Stevens' resolutions, understandably, are not to console but to confirm poetry's undeniable place in human experience, as a stay against disintegration. Thinking about what it is to think becomes a creative activity in its own right, a recreating of the fragments of the mind into a world. The act is informal meditation. Thus the "Large Red Man Reading" (CP 423), the poet grown large in his vatic role, humanizing the "coiled thorn" of reality:

> *Poesis, poesis,* the literal characters, the vatic lines,
> Which in those ears and in those thin, those spended hearts,
> Took on color, took on shape and the size of things as they are
> And spoke the feeling for them, which was what they had lacked.

In *Parts of a World* and *Transport to Summer,* Stevens regularly commemorates the world of words and the poet's realm of metaphor which he sets against the inhuman whirl. In *Auroras,* however, even the mediate forms of poetry are suspect, form standing between self and thing. Stevens is bemused by his abiding preoccupation with a theory of poetry; yet he is consciously dedicated to making his theory into poetry, by way of making poetry once more the natural rather than special analogue of experience. Even in "A Primitive Like an Orb," which is explicitly about the discoveries of poetry, the creations of metaphor are seen in experiential and almost religious terms, as a "difficult apperception," an espousal, a discovery—and thus a measuring of the imagination's capacity for discovery. And in "An Ordinary Evening in New Haven," the products of meditation are not the ideas as such but the pleasures of turning ideas over and over in the mind, until one grasps the "satisfaction underneath the sense" (CP 448). Metaphor comes to be a more natural vehicle (and tenor) of man's thinking and feeling about the world, the poem constantly becoming, moment by moment, in the mind: ". . . letters, prophecies, perceptions, clods/ Of color," in short, structures of feeling with the import of life (CP 443). But then again, these very structures miss the mark, the thing itself. The abyss between the "I" and its object is the realm of poetry, that bridge, as Stevens once put it, between "fact and miracle" (OP 232). Discovering the world to be fictive, man may will to know it absolutely, to know the ultimate poem. And willing this, he knows that he wills to know an abstraction. Thus the paradox of that bemusing exercise, "The Ultimate Poem Is Abstract" (CP 429). Wishing to know beyond categories, to know more than questions can pose, the poet conceives the ultimate Abstraction—another first idea—but only to remind himself that one cannot both know it and know of it. There is a knowledge—a knowing—in poetry's "enormous sense," in which to know is to be:

> It would be enough
> If we were ever, just once, at the middle, fixed
> In This Beautiful World Of Ours and not as now,
> Helplessly at the edge, enough to be
> Complete, because at the middle, if only in sense,
> And in that enormous sense, merely enjoy. (CP 430)

The man of imagination, however, is aware that the center to which he aspires is not to be reached at will. The forced penetrations of metaphor, like those of reason, do not in the end suffice, and the poet desires a certainty beyond metaphor:

> Our sense of these things changes and they change,
> Not as in metaphor, but in our sense
> Of them. So sense exceeds all metaphor. (CP 431)

Seeking a truth "far beyond the rhetorician's touch," Stevens has gone one step beyond the symbolic formula of "Description without Place" with its embrace of a world of words. The self not the word becomes mediate; that is, it becomes the container of the real—the "mind." The efficacy of meditation is its release of the mind from preconception. It touches the emotions which language cannot adequately speak; it manifests, that is, not only the form but also the process of feeling. It reaches to the heart of being.

This discrepancy between the literal propositions and the contexts which absorb them is perplexing. Repetitions of an idea seem to produce a new one, but this is not the purpose. The expressed concern with a theory of poetry is not so different from the world of *Transport to Summer,* but there are fewer pieces like "So-and-So Reclining on Her Couch" with its academic posturing. There is also less humor, less verbal sport. Poems like "Saint John and the Back-Ache," "Reply to Papini," "Puella Parvula," "Imago," and "Angel Surrounded by Paysans"—with its celebrated "necessary angel" passage—say much the same thing as the earlier poetry, but with much less urgency and with an awareness that the saying and not the thing said is the life of the poem. This is a religious poetry, and like the earlier verse it mocks religious forms even as it promotes its own secular belief. Who but Stevens would have thought of a dialogue between Saint John and the Back-Ache (CP 436)? Or who would have thought of discovering one's sainthood in his backache? which is to say, one's sanctity of self acutely present in his pain of self-awareness? It is Stevens' old theme, humorously realized, but the plea for imagination is most serious: the imagination whose illustrations "help us to face the dumbfoundering abyss/ Between us and the object."

Similarly "Reply to Papini" (CP 446), which begins with an epigraph from a papal letter denouncing poetry as escapism, and develops as an aggressive defense of the poet's dream as opposed to the Pope's: "The way through the world/ Is more difficult to find than the way beyond it." That way through the world is the life of poetry, a life vigorously earned, realized in a poem which tells us a great deal about Stevens' investment in his one belief:

> The poet does not speak in ruins [like the Pope]
> Nor stand there making orotund consolations.
> He shares the confusions of intelligence.
> Giovanni Papini, by your faith, know how
> He wishes that all hard poetry were true.

There are no orotund consolations either in Stevens' facing the conse-quences of his choice: for to decry the authority of ruins (with Emerson and Whitman?) is to accept one's own fate, in a hard poetry that may or may not be true, but undeniably *is*. In this two-part poem, Stevens achieves the expected resolution, but one fully earned because he has accepted the human measure as "a pastoral of endurance and of death." Refuting the Pope's forms, the poet refuses to substitute his own— asserting instead the never-ending search for any final truth: "the poem, the growth of the mind/ Of the world, the heroic effort to live expressed/ As victory."

"Angel Surrounded by Paysans" (CP 496) is a revealing example of this "poem," since it shows how perception becomes contemplation and hence the growth of the mind. Samuel French Morse has written in at least two places of its history of composition: beginning with Stevens' purchase of a Tal Coat still-life which he entitled after some musing, "Angel Surrounded by Peasants," because of the formal position in the picture of a Venetian glass bowl surrounded by several smaller glasses and bottles.[4] Finally Stevens abstracted his imaginings about the picture into a poem, one line of which was to become the title for his book of essays. Now, the "necessary angel" of the central line is at once an obvious and cryptic figure, an angel of reality and the necessary angel of earth. He is the poet as major man, an abstraction of the creative self: the angel is "one of you and being one of you/ Is being and knowing what I am and know":

> Yet I am the necessary angel of earth,
> Since, in my sight, you see the earth again,
> Cleared of its stiff and stubborn, man-locked set,
> And, in my hearing, you hear its tragic drone . . .

The angel is reality, that which speaks from beneath our man-locked forms. This is a center, the bowl without which the arrangement of glasses is formless. Thus the "necessary" angel—and the recurrent necessity for imagination which has come at last to be the measure of man's identity, the angel of reality, "a man/ Of the mind." But it is not the statement that is the poem. It is the poet's discovery—by process of contemplation—of his own angel.

The tableau of the painting is an image of essential opposites flowing into unity or form, at the center of the self, the mind. In other poems form flows into motions of the mind, as in those meditations dedicated more than nominally to autumn, that season of life when the vanishings of the physical weigh heavily upon the imagination. The result is a poetry, in the words of Stevens' Saint John, which "speak[s] below/ The tension of the lyre" (CP 437), a poetry at once too casual and too oblique. The poet seems less intent on making poems than on living within their forms—like Hans in "Page from a Tale" (CP 421), who weaves the nostalgic autumn tones of Yeats's "Lake Isle of Innisfree" through the frigid winter of his discontent, at once mocking Yeats's romantic wish and taking warmth from it. It makes for a rather private meditation in which Stevens' familiar themes collapse into an almost purely subjective rumination.

"The Auroras of Autumn" (CP 411) is a major case in point: bafflingly obscure in some of its parts, clearly Stevensian in its arresting style, as if style itself had come to suffice. It is a meditation of a mind upon itself, and thereby an act in Valéry's sense of self-reconstruction. An extreme example of Stevens' meditative style, "Auroras" is a signal instance of rhetorical poetry in which the rhetoric is directed inward rather than outward. The reader overhears rather than hears. Each of the ten poems examines a theme established in the opening lines: the search for the center of the self. Otherwise, the meditations pursue their diverse ways, sometimes creating a kind of internal counterpoint and synthesis as in poems three, four, and five. But just as one should not look for logical continuity in contemplation, he should not be surprised to find extremely personal adaptations of traditional ideas. For resolution lies in the act of contemplation itself, in an argument which like a wave progresses in rhythm but not in substance.

The poem in embryo, it seems to me, lies in the opening two stanzas:

> This is where the serpent lives, the bodiless.
> His head is air. Beneath his tip at night
> Eyes open and fix on us in every sky.
> Or is this another wriggling out of the egg,
> Another image at the end of the cave,
> Another bodiless for the body's slough?

The place, our fallen world: the imperfect paradise where the serpent-spirit of time enacts his incessant cycle. But more exactly, that place is the mind, is consciousness itself: the auroras suggesting our sense of a reality always beyond, an ultimate formlessness. Two traditional figures pose the inevitable question of *being,* that dilemma of the finite self expelled organically from the womb of nature into the consciousness of Plato's cave. The accumulation of meanings around these tropes controls the meditative maunderings, thoughts of a personal autumn about ultimate questions. The serpent, though, is shorn of his Calvinism, and of his Platonism, and given back to us as the way things are, as pure temporality, a world in which we live in "the body's slough" and desire transcendence:

> This [consciousness] is form gulping after formlessness,
> Skin flashing to wished-for disappearances
> And the serpent body flashing without the skin.

The tension between physical and metaphysical is as prepossessing as the idea of death; the constant of the serpent's world is change. In the concluding stanzas of this opening poem, man and serpent blend into the figure of the imperfect self seeking (meditating) meaning in its own imperfection.

The second meditation picks up the critical question explicitly in terms of aging man, trapped in flux and yearning for order. It begins, as do the two succeeding poems, with a sonorous acceptance, "Farewell to an idea"—possibly, as Donald Davie has suggested,[5] to summer's fiction, or to the illusion of a perpetually vital world, perhaps even to the idea of life itself, that great fiction. But more likely, it is farewell to form, acceptance of the discovery that the mind's ideas are never final and that each act of the mind kills (decreates) the previous form. Whatever, the poem is a process all its own, like the flashing boreal dawn. A progression of sharply defined images records the seasonal change which returns man once more to his last form, to the barrenness of things without spring's passionate nudity or summer's formal dress. There is nostalgia certainly, but also a vital form evident in the private meditation which moves through precise images gathering into metaphor, into form:

> The season changes. A cold wind chills the beach.
> The long lines of it grow longer, emptier,
> A darkness gathers though it does not fall
> And the whiteness grows less vivid on the wall.
> The man who is walking turns blankly on the sand.
> He observes how the north is always enlarging the change . . .

The auroras portend a last great change, and for man a polar solitude in a world no longer blue with his own light, but blue-red and polar green in the consuming mixture of death: "The color of ice and fire and solitude."

The next three poems manifest a deepening obscurity as the poet's reflections sink more deeply into the private self, each arising as it does out of the other, out of the farewell to idea. The three as a group—bound by the mother-father metaphor—are almost wrigglings out of that earlier "egg," possibly another of Plato's tropes, the mother and father suggesting respectively the subjective and objective self. Or perhaps in the allegory suggested very early, they represent the purpose of the poem (the mother) and its form (the father, who in poem four "sits/ In space"). The possibilities are extraordinary, and bewildering. Recalling Plato's severed egg, the mother and father are divided into time, like the self which must mend itself in poetry. In any event, we have in these three poems a vigorously compressed metaphor for the meditative life of the aging man, in which the poem (the uniting of mother and father) comes to stand for man's last heroic efforts to resolve his own separation from nature, to realize the experience of "form gulping after formlessness." Hence, the mother, like the imagination, and the father, like the world of change to which that imagination is married—he "measures the velocities of change" (iv)—are conjoined in poem five in a theatrical ritual, a "festival" harboring a "tragedy." This autumn activity modulates into a drama, in which the poet muses upon the texture of process. He meditates not his past history but the present making of a self, the very self that in poem two has come upon the throes of its mortal nature: "We stand," one central line has it, "in the tumult of a festival," but a festival of the mind in which "there are no lines to speak," because there is "no play." One lives the drama "merely by being here."

The obscurity is somewhat clarified in poem six, in which the mind views itself (projected upon the world, like the auroras) as a "theatre floating through the clouds," where nature dramatizes the patterns of change, the unity within natural diversity. The mind interposes itself upon flux and gives it those "half-thought-of forms" by which we endure:

> This is nothing until in a single man contained,
> Nothing until this named thing nameless is,
> And is destroyed.

Creation as decreation, the world taking on identity even as it loses its singularity in the single man—this is an old theme, but here renewed in the humility of one who has learned that the small light of man's "one candle" does not finally mute the enlarging changes: "And he feels afraid," with a Pascalian fear. (For a most significant prose gloss on the poetics of decreation, see NA 174–75, and again NA 169, for the role of the "single man.")

The remainder of the poem contends with this fear, by elevating the single man: asking first the questions of the aging ego who wills the imagination to be a god "enthroned" (vii), who desires a "time of innocence/ As pure principle" and finds it only in his own envisioning of what "should be" (viii):

> It is like a thing of ether that exists
> Almost as predicate. But it exists,
> It exists, it is visible, it is, it is.

The "frigid brilliances" of the auroral North in poem two no longer accentuate the changes; the "symbol of malice" is muted in a world of innocence. The plea for innocence, for a world of pure time outside the matrix of space, is for a total knowledge of reality, the reality of a contemplative moment, in which feeling is knowledge freed at last from Adam's curse (ix). Poem eight wills this time of innocence; and nine brings it to bear as an act of meditating purely, like the children of poem eight. (The child of the mind again, "asleep in its own life.") Nine is especially complex, for it toys obscurely with an idea of innocence as a vision which can look through change to permanence, while in the background there appears the faintest image of the "disaster" of innocence: "Shall we be found hanging in the trees next spring?"

The dialectical conclusion returns the meditation to Stevens' more familiar style, an argument that ends by accepting man's fate of being an "unhappy people in a happy world," imperfect man living with a nature which is, in and for itself, a perfection:

> In these unhappy he meditates a whole,
> The full of fortune and the full of fate,
> As if he lived all lives . . .

The poet thus reunites the mother and father by "meditating a whole," by "contriving balance"—in "Notes," one recalls, he had celebrated "not balances/ That we achieve but balances that happen" (CP 386). And "fulfilling his meditations" in "hall harridan," this autumnal world buffeted by "a haggling of wind and weather," he comes to momentary terms with the portentous lights of the North. Assuming to live "all lives," Stevens has thrust himself once more beneath his unique nature into an assumed common self, beyond which is the verging nothingness of death.

The difficulties of Stevens' late style are never more evident than in "The Auroras of Autumn." The evenness of tone is lulling; meaning gives way to private nuance, and frequent neologisms resist communication. The effect, of course, is calculated. Rhetoric becomes a mood rather than a statement, as the process of meditation transcends the decorums of ordinary poetic discourse. Rational content is largely forfeited, not for pure effect but to accentuate the quality of the mental act itself. The style of meditation, rather than reducing the flow of reality to form, tries to catch the sense of that flow, as "contained" in a single man. Whether or not Stevens has sacrificed too much for too little must be left to the reader. It is apparent that "Auroras" is easily available only to those well versed in Stevens' manner, if it is at all available. There are moments of intense feeling in this poetry, but there is also an indifferent opaqueness in the mind's involuted motions, a symbolistic quality of pure evocation—though the purpose is to contain the world, not transcend it. This kind of poetry always takes the risk of repeating itself, or blunting its impact in private nuance. It is a poetry which refuses to reveal itself without intensive and repeated perusal, and even then hardly rewards the effort.

One is left at last—until we know more about Stevens—with the poem as an immense presence, as a power struggling within the single man who is trying to make the most of his "unhappy people" (is unhappiness synonymous with consciousness?) in a "happy world," even if that happy world is a "hall harridan." One recalls "Esthétique du Mal." It is difficult to be certain where the self obtains in these meditations, but it is doubtless in the imagination's heroic engagement of first problems, in the anxious struggle to compose itself by simply verifying its own ability to think, and *be*. Coming once more upon the immense presence of death, more stark now than the "mother of beauty," Stevens is pressed to define a self that consciously bears within it the presence of its own nothingness. "The Owl in the Sarcophagus" (CP 431) is a significant poem here, in which Stevens meditates the central of his being, at the core of which is a rudimentary darkness demanding mythological light: which is to say, demanding to be contained in some form.

"The Owl in the Sarcophagus" is a parable of the mind's war with its own nature, a contemplative exercise which verifies and mocks the mythological imagination and the soothing personae it has created as a stay against mortality. The movement from the opening poem of the series, in which the bare idea of death is softened in the personification of its manifest characteristics (forms of rest), to the understanding of these images as analogous to forms of vital experience, completes the circle of the imaginative man's questioning. Death seen in the masculine images of sleep and peace, "Two Brothers," and in the mysterious "third form," as the "mother of us all," provides us (as it has traditionally served man) with a mythological preview that is comprehensible and not terrifying; but more than anything else, death is conceived in "forms" which naturalize it, satisfying the human need to dominate its fate. The habits of contemplation mythologize death by placing it within the mysterious pulsations of life, discovering, as had Yeats, that "man has created death," [6] because he has created time and hence has some need to dominate it.

The poem is a progressive meditation on this theme. Sleep and peace are the two immediate analogies of death within life: the masculine, or objective and vital, features which we understand as revivifying pauses within life's grammar, forms that are "visible to the eye that needs." But the "third form" is the mystery of death itself, the "syllable between life//And death." The meditation opens out in poem two from the enigma of these images which enfold "the ultimate intellect," forms of our knowledge molded to a "likeness of the earth." In our mind, death's forms are only conceivable as life's forms, the ultimate sleep, the ultimate peace:

> This is that figure stationed at our end,
> Always, in brilliance, fatal, final, formed
> Out of our lives to keep us in our death . . . (iv)

Sleep and peace—"Sleep realized" is an "ultimate intellect" (and a kind of death in the sense that it releases us, even as it did the Canon Aspirin, into knowledge beyond thought); and peace is our vision of form beyond process, the ultimate reality. But death as metaphor is only proximate, like the old mythologies; there remains the haunting *femme fatale* of the thing itself, "an influence felt instead of seen," an ominous, sublime presence which personification does not quite reach, who holds "men closely with discovery." She is that spouse in the deepest heart of the self with which the self is married; she is creative even as she is destructive, for she is the force that drives us to poetry, to seek the ultimate form.

Therefore, the poet discovers that his mythology of modern death, if only fictive, is a way of seeing something that cannot be seen yet must be. Bearing death in our life, we create the mythology of modern death in the poetry of merely living:

> Compounded and compounded, life by life,
> These are death's own supremest images,
> The pure perfections of parental space,

> The children of a desire that is the will,
> Even of death, the beings of the mind
> In the light-bound space of the mind . . .

Death is not transcended but contained, reincarnated within the human as the "creature" of the mind's making—for the mind like the child "sings itself to sleep" by its own creativity, its own mythmaking. No longer the mother of beauty, death in us confirms man as sole creator of the world in which he lives—the mind. Having created a mythology of modern death, we discover that we have created death, the knowledge of death as it lives in us.

The Auroras of Autumn is a volume of many things, of meditations provoked by the drop of an idea, a memory, a casual visit: a letter perhaps from José Rodríguez-Feo, correspondence with the Irish poet Tom McGreevy, an old papal letter, a still-life, the thought of death. It is all summed up in that loose-jointed, long meditation "An Ordinary Evening in New Haven," to which I will return later. *Auroras* clearly is a volume not so remarkable in its parts as in its total conception, in its majesty of tone and its orderly, confident processes. Which is to say, its strengths are likewise its weaknesses, as becomes most irritatingly obvious in the lulling repetitions and deliberate abstractness. Yet it is a poetry which talks of things, of ordinary and extraordinary things, of never-ending things and death, and at last proclaims:

> High poetry and low:
> Experience in perihelion
> Or in the penumbra of summer night—
> The solemn sentences,
> Like interior intonations,
> The speech of truth in its true solitude,
> A nature that is created in what it says,
> The peace of the last intelligence . . . (CP 490)

These are "Things of August," but really things of a time later than August. And the Stevens who composed "The Owl in the Sarcophagus," who had with all confidence come upon the discovery that as author of the life of the mind he must be author not only of the idea of death but of its mythology, had become fully aware that the time of farewell was upon him. To this end he had yet a few things to say: the *"summarium in excelsis* begins."

III

"The Rock" is an appropriately titled group of poems: *multum in parvo,* sharply etched in Stevens' personal style, stoic and tough in the face of age's pressing questions, yet tender and knowing. These poems do not depart so much from the themes of *Auroras* as critics have maintained, but rather return those themes to the intimately personal, or to as much of the personal as Stevens will allow: "Poetry is not personal" (OP 159) he once wrote, and then promptly wrote in an essay that it had to be, that it was an "indirect egotism." Mind and sky square off for one last combat, seeking the marriage of self and rock in an utterance of "fixed accord." What poetry aspires to reach in reaching beyond itself, Stevens discovers, is ironically the silence of death, the complete reconciliation of self and otherness. The section, seen as a unit, is a carefully planned farewell, what one poem describes as a "turning down toward finality" (CP 506). Preparing for his farewell, Stevens seems to come back to the intense love of the physical world that was his starting point.

As symbol the "rock" owes its origin to Stevens' desire to know the ground of things, and it may well be, as Roy Harvey Pearce maintains, the postulate of that reality "within or beneath" the surface of things, the *Ding an sich.*[7] But the rock, if a more substantial symbol than the first idea or ultimate poem, is not easily defined, nor its meaning for Stevens easily isolated. The rock, indeed, is a synthetic term, at once abstract and changing, symbolic yet vital, even I suppose in the Coleridgean (not to say the Bergsonian) sense of the *vital.* One of its aspects is the world, the world in and of itself, beyond the self—the physical in all its barren physicality. One of Stevens' favorite metaphors for the poet's life—one he was happy enough to quote later in his brief "Introduction" to *The Necessary Angel*—has to do with what he calls the "poetic act" as "an illumination of a surface, the movement of a self in the rock" (OP 241). Earlier in this essay, a short address given at Bard College in 1948, Stevens distinguished between imagination and reality in terms which might appear uncharacteristic of him:

Ordinarily the poet is associated with the word, not with the act; and ordinarily the word collects its strength from the imagination or, with its aid, from reality. The poet finds that as between these two sources: the imagination and reality, the imagination is false, whatever else may be said of it, and reality is true; and being concerned that poetry should be a thing of vital and virile importance, he commits himself to reality, which then becomes his inescapable and ever-present difficulty and inamorata. In any event, he has lost nothing; for the imagination, while it might have led him to purities beyond definition, never yet progressed except by particulars. (OP 240–41)

Cryptic as it may be, the passage is without question a repudiation of transcendence. It attaches the self to a rock that is physical before it is metaphysical, as in "Credences of Summer." Later, in one of his last addresses, he was to commit the poet to the world of Darwin, and deny him the world of Plato (OP 246). The rock, from its early appearance in *Ideas of Order* and "The Man with the Blue Guitar" through "Credences of Summer" and "An Ordinary Evening in New Haven" to the title poem of "The Rock," served a whole range of meanings from physical to metaphysical reality, from things as they are to the thing itself. Perhaps it owes something to Henri Focillon's metaphor, quoted by Stevens in "The Figure of the Youth as Virile Poet": "the living rock of some subterranean world" (NA 49), which is to say, of the poet's interior world.[8] Equally possible is Thoreau's "rock" of reality in *Walden:*

Let us settle ourselves, and work and wedge our feet downward through the mud and slush of opinion, and prejudice, and tradition, and delusion, and appearance, that alluvion which covers the globe . . . through church and state, through poetry and philosophy and religion, till we come to a hard bottom and rocks in place, which we can call *reality,* and say, This is, and no mistake; and then begin, having a *point d'appui,* below freshet and frost and fire, a place where you might found a wall or a state . . . not a Nilometer, but a Realometer. . . . Be it life or death, we crave only reality.[9]

Stevens' rock is not exactly the biblical rock of Moses, which gives forth the living waters, though it may borrow from that vital source;[10] still less is it Eliot's symbol, though it may owe its origin to an antipathy for Eliot's negation of the physical. If Stevens sees the poet as less divinely sustained than Moses, however, he sees him as one who must strike the rock and find the fountain of reality. In his Bard College address, he talks of the poet's constant engagement with life as "that miracle." Entitling the final section of his *Collected Poems* "The Rock," Stevens points to the centrality of its title poem, and to what he enunciates there as the necessity for man's "night hymns" to the "rock." The rock is that in which man must dwell, the inclusive world of thing and idea which harbors the self, and paradoxically, which the self harbors.

The striking difference between "The Rock" and *Auroras* is the increasing detachment yet emotional intensification of the former, as if Stevens had escaped from the dangers of sentimentality by holding his life in review at a metaphorical distance. His two worlds, of fact and idea, are never confused, nor ultimately fused. "The self and the earth— your thoughts, your feelings,/ Your beliefs and disbeliefs, your whole peculiar plot" (CP 501)—thus the initial poem, in which the two worlds are humanized in the sleep, or in pure being, of an "old man," who like the child is now wholly self-contained. Continuing to seek the union of the two, and thus to come upon the rock in its purest form, Stevens veritably submits his memory to the probings of imagination, arriving at last at some tentative composure. The *summa* poem of these last years, published posthumously, is "As You Leave the Room."[11] Another, less a summary of a life in poetry than an apology, is "The Planet on the Table." And in each the same kind of calm presents itself, as if Stevens has achieved that *"rêve permanent"* of meditation described by Georges Enesco, which serves as an epigraph to "The World as Meditation." Yet the one constant quality of these poems is their effect in modulating talk about the ultimate, the central, the rock, into a consummate example of how imagination actively thrives on its own creations, how the self comes to live in itself: growing, creating, and consuming itself.

Looking backward, Stevens looks not at the past so much as into the reservoir of mind—that comprehensive ego of the poet who can speak for all men—where he has been before; and the rhetoric of the earlier poems resolves itself quite naturally into the grammar of the contemplative mode. To compare a poem like "St. Armorer's Church from the Outside" (CP 529) with the very early "A High-Toned Old Christian Woman" reveals dramatically how far he has come in welding the circle. No longer defensive, nor urged self-consciously to taunt his antagonists with derisive irony, Stevens can still mock eloquently the promises of old forms, the puerile attempt to fix life in a timeless state:

St. Armorer's has nothing of this present.
This *vif*, this dizzle-dazzle of being new
And of becoming, for which the chapel spreads out
Its arches in its vivid element. . . .

Once an "immense success" (ironically), it is dead because it has denied
the "need of each generation to be itself," the need "to be actual" in a
world that is "always beginning, over and over." Repetition, not transcendence, is Stevens' cosmic prophecy: the "dizzle-dazzle of being new/ And
of becoming." The poet, standing outside, has his being within himself
and his becoming.

St. Armorer's decay repudiates once more the nostalgias, and all forms
which disallow "beginning, over and over." In "Conversation With Three
Women of New England" (OP 108), an excellent rhetorical piece written
probably too late for inclusion in the *Collected Poems,* Stevens outlines
this world without dogma, in which "the mode of the person becomes
the mode of the world." In the poet's overarching view, each of his three
women creates a perfectly acceptable world: the first, the traditional religious cosmos with a "single source" as origin and center; the second, a
naturalistic world in which things of the mind are shaped by things of
the world; and the third, the humanist world in which there are only
"man's definitions of himself." The poet is not dogmatic; he accepts all
truths as relative and the three worlds become one, not as an ideology
but in the compelling "proof" that the world can sustain all definitions,
all imaginings, because it is an imagined world:

> In which one of these three worlds are the four of us
> The most at home? Or is it enough to have seen
> And felt and known the differences we have seen
> And felt and known in the colors in which we live,
>
>   . . . . . .
>   —enough to realize
> That the sense of being changes as we talk,
> That talk shifts the cycle of the scenes of kings?

Is this not another of those condensed histories of man's belief, from
a world of Christianity to naturalism to "existentialism"? If so, however,
the poet's world is existential in the special sense of the self-creation of
mind. It is, as a title suggests, "The World as Meditation" (CP 520), in

which desire is satisfied only by knowing the proximate, never the ultimate, satisfaction, like Penelope waiting for a Ulysses and finding satisfaction in the thought rather than the fact of his coming.[12] Ulysses is the sun (the male, vital, life principle) which brings only its own presence, the essential source which the self must espouse even by proxy. He is that ever-changing thing itself for which the one longs from across the abyss of consciousness:

> She would talk a little to herself as she combed her hair,
> Repeating his name with its patient syllables,
> Never forgetting him that kept coming constantly so near.

Here, meditation effects its own reunion, or almost so; Penelope-imagination knows, however, that her "companion" is a paramour coming "constantly so near" but never to consummation. The act rather than the end of meditation becomes the mode of being for a poet come to the end of his quest for reality.

There are a number of superb considerations of this possible "world" of meditation in the volume, and the titles are occasionally as revealing as the poems: "The Poem that Took the Place of a Mountain"; "Two Illustrations That the World Is What You Make of It"; "Prologues to What Is Possible"; "Looking across the Fields and Watching the Birds Fly"; "Long and Sluggish Lines"; "Final Soliloquy of the Interior Paramour"; and, of course, that consummate eulogy for Santayana, "To an Old Philosopher in Rome." The title piece itself elaborates this compulsive need to mitigate the harshness of the rock, to embellish it with feeling, to create a poetic "icon" even when that icon is not the thing itself. In a variety of metaphors, Stevens explores the projected landscape of his meditative world and discovers once again the old truth that a truly human paradise is born in the imperfect:

> We think, then, as the sun shines or does not.
> We think as the wind skitters on a pond in a field.
>   . . . . . .
> The spirit comes from the body of the world,
>   . . . the body of a world
> Whose blunt laws make an affectation of mind. (CP 518–19)

This last stanza is pure Santayana. The poet's second world is a configuration of "hypotheses," created by the "puissant flick" of his imagination which gives "name and privilege over the ordinary of his commonplace" (CP 516, 517). Stevens' metaphors add up to one conclusion, the ultimate discovery of his aesthetic: "We say God and the imagination are one" (CP 524). After that, after having proved the self as self-creator, there is nothing left but to live out the paradox that creation is a process implying its own end.

There is assurance and serenity in these poems, and it is confidently reflected in the style. Long rhetorical periods flow easily into the aphorisms on which Stevens came to rely more and more in his late poetry. The meditative style fosters aphorism; contemplation encircles abstraction until it has distilled out some form, the form that is the act of contemplation itself. The rhetoric of meditation moves deliberately under the imagination's discipline toward the axiomatic truths inherent in the pleasures of merely thinking. The surface of this poetry, if not tendentious, is dangerously platitudinous, and tempts the poet to unearned wisdoms.[13] Yet, it should be obvious that the discovery of aphoristic truths is not the mind's goal, that there are few surprises in those pockets of rhetoric which punctuate lyric or anecdote. The experience of meditation leads its circumambulatory course toward the momentary insights from which disturbing contradictions have been mostly refined away, tracing in its rhythmic advance the ordering experience of the mind moving toward self-discovery. If the conclusion is anticipated, the processes of reaching it are nonetheless valuable. Aphorism is the end of discovery, a vision fulfilled, the "That's it" which Stevens discovers at the end of his meditative ramble in "A Primitive Like an Orb." Those of "The Rock" are most unrelenting in their repetition of a dominant idea—"The spirit comes from the body of the world"—but the particular nuance of each repetition is a renewal of the idea and a moment of repose for the man who has discovered it once again.

Long accumulating truths mellow into platitudes, rhetoric into congenial metaphor, and the poet's incessant questionings of his world begin to imply their own answers. The title poem of the collection is a most vivid example of this ruminative solemnity which comes as a reward for the faithful adherence to a single belief: that poetry and life are inseparable and thus that the total commitment of the poet to his art has been a life fullfilled. The accretions of a remembered past impinge upon the present as the poet reviews his life in the perspective of time, without either hope or despair. There is nostalgia in "The Rock" (CP 525), but without sentimentality; meditation has defended the self against itself also. The opening section, "Seventy Years Later," is autobiographical without being Tennysonian. Stevens refuses to indulge himself in lamentations for a spent life, or celebrations of its facile pleasures. The poem is as plainly about poetry as the very early "To the One of Fictive Music," but if its theme is little changed, the flesh and flashes of *Harmonium* are subdued in memory.

Stevens' review of the past in poem one is fatalistic, but without regret:

> It is an illusion that we were ever alive,
> Lived in the houses of mothers, arranged ourselves
> By our own motions in a freedom of air.
> Regard the freedom of seventy years ago.
> It is no longer air. The houses still stand,
> Though they are rigid in rigid emptiness.

There is an acute distance between the pleasures of youth and one's memory of them, between that gross universe of the rock in which youth frolicked and the shadows of a memorable past. Here, in the vivid reflection of a past that is no more, of lives that "never were" and poems that "are not," we come full upon the heroics of Stevens' self-in-poetry. For as this reminiscence must in the end deny the old sounds of the guitar, so must it ever-renew life's aesthetic and thus discard the poems of seventy years ago (which were of a world that is now but "illusion") for new poems made out of the "gray particular" of this present. Poetry is accepted as the reality and being of a moment, not a fixed and eternal form. Thus has Stevens' poetry grown and changed, to meet the needs of each day: poetry become an act of continual creation and not of nostalgic reflection.

Hence "The Poem as Icon," in which the poem is celebrated not as words in verse but as an act of the mind which issues in words or poems of the world. The poem, in short, is the form or forms by which we see reality, forms of our own making—icons in which is contained not the world but the world of the self. The icon or poem is the ultimate symbol for the marriage of mind and reality, self and world. It is a "cure" in the sense that it resolves divisions inherent in life itself:

> The fiction of the leaves is the icon
> Of the poem, the figuration of blessedness,
> And the icon is the man. The pearled chaplet of spring,
> The magnum wreath of summer, time's autumn snood,
>
> Its copy of the sun, these cover the rock.
> These leaves are the poem, the icon and the man.
> These are a cure of the ground and of ourselves . . .

Quickly the seasons pass in review—and with them a life in poetry. And now the rock remains, along with the leaves of one's last gesture, made in the "predicate that there is nothing else." Calmly, ritualistically, almost religiously, the last fiction is woven—and in the final "meanings" we perform the last acts of life:

> In this plenty, the poem makes meanings of the rock,
> Of such mixed motion and such imagery
> That its barrenness becomes a thousand things
>
> And so exists no more. This is the cure
> Of leaves and of the ground and of ourselves.
> His words are both the icon and the man.

But the imagery of a "thousand things" has disappeared from this stanza, and in its place a sound, a hymn almost, in which the icon has being but no fixed form. Here, then, does Stevens' final poetry realize the drift of his aesthetic, becoming in the sound of words the last pulse beats of a life come to full accord. He has thrust beyond the physical surface of things toward their "ground," and discovered that the ground of being is in his mind. The pun on "cure" is enormous: a process reaching from the physical to the spiritual.

Something like this is realized in the last section. "Forms of the Rock in a Night-Hymn" is well titled, a recitative as it were in which meditation becomes an iconic act, and rock and self achieve what union, what "cure," is possible. The rock as both origin and end of self is discovered to have its own origin and end in the self; for the rock of reality has meaning only in the human, in the space-time of the mind. Happy paradox this! and happier poetry:

> It is the rock where tranquil must adduce
> Its tranquil self, the main of things, the mind,

The starting point of the human and the end,
That in which space itself is contained, the gate
To the enclosure, day, the things illumined

By day, night and that which night illumines,
Night and its midnight-minting fragrances,
Night's hymn of the rock, as in a vivid sleep.

"The gate/ To the enclosure"—is this not the essential imagination of Stevens? Is it not where he started when he learned with "mon oncle" what happened to men at forty, and discovered that the fictive music springs from our happy fall into consciousness?

Returning to the "barrenness" was a recognition that the imagination too had its cycle, and its end. Yet Stevens maintains a noble, even stoic, mien in the face of this end. The ubiquitous rock is the nominal symbol for the volume, for there is a poverty which endures when the self, like the "green plant," turns "down toward finality," when the "effete vocabulary of summer" is exhausted (CP 506). The character of the section resides in the restrained yet lambent passion with which Stevens confronts "finality" or the "plain sense of things" (CP 502). The poem to which this line is also title dispassionately accepts the time when one comes "to an end of the imagination" and thus to the point of death. "It is difficult," the poet says, "even to choose the adjective/ For this blank cold," for death as fact ultimately repudiates mythology and adjectives. The calm rhetoric of "The Rock" is also sparing with adjectives, though Stevens retains enough of his imaginative "leaves" to make the barren rock tolerable. But what is most striking, and admirable, is his honest refusal to paint the rock in heavenly tones or deny the gray pallor that inheres there:

Little by little, the poverty
Of autumnal space becomes
A look, a few words spoken.

Each person completely touches us
With what he is and as he is,
In the stale grandeur of annihilation. (CP 505)

The "afflatus of ruin" pervades these poems as thickly as it fills the room where Santayana lies dying, in the poem which is without exception the grand achievement of Stevens' final years. "To an Old Philosopher in Rome" (CP 508) is not only a superb poem, it is a signal indication that Stevens did not desert his passion for life in a querulous pursuit of ideas. As if to recall his old powers, Stevens is able to identify himself and his art with the very real life of a man whose conduct both intellectually and morally was an applied act of imagination (NA 147–48), and whose philosophy, with its mutual devotion to both the real and ideal, provides the most vivid union of the imagination and life. Santayana's was a life, therefore, pregnant with humanity, repudiating the despair which has accompanied the loss of religious sanctions without supplanting one myth with another. In its triumph over loneliness and isolation, it becomes a most powerful metaphor for Stevens' belief in the redemptive powers of the secular imagination.

Here, then, in the example of Santayana, living at his acutest in the moment of death, Stevens realizes the two worlds of the self. As the old philosopher lies between life and death, amid the hushed walls of the Roman convent (Santayana died on September 26, 1952; the poem first appeared in the autumn of 1952), he lies, as the poet senses, on the "threshold of heaven," but a heaven of imagination made:

> The threshold, Rome, and that more merciful Rome
> Beyond, the two alike in the make of the mind.
> It is as if in a human dignity
> Two parallels become one, a perspective, of which
> Men are part both in the inch and in the mile.

There is a discreet blending here of Santayana's philosophy and Stevens' implicit aesthetic. Thought collapses into scene, and drama in turn becomes idea. Moreover, the effective tension throughout the poem between the orderly but vital motions in the dying man's room and the ethereal and vacant Rome, that pure heaven beyond, between the hum of life which filters in from the streets outside and the stillness toward which the spirit drifts, is a triumph of style. There is no argument, but only a muted eloquence—the eloquence of a style of mind—as the poet penetrates the scene and its drama of death, seeking "the extreme of the known in the presence of the extreme/ Of the unknown." Long periodic sentences evoke the paradox of death-in-life and life-in-death, the lambent rhythms of life counterpointed against the stasis of omnipresent death, as in this passage which is only the second half of one lengthy sentence:

Your dozing in the depths of wakefulness,
In the warmth of your bed, at the edge of your chair, alive
Yet living in two worlds, impenitent
As to one, and, as to one, most penitent,
Impatient for the grandeur that you need

In so much misery; and yet finding it
Only in misery, the afflatus of ruin,
Profound poetry of the poor and of the dead,
As in the last drop of the deepest blood,
As it falls from the heart and lies there to be seen,

Even as the blood of an empire, it might be,
For a citizen of heaven, though still of Rome.

It is in instances like this that Stevens achieved in his poetry what Santayana long aspired to realize in his.[14] Here is a rendering of Santayana's commitment to spirit and matter, and his sense of the organic origin and end of all things, including spirit. But preceding this passage is Stevens' most forceful metaphor of the life-death continuum, of the self burning out the flesh, its sustenance, the paradoxical act of life which struggles toward a purity and hence the annihilation of self:

A light on the candle tearing against the wick
To join a hovering excellence, to escape
From fire and be part only of that of which
Fire is the symbol: the celestial possible.

Stevens was never more acute in his fusion of internal and external worlds than in his projection of Santayana's spiritual into his physical life:

The sounds drift in. The buildings are remembered.
The life of the city never lets go, nor do you
Ever want it to. It is part of the life in your room,
Its domes are the architecture of your bed.

Just as Santayana's materialism binds him in love to the physical world, his imagination preserves him in detachment from its inherent chaos. Though he has denied transcendence, he has attained vision, and that after all is his most noble achievement: to transmute the tragedy of human imperfections into the dignity without which man is mere animal, to find "the afflatus of ruin." The object of life is to achieve poetry, to find a human order within nature and not without in the sentimental deference to an implausible abstraction, be it Church or State:

> It is a kind of total grandeur at the end,
> With every visible thing enlarged and yet
> No more than a bed, a chair and moving nuns,
> The immensest theatre, the pillared porch,
> The book and candle in your ambered room,
>
> Total grandeur of a total edifice,
> Chosen by an inquisitor of structures
> For himself. He stops upon this threshold,
> As if the design of all his words takes form
> And frame from thinking and is realized.

To the very end, Stevens maintains this double awareness of the mortal condition, and consequently the skepticism he shares with his old philosopher. But it is the skepticism, of course, which affords him the dignity that is otherwise denied the individual in an age in which God has suffered some crushing defeats and man has sacrificed his independence and identity for servility and security. With Santayana, Stevens embraces a humanism which is, in its civilized and refined nature, confined to that small, sophisticated group of men for whom thought and feeling are a luxury. "The Rock" is a sensitive review of this humanism, and poems like "To an Old Philosopher in Rome" bespeak an enduring quality of Stevens' poetry, from "Sunday Morning" on. It reveals likewise the limited appeal of Stevens' late style, for beyond the demands that style makes on its audience, it reminds that audience, as Santayana did his, of the expense of ease. Stevens' composition of self is not a two-week a year vacation but the life he had to live every day in poetry—or tried to. One does not discover Stevens' world on a trip to Florida or on a Guggenheim to Paris, but within the confines of the mind which has learned to explore its own loneliness.[15] It is one of the great human paradoxes that the masses of our contemporary world refuse to be lonely and are, while Santayana chose to be lonely and was not. The world he made in the imagination is very like the meditative world Wallace Stevens discovered in his late poetry. And like Santayana, Stevens did not find it without first having found the physical world, its pleasures and disappointments, its prohibitions and possibilities.

IV

"An Ordinary Evening in New Haven" (CP 465) is the last of Stevens' long poems, and appropriately it brings to composure the predilections of a lifetime. There is hardly an instance in the poem when one is not aware of that sigh with which he begins one of his last pieces: "It makes so little difference, at so much more/ Than seventy, where one looks, one has been there before" (CP 522). Coming as it did so closely following his seventieth year, "An Ordinary Evening" is without doubt an attempt at some kind of summary—not a farewell nor even a confession that the springs of imagination are giving out, but rather one of those concentrations of imaginative energy which makes the long poem a characteristic of his every volume. One feels almost certain that after "Owl's Clover" the long poem was not a problem for Stevens, that indeed it is but an extended series of shorter thematically related forms which issue from the natural act of man thinking. By the time of "Credences of Summer" he had discovered the internal "logic" of poetry to be the order of a sensibility and the music of mind.

The history of the poem is indicative of its design. It was written expressly for the one-thousandth meeting of the Connecticut Academy of Arts and Sciences; the original version, which first appeared in the Academy's *Transactions* (December, 1949), consisted of only eleven of the final thirty-one poems to appear later in *The Auroras of Autumn*. The original pieces are scattered through the final version as follows: i, vi, ix, xi, xii, xvi, xxii, xxviii, xxx, xxxi, xxix.[16] The inversion, in the final draft, of the concluding poems is revealing. The conclusion to the shorter sequence is an apostrophe to the reality of language, to "words" which effect a "change of nature," while the concluding poem of the final version offers the broader perspective of a rounded contemplative experience. Words, in the final version, become only one manifestation of the poet's imagined reality, which is more appropriately the felt thought of meditation. Theory gives way to feeling, or better to the "visibility of thought":

> It is not in the premise that reality
> Is a solid. It may be a shade that traverses
> A dust, a force that traverses a shade. (CP 489)

"An Ordinary Evening" is significant mainly for the affirmative way it brings to mythological form the final makings of a self, who knows full well it is moving from the consummations of summer through autumnal chill. Picking his way among the casually related poems, a reader can make much of what he wishes. The history of the poem's use by critics bears this out. Particularly fertile is the aphoristic style, or better, the incessant aphorisms around which the individual meditations revolve, or from which they spring. It is revealing that a number of the poem's most succinct metaphors go back several years to what Stevens called his "Materia Poetica" (most now appear in the "Adagia" of *Opus Posthumous*), indicating the poem's source in thought and feelings going back several years, through several selves. As a poem of meditation, it moves fluidly between the level of statement and the emotional clothing that makes thought visible. And in the fluid movement, it tells us a great deal about Stevens' last phase, his "grappling with rocks" and his passion to get at the reality that is not "a solid."

There is, however, an integral relation between the ideas and the external form and sequence of the poems. Moreover, unlike "Notes," it is not so rigorously or dialectically planned, and thus is at once more natural and less programmatic. Stevens no longer has to defend his aesthetic. He can merely exercise it. I should like to suggest that the poem develops by associative "blocks" of ideas, by discontinuity and *divertissement,* and is ultimately tied together only by the order of the mind itself and its natural habits of reflection, though the overall design is deliberate and not at all impulsive recording. There is an apparent progression in the poem from an abstract to a more emotional or personal questioning and resolution. But the dialectic is not progressive: poems of an almost purely theoretical nature occur intermittently; the argument builds toward no peak and requires no coda, emphasizing perhaps the casual and the ordinary of the mind's visitations as it moves from thing to thought and back again.

The poet's continuous struggle, of course, is to balance internal and external world, to find some meaningful synthesis between the self and the matrix of its residence, both actual and memorable. Meditation grows out of the images which arise from contact with a scene he has known before, that fertile compound of remembered past and vivid present. There are always flickerings of New Haven in the poet's ideas, the place itself and the associations it inspires. His response to this world, as in the second poem, is meant to absorb "these houses" into the "transparent dwellings of the self" and to obtain from this act some momentary revelation. The poem's development is thematic, not in the sense of a rigid argument but of mind distilling forms of thought:

Poems i–ii: provide the basis of meditation by presenting a problem, here most obviously of the relation of a self to the contingent environment in which it finds itself.

iii–viii: develop out of the initial problem: whether reality is the thing itself, the idea of the thing, or some balance of the two; the problem, stated simply, is the relationship of knowledge to reality, form to flux.

ix–x: conclude the questioning of reality by indicating that neither pure mind nor pure thing is conceivable, and that to opt for either (as metaphysics often does) is to distort the world for sentimental or mythological forms.

xi–xvi: elevate the I-other drama into the more abstract relation of man's physical to his metaphysical worlds, admitting the human need for the latter as well as the undeniable truth that the metaphysical is no more than the imaginative and thus human analogue of the physical.

xvii–xviii: consider the same question in terms of man's life in the commonplace world, which he loves in and for itself yet desires to transcend.

xix–xx: present the opposite problem, the life lived in the uncommon, the imaginative world which was once a religious world; but now the religious imagination distorts its reality in search of something purer, something inhuman because it is perfect and unchanging.

xxi–xxiii: respond to previous problems much in the manner of poems ix and x, but suggest that the union of pure reality and pure imagination gives us the only reality we can know.

xxiv–xxvi: explore the nature of this new reality in relation to forms of belief and find it closely associated with old mythological forms, forms of spiritual experience conceived in human images as opposed to the vague or dogmatic forms of modern religions.

xxvii–xxviii: suggest that poetry as an analogue of this new reality is therefore interrelated with life, and thus that a "theory of poetry" is a "theory of life."

xxix: celebrates language as a mediate form, and hence argues for the reality, and the life, of poetry.

xxx–xxxi: resolve the problem by returning to the experience of the aging man and the life of meditation as resistance to the rock; the meditation therefore circles back to the beginning which prompted it, the aging man's confrontation of a commonplace world which sets off the "never-ending meditation," indicating that life is just this act of a self in the rock.

There is hardly an argument here—only the blandly repeated insistence on one truth. The mind moves at will among the familiar things and ideas which have long since become a habit for it. It may well be, as Frank Doggett says, that to pursue the apparent "meanings" of the individual poems is to destroy their existence as poetry, "like telling dreams or describing music." [17] But just as in "Notes," verbality is the stuff of experience. This poem, perhaps more than any other of Stevens' long poems, is man thinking, the act of continual self-creation through poetry. Stevens here, as in all his long poems after "The Comedian as the Letter C," uses conceptual order where another poet might employ a mythical analogue. The poem progresses qualitatively rather than logically, to use Kenneth Burke's phrase, but the progression retains the linear continuity of an act of mind rather than the order of discontinuous images to which Burke refers. Stevens, indeed, most usually synthesizes the modern with the conventional, moving easily from proposition to clusters of qualification, and this is as true of "An Ordinary Evening in New Haven" as it is of the more dramatic early poems like "The Comedian as the Letter C." There are, in short, propositional gambits here, however platitudinous, obvious, and occasionally contradictory. A "visibility of thought" is not thought itself, but neither is it creation *ex nihilo*.

The first two stanzas of poem one establish the theme and direction:

> The eye's plain version is a thing apart,
> The vulgate of experience. Of this,
> A few words, an and yet, and yet, and yet—
> As part of the never-ending meditation,
> Part of the question that is a giant himself . . .

The "eye's plain version" is the first step of perception, a coming to consciousness but something short of experience, something as yet unlimned by mind. It is the experience of an "ignorant" man. The opening tropes present the motive for metaphor, the need for man to humanize reality, to grasp its fleeting and evasive nature, to pursue it with endless metaphorical "and yet[s]." Experience, beyond the "vulgate," evolves from the never-ending meditation of mind making metaphors, creating a mythological form out of the formless and incoherent, creating the "giant" or the reality which takes the shape of a self. And poem two picks up the motif in terms of the immediate situation, the ordinary New Haven and the memorable one which he transmutes into the "transparent dwellings of the self," the "impalpable habitations." This is meditation not as a special act but as a mode of being:

> In the perpetual reference, object
> Of the perpetual meditation, point
> Of the enduring, visionary love,
>
> Obscure, in colors whether of the sun
> Or mind, uncertain in the clearest bells,
> The spirit's speeches, the indefinite,
>
> Confused illuminations and sonorities,
> So much ourselves, we cannot tell apart
> The idea and the bearer-being of the idea.

The concluding statement echoes the paradox of Yeats's "Among School Children": the "idea" and its "bearer-being" are Stevens' tentative equivalents of dance and dancer, the symbolist's stasis within motion. Stevens' figure, however, is not a paradox at all but the synthesis of perceptual experience, elementary poetry as it were. Yeats's haunting vision of the inseparable conjunction of act and actor, and by extension of thing and idea, is interpreted by Stevens as the enduring oppositions from which experience springs—experience by its very nature impelling us to seek an ultimate order. The remaining twenty-nine poems are concerned primarily with the variable and possible relations of the two opposites, the variety of balances possible in the imaginative life which seeks always the ultimate order, the conjunction of idea and its bearer-being.

The qualitative flights of the succeeding argument need not be examined in detail. The next eight poems are essentially variations on the theme of poem two, each establishing its particular motif and then following it through to some resolution. They provide a variety of perspectives on the kinds or forms of man's reality, the forms we call experience. Meditation, it appears, is provoked by the awareness that we live in a world not altogether available to our reason: "The point of vision and desire are the same" (iii); "The plainness of plain things is savagery" (iv); "disillusion [is] the last illusion" (v); "Reality is the beginning not the end" (vi); "We keep coming back and coming back/ To the real" (ix); "We do not know what is real and what is not" (x). Assertion is the nominal starting point of each poem, not its conclusion. Each of the meditations re-encounters the puzzling separation of man and his world, and therefore the confusions of just what is and can be real and thereby certain. The question, as one might guess, is a point of epistemology, and more: "Reality," he discovers, is "a thing seen by the mind,"

> Not that which is but that which is apprehended,
> A mirror, a lake of reflections in a room,
> A glassy ocean lying at the door,
>
> A great town hanging pendent in a shade,
> An enormous nation happy in a style,
> Everything as unreal as real can be,
>
> In the inexquisite eye. (v)

Man's search, the poet knows, is for the "poem of pure reality, untouched/ By trope or deviation" (ix); what he discovers, on the other hand, is the paradox of his desire, that the "pure" is also the non-human and thus that man ironically wills his own nothingness:

> It is fatal in the moon and empty there.
> But, here, allons. The enigmatical
> Beauty of each beautiful enigma

> Becomes amassed in a total double-thing.
> We do not know what is real and what is not. (x)

With this discovery he once more affirms the imperfection of his real. "The brilliancy at the central of the earth" becomes the center and source of his metaphysical comforts, like the prophecy of order which lies in "four seasons and twelve months" (xi); poetry in its adherence to things of this world is found to be both vehicle for his truth and the truth itself. For poetry can at last be called the self, the self one makes in the instant of his imaginings; which is to say, his *acts* here and now:

> The poem is the cry of its occasion,
> Part of the res itself and not about it.
> The poet speaks the poem as it is,
>
> Not as it was . . .
>   . . . . . .
> In the end, in the whole psychology, the self,
> The town, the weather, is a casual litter,
> Together, said words of the world are the life of the world. (xii)

It is hardly news that Stevens' investigation of reality discovers it in poetry;[18] meditation generates its own form out of the matter (the present world plus memory) at hand. The anecdote of Professor Eucalyptus in poem fourteen is a happy example, combining as it does the light and the serious: the hierophantic yet natural name, which draws together the natural and the human yet distinguishes between them. For if man's need of sustenance issues, like nature's, in natural tropisms, he wears his title of self a little differently and somewhat comically:

> The dry eucalyptus seeks god in the rainy cloud.
> Professor Eucalyptus of New Haven seeks him
> In New Haven with an eye that does not look
>
> Beyond the object.

God is sustenance, the providential reality we seek because we need the providential, the world we dress in "paradisal parlance" and "commodius adjective" because we need "divinity." (Indeed, the Professor, seeker after the thing itself, betrays like the empiricist his own genius by looking for the genus of reality outside the self and the desire that makes him a seeker.)

One becomes increasingly aware with each poem that Stevens is traversing the same ground repeatedly, not to promote an idea but to refract it into its emotional forms, in order to get at what is human in form itself. There is, it is true, an increasing scope as the sequence of meditations progresses, but not a continuity which develops with the mock-logic of "Notes." The Professor Eucalyptus metaphor appears twice, in poems fourteen and fifteen and again in poem twenty-two, but if the second extends the argument of the first, there is no dramatic continuity in the seven poems between them. And there is no explicit advance in the inner dialectic, as it shifts and returns at will, repeating itself with surprising facility of variation. Poems twenty-one to twenty-three treat essentially the same thematic problem as poems nine and ten: the search for a reality within or beneath reality, or the point that the life of the mind is re-creation rather than creation, as poem twenty-two, echoing Coleridge, puts it. And poems fifteen and twenty-eight, though rhetorically different, develop motifs which are in general identical:

> The instinct for heaven had its counterpart:
> The instinct for earth, for New Haven, for his room,
> The gay tournamonde as of a single world
> In which he is and as and is are one. (xv)

This is an extension of Professor Eucalyptus' search, another version of Santayana's discovery. The following might well be its conclusion:

> This endlessly elaborating poem
> Displays the theory of poetry,
> As the life of poetry. A more severe,
>
> More harassing master would extemporize
> Subtler, more urgent proof that the theory
> Of poetry is the theory of life,
>
> As it is, in the intricate evasions of as,
> In things seen and unseen, created from nothingness,
> The heavens, the hells, the worlds, the longed-for lands. (xxviii)

The two quotations not only afford the poem thematic consistency, they provide its intellectual conclusion. But this is to say what all of his poems have said, in a remarkable variety of saying: that one can (and must) identify the processes of poetry with those of life, that we live in a world of metaphor, and that our heavens as well as those poems we study in school are conceived in the "intricate evasions of as," language trying to go beyond itself. But the life of the poem is something else again: it is the endless elaboration, by which out of the nothingness of a mind all alone there emerge the new forms that confirm the mind.

"An Ordinary Evening" is from the mind of a poet whose every thought is poetry, who sees the world as a poem and conceives of experience in the "shapes that it took in feeling" (xx). It is a brilliant display of metaphors and similes, and of the axiomatic truths which he has collected to defend himself against nothingness—not truths which afford him belief but truths which prove that because I imagine, I am. A combined apologia for poetry and for the poet, it is no less an apology for man. Stevens is like his poet in poem twenty-five, a man "fixed" in the eye of life, committed to his world and not beyond it. For him, the poet is a combination of Boethius and Pascal,[19] who discovers the "consolations of space" rather than its frightening silence (xxiv).

"An Ordinary Evening" is not, I think, successful as a total poem, though it presents fewer problems than the other long pieces. It is surprisingly cogent at times, being informed by the whole body of Stevens' previous work; yet it is not easily accessible, particularly in its separate parts. ("The poem should resist the intelligence/ Almost successfully," goes one of Stevens' most quoted lines.) Like so many later poems, it appeals to the body of images and symbols which have accrued with each successive volume and have come to have immense import with each recurrence. The diversity within the even meditative tone is captivating; if the poem has unity, it is a unity of its diverse style. The numerous aphorisms deliver the expected rational content, which is disturbingly simple, especially with its heavy load of platitude. Platitudes, however, give way in turn to parable, such as that of Professor Eucalyptus or his peer, the tendentious scholar in poem twenty-seven, and parable may be counterpointed against an almost pure lyric, like poem twenty-six. A juxtaposition of passages from these two poems reveals not only Stevens' diversity, but his insistent manner of saying the same thing within that diversity, yet all the while moving the mind from one transformative act or moment to the next:

> Mountains appeared with greater eloquence
> Than that of their clouds. These lineaments were the earth,
> Seen as inamorata, of loving fame
> Added and added out of a fame-full heart . . . (xxvi)

And the following picks up where transformation leaves off:

> A scholar, in his Segmenta, left a note,
> As follows, "The Ruler of Reality,
> If more unreal than New Haven, is not
> A real ruler, but rules what is unreal." (xxvii)

The concluding poems, therefore, satisfy the demands of meditation by bringing it full circle, not to an intellectual resolution, but to the artificial completeness which fullfills the poet's momentary needs to prove himself "consort to the Queen of Fact." It is, as poem thirty shows, a poem of autumn, of a man for whom the "last leaf that is going to fall has fallen," who has found himself without the old forms of belief vis-à-vis the barren rock:

> It was something imagined that has been washed away.
> A clearness has returned. It stands restored.
> It is not an empty clearness, a bottomless sight.
> It is a visibility of thought,
> In which hundreds of eyes, in one mind, see at once.

A visibility of thought—this is a precise description of the poem, and of the late poetry as a whole. As the sensuous world has disappeared, thought itself has become the poet's reality, and the act of thinking his mode of belief, beyond belief. The process of meditation is, on one level, a clothing of abstractions, blooding them with metaphor; but in the deepest sense, it is an act of self-creation, a freeing of the potential self into the actual moment of being. And so the poet, locating himself in New Haven on an ordinary night, discovers once again the uniqueness of himself at this moment, in this space and this time which precedes the inevitable future of nothingness:

>These are the edgings and inchings of final form,
>The swarming activities of the formulae
>Of statement, directly and indirectly getting at,
>
>Like an evening evoking the spectrum of violet,
>A philosopher practicing scales on his piano,
>A woman writing a note and tearing it up.

Meditation, paradoxically enough, appears to be both the search for final order (a "getting at") and defense against it. It is, however, a note written to be torn up; for all must change and none of man's forms suffice for more than their occasion.

What are we to make of this late Stevens? Is he a man satisfied with his edgings and inchings, with the swarming activities of "statement, directly and indirectly getting at"? Or, are those notes written to be torn up, those particular poems, simply notations which sustained him while he awaited the higher vision, the central poem? The question is not to be answered it seems—nor need it be. Coming upon one of Stevens' last edgings and inchings, a poem cryptically entitled "Of Mere Being" (OP 117), the critic is hard put to place his man. Does the "mere" of the title mean "simple," or "pure"? and does Stevens at last transcend (or inscend?) the physical to discover a central, the thing itself? Here is the poem:

>The palm at the end of the mind,
>Beyond the last thought, rises
>In the bronze distance,
>
>A gold-feathered bird
>Sings in the palm, without human meaning,
>Without human feeling, a foreign song.
>
>You know then that it is not the reason
>That makes us happy or unhappy.
>The bird sings. Its feathers shine.
>
>The palm stands on the edge of space.
>The wind moves slowly in the branches.
>The bird's fire-fangled feathers dangle down.

Beyond thought, beyond reason—here in the intuitive moment one perceives "mere being" but still perceives that one is perceiving. What he knows of mere being is a "palm" (a form, a faith?) beyond the physicality of tree and a bird's song without meaning. Unreal, yes!—but that

is Stevens' word for the reality of poetry, the "one of fictive music."
What one knows of mere being is an image on the edge of space, at that
point where being becomes nothingness. Is this not to prove the ultimate
creativity of self, of the mind which must always conceive a reality beyond form or metaphor, beyond thought, but nevertheless at the end of,
not outside, the mind?

In an inconsequential little poem which appeared shortly before his
death, Stevens had measured man's knowledge of the ultimate in terms
wholly human and limited, suggesting that if one could know the
thing itself and not simply ideas about the thing, what he would know
would be his power to imagine it—that *a* truth, say in metaphor, as
a part of truth, proves the availability of *the* truth:

> We live in a constellation
> Of patches and of pitches,
> Not in a single world,
> In things said well in music,
> On the piano, and in speech,
> As in a page of poetry—
> Thinkers without final thoughts
> In an always incipient cosmos,
> The way, when we climb a mountain,
> Vermont throws itself together. (OP 114)

Incipient cosmos, climbing a mountain—this is Stevens' aesthetic in
miniature. We climb mountains, it seems to say, as we write poetry,
as we live in the imagination, composing moment by moment Vermont
out of the incipient cosmos. We pitch and patch sensation into a world,
and we do it in the act of the mind. This, indeed, generates the thing
itself, the moment in which we discover that it is by the act of mind
that we make the incipient real and actual, and thus realize ourselves in
a cosmos that is *self*-sufficient.

"To be ruled by thought, in reality to govern ourselves by the truth
or to be able to feel that we were being governed by the truth, would be
a great satisfaction, as things go" (OP 235)—thus Stevens on the "great
modern faith," his "faith in the truth and particularly in the idea that
the truth is attainable." Vague word that!—but we know that the
"truth" means to Stevens the measure of the world seen humanly, the
totality of man's imaginings of reality as opposed to some encompass-

ing metaphysical formula. One of those poems from "The Rock" which break upon us with apocalyptic intensity is "Looking across the Fields and Watching the Birds Fly" (CP 517), the meditation of a modern Emerson seeking in the body of nature the old *"operandum"* and finding instead his own radical thoughts. "Mr. Homburg," as Stevens ambiguously and ironically names his mask, is a seeker of the first idea, the "new scholar" in a world which must forfeit the old "masculine myths" for humbler vision: "What we know in what we see, what we feel in what/ We hear, what we are, beyond mystic disputation." Mr. Homburg would author the modernist's "American Scholar." (Is there a pun here on humbug? or a commentary on the "scholar's" presumptuous hat, which in keeping with Stevens' symbolism is the form of the mind: in this case, round and complete, a new system mocking its German origins?) The spirit of his words is what remains of Emerson's, what remains, that is, in the inflections of modernism:

> A new scholar replacing an older one reflects
> A moment on this fantasia. He seeks
> For a human that can be accounted for.
>
> The spirit comes from the body of the world,
> Or so Mr. Homburg thought: the body of a world
> Whose blunt laws make an affectation of mind,
>
> The mannerism of nature caught in a glass
> And there become a spirit's mannerism,
> A glass aswarm with things going as far as they can.

For "scholar" read "man of imagination"; for "glass" read "poem," the old "crystal" of "Notes." And for nature read nature, the world as it is without Emerson's immanent Spirit. For in Mr. Homburg's scheme of things, so like Emerson's yet so different, to "think away" the grass and trees and clouds into spirit, rather than transforming them into "other things,/ Is only what the sun does every day."[20] In his transformative acts of mind, man has contrived his own, his masculine myths. But now he must live without "gods," in thoughts "without any form or any sense of form." In other words, the transformations he effects in imagination today are transformations of self, not of world. But consider the tone of this particular poem: the mild irony of Homburg's pretensions, yet the quiet dignity of one condemned to a world "not planned for imagery or belief." It is planned, that is, only to be itself. Still, we have Emerson's vision (his imagination) if not his innocence, and we are condemned to an "element that does not do for us/ So well, that which we do for ourselves." More self-reliant than Emerson, Mr. Homburg is equally as naive, the eternal child of the self who thinks "as the sun shines or does not." He thinks, as it were, in an "ordinariness" like the dove in "Song of Fixed Accord" (CP 519), who, a "little wet of wing and woe," pipes her trill of love: "And made much within her." Making much out of love and "sooth sorrow," making it within—this is the permanent Stevens within the changes. He is one of those priceless authors who has made the terror of nothingness meaningful to his age. Because he has been able to urge so courageously man's ability to transform nothingness into something, into "mere being."

Afterword

The Gate to the Enclosure

We come
To knowledge when we come to life.
Yet always there is another life,
A life beyond the present knowing,
A life brighter than this present splendor,
Brighter, perfected and distant away,
Not to be reached but to be known . . .
The Sail of Ulysses

Harmonium, pretty clearly, was present knowledge, and in the course of Stevens' growth and development there came the greater knowing. Not transcendental, this "distant away" was, on the contrary, a knowledge of what the self can know, what it can create, and hence what it is. This paradoxical quest for a life beyond began in mon oncle's impoverishment of the senses, and his discovery that men at forty long for the "basic slate" to replace fading pleasures of the body. And yet, he could grasp only the honey of earth. It began in the second stanza of "To the One of Fictive Music" and in the deflation of Crispin's "mythology of self." It began in poetry, in the discovery—at once comic and tragic—that the self lived apart from nature by the very awareness that it was a self, and that its relations with its world must issue in poetry. Stevens' subsequent voyage to summer and beyond, to his "Song of Fixed Accord," may be seen in one sense as an attempt to resolve the dualism, in another to maintain it by way of authenticating the self. Life was all, life involved poetry, yet poetry created a "life brighter," allowed the self emancipation from its time-

269

space matrix. It allowed worlds "not to be reached but to be known."

It is idle to attempt "placing" Stevens at this time, idle and point-less. His place in modern poetry is assured, but not yet fully assessed. In him we find no sudden and radical break with the past, no spectacu-lar gestures of rejecting tradition, no formulations or manifestoes to "make it new." He simply found it necessary to make it new, and did. The touches of decadence in *Harmonium* indicate Stevens' point of de-parture, as clearly as the undoing of Crispin's ego, and Hoon's, reveals Stevens' need to reconceive his role as poet and reassess his relation to reality. Stevens, of course, learned quickly from his contemporaries, here and abroad, and from his own eager curiosity. From the beginning, he had assimilated the modern, but with no particular urgency to ex-periment. The elegance of *Harmonium,* as I have maintained, is a strategy of the sensibility, trying on clothes of definition, changing its costume as the needs of the self change. But the volume has more drift than direction, and it exists almost exclusively on the level of "present knowledge." It is a period poetry, even if in the long run it has proved to be more. Yet this is the volume by which Stevens is mainly known. There is no denying that as individual poems his earliest ones, along with a few of his very last, are the most easily accessible. But any ultimate placement of Stevens will need to account for the continuity of his development of self, and the style of that self. And this involves an understanding of his poetics, which if implied in *Harmonium* are refined and even essentially altered by the changing and aging poet, the poet who unlike any of the masks of *Harmonium* aspired to achieve a "theory of poetry" that would be a "theory of life."

Critics have troubled for years over Stevens' flirtation with *au courant* philosophies. And most have decided that his learning was either un-fortunately infectious or that he happily escaped unmarked by thought. Reading Stevens' prose, one is struck by how much philosophy he has read and how little he has tried to understand. For his own purposes, clearly, he sought ideas to support his intuitions, but the claims of modernism I make for Stevens are not for the contemporaneity of his ideas so much as the contemporaneity of his "modes of thought," which is to say, his response to the world. Roy Harvey Pearce has re-cently placed Stevens in the "continuity" of American poetry as the most forceful and eloquent modern expression of what he calls an

Adamic mode.[1] By this he means: Stevens, in the tradition of Emersonian egocentrism, gives voice to the struggle of the poet to define himself
as creator in a world without past or tradition, a world that affords
him no identity and threatens with anonymity any self not willing to
assert its selfhood or assume its own destiny. But in the present century,
this condition is intensified by the further loss of such transcendental
faiths as could sustain an Emersonian or Whitmanesque vision. And so,
continues Pearce, Stevens' difficulties and complexities evolve from his
added task of asserting the creative self and realizing that definition in
poetry, without adequate rationale for the self and its creative potential.
He is burdened with justifying the poetry he creates, by way of justifying himself as creator. Pearce's argument for Stevens' Americanism, instructive as it is, is not to be restricted to nationalism; for if Stevens
gives expression to the last great American Adam—Adam grown old
with self-consciousness—he stands equally upon the crest of modern
thought and gives voice to the modern dilemma that transcends national
history. Perhaps, after all—as Pearce himself suggests—that is to be
the role of the American experience: to be a metaphor of the history of
the modern self, though this in its turn is an assumption I have pressed
only tentatively. If Stevens responds to Emerson and Whitman, he responds alike to Bergson and Valéry; if to Coleridge, then to Santayana
—and this does not mean at all that he devoured the thought of his
predecessors but more aptly that he, like most poets, lives in the thought
they formalized. The direct influence of Bergson, as Professor Morse
has indicated, is undeniably there in the comedy of *Harmonium,*
though it is unlikely that Stevens came to know Bergson's philosophy
until long after Bergsonian ideas had settled into his habitual way of
seeing the world and his place in it. For what there is of Bergson and
Santayana, even Whitehead and existentialism, in Stevens, is the crisis
and the triumph of modern self-consciousness.

It follows that Stevens' view of the poem as an "act of the mind"
makes him available to the kind of phenomenological scrutiny of romantic and symbolist literature exercised so effectively by continental
critics like Gaston Bachelard, J-P Richard, René Girard, and Georges
Poulet, among others. For example, Poulet's phenomenological reading
of Bergson, in his *Studies in Human Time,* offers a salient approach
to Stevens and helps to define the quality which makes the later

poetry so appropriately and revealingly modern. Bergson, for Poulet, is the key thinker in the transition from early Romantic thought to modernism, and what Poulet has to say of Bergson is eminently relevant to my argument:

In its essence as in its historical role, the thought of Bergson is transitional. Its function is to join the past and the future. On the one hand it is deeply rooted in the nineteenth century. It revives, it accentuates its themes, and resolves its difficulties. For Bergson, as for the romantics, the human being discovers himself in the depths of memory; and he no longer discovers himself there intermittently, fragmentarily, after a blind groping within the gulf of the mind, but simply in allowing himself, in a moment of pure relaxation, to be pervaded by an indelible and total memory that is always on the very verge of consciousness. Again, on the other hand, for Bergson as for the nineteenth century, all genuine thought is thought of the continuous *becoming* of things; indeed, for Bergson, to intuit their becoming is to intuit their essence. Duration is the only reality.

Nevertheless there is another aspect of Bergson's thought which already belongs to the twentieth century, since for him *becoming* no longer signifies *being changed* but *changing;* the act, that is to say, by which in transforming himself man incessantly reinvents his own being: "To exist is to change, to change is to mature, to mature is to create oneself endlessly." If the being endlessly draws its existence out of the past, it is not as one draws the consequences from a principle or as one copies the image of a pattern. It is a free adaptation of past resources to present life, in view of the future.

. . . . . .

Thus the twentieth century takes once more into account the notion of continuous creation: not necessarily in the sense of creation by God, but at any rate in the sense of creation by the mind. Each instant appears as the instant of a choice, that is to say of an act; and the root of this act is a creative decision. Every instant one acts one creates his action, and together with it one creates oneself and the world: "To make and in making to make oneself." [2]

Everywhere in Stevens' late poetry is this very sense of continuous self-creation, the emphasis on the "act" by which one not only sustains but perpetuates oneself, creating the world and the self simultaneously. *Harmonium* is a pastiche of masks and gestures, of acts which essentially add up to a self (or many faces and gestures of a self) in emergence, and in total to an act of self-discovery. The self defines itself by placing itself firmly in time and space, in a physical world it can understand and in relation to which it has being. The subsequent inner drift of Stevens' "reality" from physical to psychic may be seen, then, as a movement from the discovery of self to the full activity of self. It is movement toward the "act of the mind" as "Of Modern Poetry" announced it, an act that veritably ordained Stevens' idea of man as hero. The interlude of the thirties constitutes a most revealing period of self-definition, a holding action against the violent assaults upon the self, a resistance which culminated by authenticating the self as center and prime mover of the reality in which it lived, that is, the social and moral environment of the mind. It was a crucial period not only because it gave the anxious imago of *Harmonium* renewed purpose, but because it managed to define what Stevens had to believe was the proper ratio of creator to creation, of self to system, of imagination to order. It is with the confidence earned or asserted in "Owl's Clover" and "The Man with the Blue Guitar" that Stevens launched his last great period of contemplative action.

Everything in Stevens comes at last to the "act," to the continual process of adjusting the mind to its time-space matrix, a reality it could qualify, even psychologically create, but could not transcend. Continuous creation is a mental act; it may issue in images or metaphors or even poems, but the reality itself is process. Furthermore, the life of the mind, in so far as the thinker must distinguish between the reality he creates and sustains there and the contingencies which otherwise surround him (a nothingness, perhaps, a void, a time-space prison)—this life of the mind, as both Bergson and Santayana verified, is constantly brought into question by the world it did not create, even though it knows only the world of its own creation. The immense activity of Stevens' last years, activity in terms of theoretical speculation as well as of poetry, was an heroic attempt to sustain the self in as continuous an action as possible, to live in "knowing" the Present, that is, to *be* in the act of the mind. It seems almost as if he were constantly aware of Valéry's observation, that if one assumes that reality is the product of one's creative thought and nothing else, then one is bounded by nothingness. One is not when the mind ceases to act. This would not alone account for Stevens' great surge of creative energy in the forties and fifties, but something like that is manifest in the profusion of his poetic thoughts, his poems which seek knowledge by way of avoiding nothingness. Whatever else one finds in those essays, at once so portentously scholarly and so poetically open-ended, he must observe that they are meditative acts *pari passu* critical formulae. They are constantly involved with defining the self, whether as "noble rider" or "virile youth," as poet who acts in complement to the philosopher as a seeker after truth. They are the acts of a thinker who would discuss analogy not as things in relation to each other, but as things in relation to the mind that gives them arrangement and value. Stevens' theory of images in "Effects of Analogy" (NA 127–28), for instance, is every inch a phenomenological statement of reality as a creation of mind, though never does it suggest that this reality is the only one; or as he put it in "The Figure of the Youth as Virile Poet": "What we have under observation . . . is the creative process, the personality of the poet, his individuality, as an element of the creative process" (NA 48). What Stevens had discovered at last was the self-perpetuating imagination, that the mind truly creates in its act and that the mind contains all reality (in memory). The acts of imaginative perception or of meditating ideas were equally acts of self-creation. For to know that one can create, that is, to "know" a "life brighter than this present splendor," is to know that one's being is married to one's imperfection. And this brings us to the final twist of Stevens' modernism.

Says Poulet, speaking of the paradoxical condition of the modernist who exists so fully in his act that he does not exist otherwise, mind cannot both *be* and *know* of its *being*, for what it knows is the past, what it *was:* "If then the mind wishes to apprehend itself as creator, it must recognize in its act of creation an act of annihilation; it must create its very nothingness in order to give itself a being." [3] One recalls Professor Pearce's interesting observation that the key to Stevens' very last poetry rests in a passage from the essay "The Relations between Poetry and Painting" (NA 175), a passage in which Stevens paraphrased Simone Weil to the effect that modern reality "is a reality of decreation." [4] Pearce isolates in Stevens' very last poems the recurrent image of the child and particularly the phrase, a "child asleep in its own life." This, he says, is the ultimate thrust of Stevens' last poems, to will "his own decreation, so that, beginning at the beginning, with the uncreated, he can come to know and teach what naming is." [5] That is, he wills to establish himself once more in absolute innocence, at the origin, so that like Adam he might create his world and himself anew. In Stevens' terms, he wishes to achieve the "ultimate poem." Perhaps. But as I have argued in Chapters 1 and 6, and again here, Stevens' search for the ultimate or central or supreme speaks always in terms of possibility, of the potential of the mind and not of actuality. Rather than revealing the ultimate, or grasping the thing itself, this poetry manifests the heroic search for the real that is man's true vocation, even in a physical world. Stevens' "act of the mind," like Bergson's, generates a metaphysical comedy that is something more than the comedy Professor Morse finds in *Harmonium,* yet includes it.

There are, it is true, at least two notable poems of Stevens' last years—"The Course of a Particular" and "Not Ideas about the Thing but the Thing Itself"—which not only proclaim a discovery of the "thing" beyond the mind, but that this "thing" shares with the mind a mutual origin (in the "colossal sun"). Yet in each of these poems what is realized is the minimum knowledge which the human can have of its ambience, even as it is one with that world. The spirit, as Santayana would have it, has its origin in matter, and likewise its end; but the life it lives is a life apart. In "The Course of a Particular" (OP 96), the struggle is to define the in-human cry of the leaves which will not submit to human meanings (i.e., pantheism) and hence "concerns no one at all." The inhuman cry of nature touches "one," but the thing itself is ultimately unknown, hence "concerns" no one; for, as the poem insists, the "final finding of the ear" (I refer to the original printing, of "ear" rather than "air") can give one a knowledge that the other exists beyond the ear, but no more than that. Beyond the ear, beyond the mind, the thing exists for itself alone—"the leaves do not transcend themselves"—without meaning. This is the "new knowledge of reality," I suggest, with which Stevens concludes the *Collected Poems*—a knowledge of precisely how the self is related to the world. For what is discovered in "Not Ideas about the Thing" (CP 534) is that the self, as part of nature, shares a bodily being with the sun. But as it moves toward consciousness, the mind composes its own world, and sentimentalizes, hence loses, the thing itself. Man can know of otherness but not know it—except as he is sustained and hence contained by it. The "new knowledge," however minimal, of the world outside is an escape from solipsism, but in no sense a resolution to Stevens' problem. The human still had to make meanings of the "rock," to have ideas about the thing, and hence to compose his own world within the world. The *Collected Poems* was not a "final finding." Stevens sets one poem against the other, one probing of reality against another, not in hopes of any final finding, but as a way of sustaining the mind until it is time to say "Farewell without a Guitar" (OP 98).

One of the most obsessive of Stevens' themes, as this study has emphasized, is death. From "Sunday Morning" to "The Rock" the enigma has had to be faced, and finally effaced in acceptance. The terms of that acceptance, the "passion for yes," bound Stevens' career. Death, as in "Sunday Morning," is the essence of change, of vitality itself. He could not respond with the quiet orthodoxy of a Bryant, nor Whitman's exuberant idealism, nor Emily Dickinson's ironic conceits, nor Cummings' innocence—though like each of these he assumed that death was in the nature of things and not at the terminus. In this early poetry death was a "mother of beauty," intrinsic to change, to being, and thus a constant reminder that in being there was potential non-being. But if change were paradise enow for the poet of *Harmonium,* the aging man's confrontation of it was at once more urgent and more real: "the absence of the imagination had/ Itself to be imagined" (CP 503). This, it seems to me, is the discovery of "The Owl in the Sarcophagus," the final wisdom of death; and the poem, not without its painful evasions, comes to admit that in the "mythology" of our creation there must be a "mythology of modern death."

"The Owl in the Sarcophagus" deals with the forms by which we conceive the reality beyond "present splendor," the analogies by which we weave a mythology of death. It deals, then, with the modes of our belief (a belief beyond belief), our conceivings of death in images that are integral to the vital grammar of our lives, and thus our attempts to will a continuum of life in death. "These forms," it offers, "are not abortive figures, rocks,/ Impenetrable symbols, motionless" (CP 432). They are, rather, our sense of reality, our sense of the opposite of our being but formed out of our images of our being. The images of sleep and peace, those moments or spaces of non-being as Valéry called them, and the feminine anti-self death, are conceived as a mythology of the vital to replace the old mythology of the teleological. They are the punctuations, the commas and periods, of the rhythm of life. The poet recognizes the human need of these forms: "The children of a desire that is the will,/ Even of death, the beings of the mind. . . ." And the mind, he continues: "It is a child that sings itself to sleep,/ The mind, among the creatures that it makes,/ The people, those by which it lives and dies" (CP 436). Creator of itself, the self is the ultimate creator, creating not only the knowledge of death, but the way— the mythology—by which one can accept it. Yet the affinity with Valéry asserts itself here once more. Like Valéry, the poet discovers his being entombed in the primordial moment of his non-being, in sleep. Discovering himself to be the creator of himself, he has discovered the "child asleep in its own life" (OP 104, 106), from which state of pure or non-being the self has fallen into consciousness. This fall, as it were, into poetry is the beginning of life, of Knowledge, and the beginning of our search for the life beyond. No longer, however, can we comfort ourselves with the old mythologies, the beliefs which bind the self to a purposeful past and determined future, and to a greater inventing mind as source. "The right to know/ Is equal to the right to be" (OP 106). The exercise of this right is manifest on one level in Stevens' poems of earth, the poetry of *Harmonium*. But more important, it is realized in the later meditations, those exercises of a self—again like Valéry's—contemplating itself, seeking the center of reality that like a child asleep in its own life resides within. The child is the essentially human, not trailing clouds of glory, which is constantly being manifest in the act of imagining, in the enduring forms of poetry. The child within is one's potential being, and, in an un-Wordsworthean way, father to the man.

This may seem like an uninviting idea on which to string a poem (or a body of poetry), and indeed, one need not insist on it to explain the abstractness of Stevens' later poetry nor its enduring quality. Certainly this kind of rationale cannot make lovers of poetry lavish the same kind of attention on the later poems that they have lavished on the earlier, those poems which even while they are doing something very different give one the illusion of being concerned with the ordinary subjects of poetry: nature, feeling, love, birth, death, and taxes (the exchequer that life exacts of selves). Also, common readers are not likely to abide a poet who demands of them that they review too much of their own lives in his, or that they know his corpus entire if they are to be touched by the true wisdoms of the parts. But one need not make an exclusive choice with Stevens. Accordingly, a large part of this study is devoted to poems in isolation, outside their role in Stevens' Grand Poem. He has poems of every period which in and for themselves are great and remarkable performances; he is likewise a poet who, despite his acute self-criticism, never really culled lesser works from his books, a fact, evident in the later volumes, which contradicts that earlier debate with Williams over the finished "book." Not that Stevens grew lax in artistic discipline, this is, rather, evidence that his life of the mind enlarged to encompass more and that his "acts" in poetry became increasingly a mode of life from which very little could be excluded. Like a modern *Prelude,* and with much greater assurance that the individual self is a common (and thereby universal) self, Stevens' "book" presumes to define "man," or better, "an idea of man," in terms of his creativity. Presuming this, Stevens need not, like Wordsworth at the end of *The Prelude,* aspire to write a poem of pure mind; no more than he can argue with Wordsworth that the "mind of man becomes/ A thousand times more beautiful than the earth on which it dwells." The mind cannot be "pure"—it cannot be "cured," to recall "The Rock"—except in the very process of continuously creating itself and hence the "ground" on which it lives. It is an enormous, almost a dreadful freedom that Stevens conceives for the man of imagination, but a freedom that comes only with the acceptance of the imperfect.

"Not to be reached but to be known"—that resolves at last the anxiety of "Sunday Morning" and accepts fully man's common heroics in an "unsponsored" world. For Stevens would celebrate man as his own sponsor, nothing more or nothing less, and then deny him the false consolations that he may reach that perfection, that end, which he can conceive in imagination. In poetry, to put it another way, one realizes not the "end but the way/ To the end": "Alpha continues to begin./ Omega is refreshed at every end" (CP 469). Poetry and life—they are at once being and becoming for Stevens, all that we know, housing all that we are in a world constantly flowing away:

> And yet this end and this beginning are one,
> And one last look at the ducks is a look
> At lucent children round her in a ring. (CP 506)

Notes

INTRODUCTION

1 Stevens' reputation in the academies, which is now with the exception of Eliot's almost preeminent among American poets, was slow to develop. Among undergraduates, for whom *The Waste Land* is as common a title as *Macbeth,* Stevens is virtually unknown; and graduate students continue to "discover" him year after year. I have made a cursory investigation of publishers' blurbs, both for critical studies and anthologies which include Stevens, and rarely is his name listed with those who are likely to attract readers to the volume. In general, dictionaries which list eminent American men of letters do not include him, most notably *Webster's New World Dictionary,* which does list Amy Lowell, and Webster's *New Collegiate,* which lists Dorothy Canfield Fisher, not to say Dorothy Parker. Handbooks of literature, except for the very recent, are cautious in assessing his importance, and then usually he is rated as a poet of eccentric qualities. I doubt very much if a general listing of, say, the ten greatest American poets, made by anyone other than an informed critic or a poet himself, would dare include Stevens. Certainly no list before Stevens' death suggested he might exist in Eliot's world, or even Longfellow's. The popular reputation, of course, is of little consequence, but it indicates clearly enough that critics of Stevens are still in the position of having to make a case for their man, whose poetry is never likely to be popular.

2 Richard Eberhart, reviewing *Transport to Summer* in *Accent,* VII (Summer, 1947), 251-53, has put it emphatically: Stevens "has shown no major change in

growth, so that his late poems partake of the same kind of sensibility as his earlier ones." There are many echoes of this, most notably the remarks of A. Alvarez in his *Stewards of Excellence* (New York: Scribner's, 1958), 124–39, which conclude: "though Stevens' poetry changed a little, it hardly matured." These critics, like several of Stevens' fellow poets, fix upon his themes and discount the mutations of style as either essentially superficial or unfortunate. On the other hand, critics like Louis Martz, beginning with the same evidence, have argued for the organic growth of the canon, which gives evidence of the poet building, or rebuilding, himself through poetry. See Louis Martz, "Wallace Stevens: The World as Meditation," *Yale Review*, XLVII, N.S. (Summer, 1958), 517–36. Martz, indeed, begins by agreeing with Yvor Winters, that the poetry of *Harmonium* approaches a decadence which portends the end of poetry for Stevens, but that, contrary to Winters' belief, Stevens found a way, in the poetry of meditation, to survive and to mature. It is obvious that in this essay I agree with Martz, though I do not necessarily follow his view of *Harmonium* all the way, nor agree completely with his view of the formally meditative exercises of Stevens' very last poems.

3 The Romantics' distinction between poetry and poem can, I think, apply to Stevens. In Chapter Fourteen of the *Biographia Literaria,* Coleridge distinguishes between the poem as object (which, he adds, is different from "works of science, by proposing for its *immediate* object pleasure, not truth") and poetry in its metaphysical nature, indivisible from the poet and the poetic activity. With due regard for the differences between Stevens' and Coleridge's attitudes toward the metaphysics of imagination, one can conclude from Stevens' many remarks that he views poetry as an aspect, a most central one, of man's constant activity of consciousness: "The collecting of poetry from one's experience as one goes along is not the same thing as merely writing poetry" (OP 159).

4 See Samuel French Morse, Jackson R. Bryer, and Joseph N. Riddel, *Wallace Stevens: Checklist and Bibliography of Stevens Criticism* (Denver: Alan Swallow, 1963), for the most complete listing of Stevens' juvenilia.

5 Amy Lowell, *A Critical Fable* (Boston: Houghton, Mifflin, 1922), 97.

6 William Carlos Williams, *Kora in Hell* (Boston: Four Seas, 1920), 16–18. Reprinted in *Selected Essays* (New York: Random House, 1954).

7 John Crowe Ransom, in "The Planetary Poet," *Kenyon Review*, XXVI (Winter, 1964), 234, has remarked very recently on the significant impact of this volume on him and his fellow Nashville Fugitives: "We did not fail to exclaim excitedly over the emergence of a new poet who spoke as having authority. But it was a phenomenon for which we could not quite make out the forward drift and destination, nor the antecedent history."

8 Joseph N. Riddel, "The Contours of Stevens Criticism," *Journal of English Literary History (ELH)*, XXXI (March, 1964), 106–38.

9 Theodore Roethke has a very interesting poem on the subject, "A Rouse for Stevens," subtitled "To Be Sung in a Young Poet's Saloon," *7 Arts*, No. 3 (1955), 117, which after celebrating the more extravagant qualities of this "Imagination's Prince," concludes, "Brother, he's our father!" Several other younger poets, some of whom I have talked with, are less than enthusiastic about father's old age, following William Carlos Williams' view that Stevens' habits of thinking in the later poetry are lamentable.

10 Randall Jarrell, "The Collected Poems of Wallace Stevens," *Yale Review*, XLIV, N.S. (March, 1955), 348.

11 Cf. Jarrell's remark about the late poems: "As we read these poems, we are so continually aware of Stevens observing, meditating, creating, that we feel like saying that the process of creating the poem is the poem." Jarrell, "The Collected Poems of Wallace Stevens," 346. One wishes Jarrell had followed through on the remark, as Louis Martz did (see note 2), beyond comment on the involutions of style. The poem as process has epistemological and metaphysical significance in our time.

12 Martz, "Wallace Stevens: The World as Meditation," 517–36.

13 *The Selected Letters of William Carlos Williams,* ed. with introduction, John C. Thirlwall (New York: McDowell, Obolensky, 1957), 287.

14 Williams' "Pastoral," for example, sums up a series of more or less random perceptions and minimum conclusions from those perceptions (the "ideas" in the "things") with the lines: "These things/ astonish me beyond words." There is a similar astonishment in "Spring and All," the astonishment of a deliberately innocent and passing involvement in the emerging life of things. It might be instructive to look at Stevens' poem "Nuances of a Theme by Williams" (CP 18). It begins by quoting Williams' brief observation:

> It's a strange courage
> you give me, ancient star:
> Shine alone in the sunrise
> toward which you lend no part!

This, too, is a minimal observation, an imagistic exercise, extracting the barest idea from relationships. Stevens' two slight variations manage to generate a heightened feeling, exhorting the star to be itself, to resist being suffused in the light of humanity, to refuse to lend itself to man's wish to make meanings of it. It is a poem at once more objective than Williams' and more intensely concerned with the separation between self and thing.

15 Norman Friedman, *e.e. cummings, the art of his poetry* (Baltimore: Johns Hopkins University Press, 1960), 14.

16 Commenting on the poem, in her *Paris Review* interview, Miss Moore says that she "wouldn't call it a poem. It's truthful, it is testimony—to the fact that war is intolerable, and unjust." But it is "haphazard; as form, what has it? It is just a protest—disjointed, exclamatory. Emotion overpowered me. First this thought and then that." See *A Marianne Moore Reader* (New York: Viking, 1961), 261.

17 *A Marianne Moore Reader,* 254.

18 See Reginald L. Cook, *The Dimensions of Robert Frost* (New York: Rinehart, 1958), 79; and Robert Frost's "The Constant Symbol," *The Poems of Robert Frost* (New York: Modern Library, 1946), xvi. Williams' and Pound's hatred of the iambic is manifest abundantly in their letters and prose writings.

CHAPTER 1

1 Paul Valéry, *The Art of Poetry,* trans. Denise Folliot (London: Routledge & Kegan Paul, 1958), 77.

2 *Ibid.*, 73.

3 See Frederick J. Hoffman, *The Mortal No* (Princeton: Princeton University Press, 1964), for a contrast of Stevens and Eliot on this point. The chapter "Ecstatic Temporality" is especially important on the larger implications of the problem in modern literature.

4 This interesting literary misunderstanding draws a fundamental distinction between Williams and Stevens. Williams, of course, has no truck with the "anti-poetic" because nothing real is for him either unavailable or opposed to poetry. Stevens' use of the phrase, on the other hand, seems to call attention to the present age which can assume nothing like a poetic language, and, in contrast say to Emerson, cannot view the natural world as immanently poetic. For Williams' atti-tude toward Stevens' introduction, see *I Wanted to Write a Poem*, reported and edited by Edith Heal (Boston: Beacon, 1958), 52.

5 See Frederick J. Hoffman, "Literary Techniques and the Vanishing Self," in his *Samuel Beckett, The Language of Self* (Carbondale: Southern Illinois University Press, 1962), 56–81, especially p. 60. See also Hoffman, *The Mortal No,* especially the large section on "Self."

6 See Georgianna Lord, "The Annihilation of Art in Wallace Stevens" (Ph.D. dissertation, Ohio State University, 1962), for an extensive investigation of Stevens' attitude toward reason.

7 For parallels with Romanticism, see Newton P. Stallknecht, "Absence in Reality: A Study in the Epistemology of The Blue Guitar," *Kenyon Review,* XXI (Autumn, 1959), 545–62; James Benziger, *Images of Eternity, Studies in the Poetry of Religious Vision* (Carbondale: Southern Illinois University Press, 1962), 235–43 and *passim;* Harold Bloom, *The Visionary Company: A Reading of Romantic Poetry* (Garden City, N.Y.: Doubleday, 1961), *passim;* and Bloom, "Notes toward a Supreme Fiction: A Commentary," in Marie Borroff (ed.), *Wallace Stevens: A Collection of Critical Essays* (Englewood Cliffs, N.J.: Prentice-Hall, 1963), 76–95; and J. V. Cunningham, *Tradition and Poetic Structure* (Denver: Alan Swallow, 1960), 106–24.

8 See Sister Mary Bernetta Quinn, *The Metamorphic Tradition in Modern Poetry* (New Brunswick: Rutgers University Press, 1955), 49–88, which treats Stevens as an idealist and considers his remarks on "metamorphosis" indicative of his epistemo-gical idealism. Though she is a bit too critical of the contradiction in his devotion to both things as they are and things imagined (perhaps because she makes him too much the idealist and reads his theory of "metamorphosis" as a statement of the "shaping spirit" of imagination), her essay is sensitive and useful. Stevens' imagination, one might add here, is not a "shaping spirit" in the Coleridgean sense, but only in the sense of its transformative power over the phenomena of mind.

9 "Light" as a metaphor for imagination, of course, is common to transcendental idealism, and one must make the same distinction between Coleridge's and Stevens' use of it as he would between Emerson's and William Carlos Williams'. Perhaps the best source for the wholly secular use of the metaphor is Henry Adams' *Mont-Saint-Michel and Chartres,* in which he remarks on the use of the color blue in cathedral glass to refract the color of light. "We must chiefly remember," says Adams, "the law that light is blue," adding: "light has value only by opposition."

10 James Baird, "Transvaluation in the Poetics of Wallace Stevens," *Studies in*

Honor of John C. Hodges and Alwin Thaler (Knoxville: University of Tennessee Press, 1961), 163–73.

11 Frank Kermode, *Wallace Stevens* (London: Oliver and Boyd, 1960), 83.

12 Samuel French Morse, "Wallace Stevens, Bergson, Pater," *ELH,* XXXI (March, 1964), 1–34.

13 George Santayana, *Scepticism and Animal Faith* (New York: Scribner's, 1923), 282. Interestingly, this book appeared in the same year as *Harmonium,* and it proves to be, I think, one of the documents which justify the implicit poetics of that volume. Cf. these lines from Stevens' "Lytton Strachey, Also, Enters into Heaven" (OP 38):

> Perception as an act of intelligence
> And perception as an act of grace
> Are two quite different things, in particular
> When applied to the mythical.

14 *Ibid.,* 98.

15 *Ibid.,* 109.

16 Cf. Santayana's "Reason is itself a method of imaginative thought" in his *Dominations and Powers, Reflections on Liberty, Society, and Government* (New York: Scribner's, 1951), 463, with Stevens' "The truth seems to be that we live in concepts of the imagination before the reason has established them. If this is true, then reason is simply the methodizer of the imagination" (NA 154). Also see Stevens' remark, OP 200–201. The examples might be multiplied, but they would only prove that Stevens, facing the challenge to imagination's authority, was essentially assertive of its role in the organic mind, while Santayana could systematically go about defining the relations and interrelations of qualities of mind, and further trace the mind's independence of as well as dependence on matter. What is important is that both come back to a position that experience, or knowledge, is incipient poetry. Also cf. Emerson, in *Nature:* "The imagination may be defined to be the use reason makes of the material world."

17 Yvor Winters, *In Defense of Reason* (New York: Swallow and Morrow, 1947), 435–37.

CHAPTER 2

1 See both Harriet Monroe, *Poets & Their Art* (New York: Macmillan, 1932), 39–45, and her *A Poet's Life* (New York: Macmillan, 1938), 342–43.

2 The largest of these groups, which appeared in the September, 1914 *Trend,* consisted of eight poems titled collectively "Carnet de Voyage." One of them, "On an Old Guitar," seems to offer figurative entrance to Stevens' canon, looking forward to one of the last, "Farewell without a Guitar" (OP 98), and, of course, to "The Man with the Blue Guitar" of the middle period.

3 See Riddel, "The Contours of Stevens Criticism," 108–36, for an account of Stevens' reputation and the reception of *Harmonium.*

4 See Conrad Aiken, "The Ivory Tower—I," *New Republic,* XIX (May 10, 1919), 58–60, and Louis Untermeyer, "The Ivory Tower—II," *New Republic,* XIX (May 10, 1919), 60–61. The hassle was over Aiken's review of Untermeyer's *The New*

Era of American Poetry (New York: Henry Holt, 1919). See Riddel, "The Contours of Stevens Criticism."

5 Yvor Winters, almost alone among critics, had consistently praised Stevens' very early work. Particularly interesting is his remark, as an aside in a review of E. A. Robinson's *Collected Poems,* that Stevens was the foremost of living poets: "If the actual thought of this passage [from Robinson's *Octaves*] is not that of Wallace Stevens, nevertheless the quality of the thought, the manner of thinking, as well as the style, quite definitely is. To what extent Mr. Robinson may have influenced this greatest of living and of American poets, one cannot say. . . . Mr. Robinson's sound is inevitably the less rich, the less masterly." Winters, "A Cool Master," *Poetry,* XIX (February, 1922), 287. Taking account of Winters' tendency to praise as unrestrainedly as he damns, we should find this appraisal of Stevens, which would later be modified, an interesting footnote to the history of Stevens' reputation.

6 See Llewelyn Powys, "The Thirteenth Way," *Dial,* LXXVII (July, 1924), 45–50; and John Gould Fletcher, "The Revival of Aestheticism," *Freeman,* VIII (December 19, 1923), 355–56. One cannot resist quoting the following remark by Powys, even if it is the exception rather than the rule: "Listening to his poetry is like listening to the humming cadences of an inspired daddy longlegs akimbo in sunset light against the colored panes of a sanct window above a cathedral altar." Stevens' poetry, Powys continues, "is beyond good and evil, beyond hope and despair, beyond thought of any kind." This was meant sincerely as praise.

7 Frederick J. Hoffman, "Dogmatic Innocence: Self-Assertion in Modern American Literature," *Texas Quarterly,* VI (Summer, 1963), 156. The "dogma of style," says Professor Hoffman, is almost the sole ideological absolute held or shared by our major writers of the twenties, whose art is a concerted protest against the old gang and the old beliefs. The extremest manifestation of this dogma, says Hoffman, pointing to the influence of the French Symbolists, was the "mysticism of the 'Word,' " most clearly evident in Hart Crane's *The Bridge.* Stevens, we might note, resists the panacea of the "Word," or its ultimately mystical value, though true to the age his struggle is with words and the world.

8 See note 4, Introduction.

9 "Some of one's early things give one the creeps," Stevens remarked to Donald Hall, who collected some of them in *The Harvard Advocate Anthology* (New York: Twayne, 1950). See page 6.

10 Stevens' poem appeared anonymously in the *Harvard Monthly,* XXVIII (May, 1899), 95. Santayana's reply can be found in *A Hermit of Carmel And Other Poems* (New York: Scribner's, 1901).

11 Robert Buttel, "Wallace Stevens at Harvard: Some Origins of His Theme and Style," *ELH,* XIX (March, 1962), 90–119.

12 *Harvard Advocate,* LXIX (March 24, 1900), 18. Published under the name R. Jerries.

13 "Sonnet," *Harvard Advocate,* LXIX (May 23, 1900), 86. By R. Jerries.

14 I owe to Professor Bernard Duffey the suggestion that the relation of the Harvard Poets to the poetic renaissance of the early twentieth century was more than historians normally indicate, that these poets are more characteristically modern than is usually admitted, in both theme and style. Professor Duffey's researches bear this out, and might well lead to more extensive suggestions of Stevens' debt to the

Harvard Poets than I make here. For example, Santayana's poem "On the Death of a Metaphysician," and especially its line, "Ah, the thin air is cold above the moon!" lingers in *Harmonium,* as do many of the themes of Santayana's poems, with their resistance to transcendence, their acceptance of time, their faith in the forms of art. Take this, for instance, the last line of the third sonnet in the sequence, "Before a Statue of Achilles": "The perfect body is itself the soul." The theme of "Peter Quince at the Clavier" is here.

15 See Michel Benamou, "Jules Laforgue and Wallace Stevens," *Romanic Review,* L (April, 1957), 197–217, for an incisive evaluation of Stevens' differences from Laforgue. This essay qualifies René Taupin's claims in *L'Influence du symbolisme français sur la poésie américaine* (Paris: H. Champion, 1929) which has influenced many subsequent accounts, particularly H. R. Hays's "Laforgue and Wallace Stevens," *Romanic Review,* XXV (January–March, 1934), 242–48. See also, Daniel Fuchs, *The Comic Spirit of Wallace Stevens* (Durham: Duke University Press, 1963). There is no doubt of Stevens' knowledge of, but some question about his debt to, Laforgue. One could not have been associated with *Others* and not have known Walter Arensberg's or Maxwell Bodenheim's or Donald Evans' translations and promotions of the Frenchman. But Stevens' use of Laforgue is so different from the usual, his irony so expressly affirmative as distinct from the Pierrot's, that comparisons are not as rewarding as one might wish. It is not my purpose here to detail the analogies between Stevens and the French Symbolists. I might, however, refer the reader to the extensive work on this subject done by Benamou. My introduction to Chapter 5 takes up another aspect of Stevens' symbolism.

16 The play was published in *Poetry,* VIII (July, 1916), 163–79, as recipient of the Players' Producing Company award for the year's best one-act verse drama.

17 Hi Simons, "Wallace Stevens and Mallarmé," *Modern Philology,* XLIII (May, 1946), 256.

18 MS in Widener Library.

19 Whit Burnett (ed.), *This Is My Best* (New York: Dial, 1942), 62. Stevens calls it a "pure" poem, and hence his best.

20 Roy Harvey Pearce, *The Continuity of American Poetry* (Princeton: Princeton University Press, 1961), 404. Though Pearce's phrase applies directly to Stevens' later poetry, it is equally appropriate to *Harmonium,* in which the fall is experienced but not always admitted. This stanza of "To the One of Fictive Music," and "Le Monocle de Mon Oncle" and "The Comedian as the Letter C," are preeminent examples of this experience which Pearce relates to Emerson's remarks in his essay "Experience."

21 Stevens was asked by Renato Poggioli, who was translating some of Stevens' poems into Italian, whether there was any relation between Shakespeare's Peter Quince and the titular figure. Stevens' answer is a perfect spoof: "Is not Peter Quince in Midsummer Night Dream [*sic*]? My Shakespeare is in the attic, where it is hotter than the Sahara and I could not bring myself last night to go up and look. I think you could verify this under refrigerated conditions in the library at Harvard." See Stevens, *Mattino Domenicale ed altre Poesie,* trans. Renato Poggioli (Torino, Italy: Giulio Einaudi, 1954), with several notes in English by Stevens.

22 Fred Stocking, "Stevens' 'Peter Quince at the Clavier,'" *Explicator,* V, No. 47 (May, 1947).

23 Frederick J. Hoffman, *The Twenties* (New York: Viking, 1955), 391. Pro-

fessor Hoffman's recent book, *The Mortal No,* explores that role fully and profoundly. His title, appropriately enough, is from Stevens' "Esthétique du Mal."

24 See OP xix. Stevens' "Lettres d'un Soldat" appeared in *Poetry,* XII (May, 1918), 59–65. See Samuel French Morse, " 'Lettres d'un Soldat,' " *Dartmouth College Library Bulletin,* IV, N.S. (December, 1961), 44–50. Morse accounts for the history of the series which was, he says, planned to contain seventeen poems. Morse's story of Stevens' and Harriet Monroe's changes and deletions of the group submitted to *Poetry* is a revealing chapter in Stevens' development. According to Morse, both Stevens and Miss Monroe had second thoughts about the series before it was published, had some discussions about it, and made several changes and deletions. One discussion, Morse reports, took place at Miss Monroe's home where Stevens was supposed to have talked freely about death. Morse continues, quoting Stevens: "He was acutely embarrassed by what he had said: for although the subject absorbed him, he knew that there were 'too many people in the world, vitally involved,' for whom death was 'infinitely more than a thing to think of.' "

25 The three were "Negation," "The Surprises of the Superhuman," and "The Death of a Soldier," untitled in the original.

26 Winters, *In Defense of Reason,* 476.

27 Cunningham, *Tradition and Poetic Structure,* 120–21.

28 See Joseph N. Riddel, "Walt Whitman and Wallace Stevens: Functions of a 'Literatus,' " *South Atlantic Quarterly,* LXI (Autumn, 1962), 506–20.

29 It is impossible to verify, but one might speculate on the influence of Santayana on the theme of this passage. Cf. the following, from Santayana's *The Sense of Beauty* (New York: Dover, 1955), 188–91. "When, after the hero had been the centre and subject of so much imaginative labour, the belief in his reality lapsed, to be transferred to some other conception of cosmic power, he would have remained an ideal of poetry and art, and a formative influence of all cultivated minds. This he is still, like all the great creations of avowed fiction, but he would have been immensely more so, had belief in his reality kept the creative imagination continuously intent upon his nature.

"The reader can hardly fail to see that all this applies with equal force to the Christian conception of the sacred personalities. Christ, the Virgin Mary, and the saints may have been exactly what our imagination pictures them to be; that is entirely possible; nor can I see that it is impossible that the conceptions of other religions might themselves have actual counterparts somewhere in the universe. . . . But however descriptive of truth our conceptions may be, they have evidently grown up in our minds by an inward process of development. . . .

"The greatest feats of synthesis which the human mind has yet accomplished will, indeed, be probably surpassed and all ideals yet formed be superseded, because they were not based upon enough experience, or did not fit that experience with adequate precision. It is also possible that changes in the character of the facts, or in the powers of intelligence, should necessitate a continual reconstruction of our world. But unless human nature suffers an inconceivable change, the chief intellectual and aesthetic value of our ideas will always come from the creative action of the imagination."

30 See Morse, *et al., Wallace Stevens Checklist,* 53. The long version of "Sunday Morning" offers further evidence of Stevens' deliberate use of rhetorical balance. The first four stanzas expose and reject the lady's complacencies, leaving her to face

the reality of death with only "imperishable bliss"; but the last four ritualize that death into a new meaning, a new mythology—the implications of which will be explored later in "The Owl in the Sarcophagus." Moreover, one could argue that the poem develops, with an almost mathematical precision, by paralleling the first four stanzas with the second four: stanza five parallels, extends, and finally transforms the imagery and theme of stanza one; six does the same for two; and so on.

31 See Albert Camus, *The Myth of Sisyphus,* trans. Justin O'Brien (New York: Vintage, 1959), especially the chapter called "Absurd Creation."

32 See Elizabeth Drew, *Poetry: A Modern Guide to Its Understanding and Enjoyment* (New York: Dell, 1959), 220. Miss Drew rejects the poem as "a conception of the human condition without religious hope, and this is perhaps because of its disregard of the mind and the spirit." But this is specious reasoning, if not altogether wrong. The mind (particularly reason) and spirit, indeed, have precipitated, not allayed, that "old catastrophe" as Stevens' lady experiences it. Stevens passed beyond "Sunday Morning" simply because he found the imagination capable of grappling with that "freedom" in an "unsponsored" world to the degree that the self could become its own sponsor.

33 Richard Ellmann, "Wallace Stevens' Ice-Cream," *Kenyon Review,* XIX (Winter, 1957), 92.

34 *Ibid.,* 94.

35 See William York Tindall, *Wallace Stevens* ("University of Minnesota Pamphlets on American Writers, No. 11" [*Minneapolis: University of Minnesota,* 1961]), 14. Also Fuchs, *The Comic Spirit of Wallace Stevens.*

36 Among Stevens' books sold at auction by Parke-Bernet of New York in 1957 was a first edition of Eliot's *Prufrock and Other Observations.* "Le Monocle," of course, preceded the "agèd eagle" of "Ash Wednesday" by a decade.

37 William Fahey, "Stevens' 'Le Monocle de Mon Oncle, I,' " *Explicator,* XV, No. 16 (December, 1956). Stevens' title very clearly owes much to Donald Evans' sonnet "En Monocle," as Alfred Kreymborg has pointed out, *Our Singing Strength* (New York: Coward-McCann, 1929), 407–408.

38 Marius Bewley, "The Poetry of Wallace Stevens," *Partisan Review,* XVI (September, 1949), 909 f. See also, Kermode, *Wallace Stevens,* 36.

39 Hi Simons, " 'The Comedian as the Letter C': Its Sense and Significance," *Southern Review,* V (Autumn, 1939), 454. See also John J. Enck, "Stevens' Crispin as the Clown," *Texas Studies in Literature and Language,* III (Autumn, 1961), 389–98. Against Simons, Enck has been most outspoken, denying the poem's autobiographical reference and relating it to a convention of the modern clown. Figaro is Enck's candidate for Crispin. Offering an alternative to the autobiographical, Enck concludes, strangely, that the poem served the ends of turning "Stevens' poetic outlook away from the clown whether as doomed aspirant or the sardonic compromiser. In this sense, then, the poem does become antimythological because it fully depicts a disinherited twentieth-century comedian only to deny that this congenial imago exerts abiding power." This would appear to be an "autobiographical" interpretation of the poem's role in Stevens' canon.

40 Poggioli (trans.), *Mattino Domenicale,* 169. In the original letter to Poggioli (June 3, 1953) Stevens had written that Crispin acted in "the poetic American atmosphere," but he crossed out "American" and wrote "a" above "the."

41 See Guy Davenport, "Spinoza's Tulips, a Commentary on 'The Comedian

as the Letter C,'" *Perspective,* VII (Autumn, 1954), 147–54; Pearce, *The Continuity of American Poetry,* 424; Simons, "'The Comedian as the Letter C': Its Sense and Significance"; Enck, "Stevens' Crispin as the Clown." Those noting the Laforguean influence are legion; the influence of the harlequin is general, not specific.

42 Among Stevens' books sold at auction by Parke-Bernet was Maurice Sand's history of harlequinade, *Masques et Bouffons* (2 vols.; Paris: A. Levy, 1862), which was translated anonymously into English and published in two volumes under the title *The History of Harlequinade* (London: Martin Secker, 1915). Stevens' Crispin bears characteristics of several harlequin figures, but he cannot be identified with any one, even the French valet Crispin, whose costume is treated briefly in volume one, page 152, and who is described in volume two, pages 229–30 (both page numbers refer to the translation). Sand calls Crispin a French variation on Scaramouche, who wears no mask and dresses "in black, with boots or shoes, ruffle, gloves, a wide leather belt and a rapier." Interestingly, Stevens calls his Crispin "short shanks," but the Crispin created by the French playwright Poisson was tall and thin-legged, as was Poisson. Stevens' library included also J. A. Symonds' handsome edition of *The Memoirs of Count Carlo Gozzi* (London: John C. Nemmo, 1890), with a lengthy introduction by Symonds on Gozzi's role in the history of harlequinade as well as extensive commentary on various characters and plays in the tradition.

43 The last stanza of a minor poem "Anecdote of the Abnormal" (OP 23) offers us an antecedent of Crispin, playing as it apparently does on the two Crispins:

> Crispin-valet, Crispin-saint!
> The exhausted realist beholds
> His tattered manikin arise,
> Tuck in the straw,
> And stalk the skies.

The rise, one need add, is not miraculous, and not transcendent, but an exercise of imagination (making saints out of servants!).

44 Davenport, "Spinoza's Tulips."

45 Kermode, *Wallace Stevens,* 48.

46 See Pearce, *The Continuity of American Poetry,* 388. See also Tindall, *Wallace Stevens,* 26, who indicates that both "clipped" and "relation" are puns.

47 Bewley, "The Poetry of Wallace Stevens," 895–915.

48 Kermode, *Wallace Stevens,* 27.

49 Pearce, *The Continuity of American Poetry,* 424–26.

CHAPTER 3

1 Stevens, of course, did write some poetry during the period, though it is impossible to know how much. A letter to Louis Untermeyer (June 11, 1929) contains the poem "Annual Gaiety" (now collected in OP, 32) which Stevens contributed to Untermeyer's *Modern American Poetry: A Critical Anthology* (New York: Harcourt, Brace, 1930), 340. Also, six of the fourteen new poems Stevens included in the 1931 edition of *Harmonium* were first printings, suggesting that they were written after 1924, when Stevens apparently ceased to publish in journals. (All letters cited in this study are in the possession of Holly Stevens Stephenson.)

2 William Carlos Williams, review of *The Man with the Blue Guitar and Other Poems*, in *New Republic*, XCIII (November 17, 1937), 50. Other reviews of Stevens' poetry at this time which found him delinquent in social consciousness include Theodore Roethke, review of *Ideas of Order*, in *New Republic*, LXXXVII (July 15, 1936), 304–305; Dorothy Van Ghent, "When Poets Stood Alone," *New Masses*, XXVI, Sec. II (January 11, 1938), 41–46.

3 Stanley Burnshaw, "Turmoil in the Middle Ground," *New Masses*, XVII (October 1, 1935), 42. For a revealing commentary on the motivations behind the Burnshaw review, and Stevens' subsequent response, see Burnshaw, "Wallace Stevens and the Statue," *Sewanee Review*, LXIX (Summer, 1961), 355–66. Though Burnshaw does not explain away the stringency of his attack, he does indicate very clearly that he did not intend for his review to be so severe, and indeed that he had only the greatest respect for Stevens as a poet. Probably so, but the urgency of the decade speaks in the review, and Stevens knew it. When he came to answer Burnshaw, in the second poem of the long version of "Owl's Clover," he was not answering the man but the idea. Burnshaw had come to be the voice of that idea in all its violent fear of poetry.

4 "I hope I am headed left, but there are lefts and lefts, and certainly I am not headed for the ghastly left of MASSES. The rich man and the comfortable man of the imagination of people like Mr. Burnshaw are not nearly so rich nor nearly so comfortable as he believes them to be." Letter to J. Ronald Lane Latimer, publisher of the Alcestis Press, who had printed the first edition of *Ideas of Order*, and who was to print the long version of "Owl's Clover," dated October 9, 1935, eight days after the appearance of Burnshaw's review.

5 "We are confronting . . . a set of events, not only beyond our power to tranquillize them in the mind, beyond our power to reduce them and metamorphose them, but events that stir the emotions to violence, that engage us in what is direct and immediate and real, and events that involve the concepts and sanctions that are the order of our lives and may involve our very lives; and these events are occurring persistently with increasing omen, in what may be called our presence. These are the things that I had in mind when I spoke of the pressure of reality, a pressure great enough and prolonged enough to bring about the end of one era in the history of the imagination and, if so, then great enough to bring about the beginning of another. It is one of the peculiarities of the imagination that it is always at the end of an era. . . . To sum it up, the pressure of reality is, I think, the determining factor in the artistic character of an era and, as well, the determining factor in the artistic character of an individual. The resistance to this pressure or its evasion in the case of individuals of extraordinary imagination cancels the pressure so far as those individuals are concerned" (NA 22–23).

6 See especially Christopher Caudwell, *Illusion and Reality* (London: Lawrence & Wishart, 1946), 30 and *passim;* first published in 1937. See also Caudwell's *Studies in a Dying Culture*, ed. John Strachey (London: Bodley Head, 1938), and *Further Studies in a Dying Culture*, ed. Edgill Rickword (London: Bodley Head, 1949). It is true that very few Marxists had time for the niceties of aesthetics, preferring instead the blunt and literal dogma that art must reflect the social crisis, with proper emphasis of course on the ideological rights and wrongs, blacks and whites. Caudwell, however, could not be satisfied with the ideological subordination of poetry to politics. And it is interesting to contemplate how much his dialectics might have

satisfied a Trotsky, and equally irritated a Stalin. For Caudwell's argument, remarkably similar in purpose to that of the Agrarians as I have mentioned, places poetry at the center of man's spiritual economy, as a kind of surrogate religion, if not, in fact, the pure expression of religion before it is converted into a doctrine for the bourgeois state. But Caudwell was realist enough to know the adjustments of poetry to reality that need be made to appeal to man in the "complex" of modern society, that it could no longer serve the old primitive, ritualistic needs. Unlike the Agrarians, of course, he could not think of slowing down the industrial push toward the future. He would make poetry the instrument by which man seeks the ideal future, or envisions the ideal he materially seeks; if the more enlightened Agrarians cannot honestly be accused of seeking an ideal past, they nevertheless yearn for the stillness not heard since Appomattox, the order achieved in the forms of art and literature and religion which contain rather than accelerate time. One might, playing with dialectics, insist that Stevens is a man of the Present, seeking a way between the ideal Future and the ideal Past.

7 Williams, review of *The Man with the Blue Guitar and Other Poems,* 50.

8 Statement from front flap of dust jacket, *Ideas of Order* (New York: Knopf, 1936).

9 Note Stevens' remarks on the "pure," in an essay written shortly after the appearance of *Ideas of Order:* "In spite of M. Brémond, pure poetry is a term that has grown to be descriptive of poetry in which not the true subject but the poetry of the subject is paramount. All mystics approach God through the irrational. Pure poetry is both mystical and irrational. If we descend a little from this height and apply the looser and broader definition of pure poetry, it is possible to say that, while it can lie in the temperament of very few of us to write poetry in order to find God, it is probably the purpose of each of us to write poetry to find the good which, in the Platonic sense, is synonymous with God. One writes poetry, then, in order to approach the good in what is harmonious and orderly" (OP 222).

10 The first edition was published by Alcestis Press, July, 1935; the second, and trade edition, by Knopf, October 19, 1936.

11 This poem was originally published in *Broom,* V (November, 1923), 201–203, under the title, "Discourse in a Cantina at Havana," later reprinted in *The Hound and Horn,* III (Fall, 1929), 53–56, under the present title.

12 Quoted in Kimon Friar and John Malcolm Brinnin (eds.), *Modern Poetry* (New York: Appleton-Century-Crofts, 1951), 538.

13 Ramon Fernandez, *Messages,* trans. Montgomery Belgion (New York: Harcourt, Brace, 1927), 42–43.

14 Burnshaw, "Turmoil in the Middle Ground," 42.

15 F. O. Matthiessen, "Society and Solitude in Poetry," *Yale Review,* XXV, N.S. (March, 1936), 604–607.

16 William Van O'Conner, *The Shaping Spirit* (Chicago: Regnery, 1950), 60.

17 Statement by Stevens on front flap of dust jacket, *The Man with the Blue Guitar and Other Poems* (New York: Knopf, 1937).

18 Stevens' reference most probably is to Schwarz's large New York toy store.

19 While problematic, the relation of Stevens' use of Africa to Laforgue's, even as a possibility, is interesting. Warren Ramsay, in his *Jules Laforgue and the Ironic Inheritance* (New York: Oxford University Press, 1953), 84–85, 252–53n, has pointed out Laforgue's interest in the interior Africa of the self, and has isolated

and translated a revealing passage, first published, interestingly enough, in a journal entitled *Entretiens Politiques et Littéraires,* IV (February, 1892), 49. But the identification of Africa, primitivism, and the like with the interior self is no doubt too commonplace for Stevens to have needed a specific source. A cursory acquaintance with the literature of his time would have served as precedent.

20 See Irving Howe, "Another Way of Looking at a Blackbird," *New Republic,* CXXXVII (November 4, 1957), 16–17, for an interesting assessment of the poem's failure to comprehend the political crisis. Professor Howe's essay—a review of *Opus Posthumous*—is astute, but it does not admit Stevens' defense of poesy, and the essential nonpolitical nature of it.

21 Statement by Stevens on front flap of dust jacket, *The Man with the Blue Guitar and Other Poems.*

22 Kenneth Burke, "Revolutionary Symbolism in America," *American Writers' Congress* (New York: International Publishers, 1935). Now most easily available in F. J. Hoffman (ed.), *Perspectives on Modern Literature* (Evanston: Row, Peterson, 1962), 180–86.

23 Poggioli (trans.), *Mattino Domenicale,* 174.

24 This is the phrase Stevens uses in poem fifteen of "Blue Guitar." In his essay "The Relations between Poetry and Painting," however, he uses what is perhaps a more apt term, "horde of destructions," suggesting the painting's imposition of order upon diverse fragments. Says Stevens in a letter to Renato Poggioli (July 1, 1953), "I had no particular painting of Picasso's in mind." Earlier (June 25, 1953), he had remarked: "The words hoard of destructions, as I remember, were either from a group of dicta by Picasso which were published some years ago by Christian Zervos or by a comment from Zervos on Picasso." The section of the poem speaking of the Picasso painting appeared in May, 1937, before *Guernica,* which obviously precludes a direct allusion to that painting.

25 Poggioli (trans.), *Mattino Domenicale,* 174.

26 *Ibid.*

27 *Ibid.,* 175.

28 *Ibid.,* 176.

29 *Ibid.,* 176–77.

30 *Ibid.,* 178.

31 *Ibid.,* 179.

32 *Ibid.*

33 *Ibid.,* 182. Says Stevens: "Religious ceremonies and delights are evasions of reality. External life, the opposite, is all a wedding with reality. The ancient argument goes on forever. It is like a comparison of masks."

34 See Samuel French Morse, "The Motive for Metaphor—Wallace Stevens: His Poetry and Practice," *Origin V,* II (Spring, 1952), 16.

35 For the philosophical implications of this, see the Afterword.

CHAPTER 4

1 Cf. T. S. Eliot's remark from, "Yeats," in his *On Poetry and Poets* (New York: Farrar, Straus and Cudahy, 1957), 297: ". . . it is my experience that towards middle age a man has three choices: to stop writing altogether, to repeat himself with perhaps an increasing skill of virtuosity, or by taking thought to adapt himself

to middle age and find a different way of working." He goes on to speak of the late long poems of Browning and Swinburne, saying that they are not read today because the essential Browning and Swinburne are in their earlier poems. It is evident that Stevens never stopped writing, but he has been accused of repeating himself. Yet I think that he found a new way of working. In any event, Stevens cannot be found altogether in his earlier poems. "Maturing as a poet," Eliot goes on, "means maturing as the whole man, experiencing new emotions appropriate to one's age, and with the same intensity as the emotions of youth." *Parts of a World* is groping and repetitious, but in "Notes toward a Supreme Fiction" a new way of feeling begins to emerge, to reach its intensest in "The Rock."

2 Of all Stevens' volumes *Parts of a World* was received most indifferently. Perhaps the characteristic judgment is that of Marius Bewley, "The Poetry of Wallace Stevens," *Partisan Review,* XVI (September, 1949), 895-915, which in retrospect condemned it for containing too many practice poems. Practice to Stevens, however, was not simply pruning one's style. It was an exacting commitment of the self. These poems are something like a holding action, which puts out tentative feelers toward a new mode, until finally it secures enough high ground to launch another attack against the pressures of reality.

3 *Parts of a World* was published September 8, 1942, by Knopf. *Notes toward a Supreme Fiction* received limited printing in volume form by the Cummington Press, Cummington, Massachusetts, in November, 1942. *Notes* was printed as early as September, 1942.

4 Ernst Cassirer, *Philosophy of Symbolic Forms,* trans. Ralph Mannheim (New Haven: Yale University Press, 1953), II, 197.

5 See Michel Benamou, "Le Thème du héros dans la poésie de Wallace Stevens," *Études Anglaises,* XII (Juillet-Septembre, 1959), 222–30. Benamou observes that the seedling idea of the hero is probably represented in the opposing masks of Hoon and Crispin in *Harmonium,* the one a transcendent self, living in a self-contained imagination, the other the common self, whose intelligence is his soil. It is an interesting suggestion, and might be extended to include most of the personae of *Harmonium,* even the poet's developing sense of his total self as representative man.

6 Stevens' many references to the gods as poetic creations are apt here. One will suffice: ". . . if we say that the idea of God is merely a poetic idea, even if the supreme poetic idea, and that our notions of heaven and hell are merely poetry not so called, even if poetry that involves us vitally, the feeling of deliverance, of a release, of a perfection touched, of a vocation so that all men may know the truth and that the truth may set them free—if we say these things and if we are able to see the poet who achieved God and placed Him in His seat in heaven in all His glory, the poet himself, still in the ecstasy of the poem that completely accomplished his purpose, would have seemed, whether young or old, whether in rags or ceremonial robe, a man who needed what he had created, uttering the hymns of joy that followed his creation" (NA 51). Stevens' fascination with the old gods of mythology, as opposed to the God of Christianity, was with their humanity; and even though he eschews the anthropomorphic, refusing to believe that the imagination can ever again be satisfied with such creations, his own myth of the hero, man beyond symbol, reminds him of what has been lost, and the challenge to the poet confronting modern reality.

7 See Roy Harvey Pearce, *The Continuity of American Poetry,* 426 n. Pearce

would fix Stevens' interest in Klee as early as before *Harmonium,* though he acknowledges the contention of Samuel French Morse that there is no evidence Stevens knew of Klee before 1930. In 1923, Klee did publish an essay, in a collection produced by the Bauhaus, entitled "Wege des Naturstudiums," in which he commented at length on the new role of the artist as a "creature living on the earth, a creature living at the center of the universe—that is to say a creature on a star among other stars." See B. Di San Lozzaro, *Klee,* trans. Stuart Hood (New York: Praeger, 1957), 117–22. See also Stevens' quotation from Klee on the artist who established " 'himself there where the organic center of all movement in time and space—which he calls the mind or heart of creation—determines every function' " (NA 174). The phrase "heart of creation," which seems to be not a part of this quotation but an interpolation of Stevens, is from the epitaph on Klee's grave (see Lozzaro, *Klee,* 232).

8 Says Stevens: ". . . the great poems of heaven and hell have been written and the great poem of the earth remains to be written. I suppose it is that poem that will constitute the true prize of the spirit and that until it is written many lesser things will be so regarded, including conquests that are not unimaginable" (NA 142).

9 See Louis Martz, "Wallace Stevens: The World as Meditation," 529, for comment on the actor and audience of meditation in this poem. Martz points out that they are two aspects of the poet's self, an observation pertinent to many of Stevens' later poems, e.g. "The House Was Quiet and the World Was Calm," that exercise in introspective analysis that recalls at once Valéry and Santayana.

10 *Parts of a World* (New York: Knopf, 1942), n.p.

11 In a letter to Oscar Williams (November 18, 1940), Stevens remarks abou. "Extracts," which he was submitting for publication in Williams' anthology, *New Poems: 1940, An Anthology of British and American Verse* (New York: Living Age Book, 1941), 200–207: "One of the characteristics of the world today is the lightness with which ideas are asserted, held, abandoned, etc. That is what this poem grows out of."

12 Stevens used the figure of "Ananke" in some stanzas which were intended presumably for the poem. Samuel French Morse has preserved them in *Opus Posthumous,* 83. In these stanzas, too, we learn that the hero is "a man among other men, divested/ Of attributes, naked of myth, true . . ."

13 R. P. Blackmur, "Wallace Stevens: An Abstraction Blooded," in his *Language as Gesture* (New York: Harcourt, Brace, 1952), 250, a review of "Notes" first published in the *Partisan Review,* X (May-June, 1943), 297–300.

14 At least one of Stevens' essays (see OP 191–92) indicates a knowledge of Alfred North Whitehead's *Science and the Modern World* (New York: Macmillan, 1925), and particularly that important chapter on "The Romantic Reaction." The passage which Stevens quotes from Whitehead, to the effect that "everything is everywhere at all times, for every location involves an aspect of itself in every other location," is significant, it would seem, for Stevens' concern with the central and with the poetry of the center (see NA 115–16).

15 Kermode, *Wallace Stevens,* 111–12. If Kermode means here, however, that Stevens' processes of thought are forever saying farewell to an idea, continually dissolving one image in order to create another, the comment is astute, not evasive. Kermode, by the way, has an extensive set of notes on the possibilities of the

"verbality": in *Annali dell'Istituto Universitario Orientale: Sezione Germanica* (Naples), (1961), 173–201.

16 Also, Stevens' abstraction has its echo of Whitehead's involved discussion of abstraction from possibility and abstraction from actuality in *Science and the Modern World,* 241 ff. One wonders, too, if there is any influence of Bradley's view of levels of reality and truth in Stevens' abstractions.

17 Santayana, *Scepticism and Animal Faith,* 109 and *passim.*

18 See especially Whitehead's chapter, "God," in his *Science and the Modern World;* also Alfred N. Whitehead, *Process and Reality* (New York: Macmillan, 1929).

19 Santayana, *Scepticism and Animal Faith,* 109.

20 Charles Feidelson, *Symbolism and American Literature* (Chicago: University of Chicago Press, 1953).

21 *Ibid.,* 72–73.

22 Warren Carrier, "Wallace Stevens' Pagan Vantage," *Accent,* XIII (Summer, 1953), 165–68.

23 Glauco Cambon, *The Inclusive Flame* (Bloomington: Indiana University Press, 1963), 111, suggests a painting as source, but then draws back to call it an "hermetic lyric." He also suggests the Orpheus-Christ myth, but it is obvious, even with the strong suggestion of the Orpheus legend, that this poem ascribes to no mythical analogue.

24 See Bloom, *"Notes toward a Supreme Fiction:* A Commentary," in Borroff (ed.), *Wallace Stevens,* 91–92, for a curious defense of the Canon as an exponent of "major man" rather than as one who lives by preconceived order. Bloom has some difficulty with his reading, finally admitting that the Canon does not fit all the requirements for the imaginative man. Bloom reads the Canon's ambiguous name as a barbituate for "the headache of unreality." But what of the possible pun on Aspirin-aspire, man aspiring beyond life? and the extensive pun on Canon, his canon law which aspires to be a kind of central poem? The Canon is a man of pleasure, it is true, but one bound by imposed forms (his "fugue" is too formal, not a freedom; and he denies himself the freedom of dreams). In any event, it is hard to read him as even an exponent of "major man," but only as a failed possibility, one who surrenders to a law not his own.

25 Willard Arnett, *Santayana and the Sense of Beauty* (Bloomington: Indiana University Press, 1957), 140.

CHAPTER 5

1 See note 15, Chapter 2, for criticism relating Stevens and Laforgue. The Verlaine influence is less pronounced, and not so evident in criticism, though one commentator called him "Verlaine in Hartford," *View,* I (September, 1940), 1, 6. Also, Fuchs, *The Comic Spirit of Wallace Stevens,* and Tindall, *Wallace Stevens,* offer some significant analogies of theme and symbol. For the Mallarmé influence, see Hi Simons, "Wallace Stevens and Mallarmé," 235–59; and Michel Benamou, "Wallace Stevens and the Symbolist Imagination," *ELH,* XXXI (March, 1964), 35–63.

2 The most recent, and most thorough, of Benamou's essays, "Wallace Stevens and the Symbolist Imagination," is a revision and enlargement of his "Sur le prétendu

'Symbolisme' de Wallace Stevens," *Critique* (Paris), XVII (Décembre, 1961), 1029–45. See also, Benamou, "Le Thème du héros dans la poésie de Wallace Stevens," 222–30, and "Jules Laforgue and Wallace Stevens," 107–17.

3 Benamou, "Wallace Stevens and the Symbolist Imagination," 50. Cf. R. P. Blackmur, "The Substance that Prevails," *Kenyon Review,* XVII (Winter, 1955), 102–103: ". . . he is not a symbolist . . . : the iconography of his mind was immediate and self-explanatory *within* his vocabulary." Also see Pearce, *The Continuity of American Poetry,* 386, referring to the poems of *Harmonium:* "These are not 'symbolist' poems—since the data which compose the experiences of their protagonists 'correspond' to nothing outside the closed systems of meaning which are the poems." The only argument I would have with Benamou's essay is that it draws its conclusions too often from word and image counts, and occasionally fails to account for the changing meanings of Stevens' metaphors. This is a common problem of phenomenological criticism which, attending to clusters of images, may violate larger contexts. For example, Stevens' metaphor of the "rock" appears in his poetry during the thirties and comes to maturity in his very last poems; its value as metaphor changes radically, as does the meaning of Stevens' several metaphors of the first idea, ultimate poem, and so on.

4 The reviews of *Transport* were at best uneven. It appeared almost concurrently with a reissue of *Harmonium,* evoking this representative comment from Peter Viereck, *Kenyon Review,* X (Winter, 1948), 155: ". . . an invidious comparison insists on being made." F. O. Matthiessen, in the *New York Times Book Review* (April 20, 1947), 4, 26, praised its maturity; as did Louis Martz, in the *Yale Review,* XXXVII, N.S. (December, 1947), 339–41. Richard Eberhart, representing the poets' view, along with Viereck, was uncertain about the abstractness, and questioned Stevens' maturity, in his review of *Transport to Summer,* in *Accent,* 251–53.

5 Feidelson, *Symbolism and American Literature.*

6 Quoted from Henri Focillon, *The Life of Forms in Art,* trans. Charles B. Hogan and George Kubler (New Haven: Yale University Press, 1942), 52.

7 *Ibid.,* 55.

8 *Ibid.,* 58.

9 Both Pearce, in *The Continuity of American Poetry,* and Kermode, in *Wallace Stevens,* consider the shorter poems footnotes to the longer.

10 This may refer to Rossini's *Semiramide.* Semiramis, a mythical Assyrian queen, and legendary founder of Babylon, combines wisdom with voluptuousness. Perhaps the allusion recalls, also, Valéry's *Air de Semiramis.* The reference here seems to be to the act of making, creating oneself in the architecture of words.

11 See Pearce, *The Continuity of American Poetry,* 426, for a use of "The Lack of Repose" as a commentary on the American experience, and particularly on Stevens' repudiation of the comforting traditionalism on which this "Andrew Jackson Something" lives.

12 George Santayana, *The Realm of Spirit* (New York: Scribner's, 1940), p. 266.

13 Valéry, *The Art of Poetry,* 226–27.

14 Stevens read "Description without Place" as the Harvard Phi Beta Kappa poem, June, 1945, accounting perhaps for its intellectual posture, though as Auden's "Under Which Lyre" indicates, and John Crowe Ransom's "Address to the Scholars of New England" likewise, the intellectual tone of an occasional poem need not

preclude irony and high humor. One would hesitate, however, to call this poem occasional.

15 Martz, "Wallace Stevens: The World as Meditation," 517–36.

16 Cf. "Recitation after Dinner" (OP 86) on the continuity of tradition, a poem Stevens did not preserve for his *Collected Poems,* perhaps because it was too much like its opening lines: "A poem about tradition could easily be/ A windy thing."

17 The title is a possible combination of *Les Fleurs du mal* and *Curiosité esthétique.* But if so, the debt to Baudelaire is by no means a key to the poem. In another version of this reading, I suggested that the "Spaniard of the Rose" might possibly owe something to Baudelaire's "Don Juan aux enfers." But Samuel French Morse, who should know, says it refers to Señor Pedro Dot, a hybridizer of roses (see Fuchs, *The Comic Spirit,* 176 n.). Roger Mitchell, in *Notes and Queries,* X, N.S. (October, 1963), 381, makes a case for William Carlos Williams as the Spaniard. Like most of Stevens' allusions, however, the meaning depends on no external reference. Though there is no particular association, Stevens' use of "my semblables" in "Dutch Graves in Bucks County" recalls Baudelaire's famous implication of the reader in his blighted flowers. If so, this is just another example of Stevens' self-contained allusions.

18 See Stallknecht, "Absence in Reality: A Study in the Epistemology of the Blue Guitar," 545–62, for an extended treatment of Stevens' neo-romantic epistemology in relation to Wordsworth and Coleridge.

19 See Pearce, *The Continuity of American Poetry,* 404; and Louis Martz, *The Poetry of Meditation* (New Haven: Yale University Press, 1954), 68.

20 Letter to Renato Poggioli, June 3, 1953.

21 Martz, "Wallace Stevens: The World as Meditation," 520.

CHAPTER 6

1 Randall Jarrell, "Reflections on Wallace Stevens," *Partisan Review,* XVIII (May–June, 1951), 341–42. Reprinted in Jarrell's *Poetry and the Age* (New York: Knopf, 1953).

2 Louis Martz's essay, "Wallace Stevens: The World as Meditation," 517–36, is indispensable for understanding the mode of this poetry, though I will not agree completely in the following pages with Martz's view of the formal meditative exercises, by which he links Stevens' secular poetry with an earlier religious tradition. Stevens, indeed, used the term meditation in the loosest way, to describe the imaginative activity of playing upon the reservoir of memory and present association.

3 See Pearce, *The Continuity of American Poetry,* 404–19, and especially 412–13, for Stevens' special sense of "modern reality as a reality of decreation." Though I would not agree totally with Pearce here, believing as I do that Stevens' search for the central was for the creative center of self rather than for some ultimate *Ding an sich,* I find his suggestions stimulating. Especially important is his argument for Stevens' development, which again I do not fully accept but surely respect.

4 See especially "Introduction," *Poems by Wallace Stevens,* ed. with introduction Samuel French Morse (New York: Vintage, 1959), xvii–xx.

5 Donald Davie, " 'The Auroras of Autumn,' " *Perspective,* VII (Autumn, 1954), 125–36.

6 *The Collected Poems of W. B. Yeats* (New York: Macmillan, 1954), 230. Yeats's poem concerns not only the tragedy of consciousness, but of human violence.

7 Pearce, *The Continuity of American Poetry*, 409–12.

8 See Focillon, *The Life of Forms in Art*, 58.

9 The passage comes near the conclusion of "Where I Lived and What I Lived For," chapter 2 of Thoreau's *Walden*.

10 See Ralph J. Mills, Jr., "Wallace Stevens: The Image of the Rock," *Accent*, XVIII (Spring, 1958), 75–89.

11 See Kermode, *Wallace Stevens*, 18, for a brief mention of the poem in relation to Yeats's "The Circus Animals' Desertion." Like Yeats's, Stevens' poem weaves together old forms, including strands of old poems and themes, into a new, perhaps the last, discovery. But it is not difficult to see that Stevens is no equal of Yeats in this mode. Or at least not in this poem.

12 See Martz, "Wallace Stevens: The World as Meditation," 533–34.

13 On the aphoristic quality of this poetry, see Frank Doggett, "Wallace Stevens' Later Poetry," *ELH*, XXV (June, 1958), 139, 146.

14 See Norman Holmes Pearson, "Wallace Stevens and 'Old Higgs,'" *Trinity Review*, VIII (May, 1954), 35–36. Santayana was aware of his deficiencies as poet, and in terms which might explain Stevens' superiority in giving voice to similar sentiments, if not similar experiences: "Of impassioned tenderness or Dionysiac frenzy I have nothing, nor even of that magic and pregnancy of phrase—really the creation of a fresh idiom—which marks the high lights of poetry. Even if my temperament had been naturally warmer, the fact that the English language (and I can write no other with assurance) was not my mother-tongue would of itself preclude any inspired use of it on my part; its roots do not quite reach to my centre" ("Preface," *Poems*, New York: Scribner's, 1928, vii–viii). One thinks of Bertrand Russell's remark that Santayana's philosophy represents "emotional privation," and how some critics of Stevens have virtually accused him of the same.

15 See Robert Lowell, "Imagination and Reality," *Nation*, CLXVI (April 5, 1947), 400–402. Lowell, after comparing Stevens with Santayana, accuses both of championing an art that is available only to the comfortable, that demands a slave society to support it.

16 The shorter version of the poem first appeared in *Transactions of the Connecticut Academy of Arts and Sciences*, XXXVIII (December, 1949), 161–72. It is now included in Morse's selections, *Poems by Wallace Stevens*, 145–52.

17 Doggett, "Wallace Stevens' Later Poetry," 153.

18 Kermode, *Wallace Stevens*, 109, 121 n., relates the quotation directly to a passage in Santayana.

19 Doggett, "Wallace Stevens' Later Poetry," suggests the Boethius allusion in relation to Boethius' method of personifying the consolations of philosophy.

20 See Santayana, "The Genteel Tradition in American Philosophy," in his *Winds of Doctrine* (New York: Scribner's, 1913), 168–215, especially his comment that the Transcendentalists turned Romantic philosophy's "conscientious critique of knowledge . . . into a sham system of nature" (p. 195).

AFTERWORD

1 Pearce, *The Continuity of American Poetry*, 376–419, especially 376–81.

2 Georges Poulet, *Studies in Human Time*, trans. Elliott Coleman (Baltimore: Johns Hopkins University Press, 1956), 34–35.

3 *Ibid.*, 36.

4 Pearce, *The Continuity of American Poetry*, 412–13.

5 *Ibid.*, 419. See also his more recent essay, in many ways the best single piece on Stevens in print: "Wallace Stevens: The Lesson of the Master," *ELH*, XXXI (March, 1964), 65–85. Pearce somewhat qualifies his view of the extreme thrust of Stevens' later poetry toward a grasp of the thing itself. At least he withdraws his earlier observation that a very late poem like "Not Ideas about the Thing but the Thing Itself" realizes its title, and alters his argument along the lines of that I have offered here and, simultaneously with but independently of his essay, in an essay in that same volume of *ELH*. In the end, we agree, Stevens found a "cure" for the "ground" and a "satisfaction" for the mind not at the end of the act, but within the act of the mind. As Pearce put it: "At the end, or almost at the end . . . the mind's sole creation was the mind, the revelation that its sole creation was itself. . . . In the seeking itself lay the source of support" (85). As I put it: "Even though this last poetry evidences the wish to get beneath appearances to a thing-itself, even though its own style seems intent on pulverizing the metaphors and myths by which mind clothes reality, even though it occasionally asserts that the self must push itself toward the purity of the ultimate abstraction—even though all these are given voice, what remains vital in this poetry is the tension . . . between what is desired and what is finally accepted as possible. Stevens' final composure, then, need not be explained as achieving what it willed (to 'know' the 'thing itself'). Rather, it would seem to be a final affirmation of the power of the self to *be,* to conceive and meditate a reality other than that which ordinary experience affords, and to find its *being* in the act of the mind that can create abstractions. . . . Here at last for Stevens poetry and life became one, poetry and life being 'good' even in their limitation, even in their dependence on the mind's being able to conceive a reality beyond form, and thus to conceive a reality that is a negation of poetry and life" (136–37).

Indexes

299

SUBJECT INDEX